Consumer Credit Models: Pricing, Profit, and Portfolios

Consumer Credit Models: Pricing, Profit, and Portfolios

LYN C. THOMAS

UNIVERSITY PRESS

OXFORD
UNIVERSITY PRESS

Great Clarendon Street, Oxford, OX2 6DP,
United Kingdom

Oxford University Press is a department of the University of Oxford.
It furthers the University's objective of excellence in research, scholarship,
and education by publishing worldwide. Oxford is a registered trade mark of
Oxford University Press in the UK and in certain other countries

Published in the United States of America by Oxford University Press
198 Madison Avenue, New York, NY 10016, United States of America

British Library Cataloguing in Publication Data

Data available

Library of Congress Cataloging in Publication Data

Data available

ISBN 978–0–19–923213–0

To Margery with love and thanks,
and to the portfolio of Abi, JJ, Tom, Olivia and siblings, and cousins yet to come.

Preface

Consumer lending is the sleeping giant of the financial sector. The growth in consumer credit over the last 50 years is truly spectacular. The marketplace for total retail banking and consumer lending is enormous; it exceeds corporate debt by more than 50% in many countries. It was only with the US sub-prime mortgage crisis of 2007 and the consequent worldwide credit crunch that consumers, lenders, and banking regulators really woke up to its importance. Yet the literature on consumer lending and consumer credit modelling is minimal compared with that on corporate lending or the exotic equity-based derivatives. Part of this is because credit scoring, the risk assessment approach introduced in the 1950s, has worked so well since then that there has been little reason to analyse it deeply. Its success has been down to the fact that it focused on one objective—to assess the default risk of prospective and existing borrowers in the next year—and one decision—whether to accept an applicant for a loan. The extension from acceptance scoring to behavioural scoring allowed other decisions on whether to extend further credit or whether to try and cross-sell another product to the borrower but as we have shown this can be reinterpreted as another form of the acceptance decision.

Slowly over the years, with much more momentum since the millennium, lenders have recognized that they need to extend the range of decisions that consumer credit risk assessment should be used in. This will mean changing the methodology used to build the assessment systems, changing the business measures used to assess the borrowers, and most of all, developing models to address the new decisions that credit scoring can be used for.

This is the first book to address these new issues that lenders are beginning to grapple with in credit cards, mortgages, personal, equity, and auto loans. There are three major developments: first, how to move from default-based scoring to profit scoring, that is, to develop models/techniques which assess not just the default risk of borrowers but also their profitability. This involves dynamical models of their likelihood to purchase additional financial products and the chance of moving to other lenders or prepaying their loans. Second, because of the changes to more private application channels like the telephone and the internet, lenders are able to customize the loan offers they make to prospective borrowers. This raises the problem of how to model such variable pricing decisions which are related to similar problems in yield management. In the consumer lending content, the obvious question is how lenders should price for the different default risks of the borrowers. Third, the Basel II regulatory regime for lending requires lenders to model the default risk of portfolios of loans and not just individual loans. This means that one needs to consider how the methodologies giving rise to the credit risk assessment of individual consumer loans can be extended to portfolios of such loans. Another impetus for modelling portfolio credit risk for consumer loans is the need to price portfolios of consumer loans as part of the securitization process, where existing ad hoc methods have proved conspicuous failures, leading to the temporary demise of the asset-backed securities market. This book will give practitioners a series of new models and techniques that suggest ways to address these issues. These models are gleaned from our experience of helping practitioners and researchers think about such problems.

The book will also review the current models and techniques used in credit scoring and the ways the resulting risk assessment systems can be measured. It gives practitioners, researchers, and students new insights into the meaning of scores and how they should be measured. The majority of the book though will help those three groups of readers address the new modelling problems that will dominate consumer credit lending for sometime into the future.

The book is divided into five chapters. Chapters 1 and 2 describe the current situation of what scoring systems are, what they are used for, and how scoring systems are measured. The first chapter uses decision trees to model the acquisition decision and points out how scoring is used to make this decision. It discusses carefully what is meant by a score, the importance of log odds scores, and how a score relates to concepts like weights of evidence, information value, business performance, and decision-maker objectives. To our knowledge, this has not been explained clearly before in the credit scoring context, and so should greatly benefit both those who build scorecards and those who use them in portfolio acquisition and management. The chapter also shows how one can model the acquisition decisions using rates of return on the funds lent rather than total revenue and that such an interpretation clarifies some of the decisions being made. The first chapter also gives an overview of the way scorecards are currently built outlining the different steps and analysis involved and the alternative methodologies that have been used.

Chapter 2 looks at the different ways scorecards can be measured and points out clearly but rigorously what is being measured by each performance measure and what is the relationship between them. Three quite different features of a scorecard are measured—its ability to discriminate between the good and bad borrowers, the accuracy of its probability prediction of the chance of a borrower defaulting, and the errors that arise in the categorical predictions of a borrower being a good or a bad, which follow from using the scorecard and a particular cut-off score. Understanding these different types of measurement has taken on increasing importance because of the need to validate scorecards as required by the Basel New Accord which specifies risk and capital requirements for banks and financial institutions.

Each of the remaining three chapters looks at some of the new challenges that consumer credit will have to address. Chapter 3 looks at ways in which the traditional cut-off policies for acquisition decisions can be extended to include variable pricing. So the question then is not whether to offer a loan to a potential borrower but what interest rate to charge the borrower. The chapter examines some of the problems that arise as a result of preferences and uncertain responses by borrowers. The effects of adverse selection are studied and incorporated in the pricing policies.

Chapter 4 looks at how one can develop profit management systems by introducing dynamic scoring models of the performance of borrowers. It starts with the simplest models of risk/return matrices which some lenders use and shows how these can be developed into much more objective and analytic systems by incorporating relatively simple stochastic processes. In particular, it looks at the use of Markov chains and Markov decision process models, which have proved successful in other application areas. With these models one can build profitability models which will support decisions on credit limit adjustments and even introduce Bayesian ideas so that the belief about an individual's default risk depends on that individual's repayment performance. Perhaps even more important is the approach based on survival analysis which seeks to estimate when default or other negative events occur rather than if they occur. Using Cox's proportional hazard models in this approach leads to an alternate hazard score, which is proving an effective risk assessment statistic, particularly when the objectives do not have fixed time horizons. Thus it comes into its own when building customer lifetime value models, particularly when used with the competing risk ideas of survival analysis.

Chapter 5 looks at the credit risk of portfolios on consumer loans and is motivated by the new Basel Accord regulations and the growth in securitization, both of which seek to assess such risks. It has a concise but comprehensive review of the Basel Accord as it is applied to consumer (retail) lending and then looks at the types of portfolio consumer credit risk models that are being developed and how they could be used for tasks such as stress testing the parameters as required in the New Accord.

This book emphasizes the policies and decisions that can be made under various operating restrictions, under different financial regulations, and with different financial objectives. Once a lender has a scorecard, the score can be used to make good financial decisions that increase profit, market share, and return on equity, rather than concentrating exclusively on risk. The book also develops models to address pricing issues, that is, what to charge a borrower at a given level of risk and how to manage existing portfolios when new uncertainties of attrition and default arise. It concentrates on modelling and decision making and thus has more emphasis on probability models and less on statistical techniques than previous books on credit scoring.

The tone of the book is to explain ideas clearly but rigorously using simple probability models and logical arguments. We believe the statistical and probabilistic ability of credit analysts in industry and students in management science, operational research, and banking and finance masters courses will find this combination comprehensible and appealing.

Contents

Acknowledgements

I would like to thank those who helped shape this book. When I started writing the book, I invited Bob Oliver to become a joint author with me. In the end it did not turn out to be possible, but our collaboration over several years was extremely influential in shaping my thoughts on the subject matter of the book. He brought a wealth of practical knowledge and a keen sense of mathematical rigour to our discussions and we often concluded a session around a white board having both learnt a great deal from the interchange. In particular, the definition of what is meant by a score and the ways it can be extended which are to be found in Sections 1.5 and 1.6, the "rate" model of the acceptance decision introduced in Section 1.7 but found thereafter throughout the book, and the ideas of the business objectives of lenders found in Section 1.3, all of which developed through many cross Atlantic revisions owe much to his insights. As we had both contributed to many early drafts of these sections, we agreed that it would be acceptable to republish portions of the first appearing text that would be relevant to a later publication. I am very grateful to him for his interaction with the project.

I am also grateful to Jonathan Crook, David Edelman, David Hand, Alan Lucas, and Bob Phillips for conversations concerning various aspects of the book. Also, thanks go to my colleagues at Southampton, Christophe Mues and Bart Baesens, for many discussions concerning credit scoring and consumer credit. I am especially grateful to Ania Matuszyk, Madhur Malik, and Ross McDonald who read and commented on various chapters of the book. Finally, my thanks go to Alison Jones and Dewi Jackson at the Oxford University Press for encouraging me and persevering with me through this venture.

1

Introduction to consumer credit and credit scoring

1.1   Introduction: importance and impact of consumer credit

The word credit is derived from the Latin word creditum – to have trusted – and for 4000 years, people have trusted one another by lending money or goods. There is a Sumarian clay tablet dated from around 2000 BC which records the transaction of two farmers who have borrowed money against the harvest.

Sin-Kalama-idi, son of Ulamasha, and Apil-ilu-shu, Son of Khayamdidu, have borrowed from Arad-Sin sixteen shekels of money for the garnering of the harvest. On the festival of Ab they will pay the wheat.

A little later during the old Assyrian empire, the Kültepe texts record the transactions of a trading route from cities on the Tigris to the Anatolian region of Turkey. The sellers at the far end of the route were being charged 33% interest on the goods sent because of the hazards involved in transporting the goods. So risk-based pricing was in operation even then.

Although the Code of Hammurabi (1792–1750 BC) established the first laws regulating lending to consumers, it took until the fifteenth century AD for there to be an industry of lending to consumers when public pawnshops (*monts-de-pières*) were established in medieval Italy. In the intervening years, there was a philosophical debate on whether one should make money from credit. This was because lending money was equated with usury-lending at rates that are unreasonable to the borrower. Aristotle in his Politics said 'for usury is most reasonably detested, as it is increasing our fortune by money itself, and not employing it for the purpose it was originally intended, namely exchange'. This lack of understanding of the time value of money was such that both the Catholics and the Moslems forbad the charging of interest. Saint Thomas Aquinas argued that money was sterile unlike animals and so 'money does not beget money'. In Section 275 of the Koran, it says 'But God hath permitted trade and forbidden usury'.

The founding of the Bank of England in 1694 was one of the first signs of the financial revolution which would allow mass lending. Over the next 150 years, banks began lending to the nobility and gentry. Then lending slowly begun to be offered by manufacturers as well as banks so that by the 1850s the Singer Sewing Machine Company was selling its machines on hire purchase. However, unsecured lending really started in the 1920s when Henry Ford and A. P. Sloan recognized that in order to sell cars to a mass market one had also to find ways of allowing consumers to finance their purchase, and so developed finance houses. With the introduction of the credit card in the 1950s and 1960s, consumers had a product that allowed them to use credit for almost all their purchases from snack food bites to airline flights.

Now at the start of the twenty-first century consumer credit is the driving force behind the economies of most of the leading industrial countries. Without it, the phenomenal growth in home ownership and consumer spending of the last 50 years would not have occurred.

In 2007, the total debt owed by consumers in the USA was $13 trillion ($13,009,000,000,000), of which $9.8 trillion was on mortgages and $2.4 trillion on consumer credit (personal bank loans, credit cards, overdrafts, and motor and retail loans). This is now 40% more than the $9.2 trillion owed by all US industry and more than double the $5.8 trillion of corporate borrowing (the rest being borrowing by small and medium-sized companies and agricultural organizations). Figure 1.1.1 shows the growth in this borrowing since the 1960s in the USA and emphasizes how consumer credit has been growing faster than corporate borrowing for most of that period. Figure 1.1.2 shows that although revolving credit (credit and store cards) did not really start until 1966, they now account for 40% of the non-secured consumer credit market.

Consumer debt in the USA has exceeded the national annual income for most of the period since 2000 and in 2007 household consumer debt was over 130% of disposal income. Although the total US consumer debt is the highest of all the countries in the world, some other countries approach this level on a debt per

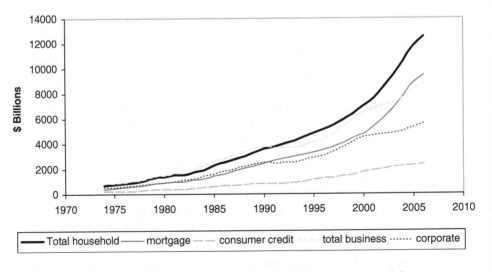

FIG. 1.1.1. Comparison of US household and business debt.

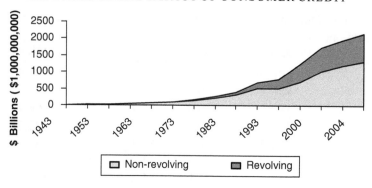

F<small>IG</small>. 1.1.2. Split between revolving and non-revolving US consumer credit.

consumer basis. In Canada, for example, consumer debt is 813 billion Canadian dollars ($666 billion), with 69% of it due to mortgages and 31% due to other forms of consumer credit. This means the consumer credit per household is 110% of the annual aggregated household income.

The UK and Germany are the European countries with the largest total amount of consumer credit. In the UK, the total debt outstanding passed 1 trillion pounds (£1,000,000,000,000) in July 2004 and by the end of 2007 it was over £1.4 trillion. Lending for house purchase accounts for £882 billion of this and consumer credit for £183 billion. This averages out at £17,891 ($35,000) per person not far from the US figure, with £4000 of this coming from unsecured credit (£1300 on credit cards, £1890 on personal loans, and £810 on overdrafts and motor or retail finance).

In other European countries the growth in consumer credit has not been at quite this level over the last decade or if it has it started from a much lower level. Table 1.1.1 (Mizen 2002) shows this growth in unsecured consumer credit during the 1990s. Traditionally there has been a north–south split with the Northern Europeans led by the UK saving less and spending more on credit and Southern Europe doing the reverse. However, by 2000 the growth rates for consumer credit in Italy and Spain are matching those of any other European country.

The total level of consumer credit in other countries does not match that in North America and Europe, but the growth in these areas is phenomenal. Until recently credit cards were unheard of in China but now they use plastic for more than $200 billion worth of transactions annually and the government is laying the legal frame work for setting up credit reference bureaus. Thailand and South Korea are other examples where consumers have rapidly changed from a savings culture to a consumer credit one. South Koreans were still saving 30% of their gross domestic product (GDP) in the mid-1990s but within 10 years were in a consumer credit crisis with each consumer having an average of four credit cards.

TABLE 1.1.1. Outstanding unsecured consumer credit (in euro billions) in Europe in the 1990.

Year	Germany	Belgium	Spain	France	UK	Italy
1993	176.9	10	30.8	58.7	83.5	16.8
1994	186.1	9	32	60.2	90.9	17.4
1995	189.5	9.3	36.7	63.8	106.7	18.3
1996	198.8	9.6	38.6	69.3	121.2	20.4
1997	204.3	10.2	42.3	74.9	138	23.8
1998	216.7	11.1	52.3	80.8	159.8	28.5
1999	215.7	11.9	54.6	89.5	185.2	32.2
2000	226.6	12.2	58.6	97.8	186.2	38.5
Per head 1993	2185	1000	788	1020	1438	295
Per head 2000	2709	1192	1486	1651	3123	667

TABLE 1.1.2. Credit and debit card circulation in 2003.
Visa/MC (credit + debit) (cards in circulation) 000s

Rank	Country	Cards
1	USA	755,300
2	China	177,359
3	Brazil	148,435
4	UK	125,744
5	Japan	121,281
6	Germany	109,482
7	S. Korea	94,632
8	Taiwan	60,330
9	Spain	56,239
10	Canada	51,100
Top 10	Total	1,699,902
Global	Total	2,362,042

Top 10 represent 72% of global Visa/MasterCards.

Although the mortgage and secured lending market involves consumers in the most credit outstanding, it is the unsecured lending market, especially the credit card market that produces the most volume of transactions and has the highest profile with consumers. Table 1.1.2 gives the total number of credit and debit card under the Visa and MasterCard (MC) label in circulation in 2003. Note that only about 5 million of the cards in China are credit cards, whereas in Brazil, with 177 million population and the world's eighth largest economy, the penetration of credit cards among the A/B socio-economic classes is more than 90%. Among those not in the top 10, India is experiencing 25%+ annual growth in credit and debit cards and is fast approaching the 50 million card mark, though most of these are debit cards.

Thus it is clear that the demand for consumer credit is worldwide and continuing to grow at extremely high rates. To cope with this one needs decision-making systems that allow lenders to automatically assess the risks they are taking in 'trusting' a consumer. Credit scoring, which was developed just in time to allow the mass introduction of credit cards, has for the last 50 years proved such a system.

1.2   Historical background of default-based credit scoring

Credit scoring began in the 1950s when it was realized that Fisher's work in the 1930s on statistical methods of classification (Fisher 1936) could be applied in classifying good and bad loans. Henry Wells of the Spiegel mail order catalogue company and David Durand (Durand 1941) for the National Bureau of Economic Research had already recognized this but it was the formation of a consultancy by Bill Fair and Earl Isaac in San Francisco that made it into a commercial product. Initially the approach was taken up by the finance houses and the mail order catalogue companies, where Montgomery Ward was to the fore. The trigger for the expansion in credit scoring was the development of the credit card. The first such card was the BankAmericard, which was also launched in the San Francisco area in 1958. The expansion in the credit card market in 1966, when the BankAmericard was franchised all over the USA and the first credit card, Barclaycard, was launched in the UK, could only happen because credit scoring had proved its worth as an automatic way of estimating default risk for consumer credit.

Credit scoring was shaped by the decision it initially sought to support, namely, should one grant credit to a new applicant. Application scoring, as we shall call this branch of credit scoring from now on, sought to make such decisions consistent and automatic so that one could process a high volume of applicants. Its philosophy was pragmatic, in that it only wanted to predict not to explain, and so anything that increased the predictive power of the system could be used, provided it was not illegal. Moreover, it assumed that the factors implying credit worthiness were relatively stable at least over time intervals of a few years. The idea was to use the lender's data on past applicants to rank the current applicants in order of risk of defaulting. So data on those who applied for credit 1 or 2 years ago, together with their subsequent credit history, was used to build the application-scoring model that would be used to determine for the next 2 years or so which credit applicants to accept.

Application scoring traditionally has assessed a very specific default risk. The most common risk considered is the chance that an applicant will go 90 days overdue on their payments in the next 12 months. What would happen over other time periods and whether the customer is proving profitable to the lender are aspects not considered in this assessment. Moreover, the actual values of the probability of defaulting do not matter, provided the relative ordering of the applicants is correct. The decision of how many or what percentage of applicants to accept is a managerial decision by the lender involving trade-offs between the business measures such as expected profits, expected losses, and market share. Thus the cut-off score, the point at which applicants are accepted, is made subjectively or at most using empirical evidence like the marginal good:bad odds at that score – the ratio of the extra goods to the extra bads that would be accepted if the cut-off score was dropped a small amount. So the actual estimated default risk does not come directly into the final decision.

The data available for application scoring was greatly enhanced with the development of credit bureaus. These organizations pooled data on the performance of a consumer with different lenders with the official information, such as electoral roll and court documents concerning bankruptcy proceedings, available on the consumer. The data held by such bureaus varies enormously from country to country. At one extreme is the USA where information is available on almost all the credit lines held by an individual while at the other end there are European countries where, because of data protection legislation, bureaus only hold openly available official information.

Behavioural scoring revolutionized the credit scoring environment in the early 1980s. It is an obvious extension of application scoring. In it, one uses information on the payment and purchase behaviour of current customers in the recent past called the observation period (typically the past year). One can also use current information available from the credit bureau as well as the data used in application scoring. All these data are used to forecast the default risk of a customer over the next 12 months or some other fixed future time horizon. Lenders usually update such behavioural scores monthly and in most cases the information on recent performance and current credit bureau information is much more powerful than the application data. However, one could argue that behavioural scoring was the revolution that was not.

One way of viewing application scoring is to say that it tries to match a photograph of the consumer on application with a photograph of their status after a fixed time period of borrowing. It is a classification problem which compares static characteristics on application with a static performance indicator at some fixed time period in the future. In this analogy, behavioural scoring would be considered as trying to match a video clip of the dynamics of consumers' performances in the recent past with photographs of their status at some future time point. However, behavioural scoring uses exactly the same approach as application scoring by translating the consumer's dynamics during the observation period into a set of statistics – average balance, maximum credit payment, number of times over the credit limit – and then matching these statistics with future status; that is, translating the video clip into a set of measurements of behaviour. Granted, there may be a lot more variables involved, with some lenders generating more than 1000 variables to describe the recent performance of a consumer, but the subsequent analysis is the same as that of application scoring and the risk measured – that is, the chance of defaulting within some fixed time period in the future – is the same.

There were two opportunities that behavioural scoring ignored. First, instead of building a static classification model, behavioural scoring could have been developed by using the dynamics of consumers' past behaviour to build a dynamic model of their future behaviour. That is, it would try to match a video clip of the consumers' past performances with a video clip of their future performances or at least with a snapshot of the status at some fixed future time point. Second, behavioural scoring could have changed the risk measure it was estimating. What are the decisions for which one uses behavioural scoring? It cannot be used to decide whether to give borrowers their existing credit, as that has already been done. It is used to decide whether to advance them further credit, what terms to offer it at, whether to try and cross-sell other products to them, or whether to improve their existing terms because they are likely to move their custom elsewhere (attrition). It is not clear that ranking consumers by their chance of defaulting in a given time period on the loan amount they had in the past, under the lending limitations they had in the past, and the market and economic conditions that held then, is the best way of deciding these more complex decisions.

We are now in the throes of the third revolution in credit scoring, which is characterized by the changes in lenders' objectives, in consumers' choices and expectations, and in regulatory pressure. Lenders are now much more clearly focussed that their lending strategies must meet their business objectives like profitability or market share. They want to optimize all the decisions related to lending to a consumer with respect to these business objectives rather than just forecast the default risk on some standard (vanilla) lending product. They realize they can choose the credit limit, the interest rate (the price of the product), and the other product features to offer a consumer so as to maximize the profitability of that consumer to them. The new application channels of the telephone and the internet mean the lender can customize the offer to the individual consumer without the information being widely disseminated to other consumers. Moreover, the lending process does not end once the lending product has been accepted. The way the lenders operate the relationship with the borrowers (shades of customer relationship management) will affect the profitability of the consumer to them. The techniques that support the lending and operating decisions, measured under business-oriented objectives, are called profit scoring systems. Returning to the photographic analogy, it is now clear that to estimate future profit we need a video clip of the future behaviour of the customers not just their status at some fixed time point. Thus these systems will need to connect the video clip of customers' past behaviour (or a snapshot of a new applicant) with the video clip of their future behaviour which will be needed to estimate their profitability. Thus, in this revolution there is no escaping the need to build dynamical models rather than to perform static classifications.

Two trends are changing what consumers expect from their lending products. The first is the move to customization. This means consumers are looking for the variation of the standard lending product, be it credit card, personal loan, or mortgage, which most suits their needs. This variation could also be in the price, where for most products the price is really the interest rate charged. Second, in countries with well-developed consumer lending, such as those in Table 1.1.2, with the exception of China and Brazil, the market is close to saturation. Consumers are not seeking more credit but are checking whether it is better to stay with their existing lender or move (attrite) to another who is offering a more attractive product. Thus, the pricing and customization of the lending products is becoming more important.

Traditionally consumer credit modelling has modelled each loan in isolation but lenders are really interested in the characteristics of their portfolio of loans to consumers (usually called a retail portfolio). The importance of the credit risk (how much of the money lent will be lost because of borrowers defaulting) of a portfolio of consumer loans has been increased by the changes in banking regulations incorporated in the New Basel Capital Accord. This Accord was implemented in 2007 and is sometimes called Basel II since it is the second such capital accord. It allows banks to use internal rating-based models to help determine how much capital they need to set aside against possible losses in their loan portfolio. For retail portfolios, credit scoring systems are such internal rating-based models. However, using them for this purpose does change some of the requirements on the scoring systems. No longer is it enough for the scoring systems just to correctly rank the consumers. Now since the forecasted probability of default given by the scoring system is used to set the capital needed to be set aside, these forecasts need to be accurate as possible. Moreover the model of the credit risk for portfolios of loans used in the New Basel Capital Accord calculation is one derived from lending to companies. Its use highlights the fact that there is currently no accepted model of the credit risk for portfolios of consumer loans.

This book seeks to outline the models and the underpinning theory which support the current usage of credit scoring and to explore some of the models one can use to develop this third revolution in credit scoring. Thus the reminder of this chapter describes why and how one constructs and uses default-based credit scorecards. It uses decision trees to explain the problems that are being addressed and how they require estimates of the risk of borrowers defaulting and ways of measuring the profitability of, or the return on, the loan. This means understanding what a score actually is and how it relates to the probability of a borrower defaulting. The chapter concludes with a brief review of the methodology and main techniques used in building such default-based scorecards. Until recently there were hardly any books which described the use of credit scoring and the methodologies underpinning it. Lewis's book (Lewis 1992) was an interesting introduction from an experienced practitioner, while Thomas et al. (1992) was a set of edited papers from a conference on the subject. More recently there have been a few texts which cover the methodologies used in credit scoring and the standard applications of scoring, such as Mays (1998, 2004), McNab and Wynn (2000), Thomas et al. (2002, 2004), Siddiqi (2005), and Anderson (2007). Chapter 1 summarizes the current approach to building scorecards. Chapter 2, on the other hand, looks at how one measures how good a scorecard is, and emphasizes that one can measure a scorecard in three different ways – by its discriminating ability, by the accuracy of its probability predictions and by the correctness of its categorical forecasts.

The remaining three chapters of the book look at three of the new challenges to credit scoring posed by this third revolution. Chapter 3 discusses the models needed to understand and implement risk-based pricing. It points out how default-based risk scores could be used in this context but that one will also need to develop response scores to estimate the probability that a potential borrower will in fact take up the loan offer made. It also points out that one will need to be careful in implementing these ideas because one is dealing with potential borrowers who make intelligent decisions and so issues like adverse selection can arise. In Chapter 4, we look at how one can build models for profit scoring by introducing the dynamics of borrowers' repayment and usage behaviour. These require new modelling approaches and we discuss the use of Markov chain models and proportional hazard survival analysis approaches in this context. Lastly, in Chapter 5, we look at the credit risk for portfolios on consumer loans. Currently there are good models for estimating the default risk of an individual borrower, but how can these be expanded to deal with the correlation in default risks of different borrowers. This has become one of the most important uses of credit scoring because of the emphasis on internal rating-based models in the Basel Accord requirements for regulatory capital. In this last chapter, we discuss the details of the Accord as it concerns consumer (retail) lending and, as mentioned previously, highlight the current lacunae in modelling credit risk of portfolios of consumer loans, which the Accord has exposed.

1.3 Objectives of lenders

Consumers borrow money from a wide range of lenders. When we think initially of lenders, we think of banks, mortgage companies, and credit and store card organizations. However, consumers also borrow from finance houses and car/auto finance companies to finance the purchase of cars and white goods; from utility companies when they pay for their electricity or telephone usage in arrears; mail order companies which were some of the first into credit scoring, and insurance companies when payment for an insurance product is spread over the lifetime of the product. Most consumers' borrowing is on secured loans so as to buy specific items like houses or cars, which the lender can legally repossess if the loan is not repaid. Consumers also take out unsecured loans or use revolving credit facilities like credit cards, in which case the lender does not know what is being purchased and has no right to the goods purchased but only to the money lent. In the case of utilities the consumer uses the commodity supplied by the lender before paying for it and so this is again essentially an unsecured loan since the lender will not be able to recover the amount of the commodity used by the consumer. We will use a shorthand throughout the book and refer to the lender as a bank and to the user of the lending product as a borrower. A loan is booked when both the bank and the borrower agree to it. The bank has the right to accept or reject the proposal made by the applicant for a loan while the applicant can take or not take the loan offered by the bank. A loan portfolio is a collection of booked loans.

Objectives of lender

The main objective for a bank is to maximize the profit achieved on its lending, but on an individual loan the bank needs to do this by considering the return achieved – how much profit was achieved compared with the amount of the loan that was borrowed. A loan with a profit of £100 when £1000 is tied up in the loan is not as good as one when £60 is achieved on a loan of £500. One has to be careful though because the amount of profit on a loan is not certain. There is a risk that the borrower will not repay the loan, in which case the lending leads to a substantial loss and not to the expected positive return. So risk might be quantified by the default rate expected in the portfolio, or the losses these defaults lead to. Thus an alternative objective for the bank would be to keep the risk and return profiles of its lending within pre-agreed limits. A third objective might be to increase the size of the lending portfolio either by increasing the number of loans of particular types that are made or by increasing the different types of lending undertaken. This objective can be considered to be increasing the market share of the bank, and that is considered attractive because the more customers a bank has, the more opportunities it has to sell its other products.

It seems as if it is the managers and directors of the bank who set the objectives. However, the managers have to be mindful of the other stakeholders who are interested in the lending decisions the bank makes, namely the equity holders, the holders of the bank's debts, its depositors, and its borrowers. If the equity holders do not like the objectives set, they can sell their equity; if the debt holders are unhappy, they will not lend to the bank; if the depositors disapprove of the bank's strategy, they could close their accounts with the bank. All this puts pressure on the managers that they may lose their posts either by the actions of more senior managers or the bank's directors or by the bank being taken over by a rival organization. The problem is that the different stakeholders may have different priorities and so a bank often has to seek to meet a number of sometimes conflicting objectives. Finding the appropriate trade-off between the different objectives is one of the main skills of senior managers.

There are two major trade-offs that recur in bank lending – one is between risk and return and the other is between profit and market share or volume. With return one is concerned with the expected return or expected profit, which is what the bank would get on average if it could repeat the lending many times. This needs to be compared with the risk, which should be some way of measuring the uncertainty in what the return on the lending might be.

The other main strategic trade-off is between profit and volume or market share. If one has an application scorecard, then each cut-off score gives a different combination of these two objectives. This is shown in Fig. 1.3.1, which plots profit against market share. The current operating point is taken to be O but by changing the cut-off point one can move to any other point on the curve AOB given by the current credit scorecard. Point A corresponds to the situation where the bank sets so high a cut-off that it accepts no one who applies but still has costs involved in advertising and running the lending operation. Dropping the cut-off, the bank starts to accept the least risky borrowers and so profits should go up steadily as volume increase. At some point though in order to increase the volume of borrowers accepted further, the bank will have to start taking customers whose chance of defaulting is sufficiently high that they are not profitable. From there on in order to increase the volume of the portfolio of accepted borrowers the bank will have

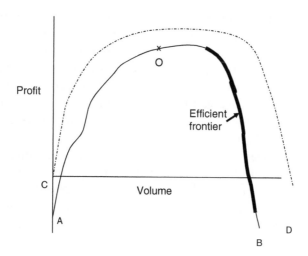

FIG. 1.3.1. Trade-offs between profit and volume.

to keep losing profit until it gets to point B. One might expect to choose cut-offs that are in the efficient part of the curve, that is, where there is no other cut-off which leads to as much or more volume and a higher profit, but sometimes as here with point O in Fig. 1.3.1, the organization has opted for a more conservative choice.

However, as well as deciding on what is the optimal current trade-off on the current trade-off curve AOB, one could try to move the curve so that the bank gets more profit from the same size of portfolio. For example, the trade-off curve might become CD where there are points with more profit and more volume than any current choice. In this book, we will address three ways in which this might happen. In the last part of this chapter, we discuss how to build scorecards and, in Chapter 2, how to measure them. So the bank may decide to build a new credit scoring system which is better than the current system and so will lead to fewer losses and hence more profits for the same size of portfolio accepted. In Chapter 3, we discuss the ideas of risk-based pricing which allows banks to adjust the interest rates charged to reflect the risks involved. This could again mean one ends up with more profitability for the same size of portfolio accepted. In Chapter 4, we discuss profit scoring systems which aim to estimate the profit the bank will make from each borrower and not the default risk of that borrower which is what the current systems do. Again moving to such systems might increase the profits the bank can make and so move the trade-off curve between profit and volume from AB to CD in Fig. 1.3.1.

Lending process

One way of describing the operations of a bank is that it assesses and repackages financial risk, by balancing its debts with its assets. A bank can acquire money in a number of different ways. Its equity holders pay money in return for the ownership of the bank; it can borrow money from other financial organizations in the money markets; it can borrow money from its depositors at agreed rates of interest; it can use the money its current account holders have in their accounts in exchange for the services it provides for them. This money is used to acquire assets, including its consumer loan portfolio.

With a consumer loan portfolio the first stage is the acquisition of the portfolio of borrowers. The bank then needs to manage the portfolio so that it produces profits. This gives the return on the money used to finance the loans given to the borrowers. At some stage a bank may decide that it wants to realize some of the money that is being used to finance the loans, often because it has run out of cash to fund further loan portfolios. It can do this in a number of ways. One is to issue corporate bonds which will increase the bank's corporate debt. Second, it can sell the portfolio of loans to another investor but more commonly it will securitize (convert) the loans into asset-backed or mortgage-backed securities where they are bundled together, and sold in the marketplace.

This book is concerned with the acquisition and management of consumer loan portfolios. However, the sub-prime crisis in the USA in 2007 showed how problems with the acquisition and management process can have knock effects throughout the whole of the financial world. Since there had been very few losses in mortgage lending for most of the previous decade, mortgage lenders chased volumes by lending to more and more risky customers and offered products with very attractive initial lending terms. Thus losses on these mortgages only started to appear when borrowers had to move to the standard repayment rates. However, the mortgages had already been securitized and so organizations who had bought these securities, as well as the original lenders started to post heavy losses. This led to the financial markets taking fright of risky loans wherever they appeared and so many of the private equity buyouts, which had been fuelling the rise in the stock markets, had to be stopped. One reason for the spread of the problem was that not all the information available from the initial risk assessment was used by those buying the securitized products to decide whether the price of those securities was a fair one.

So to reiterate, in the acquisition and management process application scoring is used to asses the risk of a prospective loan. A bank can improve its profits by improving the assessment of the risk and also by using this information to change the 'price' of the loan, that is, the interest rate charged on the loan, which leads to risk-based pricing. Currently banks use behavioural scoring to assess the probability of a customer defaulting, but if they can assess the cash flow likely to be obtained from a borrower, they can translate that into the expected future worth of the borrower. Identifying what are the factors that are predictive of a borrower's profitability, and what operational decisions the lender can make to enhance this profitability, leads to profit scoring and customer lifetime value models.

The main objectives used in this book are all expected values of random variables, be it returns or profits or costs. Implicit in this is that the bank has a sufficiently large portfolio that the law of large numbers will mean the average over the portfolio is the corresponding expectation. However, in Chapter 5 we will return to the issue of the credit risk in portfolios of consumer loans, as this is fundamental to the changes in the banking regulations brought about by the Basel Accord introduced in 2007. At that point, we will need to consider in more detail the distribution of the losses not just the expected value of the losses.

1.4   Tools for modelling lending decisions: influence diagrams, decision trees, and strategy trees

Lending to a borrower, be it giving a credit card, mortgage, or personal loan to a new applicant or extending the credit limit on an existing facility, is a decision problem for the bank. In trying to understand what information would be useful in making such a decision, what is the sequence of events that could occur during and after the decision process and the possible outcomes of the decision, it is useful to have some coherent way of thinking about the whole decision. Influence diagrams help one to visualize graphically how the decisions, the uncertainties, the information, and the outcomes are interrelated. They help decision makers derive structure for a model of the problem and can be used in any sort of decision problem, not just consumer credit. Once a model structure has been agreed, one can then use a second tool – decision trees – to put some more flesh onto this structure by identifying the different options open to the decision maker and the different outcomes that may occur. Decision trees identify what are the optimal decisions under certain objectives and explain the sequence in which decisions have to be made and the sequence in which the information becomes available during the decision process. The decision at the end can be quite complex with different options being chosen depending on the characteristics of the consumer and other relevant information. To understand such a complex strategy one can use the decision tree format to clarify which decisions are made to which group of borrowers.

Influence diagrams

Influence diagrams have two important roles in structuring decision problems. They give a framework so that those involved in the decision making can communicate with each other their view of the important aspects of the decision. This facilitating role can be found in many qualitative modelling techniques which go under the name of 'soft systems' and should not be underestimated as the basis for good consistent decision making. Second, influence diagrams identify what data is relevant to the decisions and to which aspect of the decision making it is related. This is particularly important in the area of consumer lending where there is a great deal of information available.

An influence diagram consists of a graph with three types of nodes connected by arcs. The nodes describe:

- decisions (usually represented by rectangular nodes)
- uncertain events (usually represented by circular nodes)
- outcomes (usually represented by diamond nodes).

If one of these events or decisions has an impact on or influences another event, decision, or outcome, a directed arc (arrow) is drawn from the node that does the influencing to the node that is influenced. So if one has an arc from X to Y then we say that X influences Y. This does not mean that it causes Y to happen but only that, if Y is a random event, the conditional probability $\Pr\{Y|X\}$ is not the same as the unconditional probability $\Pr\{Y\}$. If Y is an outcome or decision, it means that

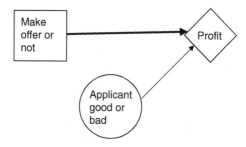

FIG. 1.4.1. Influence diagram for simple consumer lending decision.

the outcome will be affected by X and if Y is a decision the information in X could change the decision. One has to be careful of the timing of the events because even though our initial instinct may be to say X influences Y, if Y occurs before X, we must assume that Y influences X.

Application decisions in consumer credit

If one considers the simplest decision in consumer credit, whether or not to give credit to a new applicant, one could represent it by the influence diagram of Fig. 1.4.1. In this there is a decision by the bank whether to grant credit or not, and there is a random event (as far as the bank is concerned) on whether the applicant's repayment performance will be satisfactory (good) or not (bad) and these two events affect the profitability of the applicant to the bank.

The way to build such a diagram is to first list the decisions involved and the random events that will affect the decisions. Then identify the way in which the results of the decisions will be measured. Represent the random events and the decisions by square and circular nodes where, if possible the events should flow in time from left to right. Identify the dependencies and influences between the different nodes and insert directed arcs (arrows) to represent these dependencies. Check that if there are two decisions at different times there is a path going from the earlier to the later decision and that if a chance node is known and affects the earlier decision then it also is known and affects the later decision. Finally check that there are no directed cycles in the diagram (a path of arcs that returns to its start node), since this says that the outcome of a decision can affect the decision which is nonsensical.

In reality of course, the lending decision is somewhat more complicated than suggested in Fig. 1.4.1. First of all, the bank can use the information available about the applicant – from the application form and from credit bureaus – to make a forecast of whether the applicant's performance will be good or bad. Second, the applicant may decide not to accept the offer made. The forecast is a random event in that the bank cannot decide what the forecast will say about a particular

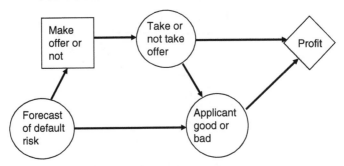

FIG. 1.4.2. Influence diagram for standard consumer lending decision.

applicant and it is reasonable that it will influence both the offer decision and have an impact on whether the applicant will subsequently be a good or a bad. Similarly the decision by the applicants whether to accept (take) the offer or not to take it must have an influence on their profitability to the bank and in turn must be influenced by the offer made. It is also reasonable to assume that there is a relationship between whether the applicant will accept the offer or not and whether the applicant will subsequently default. Applicants who are good may have so many offers of credit that they can be choosy, while those who are highly likely to default may not be getting many offers. The bank's perception is that taking the offer is information which then changes the applicant's chance of defaulting, since the bank immediately sees the decision on whether the applicant has taken the offer but will have to wait some time before finding out whether the applicant will default. This is shown in the influence diagram in Fig. 1.4.2.

A more sophisticated bank may also develop a forecast on whether the applicant will take the offer as well as the default risk. The real lending decision is of course even more complicated because we have not considered how the applicant came to apply and how the bank will manage the relationship once it is established. For example, if the application came about because of direct mailing, then there was the bank's initial decision on to whom to mail and the applicant's decision about whether to respond to the mailing. In this case as well as forecasting the default performance of the applicant, banks also forecast whether the applicant will respond to the mailing (response rate), accept the offer made, use the lending facility (usage), change to another bank after a relatively short time (attrition), or buy other products from the bank (cross-selling). All these forecasts can be made either before the mailing decision or before the offer decision. When the borrower accepts the loan facility, all the uncertainties mentioned earlier – usage, attrition, and cross-selling – will become resolved. They will all though have an impact on the profitability of the applicant to the bank as shown in Fig. 1.4.3.

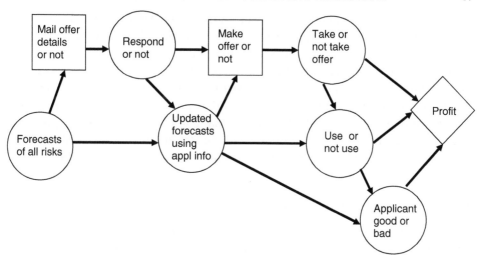

FIG. 1.4.3. Influence diagram for more realistic consumer lending process.

Decision trees

We now consider how one can build decision tree models of the decision structure visualized in the influence diagrams. A decision tree has a similar structure to influence diagrams consisting of nodes joined by arcs. In a decision tree, there are again three types of events depicted:

- Decisions – represented by rectangular nodes
- Chance events – represented by circular nodes
- Pay-off events – represented by numerical values at the end of each path.

The first represents points in time where the decision maker makes a choice. The second represents points in time where uncertainty gets resolved and the outcome of a chance event is revealed, while the third represents the final outcome of the decision process. The arcs out of the decision nodes represent the different actions that the decision maker can perform at that decision point, while the arcs out of the chance nodes represent the different way that uncertainty can be resolved. One gives a weight to each arc from a chance node to represent the probability of that outcome being the one that occurs. The pay-off value is the profit or cost to the decision makers but can also represent the utility to them of that outcome. The diagram is called a tree because none of its branches can join back together and so form cycles in the tree. This is because once a decision is made or a chance event resolved that information is available to all future decisions. One can solve the tree under the expected monetary value (EMV) criterion by starting at the end of each of the branches and working backwards in time though all the decision and chance event nodes. The value of the problem at each chance event node is the expected pay-off at that node which is calculated by weighting the values at the end of each arc out of that chance event by the probability of that outcome occurring and summing the result over all the arcs out of that node. The value at each decision node is the maximum value in the nodes at the end of the arcs leaving that node. This corresponds to choosing the decision that maximizes the expected profit. In each tree one can work back to the start of the tree and then identify the strategy that maximizes the profit by marking the options chosen at each decision node.

Decision trees for consumer credit decisions

One can represent the simple consumer credit decision of Fig. 1.4.1 by the decision tree in Fig. 1.4.4. There is an initial decision by the bank of whether to offer credit to the applicant. If it is not offered, the pay-off to the bank is taken to be 0. If credit is offered, there follows a chance event as far as the bank is concerned, which is whether the borrower's repayments are satisfactory ('good') or unsatisfactory, in that the borrower defaults ('bad').

Consider the situation where the profit to the bank if a borrower repays is 10 while the loss the bank incurs if the borrower defaults is 100. If one believes the chance of default is 5%, this is the same as saying the chance the borrower is a good is 0.95. In that case if one offers the loan then under the EMV criterion (that is average profit over all applicants) the expected profit from the borrower if the bank accepts them is

$$0.95.10 + 0.05(-100) = 4.5$$

while if the bank rejects the borrower the profit is 0. So the decision tree suggests that the bank should accept the borrower.

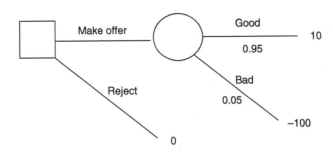

FIG. 1.4.4. Decision tree of simple consumer lending decision with numerical pay-offs.

If the probability of default changes to 10% and so the probability the borrower is good is 0.9, then the expected profit to the bank if the borrower is accepted is

$$0.9(10) + 0.1(-100) = -1.$$

So now the decision tree suggests that the bank should refuse the loan to the borrower.

In general let g be the profit made by the bank from repaying borrowers, and l be the loss the bank suffers because of the borrower defaulting. If we assume the probability the borrower will be good is p then we get the decision tree in Fig. 1.4.5. Here the weight on the arc that the borrower will repay by p and the arc that the borrower will default is given the probability weight of $1 - p$.

Using the EMV criterion, the expected profit per loan if the bank accepts everyone is $pg + (1-p)(-l)$ and is 0 if the bank rejects everyone. Thus, under this EMV criterion, the bank accepts applicants provided

$$pg - (1-p)l > 0 \text{ or that } p/(1-p) > l/g \qquad (1.4.1)$$

$p/(1-p)$, the chance of being good divided by the chance of being bad is called the good:bad odds.

The decision tree for the standard consumer credit decision is more complicated. The initial event is receiving the forecast of the probability that the applicant will repay (that is a 'good'). This could have many braches but to keep the decision tree simple we will assume in the decision tree in Fig. 1.4.6 that there are just two forecasts of this probability – high chance of repaying (H) and low chance of repaying (L). These forecasts are usually represented by a 'sufficient statistic', the default score, which we consider in more detail in the next section. In each case the bank then has to decide whether or not to make an offer. The next event is whether the applicant accepts the offer or not. This is a decision by the applicant but as far as the bank is concerned this is a chance event. Set the probability of take – that is that the offer is accepted – to be q. Later in Chapter 3, we will recognize that this

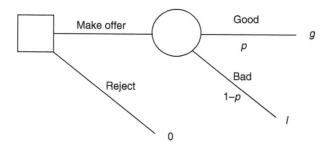

FIG. 1.4.5. Decision tree of simple consumer lending decision with general pay-offs.

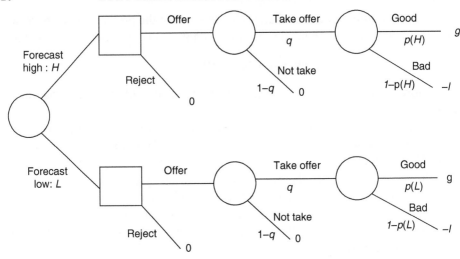

FIG. 1.4.6. Decision tree of standard consumer lending decision.

is a decision by the applicant and that the problem has became a game – a model involving two or more decision makers – and the decision tree will evolve into the extensive form model of games. The bank may also be able to obtain forecasts of whether the applicant will take the offer. These forecasts could take the form of response scores in the same way as the default forecasts could be given by default scores. We will ignore these extensions in Fig. 1.4.6. So, in that decision tree, we see that leading from the branch of the tree where applicants were made offers and then accepted them, there is one final chance event, namely whether the applicant turns out to be a good or a bad. The probabilities of these outcomes are set as $p(H)$ and $1 - p(H)$ if the original forecast was that the applicant had a high chance of repaying and $p(L)$ and $1 - p(L)$ if the forecast was that the chance of repayment was low. Working back through the tree under the EMV criterion one would accept applicants with high repayment forecasts if

$$q(p(H)g + (1 - p(H))(-l)) > 0 \tag{1.4.2}$$

and accept applicants with low repayment forecasts provided

$$q(p(L)g - (1 - p(L))l) > 0. \tag{1.4.3}$$

As it stands the take probability q does not seem to affect the decision. The rule for accepting an applicant is to accept those whose risk forecast X satisfies

$$\frac{p(X)}{1 - p(X)} > \frac{l}{g}. \tag{1.4.4}$$

If one defines $p(G|X) = p(X)$ to be the probability that someone with a forecast X is a good and $p(B|X) = 1 - p(X)$ to be the probability that someone with forecast X is a bad then

$$\frac{p(G|X)}{p(B|X)} \triangleq o(G|X) > \frac{l}{g} \tag{1.4.5}$$

where $o(G|X)$, the odds of being good is the probability of being good divided by the probability of being bad. This would extend to the situation where there are a whole range $x \in \mathcal{X}$ of different outcomes. In that case the lender maximizes the profit by accepting those who forecast are in the set $\mathcal{A}$ where

$$\mathcal{A} = \left\{ x \in \mathcal{X} \,|\, o(G|x) > \frac{l}{g} \right\}. \tag{1.4.6}$$

If though it was assumed those who were made offer but then rejected them cost the bank c in administration, a cost which is already incorporated in g and l for those who took the offer, then the bank should only accept a group if

$$q(pg + (1-p)l) - (1-q)c > 0 \tag{1.4.7}$$

and the acceptance probability is now impacting on the decision.

A decision tree model which tries to cover all the aspects of the lending decision would become far too unwieldy to use for computing the optimal strategy. However, like influence diagrams the exercise of drawing such a tree even with very crude outcomes for the chance events helps understand the sequence of decisions that are involved in the process. It also clarifies when information becomes available and when one would have liked it to be available. Figure 1.4.7 is representative of the decision tree that might be developed if one wanted to include some of the events

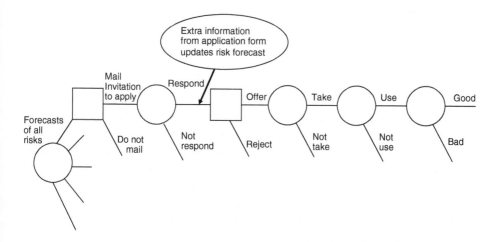

FIG. 1.4.7. Decision tree for the more realistic lending model in Fig. 1.4.3.

like usage, and response probabilities which were identified earlier in the influence diagram of Fig. 1.4.3 as affecting profitability.

Once the bank accepts an applicant, it is not the end of the decision making involving that borrower. The bank has do to decide what operating policy it should employ. The most obvious aspect of this is what credit limit to allow for revolving credit products like credit cards, or whether to allow or invite refinancing of the loan at a different interest rate and different terms for fixed loan products like auto loans and mortgages. The difference now is that the forecast of the probability of the borrower defaulting uses information on the repayment behaviour and current arrears status of the borrower rather than that available when they applied. If such information is translated into a score in the way which will be described in Section 1.5, this is called a behavioural (default) score, whereas that using the information available at application is not surprisingly called the application score.

Example 1.4.1

Consider a very simple case which is represented by the decision tree in Fig. 1.4.8. Here the forecast from the behavioural information again only take two values – high chance of repaying (H) and low chance of repaying (L). If there is no change in the credit limit, the profit to the bank if there is no default is g_0 and the loss if there is default is l_0. If the credit limit is increased then it is likely the profit, if no default will increase to g_1 but the loss if there is a default may also increase to l_1. Assume the change in credit limit does not affect the probability of repayments, which are $p(H)$ if the forecast was the high one (H) and $p(L)$ if the forecast was the low one (L). This leads to the decision tree in Fig. 1.4.8.

If the forecast is S (S is either H or L), assume the chance of repaying is $p(S)$, the bank should be willing to increase the credit limit if

$$g_1 p(S) + (1 - p(S))(-l_1) > g_0 p(S) + (1 - p(S))(-l_0)$$

$$\text{or} \quad \frac{p(S)}{1 - p(S)} > \frac{l_1 - l_0}{g_1 - g_0}. \tag{1.4.8}$$

This corresponds to the good:bad odds given the forecast being greater than the ratio of the increase in the loss on a default divided by the increase in profitability on a good. So the solution of this credit limit problem is equivalent to that of deciding whether to accept an applicant (or in this case accept more of the potential profit and the potential risk of a borrower) when the profit from the applicant is $(g_1 - g_0)$ and the loss if the applicant defaults is $(l_1 - l_0)$. The decision tree formulation shows that the credit limit increase decision is equivalent to the application decisions, but where one is deciding whether to take 'more' of the borrower.

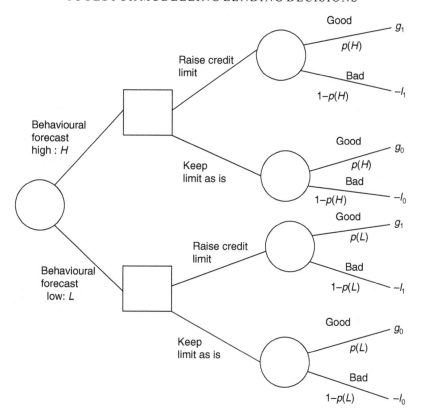

FIG. 1.4.8. Decision tree for higher credit limit decision.

Strategy trees

Strategy trees are ways of describing the strategies or sequence of decisions that one has decided to implement in the decision-making situation. This may be the optimal set of decisions obtained using a decision tree. So they have the same arcs as would appear in a decision tree but only the arcs describing the specific decision chosen at each particular node are included. The strategy tree will also ignore any chance event occurring after the last decision point. The aim is to give a clear description of the strategy involved in terms of what information must be looked at, and which decision made in the light of that information. Such a strategy tree could then be automated in the software used to process the application process. So a strategy tree for the more realistic lending decision described in the tree in Fig. 1.4.7 would look like Fig. 1.4.9.

In this case there were two decisions – whether to mail information about the loan offer to a prospective borrower and whether to accept the borrower if they

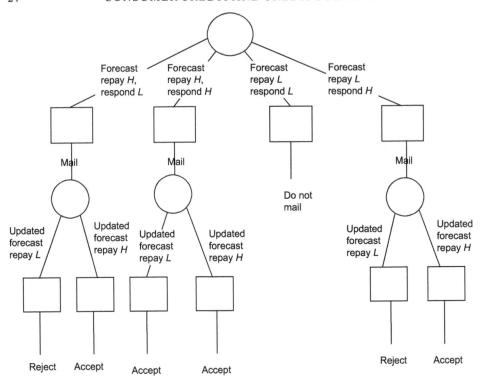

Forecast
repay H,
respond L

Forecast
repay H,
respond H

Forecast
repay L
respond L

Forecast
repay L
respond H

Mail

Mail

Mail

Do not
mail

Updated
forecast
repay L

Updated
forecast
repay H

Updated
forecast
repay L

Updated
forecast
repay H

Updated
forecast
repay L

Updated
forecast
repay H

Reject   Accept

Accept

Accept

Reject   Accept

FIG. 1.4.9. Strategy tree for more realistic lending model.

subsequently applied for the loan. In this case there are forecasts of the likely probability of the potential borrower repaying the loan and of responding to the mailing of the loan offer. To simplify matters we assume each of these forecasts is that the chance is either high (H) or low (L). For those who respond to the invitation by sending back the application form, the repayment forecast can be updated in the light of this information. It is this updated repayment forecast together with the earlier forecasts that is used to make the accept/reject decision. The strategy being suggested here is not to mail to those who have low forecasts of both the chance of responding to the offer and of then repaying the loan. Mail to the other possible applicants and reject those whose updated repayment forecast is low except for those whose original forecast was high for both repayment and response. In this hypothetical situation, one possible reason for taking this last group is that they are likely to be good targets for cross-selling opportunities.

Strategy trees are used to clarify what combination of chance events are considered in making the decision and what decision is made in the light of each combination. It is useful in the consumer credit case, where the chance events are the characteristics of and the forecasts concerning the borrower and these split the borrower population into a large number of groups and a different strategy is applied to each group. The strategy tree makes it clear which strategy is being applied to which group.

1.5 Probabilities, odds, information, and scores

It is clear from the last section that quantifying the chance of a borrower defaulting is critical in deciding whether a bank should advance credit or not and, if so, under what terms. Banks would like to produce well-informed forecasts of the chances that a borrower will repay on time and in the manner specified by the loan contract. Hopefully these forecasts would have more gradations than just the high and low levels of probability of being good which were used to illustrate the ideas in the previous section. It is in their best interests to have good techniques to assess the chance of a borrower being good.

There are three interrelated ways of describing the chance of a borrower being good. The first is the familiar one of estimating the probability that an event occurs; the second is to consider the odds of its occurrence; and the third is to prescribe a score or index, which contains all the information needed to estimate these odds. We want to understand how probabilities, odds, and scores are related to one another. Traditionally credit scorers have been primarily concerned with risk scores, that is, scores that measure the risk of defaulting, not paying on time, entering into a fraudulent transaction or other events that directly bear on whether the bank will be paid in accordance with a loan contract. As the examples in Section 1.4 showed there are also other uncertainties that are important to estimate when deciding on whether to accept a borrower, such as whether the borrower is likely to take the offer, and whether the borrower will use the credit card or loan facility when they have it. We concentrate on default risk but exactly the same analysis and resultant connection between probability, odds, and score hold for these other uncertainties.

Probabilities and odds

In credit scoring, one can analyse the historical data on past borrowers and use it to predict the likely future behaviour of prospective borrowers. To do this one assembles relevant data on the past borrowers from application forms, credit bureaus, accounting and financial records, as well as marketing information. The borrowers are then classified into two risk groups: good and bad. The bads refer to the individuals that default, go bankrupt, make late payments, and so on and the goods are ones who meet their financial obligations in full and on time. The probabilities of being good depend on the characteristics, $X = (X_1, X_2, \ldots, X_m)$, of the borrower that influence the repayment behaviour of the borrower. These characteristics can include socio-economic characteristics, like the age, residential status, and employment of an individual, their past credit performance including late or missed payments, and their existing debt obligations. Typically they have not usually included the environmental and economic conditions, but as we argue later these may provide extra useful information and could be included. The outcomes of each characteristic are called attributes and we will use X as our notation when we are discussing the characteristics in general and $\mathbf{x} = (x_1, x_2, \ldots, x_m)$ when we are dealing with the vector consisting of a specific set of outcome attributes of the characteristics. There may be a large number of different combination of attributes each of which gives a different vector $\mathbf{x}$ and we define $\mathcal{X}$, to be the set of all possible combination of attributes. In our illustrative examples though, we typically work with a small number of characteristics. The idea is to use the vector of attribute values of the characteristics, $\mathbf{x}$, of a borrower to estimate the probability that they will be a good that is, $\Pr\{\text{good}|\text{data } \mathbf{x}\}$. We write the conditional probabilities of good or bad given the relevant data $\mathbf{x}$ as

$$\Pr\{\text{good}|\text{data } \mathbf{x}\} = p(G|\mathbf{x}); \quad \Pr\{\text{bad}|\text{data } \mathbf{x}\} = p(B|\mathbf{x})$$

$$p(G|\mathbf{x}) + p(B|\mathbf{x}) = 1 \quad \mathbf{x} \in \mathcal{X}. \tag{1.5.1}$$

When dealing with probabilities it is often easier in practice to consider the odds of the event – the chance of the event happening divided by the chance of it not happening. Horse racing is a good example of where this occurs. Similarly with default risk one can assess the chance of a good or bad outcome by the odds of a good or bad, where we define the odds as the ratio of the probability of a good (bad) outcome to a bad (good) outcome:

$$o(G|\mathbf{x}) \triangleq \frac{p(G|\mathbf{x})}{p(B|\mathbf{x})} \quad \text{and} \quad o(B|\mathbf{x}) \triangleq \frac{p(B|\mathbf{x})}{p(G|\mathbf{x})} = \frac{1}{o(G|\mathbf{x})} \tag{1.5.2}$$

Let us see how one can use data on past borrowers to estimate these probabilities and odds.

Example 1.5.1 Probabilities and likelihoods from Bank of Southampton (Appendix B) data

Consider an example based on the hypothetical data in Appendix B, which we shall call the Bank of Southampton from now on. In this case one has a sample of 1000 previous borrowers and there are three characteristics available on each of them – age, residential status, and ownership of a credit card. Each borrower has been classified as good or bad. In this hypothetical example the number of goods is 900 and the number of bads is 100, making a total of 1000. We will concentrate only on one characteristic – the residential status – which has three attributes – owner, renter, or others. Consider the counts of owners, renters, and others in Table 1.5.1.

TABLE 1.5.1. Counts of residential status
from Appendix B data.

Attribute	Number good	Number bad
Owner	570	30
Renter	150	50
Other	180	20
Total	900	100

Using the table, a simple way to estimate whether an owner would be a good is to calculate the fraction of times (or the odds) that owners have good rather than bad outcomes.

Similarly we can estimate the chance of being good for renters and for others to get in the three cases:

$$p(G|owner) = \frac{570}{570 + 30} = 0.95 \qquad o(G|owner) = \frac{570}{30} = 19.0$$

$$p(G|renter) = \frac{150}{150 + 50} = 0.75 \qquad o(G|renter) = \frac{150}{50} = 3.0 \qquad (1.5.3)$$

$$p(G|other) = \frac{180}{180 + 20} = 0.90 \qquad o(G|others) = \frac{180}{20} = 9.0$$

Similar calculations can be made for the conditional probability or odds of a bad.

We are also interested in the distribution of the applicant's characteristics among the good and the bad populations separately. We can get these from the probabilities in (1.5.1) by using Bayes' theorem if we have some a priori view of the chance of applicants being good or bad. If we assume a priori that the chance an applicant will be a good is p_G and the chance they will be bad is p_B, which is equivalent to assuming that these are the fractions of goods and bads in the applicant population, then we can use Bayes' theorem as a way of turning the conditional probabilities around.

Bayes' rule says that if we have uncertain events E and F, then

$$Pr\{E|F\} = \frac{Pr\{F|E\} \times Pr\{E\}}{Pr\{F\}} \qquad (1.5.4)$$

This is obvious if you think of the chance of both E and F occurring. Depending on which event you think of first this probability is both $Pr\{E\} \cdot Pr\{F|E\}$ and $Pr\{F\} \cdot Pr\{E|F\}$. The equality of these two probabilities gives the Bayes' result.

Applying Bayes' rule in the case of the probability of a good or a bad having attributes $\mathbf{x}$ with the distribution of goods and bads in the population given by p_G

and p_B, respectively, gives

$$\Pr\{\text{data } \mathbf{x}|G\} = f(\mathbf{x}|G) = p(G|\mathbf{x})f(\mathbf{x})/p_G;$$

$$\Pr\{\text{data } \mathbf{x}|B\} = f(\mathbf{x}|B) = p(B|\mathbf{x})f(\mathbf{x})/p_B \forall \mathbf{x} \in X \qquad (1.5.5)$$

where $f(\mathbf{x})$ is the (very small) probability that an applicant will have attributes $\mathbf{x}$.

$f(\mathbf{x}|G)$ and $f(\mathbf{x}|B)$ are called likelihood functions, and describe how likely the attributes $\mathbf{x}$ are in the good (and bad) populations. They are also conditional probabilities like $p(G|\mathbf{x})$ but in order to avoid confusion, and because if X was an infinite set they could be density functions, we will denote them as $f(\mathbf{x}|.)$

If we return to the data in Example 1.5.1, we can calculate the likelihood that a good (or bad) will be an owner, renter, or other as follows:

$$f(\text{owner}|G) = \frac{570}{900} = 0.633 \qquad f(\text{owner}|B) = \frac{30}{100} = 0.3$$

$$f(\text{renter}|G) = \frac{150}{900} = 0.167 \qquad f(\text{renter}|B) = \frac{50}{100} = 0.5 \qquad (1.5.6)$$

$$f(\text{others}|G) = \frac{180}{900} = 0.20 \qquad f(\text{others}|B) = \frac{20}{100} = 0.2.$$

Information odds and population odds

There is one particular odds that keeps recurring in credit scoring and that is the population odds o_{Pop} defined by

$$o_{\text{Pop}} \triangleq \frac{p_G}{p_B} = \frac{p(G)}{p(B)}. \qquad (1.5.7)$$

It reflects the initial belief about the chance a borrower will be good before there is any information available on the borrower. Then when the information $\mathbf{x}$ is available about the borrower the posterior probabilities of good and bad are given by $p(G|\mathbf{x})$ and $p(B|\mathbf{x})$. We can divide the two expressions in Eq. (1.5.5) by one another and get the result that the *posterior odds* of an individual being good is obtained from Bayes' rule by

$$o(G|\mathbf{x}) = \frac{p(G|\mathbf{x})}{p(B|\mathbf{x})} = \frac{p_G f(\mathbf{x}|G)}{p_B f(\mathbf{x}|B)} \equiv o_{\text{Pop}} \times I(\mathbf{x}), \quad \mathbf{x} \in X \qquad (1.5.8)$$

where it can be recalled that $f(\mathbf{x}|G)$ and $f(\mathbf{x}|B)$ are the *likelihoods* of the data $\mathbf{x}$ conditioned on the borrower being good (bad). $I(\mathbf{x})$, the ratio of the conditional likelihood of a good having attributes $\mathbf{x}$ divided by the likelihood of a bad having attributes $\mathbf{x}$, is referred to as the *information odds*.

Equation (1.5.8) shows that the odds of a borrower with attributes $\mathbf{x}$ is the product of the prior population odds, which is independent of the individual borrower's attributes and the information odds, which depend on the attributes of the borrower.

Information odds $I(\mathbf{x})$ greater than 1 suggest that the borrowers with those attributes $\mathbf{x}$ are more likely than the general population to be good; information odds $I(\mathbf{x})$ less than 1 suggest that the corresponding borrowers are less likely to be good than the general population. We will find subsequently that the log of the information odds, $\ln(I(\mathbf{x}))$, is also a useful way of assessing the information that the data $\mathbf{x}$ carries about the probability of the borrower being good and it is called the weights of evidence provided by $\mathbf{x}$.

Example 1.5.1 (continued)

We can check the results of Bayes' rule by noting that in Table 1.5.1 of Example 1.5.1, we have immediately that $p_G = 900/1000 = 0.9$ and $p_B = 100/1000 = 0.1$. Also note that $p(\text{owner}) = 600/1000 = 0.6$. $p(\text{renter}) = 200/1000 = 0.2$, and $p(\text{others}) = 200/1000 = 0.2$. Then:

$$p(G|\text{owner}) = \frac{f(\text{owner}|G)}{p(\text{owner})} p_G = \frac{0.633}{0.6} 0.9 = 0.95 \quad \text{and}$$

$$p(B|\text{owner}) = \frac{f(\text{owner}|B)}{p(\text{owner})} p_B = \frac{0.3}{0.6} 0.1 = 0.05$$

$$p(G|\text{renter}) = \frac{f(\text{renter}|G)}{p(\text{renter})} p_G = \frac{0.167}{0.2} 0.9 = 0.75 \quad \text{and}$$

$$p(B|\text{renter}) = \frac{f(\text{renter}|B)}{p(\text{renter})} p_B = \frac{0.5}{0.2} 0.1 = 0.25$$

$$p(G|\text{other}) = \frac{f(\text{other}|G)}{p(\text{other})} p_G = \frac{0.2}{0.2} 0.9 = 0.9 \quad \text{and}$$

$$p(B|\text{other}) = \frac{f(\text{other}|B)}{p(\text{other})} p_B = \frac{0.2}{0.2} 0.1 = 0.1. \tag{1.5.9}$$

The population odds in the example is $o_{\text{Pop}} = 900/100 = 9$ and so Eq. (1.5.8) becomes:

$$o(G|\text{owner}) = o_{\text{Pop}} \times \frac{f(\text{owner}|G)}{f(\text{owner}|B)} = 9 \times \frac{0.633}{0.3} = 19$$

$$= o_{\text{Pop}} \times I(\text{owner}), \quad \text{where} \quad I(\text{owner}) = 2.11$$

$$o(G|\text{renter}) = o_{\text{Pop}} \times \frac{f(\text{renter}|G)}{f(\text{renter}|B)} = 9 \times \frac{0.167}{0.5} = 3$$

$$= o_{\text{Pop}} \times I(\text{renter}), \quad \text{where} \quad I(\text{renter}) = 0.33 \tag{1.5.10}$$

$$o(G|\text{others}) = o_{Pop} \times \frac{f(\text{others}|G)}{f(\text{others}|B)} = 9 \times \frac{0.2}{0.2} = 9$$

$$= o_{Pop} \times I(\text{others}), \text{ where } I(\text{others}) = 1.0.$$

Forecasting using information odds

In the early days of credit risk scoring, the information odds could be used to improve judgemental cut-off rules for acquisition. By trial and error a bank could use a score based solely on information odds to determine the relative risk of the borrowers. Determination of PopOdds was not critical since it just wanted a ranking of the borrowers in relative risk. However, this approach only works if there are a few characteristics to consider because otherwise the calculations get too severe.

Using the chain rule to express the joint probabilities in Eq. (1.5.8), we can write the odds as

$$o(G|x_1, x_2, \ldots, x_n) = \frac{p_G}{p_B} \times \frac{f(x_1, x_2, \ldots, x_n|G)}{f(x_1, x_2, \ldots, x_n|B)}$$

$$= \frac{p_G}{p_B} \times \frac{f(x_1|G)}{f(x_1|B)} \times \frac{f(x_2|G, x_1)}{f(x_2|B, x_1)} \times \cdots \times \frac{f(x_n|G, x_2, \ldots, x_{n-1})}{f(x_n|B, x_2, \ldots, x_{n-1})}.$$

$$(1.5.11)$$

One could, in principle, build contingency tables of ever-increasing dimension to estimate the likelihood functions needed for Eq. (1.5.11). Bank's databases though often contain records of 150 or more characteristics on each borrower or loan applicant, and so this approach is really not practical. Estimating the densities $f(\mathbf{x})$ for these high-dimensional contingency tables is the heart of the problem. For problems with 10 characteristics, each with five attributes, we see that $5^{10} = 9,765,625$ cells are needed to calculate all the information odds needed. If there are 100 characteristics each with two attributes (that is binary outcomes), then 2^{100} or approximately 1.3×10^{30} cells are required. To further complicate the problem many of the cells of these high-dimensional contingency tables will have counts of zero as most attribute combinations are never observed. Even with current advances in computing technology, it is impossible to obtain statistical estimates of this number of likelihood probabilities.

What is needed is an efficient, reproducible, and accurate scoring technology which, once calculated, represents each borrower with a scalar number, instead of the vector $\mathbf{x}$ of attributes of the characteristics. This is what a score does.

Score as a sufficient statistic

A score, $s(\mathbf{x})$, is a function of the characteristics' attributes $\mathbf{x}$ of a potential borrower which can be translated into the probability estimate that the borrower will be good.

The critical assumption in credit scoring is that the score is all that is required for predicting the probability of the applicant being good. In some ways the score is like a sufficient statistic. It is also usual to assume that the score has a monotonic increasing relationship with the probability of being good – in that case the score is called a **monotonic score**. Such scores preserve rankings so if a borrower has a higher score than a second borrower, the first borrower has a higher probability of being good than the second.

We assume that a **proper** or **sufficient score** $s(x)$ captures as much information for predicting the probability of a performance outcome, say good/bad, as does the original data vector, $\mathbf{x}$. We will assume throughout the book that we have proper scores. This assumption that the risk score includes all the information required to predict good/bad outcomes means that

$$\Pr\{\text{good}|\text{score based on } \mathbf{x}\} = p(G|s(\mathbf{x})) = p(G|s(\mathbf{x}), \mathbf{x}) = p(G|\mathbf{x}) \ \forall \mathbf{x} \in \mathcal{X} \tag{1.5.12}$$

So with a proper score we can replace the multi-dimensional characteristics $\mathbf{x}$ describing a borrower by the scalar value $s(\mathbf{x})$ and this does not change the forecasted probability that the borrower will be a good. If one used a different set of characteristics, with attribute combinations $\mathbf{y}$ where $\mathbf{y} \in \mathcal{Y}$, one could develop another proper risk score $s(\mathbf{y})$. The two scores might agree on all borrowers or they might not, but they would give rise to the same probability of a borrower being a good.

From now on we will often drop the $\mathbf{x}$ dependence of the score and write

$$p(s) = p(G|s(\mathbf{x})) \quad \text{and} \quad 1 - p(s) = 1 - p(G|s(\mathbf{x})) = p(B|s(\mathbf{x})) \ \forall \mathbf{x} \in \mathcal{X} \tag{1.5.13}$$

Similarly we would drop the $\mathbf{x}$ dependence in the likelihoods and use

$$f(\{\mathbf{x}|s(\mathbf{x}) = s\}|G) = f(s|G); f(\{\mathbf{x}|s(\mathbf{x}) = s\}|B) = f(s|B); f(\{\mathbf{x}|s(\mathbf{x}) = s\}) = f(s)$$

If a score $s(\mathbf{x})$ is a proper score, then we can extend the result in Eq. (1.5.8) that the odds of a borrower with characteristics $\mathbf{x}$ is the product of the population odds and the information odds to a similar result for scores, namely,

$$o(G|s) \equiv o(G|\{\mathbf{x}|s(\mathbf{x}) = s\}) = \frac{p_G f(\{\mathbf{x}|s(\mathbf{x}) = s\}|G)}{p_B f(\{\mathbf{x}|s(\mathbf{x}) = s\}|B)} = o_{\text{Pop}} \frac{f(s|G)}{f(s|B)} = o_{\text{Pop}} \times I(s) \tag{1.5.14}$$

where $I(s) = f(s|G)/f(s|B)$ is the information odds provided by the score s.

Log odds score

The odds function $o(G|\mathbf{x})$ as defined in (1.5.8) can be though of as a score since it contains all the information in $\mathbf{x}$ that is useful in estimating the probability of a borrower being good. Moreover one can always extract the original probability from the odds, and it has the property that as the odds increase so does the probability of the borrower being good. However, there is another score function – the log odds score – which has come to dominate credit scoring both because it has such attractive theoretical properties and also because one of the main approaches to building scorecards – logistic regression, described in more detail in Section 1.9 – will give scorecards which are of that type.

We define the log odds score as

$$s(\mathbf{x}) \triangleq \ln o(G|\mathbf{x}) = \ln \frac{p(G|\mathbf{x})}{p(B|\mathbf{x})} \qquad p(G|\mathbf{x}) + p(B|\mathbf{x}) = 1 \qquad \mathbf{x} \in \mathcal{X}. \quad (1.5.15)$$

where ln is log to the base e (it is not necessary to take this base but it has become standard practice). Log odds stretch the scale of measurement for extremely small or large probabilities. The emphasis on rare events and very small probabilities is important as the probability of default for an individual borrower is small but the loss consequence for most bank portfolios is very large.

The definition of a log odds score should not be confused with the estimation procedure commonly referred to as logistic regression. Logistic regression attempts to find a score function that is a sum of attribute level scores and has the log odds score properties. There are other ways of building score functions as discussed in Section 1.10, and in some of these one can transform or scale the score function so that it is approximately a log odds score.

Specifying the odds or score of an event is equivalent to specifying its probability because we can write the probability in terms of odds:

$$p(G|\mathbf{x}) = \frac{o(G|\mathbf{x})}{1 + o(G|\mathbf{x})} \qquad p(B|\mathbf{x}) = \frac{1}{1 + o(G|\mathbf{x})}$$

or, in terms of score:

$$p(G|\mathbf{x}) = \frac{o(G|\mathbf{x})}{1 + o(G|\mathbf{x})} = \frac{e^{s(\mathbf{x})}}{1 + e^{s(\mathbf{x})}} = \frac{1}{1 + e^{-s(\mathbf{x})}}. \quad (1.5.16)$$

Log odds score separates weights of evidence and population odds

The most important theoretical feature of a log odds score is that it separate out completely the information about the population from the idiosyncratic information about the individual borrower being scored. If we take the log of the Bayes' rule in Eq. (1.5.8), we get a log odds score which splits into two components: one term depending on population odds and another on information odds:

$$s(\mathbf{x}) = \ln o(G|\mathbf{x}) = \ln \left(\frac{p_G f(\mathbf{x}|G)}{p_B f(\mathbf{x}|B)} \right) = \ln \left(\frac{p_G}{p_B} \right) + \ln \left(\frac{f(\mathbf{x}|G)}{f(\mathbf{x}|B)} \right)$$

$$= \ln o_{\text{Pop}} + \ln I(\mathbf{x}) = s_{\text{Pop}} + s_{\text{Inf}}(\mathbf{x}) \qquad (1.5.17)$$

where $s_{\text{Inf}}(\mathbf{x}) \stackrel{\Delta}{=} w(\mathbf{x}) \stackrel{\Delta}{=} \ln I(\mathbf{x})$.

This says that the log odds score is the sum of a term depending only on the population odds ($s_{\text{pop}} = \ln o_{\text{pop}}$) and a term which depends on the information on the borrower $\mathbf{x}$. The first term on the right-hand side (RHS) of (1.5.17) can be thought of as the 'prior' score – that is, the score of a randomly selected individual from the population; this score is then increased or decreased by the score which is based on the data that is unique to a particular individual.

The latter term, the log of $I(\mathbf{x})$, is called the weights of evidence of the information in $\mathbf{x}$, $w(\mathbf{x})$. There is a similar definition for the weights of evidence for a score s, so that

$$w(\mathbf{x}) = \log I(\mathbf{x}) = \log \left(\frac{f(\mathbf{x}|G)}{f(\mathbf{x}|B)} \right) = \log \left(\frac{P(G|\mathbf{x})f(\mathbf{x})/p_G}{P(B|\mathbf{x})f(\mathbf{x})/p_B} \right)$$

$$= \log \left(\frac{P(G|\mathbf{x})/P(B|\mathbf{x})}{p_G/p_B} \right)$$

and

$$w(s) = \log I(s) = \log \left(\frac{f(s|G)}{f(s|B)} \right) = \log \left(\frac{P(G|s)f(s)/p_G}{P(B|s)f(s)/p_B} \right)$$

$$= \log \left(\frac{P(G|s)/P(B|s)}{p_G/p_B} \right). \qquad (1.5.18)$$

So the weights of evidence is the log of the ratio of the good:bad odds for the groups with that information $\mathbf{x}$ or score s, compared with the original population odds. If it is positive it suggests that this group is better than the overall population and if it is negative it suggests the good rate for this group is worse than for the whole population.

The above result that the log odds score separates so naturally in (1.5.17) makes log odds and this equation so useful. Note again that the information odds score depends on characteristics of the individual, but the PopOdds score does not. Another reason why log odds are more useful than just the odds themselves is that if one takes the obvious estimator of log odds by taking samples of the data, the estimator can be approximated by a normal distribution when the sample size is much smaller than is necessary to get the odds estimator to have a normal distribution (Hosmer and Lemeshow 1989, p. 44).

Let us see how we construct a log odds score using the data from the Bank of Southampton in Appendix B.

Example 1.5.2 Log odds score using Bank of Southampton data (Appendix B)

The Southampton bank has a sample of 1000 cases to build a log odds score, and there were three different characteristics – residential status, age, and credit card. The data for residential status was given in Table 1.5.1, but we repeat it in Table 1.5.2 together with the data on age. The age characteristic has four attributes – under 30, 30–39, 40–49, and over 50.

First let us construct the weights of evidence, $w(\mathbf{x})$ and the log odds score, $s(\mathbf{x})$ for the residential status attributes. The resultant score is what we would have to use if residential status is the only characteristic available. We can use the results of (1.5.4) or (1.5.10) in the calculation:

$$s_{\text{Pop}} = \ln(o_{\text{Pop}}) = \ln(900/100) = 2.197$$

$$w(\text{owner}) = s_{\text{inf}}(\text{owner}) = \ln(I(\text{owner})) = \ln\left(\frac{f(\text{owner}|G)}{f(\text{owner}|B)}\right)$$

$$= \ln\left(\frac{0.633}{0.3}\right) = 0.747$$

$$s(\text{owner}) = s_{\text{Pop}} + w(\text{owner}) = 2.197 + 0.747 = 2.944$$
$$= \ln(570/30) = \ln(o(G|\text{owner}))$$

$$w(\text{renter}) = s_{\text{inf}}(\text{renter}) = \ln(I(\text{renter})) = \ln\left(\frac{f(\text{renter}|G)}{f(\text{renter}|B)}\right)$$

$$= \ln\left(\frac{0.167}{0.5}\right) = -1.099 \tag{1.5.19}$$

$$s(\text{renter}) = s_{\text{Pop}} + w(\text{renter}) = 2.197 - 1.097 = 1.10 = \ln(150/50)$$
$$= \ln(o(G|\text{renter}))$$

$$w(\text{others}) = s_{\text{inf}}(\text{others}) = \ln(I(\text{others})) = \ln\left(\frac{f(\text{others}|G)}{f(\text{others}|B)}\right) = \ln\left(\frac{0.2}{0.2}\right) = 0.0$$

$$s(\text{others}) = s_{\text{Pop}} + w(\text{others}) = 2.197 + 0.0 = 2.197$$
$$= \ln(180/20) = \ln(o(G|\text{others})).$$

So we end up with weights of evidence of 0.747, -1.097, and 0 for owners, renters, and others, respectively, which reflect the fact that owners are more likely to be good than others, who in turn are more likely to be good than renters. The log odds score values are 2.944, 1.10, and 2.197, respectively.

TABLE 1.5.2. Residential status and age data from Bank of Southampton (Appendix B).

Residential status attribute	Number good	Number bad	Age attributes	Number good	Number bad
Owner	570	30	Under 30	175	26
Renter	150	50	30–39	175	30
Other	180	20	40–49	175	15
Total	900	100	Over 50	375	29

Suppose in fact this was only a random sample from the original application population or rather a random sample of the goods. In the original population there were in fact 5000 goods, not just the 900 in the sample but only the 100 bads used in the sample. How would this affect the log odds score The change in the population odds does not change the information odds and hence the weights of evidence at all and so the only change will be in the population odds. So the scores would become

$$s_{Pop} = \ln(o_{Pop}) = \ln(5000/100) = 3.912$$

$$s(\text{owner}) = s_{Pop} + w(\text{owner}) = 3.912 + 0.747 = 4.659 = \ln(o(G|\text{owner}))$$

$$s(\text{renter}) = s_{Pop} + w(\text{renter}) = 3.912 - 1.097 = 2.815 = \ln(o(G|\text{renter}))$$

$$s(\text{others}) = s_{Pop} + w(\text{others}) = 3.912 + 0.0 = 3.912 = \ln(o(G|\text{others})).$$

$$(1.5.20)$$

Obviously the presence of a large PopOdds increases the overall score but the information odds score does not change.

Suppose instead the only characteristic available was age, but the population was back to 900 goods and 100 bads then the weights of evidence and log odds scores would then be calculated as follows:

$$s_{Pop} = \ln(o_{Pop}) = \ln(900/100) = 2.197$$

$$w(\text{under 30}) = s_{\text{inf}}(\text{under 30}) = \ln\left(\frac{f(\text{under 30}|G)}{f(\text{under 30}|B)}\right)$$

$$= \ln\left(\frac{175/900}{26/100}\right) = \ln\left(\frac{0.1944}{0.26}\right) = -0.291$$

$$s(\text{under 30}) = s_{Pop} + w(\text{under 30}) = 2.197 - 0.291 = 1.906$$

$$= \ln(175/26) = \ln(o(G|\text{under 30}))$$

$$w(30 - 39) = s_{\text{inf}}(30 - 39) = \ln\left(\frac{f(30 - 39|G)}{f(30 - 39|B)}\right)$$

$$= \ln\left(\frac{175/900}{30/100}\right) = \ln\left(\frac{0.1944}{0.30}\right) = -0.434$$

$$s(30 - 39) = s_{\text{Pop}} + w(30 - 39) = 2.197 - 0.434 = 1.763$$

$$= \ln(175/30) = \ln(o(G|30 - 39))$$

$$w(40 - 49) = s_{\text{inf}}(40 - 49) = \ln\left(\frac{f(40 - 49|G)}{f(40 - 49|B)}\right)$$

$$= \ln\left(\frac{175/900}{15/100}\right) = \ln\left(\frac{0.1944}{0.15}\right) = 0.259$$

$$s(40 - 49) = s_{\text{Pop}} + w(40 - 49) = 2.197 + 0.259 = 2.456$$

$$= \ln(175/15) = \ln(o(G|40 - 49))$$

$$w(\text{over } 50) = s_{\text{inf}}(\text{over } 50) = \ln\left(\frac{f(\text{over } 50|G)}{f(\text{over } 50|B)}\right) = \ln\left(\frac{375/900}{29/100}\right)$$

$$= \ln\left(\frac{0.4167}{0.29}\right) = 0.362$$

$$s(\text{over } 50) = s_{\text{Pop}} + w(\text{over } 50) = 2.197 + 0.362 = 2.559$$

$$= \ln(375/29) = \ln(o(G|\text{over } 50)). \tag{1.5.21}$$

We now have two predictions for odds of a good, one based on age and the other based on residential status. They are very different from one another. How do we combine these different results to obtain a prediction which makes use of the information in both age and own/rent status The simplest approach is to use Bayes' rule in a very naïve way.

Naïve Bayes' scorecard building

In general, Bayes' rule applies even when we have two or more predictive factors. For example with our data on owners/renters and age, we can write

$$o(G|x_1, x_2) = \frac{p(G|x_1, x_2)}{p(B|x_1, x_2)} = \frac{p_G f(x_1, x_2|G)}{p_B f(x_1, x_2|B)}. \tag{1.5.22}$$

If we could make the strong assumption that the attributes of residential status (x_1) and age (x_2) were independent of one another, the likelihood $f(x_1, x_2|G)$ of x_1 and x_2 can be factored into two parts: one depending only on x_1 and the other only on x_2 so that the joint likelihood depends only on the outcomes of age and the outcomes of residential status. In this case the odds could be rewritten as

$$o(G|x_1, x_2) = o_{Pop} \frac{f(x_1|G) f(x_2|G)}{f(x_1|B) f(x_2|B)}. \qquad (1.5.23)$$

The product of the first two factors on the RHS are the odds obtained when information on age is unavailable; we can now write the conditional odds of a good conditional on both characteristics as the conditional odds on one times an adjustment that is the likelihood ratio for the second characteristic.

$$o(G|x_1, x_2) = o_{Pop} \frac{f(x_1|G) f(x_2|G)}{f(x_1|B) f(x_2|B)} = o(G|x_1) \times \frac{f(x_2|G)}{f(x_2|B)} = o(G|x_2) \times \frac{f(x_1|G)}{f(x_1|B)}.$$

Taking logs gives:

$$\ln(o(G|x_1, x_2)) = \ln(o_{Pop}) + \ln\left(\frac{f(x_1|G)}{f(x_1|B)}\right) + \ln\left(\frac{f(x_2|G)}{f(x_2|B)}\right)$$

$$= \ln(o(G|x_1)) + \ln\left(\frac{f(x_2|G)}{f(x_2|B)}\right)$$

$$= \ln(o(G|x_2)) + \ln\left(\frac{f(x_1|G)}{f(x_1|B)}\right)$$

$$\Rightarrow s(x_1, x_2) = s_{Pop} + w(x_1) + w(x_2)$$

$$= s(x_1) + w(x_2) = s(x_2) + w(x_1). \qquad (1.5.24)$$

This result generalizes in the sense that if we have n independent characteristics numbered $x_1, x_2, \ldots, x_n$ rather than x_1 and x_2 then we can write the odds formula as

$$o(G|\mathbf{x}) = o(G|x_1, x_2, \ldots, x_n) = o_{Pop} \frac{f(x_1|G) f(x_2|G)}{f(x_1|B) f(x_2|B)} \cdots \frac{f(x_n|G)}{f(x_n|B)} \qquad (1.5.25)$$

and, therefore, the score can be written as

$$s(\mathbf{x}) = \ln o_{Pop} \frac{f(x_1|G) f(x_2|G)}{f(x_1|B) f(x_2|B)} \cdots \frac{f(x_n|G)}{f(x_n|B)}$$

$$= \ln o_{Pop} + \ln \frac{f(x_1|G)}{f(x_1|B)} + \ln \frac{f(x_2|G)}{f(x_2|B)} + \cdots + \ln \frac{f(x_n|G)}{f(x_n|B)} \qquad (1.5.26)$$

$$= s_{Pop} + (w_1(x_1) + w_2(x_2) + \cdots + w_n(x_n)) = s_{Pop} + s_{Inf}(\mathbf{x}).$$

This is another surprising result in that it says that with these assumptions the log odds score for an individual borrower is the sum of the log of the population odds and the weights of evidence for each of the attributes of that borrower. So all one needs to do is to calculate the weights of evidence for each attribute and add the appropriate ones to get a score function. The function is a linear combination of the weights of evidence of the attributes.

A score is defined to be **additive** if it is the sum of attribute values where each value depends only on the one attribute. Thus an additive score would satisfy

$$s(\mathbf{x}) = v_0 + v_1(x_1) + v_2(x_2) + \cdots + v_m(x_m), \mathbf{x} \in \mathcal{X}. \qquad (1.5.27)$$

So the naïve Bayes' score is an example of an additive score. Additive scores are much preferred in practice because it is clear what the effect of each attribute in the scorecard is.

Recall that the calculation of the probability of being good from the underlying score must always include the relevant PopOdds, as in

$$p(G|s(\mathbf{x})) == \frac{1}{1 + e^{-s(\mathbf{x})}} = \frac{1}{1 + e^{-s_{Pop}} e^{-s_{Inf}(\mathbf{x})}}. \qquad (1.5.28)$$

Example 1.5.2 (continued) Naïve Bayes' applied to Southampton Bank data

In Example 1.5.2 we ended up with weights of evidence and log odds scores for a scorecard based on residential status only in (1.5.18) and on age only in (1.5.20). If we wanted a scorecard based on information about age and residential status, then if we assume that these two characteristics are independent, we can use the naive Bayes' formula to get the scorecard defined in (1.5.26). The scores $s(x_1, x_2)$ for each of the 12 different combinations of residential status and age attributes are given in Table 1.5.3, where $s_{Pop} = 2.197$.

Thus the second column shows that for those who are owners and under 30, the resulting score, which is the sum of the log of the population odds (2.197) and the weights of evidence for being an owner (0.747) and of being under 30 (-0.291), is 2.654. This corresponds to good:bad odds of 14.21:1, which is $e^{2.654}$:1. Looking at the different groups the ones with the highest score are those who are owners over 50, who have a score of 3.307. Using (1.5.16), this means that the probability of being good for this group is

$$P(G|\text{owner, over 50}) = \frac{1}{1 + e^{-3.307}} = 0.965.$$

The ones with the lowest score are renters, aged between 30 and 39 who have a score of 0.665. For these the probability of being good is

$$P(G|\text{renter, 30–39}) = \frac{1}{1 + e^{-0.665}} = 0.660.$$

The last three rows of Table 1.5.3 show the actual numbers of goods and bads in that group and so the actual odds. Comparing these with the odds obtained from the score show significant differences in some cases. For example, in the last column of Fig. 1.5.3 – the 'others' aged over 50 – the odds from the score were 13:1 whereas the actual odds were 20:1. This is because the assumption of independence between

TABLE 1.5.3. Results of applying naïve Bayes' approach to Bank of Southampton data.

Owner $w(x) = 0.747$	1	1	1	1	0	0	0	0	0	0	0	0
Renter $w(x) = -1.099$	0	0	0	0	1	1	1	1	0	0	0	0
Others $w(x) = 0$	0	0	0	0	0	0	0	0	1	1	1	1
Under 30 $w(x) = -0.291$	1	0	0	0	1	0	0	0	1	0	0	0
30–39 $w(x) = -0.434$	0	1	0	0	0	1	0	0	0	1	0	0
40–49 $w(x) = +0.259$	0	0	1	0	0	0	1	0	0	0	1	0
Over 50 $w(x) = 0.362$	0	0	0	1	0	0	0	1	0	0	0	1
Score: $s(x) = 2.197 + w(x_1) + w(x_2)$	2.654	2.511	3.204	3.307	0.808	0.665	1.358	1.461	1.907	1.764	2.457	2.560
Odds from score: $o(G|x) = e^{s(x)}$	14.21	12.31	24.63	27.30	2.24	1.94	3.89	4.31	6.73	5.83	11.67	12.93
Actual numbers of goods	65	125	145	235	53	20	17	60	57	30	13	80
Actual number of bads	5	8	8	9	16	14	4	16	5	8	3	4
Actual odds	13.00	15.63	18.13	26.11	3.31	1.43	4.25	3.75	11.40	3.75	4.33	20.00

age and residential status was not valid in this case. In fact these numbers were constructed to ensure that there were strong interactions between the characteristics, probably stronger than one gets in reality. However, it shows that the naïve Bayes' approach is not robust enough to build practical scorecards. In Sections 1.8, 1.9, and 1.10, we discuss the methodology and techniques that are currently most commonly used to build scorecards. In these methodologies one tries to ensure that the characteristics that remain in the final scorecard are not strongly correlated. The techniques used try to compensate for the remaining dependencies by choosing score values for the attributes which are not just their weights of evidence.

Score distributions

To get a feel for how good the score is in distinguishing goods from bads in a population of borrowers, one needs to describe the distribution of the scores among the goods and among the bads. The conditional distributions of scores, that is, the distribution of scores for the good and bad risk sub-groups given the observed performance, are of theoretical and practical interest. The conditional distribution functions are denoted by

$$\Pr\{\text{score} \leqslant s | G\} = F(s|G) = \int_{-\infty}^{s} f(u|G)du \quad \text{and} \quad F(s|B) = \int_{-\infty}^{s} f(u|B)du.$$

$$(1.5.29)$$

Having constructed a score, one can describe the riskiness of the population of borrowers by describing the distribution function of the scores on the whole population. This can be obtained from the conditional distribution functions by

$$F(s) = p_G F(s|G) + p_B F(s|B). \tag{1.5.30}$$

We often have to make a notational decision about whether the scores and applicant characteristics should be represented as discrete or continuous entities. Typically, each characteristic contains only a finite number of attribute values – even the apparently continuous ones such as age and income – and only a finite number of characteristics; it is therefore correct to consider scores as discrete quantities and deal with the probability of them taking on specific values. For example, the discrete version of the cumulative distribution function for scores could, in these cases, be written as

$$F_i(G) = \Pr\{\text{score} \leqslant s_i | G\} = \sum_{j=0}^{i} f_j(G)$$

where the score bins are enumerated by the index i or j. In our experience, model formulations and the mathematical analyses of these models are considerably simplified by formulating the scoring models in continuous terms. Once the formulas and insights have been obtained, it is usually a straightforward matter to reformulate and make computations for the discrete equivalents.

1.6   Modifying scores: scaling, multiple levels, and time dependency

Scores are modified and extended in a number of different ways. In this section we look at three of these: how and why to scale or recalibrate a score; how and why to build a multi-level scoring system where some of the attributes that make up a score are themselves scores from a different scorecard; and how to introduce time-dependent scores.

Scaling of natural scores

It may be important in business applications to specify scores on different scales rather than to use the natural log odds scores we introduced in the previous section. The reasons are often to give a better understanding of the score to non-experts. For example we had a score in the last section which went from 0.665 to 3.307, which psychologically may make non-experts think there is not much difference in the results whereas if we multiply the score by 200 so it went from 133 to 661 they might think this implies a significant difference. Scales are common in a number of other areas and have a variety of properties. For example, temperature is taken as an ordinal scale with two fixed points given specific values: the temperature of freezing water is set at 0°C and of boiling water at 100°C. The centigrade scale has the property that a difference of 5°C corresponds to the same difference in heat energy at all points on the scale. In fact one has a second scale for temperature where the freezing point of water is set as 32°F and the boiling point of water is 212°F. One can transform a value on the centigrade scale to a value on the Fahrenheit scale by the linear transformation:

$$F = 1.8C + 32$$

or its inverse,

$$C = 0.555F - 17.77.$$

Stock market and other financial and economic indices define the ratio of the current position to one at a fixed date in the past to reflect growth over time. Intelligence quotient (IQ) is also an ordinal scale but with one fixed point (100 is supposed to be the IQ of the average person at some date in the past). The other features of the IQ rating are unclear to the public. When local authorities used scoring to prioritize who would get the first available local authority housing, it was important from a political point of view that no attribute was given a negative point value. These examples illustrate the different properties of scales that are in general use though it is not clear which ones the general public understand or which properties they prefer. So which properties of scales should a credit score have? The following properties of scores have been advocated by various lenders.

- Total score is positive.

This means that the final score given to someone $s = s_{Pop} + s_{inf}$ should be a positive value. This does not automatically happen for a log odds scores since it would require that

$$\log\left(\frac{p(s)}{1-p(s)}\right) = s > 0 \Leftrightarrow \frac{p(s)}{1-p(s)} > 1 \Leftrightarrow p(s) > 0.5. \qquad (1.6.1)$$

And there may be scores where there is less than an even chance of being good.

- There is one or more reference (or anchor) score which have specified good:bad odds.

For the log odds score, $\log\left(\frac{p(s)}{1-p(s)}\right) = s \Leftrightarrow \frac{p(s)}{1-p(s)} = e^s \Leftrightarrow o_m(s) = e^s$ and so there is the obvious relationship between score and odds.

- Differences in scores have constant meaning throughout the scale.

For a log odds score, this property also will always hold, because if one considers the scores s and $s + h$, then

$$e^s = \left(\frac{p(G|s)}{p(B|s)}\right); \; e^{s+h} = \frac{p(G|s+h)}{p(B|s+h)} \Rightarrow$$
$$e^h = \frac{p(G|s+h)}{p(B|s+h)}\bigg/\frac{p(G|s)}{p(B|s)} = \frac{o(G|s+h)}{o(G|s)} \qquad (1.6.2)$$

and so the ratios of the odds at s and $s + h$ depend only on h. So a difference of h in the scores has the same meaning throughout the scale.

The two requirements that are used most in practice are to have one reference point and to try and ensure that differences in scores have constant meaning throughout the range. If one chooses the reference score appropriately though one can also ensure all scores are positive. If a business user wants these properties or may be wants scores specified on a scale of 0 to 100, 0 to 1000, or between 500 and 1000, this can be achieved by applying a linear transformation to the log odds score so that

$$s_{Scaled} = a + bs_{original} \qquad (1.6.3)$$

where s_{Scaled} is the scaled score, and a and b are constants representing the intercept and slope of the straight line. For example, behaviour scores typically cover a range of values from 500 to 850 rather than values between -4 and $+4$.

Suppose one wants to scale a log odds score so that in the new score a value of 600 occurs when the odds are 15:1 and that an increase in the scaled score of 20 points corresponds to a doubling of the odds. With odds of 15:1 a log odds score would have a value $\ln(15)$, while doubling the odds changes a log odds score from h to $h + \ln(2)$. Thus we would require a scaling where

$s_{\text{Scaled}} = a + bs$ with the properties

$s_{\text{Scaled}} = 600 = a + b \ln 15$

$$20 = (a + b(h + \ln 2)) - (a + bh) = b \ln 2 \qquad (1.6.4)$$

$$\Rightarrow b = \frac{20}{\ln 2} = \frac{20}{0.693} = 28.860 \Rightarrow a = 600 - (28.86)\ln(15) = 521.85.$$

This calculation for the scaled score means that it can be expressed in terms of the original score as

$$s_{\text{Scaled}} = 521.85 + 28.86s.$$

Just as we can convert from Fahrenheit to centigrade and vice versa, we can also calculate the natural score from its scaled score or vice versa. In the above example,

$$s = 0.034s_{\text{Scaled}} - 18.082.$$

Example 1.6.1 Scaling of scores from run book in Appendix A

Appendix A presents the run book, which describes the numbers of goods and bads in different score bands, for a particular scoring system. The first column gives the different score bands, which go from 143 to more than 449. The other columns describe, respectively, the number of goods and the number of bads in the band; the marginal odds of goods to bads in the score band; the cumulative number of goods and bads with scores in or below that band; the proportion of goods and of bads with scores in or below that band; and the cumulative good:bad odds for those with scores in or below that score band. The population odds of the sample is $18{,}234/883 = 20.65{:}1$. Looking at the data we can plot the graph of the log of the marginal odds against the score and we do this in Fig. 1.6.1 for the score range 200 to 420 (before we start having to adjust the marginal odds by adding 0.5 to the numbers of goods and bads in that score band to prevent the marginal odds becoming infinite).

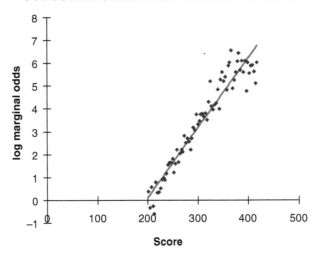

Fɪɢ. 1.6.1. Plot of log of marginal odds against score and corresponding regression line.

The corresponding regression line of the log of marginal odds against score s gives the relationship:

$$\text{Ln (marginal odds)} = -5.997 + 0.030588 \, s \qquad (1.6.5)$$

The original score was built with the idea that a score of 200 would correspond to odds of 1:1 and a score of 400 would correspond to odds of 500:1 Neither of those works out quite correctly using equation (1.6.5) since a score of 200 corresponds to log marginal odds of 0.120 which gives marginal odds of $e^{0.120} : 1 = 1.13 : 1$, while a score of 400 corresponds to log marginal odds of 6.238 which gives marginal odds of $e^{6.238} : 1 = 512 : 1$

Suppose one wanted to scale the score so instead it had the properties that an increase of 30 in the score doubled the log odds (so the log odds to score gradient should be ln(2)/30=0.023105) and that a score of 150 would correspond to marginal odds of 1:1, which is the same as log marginal odds of 0. If one used equation (1.6.3) where

$$s_{scaled} = a + bs_{original}$$

then the gradient of the log odds to the score for the scaled score is 1/b times the gradient of the log odds to the original score, i.e.(0.030588/b) where the gradient of the original score is given by equation(1.6.5). Thus to rescale the gradient we require

$$\frac{0.030588}{b} = \frac{\ln(2)}{30} \Rightarrow b = 1.324.$$

To get the anchor point of marginal odds of 1:1 at a score of 150, one needs to note that in the current score those marginal odds occur at a score of 196. This can be checked because marginal odds of 1;1 is equivalent to log marginal odds of 0 and from equation (1.6.5) that occurs at a score of $5.997/0.030588 = 196$. Thus a value of 196 on the original score needs to be transformed to 150 on the scaled score and so

$$150 = a + b(196) = a + 1.324(196) \Rightarrow a = -109.5$$

$$\Rightarrow s_{scaled} = -109.5 + 1.324 s_{original}.$$

(1.6.6)

This type of scaling has been adopted by a number of credit bureaus and score vendors for many years, although the precise details of the reference (anchor) point or the slope are usually proprietary. What we learn from this scaling is that the sensitivity of the scaled score to the change in odds affects the determination of b whereas the PopOdds only affects the intercept, a.

If a scorecard is applied to a new population of borrowers where the PopOdds changes but the information odds does not, the new fitted odds can be easily computed by noting that

$$o(G(\mathbf{x})) = \frac{p_G f(s(\mathbf{x})|G)}{p_B f(s(\mathbf{x})|B)} \quad o'(G(\mathbf{x})) = \frac{p'_G f(s(\mathbf{x})|G)}{p'_B f(s(\mathbf{x})|B)} \Rightarrow o'(G(\mathbf{x}))$$

$$= \frac{p'_G \, p_B}{p'_B \, p_G} o(G(\mathbf{x})) = \frac{o'_0}{o_0} o(G(\mathbf{x})).$$

(1.6.7)

If one assumes the original scorecard gave a log odds score

$$s(x) = \ln\left(\frac{p_G}{p_B}\right) + \ln\left(\frac{f(s(\mathbf{x})|G)}{f(s(\mathbf{x})|B)}\right) = s_{Pop} + s_{Inf}(\mathbf{x}),$$

then the score on the new population can be rescaled to be a log odds score by adding a constant, since

$$s'(\mathbf{x}) = \ln\left(o'(G(\mathbf{x}))\right) = \ln\left(\frac{p'_G}{p'_B}\right) + \ln\left(\frac{f(s(\mathbf{x})|G)}{f(s(\mathbf{x})|B)}\right)$$

$$= \ln\left(\frac{p'_G}{p'_B}\right) + \left(s(x) - \ln\left(\frac{p_B}{p_G}\right)\right)$$

$$= (s'_{Pop} - s_{Pop}) + s(\mathbf{x}) = a + s(\mathbf{x}).$$

(1.6.8)

Scaling normally distributed scores to make them log odds scores

One of the first approaches to building a score – linear regression, which we will discuss in more detail in Section 1.9 – assumed that scores were such that the conditional good and bad score distributions were normally distributed. This means that the density functions for the good sub-population could be written as

$$f(s|G) = \frac{1}{\sigma_G \sqrt{2\pi}} \exp -\frac{1}{2}\left(\frac{s - \mu_G}{\sigma_G}\right)^2$$

(1.6.9)

The expression for the conditional bad density is identical except that the subscript B is used for mean and variance. If s is a proper score but not necessarily a log odds score for a given database, then the log of the likelihood ratio of good and bad scaled scores – the weights of evidence at score s – satisfies:

$$\ln\frac{f(s|G)}{f(s|B)} = \left(\ln\frac{\sigma_B}{\sigma_G} - \frac{1}{2}\left(\frac{s-\mu_G}{\sigma_G}\right)^2 + \frac{1}{2}\left(\frac{s-\mu_B}{\sigma_B}\right)^2\right) \qquad (1.6.10)$$

which is seen to be quadratic in the score with coefficients expressed in terms of the means and variances of the conditional distributions. The standard assumption in the linear regression approach to building a scorecard is that the variances are equal, that is, $\sigma_G = \sigma_G = \sigma$. In that case, the weights of evidence become linear in the score since

$$\ln\frac{f(s|G)}{f(s|B)} = \frac{1}{2\sigma^2}\left(2(\mu_G - \mu_B)s - (\mu_G^2 - \mu_B^2)\right) = a + bs. \qquad (1.6.11)$$

In practical applications, weights of evidence are often found to be approximately linear in the score over large ranges of score values even when the assumption of normality with equal variances would not appear to be a good assumption. Assuming Eq. (1.6.11) holds then this original score can be scaled so that it becomes a log odds score as follows:

$$s_{\text{log odds}} = \ln\frac{p_G}{p_B} + \ln\frac{f(s|G)}{f(s|B)} = \left(\ln\frac{p_G}{p_B} - \frac{(\mu_G^2 - \mu_B^2)}{2\sigma^2}\right) + \frac{\mu_G - \mu_B}{\sigma^2}s = a + bs.$$
$$(1.6.12)$$

So scaling can transfer a proper score, which has normally distributed score distributions for the goods and the bads, or weights of evidence which are linear in the score into a log odds score. Several approaches to building a scorecard produces scores which are not log odds scores but have score distributions close to normal for the goods and the bads, with roughly equal variances in the two cases. Scaling is a way of changing such scores into approximately log odds score.

The most common use of scaling though is to have scores with an anchor point and an agreed meaning for the gradient of the score – doubling the log odds every 10 points say. So even if a non-log odds score is changed into an approximately log odds score by scaling it is probably scaled further (often the two scaling processes are done in one exercise) to arrive at these properties.

Multiple-level scorecards using information from different sources

Banks have access to a number of sources to acquire information to build scorecards. Obviously a bank will have the applicant's application form data available, and for existing borrowers they have the records of their performance which they can use to improve their estimates of the risk score or make decision about increasing the credit limit, repricing the loan or trying to cross-sell another product. Banks can also pay for the credit bureau information on the borrower which describes their default records and in some countries their positive performance on other loans. Also if a borrower has several products with the bank they may have a record on the primary product – say, their current or checking account – which they want to use on deciding the risk of lending on other products.

If one has two data sets of attributes of different characteristics $\mathcal{X}$ and $\mathcal{Y}$, how should one build a scorecard One obvious way is to amalgamate the data sets and derive a score based on $\mathcal{X} \cup \mathcal{Y}$. There may be a number of reasons why a bank does not want to do this. First, they may want to use a scorecard based only on $\mathcal{X}$ for other purposes, and may well have already built such a scorecard. For example it may be the data used for building an application scorecard, and they are thinking of using it in behavioural scorecards as well. Second, they may have to pay for the extra data in $\mathcal{Y}$. They will not want to pay for the data for those borrowers where from the score based on the database $\mathcal{X}$ the risk of the borrower defaulting is so small (or so large) that it is clear what decision the bank should make about such a borrower. Thirdly the bank may feel that the quality of the data in one data base is so superior to that in another that they want to have a score based on the superior data as well as on the combined data. This superiority could be because one set of data changes much more slowly than the other. So for example if the bank is trying to build a response score but wants to use the data appropriate for default risk $\mathcal{X}$ as well as data $\mathcal{Y}$ on response rates under current market conditions, the latter are likely to change much more quickly than the former.

For these reasons, lenders have become accustomed to building a scorecard on $\mathcal{X}$ and then using the score from that scorecard $s(\mathbf{x}), \mathbf{x} \in \mathcal{X}$ as one of the characteristics in a new database on which to build a new score $s_2(\mathbf{y}, s(\mathbf{x}))$, where $(\mathbf{y}, s(\mathbf{x})) \in \mathcal{Y} \cup s(\mathbf{x})$. This exploits the proper property of the score $s(\mathbf{x})$ which says that it contains all the information in $\mathcal{X}$ needed to assess the risk under question. Some of the popularity of this model stems from the fact that if the $\mathbf{x}$-data contains m characteristics and the $\mathbf{y}$-data contains n characteristics, the scoring estimation problem has been reduced from a problem with $m + n$ characteristics to a problem with $n + 1$ characteristic, one of which is the original score. Quite often the new data $\mathbf{y}$ has low dimensionality compared to the original so that $n + 1$ is very much smaller than $m + n$.

One can repeat this process at a higher level. If $s_2(\mathbf{y}, s(\mathbf{x}))$, where $(\mathbf{y}, s(\mathbf{x})) \in \mathcal{Y} \cup s(\mathbf{x})$ is the score built at this second level one can add it to another data base $\mathcal{Z}$ to build a third level score $s_3(\mathbf{z}, s_2(\mathbf{y}, s(\mathbf{x})))$, where $(\mathbf{z}, s_2(\mathbf{y}, s(\mathbf{x}))) \in \mathcal{Z} \cup s_2(\mathbf{y}, s(\mathbf{x}))$. A common occurrence of three levels of scores is when the bank buys a generic score from a credit bureau, which the credit bureau has built using the data it has available. This score is then added to the information that the lender has about the performance of a customer on their primary account, which is often not a loan product but a current or checking account, to build a second-level customer score. This customer score is then added to the information of the borrower on a particular loan product like a mortgage or personal loan to build a third-level risk score for that borrower on that product.

Hazard rates and time-dependent scores

So far the probability, odds and score have not considered the time period over which the borrower goes bad. Borrowers are either good or bad and it does not matter when they go bad. When in Chapter 4, we start considering the time dependence of events, we need to look at how scores can be used to help estimate when events will occur. In reality, time will be discrete – since banks only record the month when a borrower defaulted, and not when within that month it occurred. However, when dealing with such survival analysis ideas of when events occur, it is clearer to give the definitions in continuous time and recognize we can then construct the discrete time equivalents – usually by replacing integration by summation.

In a continuous time-dependent model of default, let T be the instant of time at which default occurs, which we think of as the instant the borrower went bad. The probability that this will happen before time t is given by

$$P_B(t) = \Pr\{T < t\} \tag{1.6.13}$$

and so the probability of default in $(t, t + \delta t]$ is

$$\Pr\{t < T \le t + \delta t\} = P'_B(t)\delta t.$$

The probability survival function that default will occur after t equals the probability that there has been no default in $(0,t]$ which can be written as

$$P_G(t) = 1 - P_B(t) = \Pr\{T \ge t\} = \Pr\{\text{default occurs at or after } t\} = \int_t^\infty P'_B(u)du. \tag{1.6.14}$$

Implicit in this equation is the idea that every borrower will eventually default, that is, $P_B(\infty) = 1$. Of course this is really semantics because loans do not last long enough nor borrowers live long enough for this condition ever to be checked. If a lender has a strong objection to this statement though one can always say

$$\lim_{t \to \infty} P_B(t) = P_B^{ever}$$

and then add a point mass of $1 - P_B^{ever}$ at $t = \infty$.

Define the default hazard rate or hazard function, $h(t)$, as the rate where $h(t)\delta t$ is the conditional probability of default in $(t, t+\delta t]$ given there has been no default in $(0,t]$:

$$h(t) = \Pr\{t \le T < t + \delta t | T \ge t\} \stackrel{\Delta}{=} \frac{P'_B(t)}{1 - P_B(t)}$$

$$= -\frac{d}{dt} \ln(1 - P_B(t)) = -\frac{d}{dt} \ln(P_G(t)). \tag{1.6.15}$$

This is not the probability that borrowers will default at a time t into the loan but rather the probability that given the borrowers is still active at time t they will default in the next instant of time. (The equivalent in human mortality is not that someone will die aged 85 but rather the probability that someone on their 85th birthday will die in the next year.) If one integrates the relation between hazard rate and the derivative of the survival function shown in Eq. (1.6.15), one gets a relationship between the cumulative hazard function and the survival function as follows. Define the cumulative hazard function, $H(t)$, by

$$H(t) \stackrel{\Delta}{=} \int_0^t h(u)du. \tag{1.6.16}$$

Then by integrating Eq. (1.6.15), the survival probability and the probability of default can be expressed in terms of the cumulative hazard function to get

$$P_G(t) = 1 - P_B(t) = e^{-H(t)} \quad \text{or} \quad P'_B(t) = h(t)e^{-H(t)}. \tag{1.6.17}$$

Note that the odds of not defaulting before time τ is

$$o(\tau) = \frac{1 - P_B(\tau)}{P_B(\tau)} = \frac{1}{e^{H(\tau)} - 1}. \tag{1.6.18}$$

This suggests that we can define a score not just for the good:bad odds in some fixed period in the future but for any period $[0,\tau)$ in the future. Define the time-dependent score $s(0,\tau)$ by the log of the odds of the chance of being good (that is not defaulting) during the period $[0,\tau)$ divided by the chance of becoming bad (that is defaulting) during that period. Then

$$s(0, \tau) = \ln\left(\frac{P_G(\tau)}{P_B(\tau)}\right) = \ln o(\tau) = -\ln\left(e^{H(\tau)} - 1\right). \tag{1.6.19}$$

In fact one could extend this definition to define a score over any time interval in the future not just the ones that start at the current time. Define $s(t,\tau)$ by

$$s(t, \tau) = \ln\left(\frac{\Pr\{T \ge t + \tau | T \ge t\}}{\Pr\{t \le T < t + \tau | T \ge t\}}\right) = \ln\left(\frac{P_G(t + \tau)}{P_B(t + \tau) - P_B(t)}\right)$$

$$= -\ln\left(e^{H(t+\tau) - H(t)} - 1\right). \tag{1.6.20}$$

Example 1.6.2 Exponential default rate: constant hazard rate

Let us assume that the hazard rate is constant exponential, so that

$$h(t) = \lambda \quad \text{and} \quad H(t) = \lambda t.$$

Assume that $H(0) = 0$. It follows that

$$P_{\mathrm{B}}(t) = \Pr\{\text{default before } t\} = 1 - e^{-H(t)} = 1 - e^{-\lambda t}.$$

The time-dependent score is given by

$$s(t) = \ln o(t) = -\ln\left(e^{H(t)} - 1\right) = -\ln(e^{\lambda t} - 1), \qquad (1.6.21)$$

which starts at $t = 0$ at a value close to $+\infty$ and falls monotonically until $s(\infty) = -\infty$.

This is an example of a borrower whose risk of defaulting does not depend on how long the loan has been running – the 'months on books' of the loan.

Example 1.6.3 Weibull distribution hazard rate

If one wants a varying hazard rate, then an obvious possibility is the Weibull distribution. This has two parameters, the shape λ and the scale α. For values of $\lambda < 1$, the hazard rate is monotonically decreasing, while if $\lambda > 1$ it is monotonically increasing. For $\lambda = 1$, the Weibull distribution reduces to the exponential distribution with constant hazard rate. For the general Weibull distributions, the hazard rate and cumulative hazard function become

$$h(t) = \frac{\lambda}{\alpha}\left(\frac{t}{\alpha}\right)^{\lambda-1} \quad \text{and} \quad H(t) = \left(\frac{t}{\alpha}\right)^{\lambda}.$$

Assume that $H(0) = 0$. It follows that

$$P_{\mathrm{B}}(t) = \Pr\{\text{default before } t\} = 1 - e^{-H(t)} = 1 - e^{-\left(\frac{t}{\alpha}\right)^{\lambda}}.$$

The time-dependent score is given by

$$s(t) = \ln o(t) = -\ln\left(e^{H(t)} - 1\right) = -\ln(e^{\left(\frac{t}{\alpha}\right)^{\lambda}} - 1), \qquad (1.6.22)$$

which again starts at $t = 0$ at a value close to $+\infty$ and falls monotonically until $s(\infty) = -\infty$.

Figure 1.6.2 shows the form of the hazard functions for the two different cases (a) $\lambda = 2, \alpha = 5$ and (b) $\lambda = 0.5, \alpha = 2$.

The estimation and calibration of hazard rates, scores, and fitted odds is a difficult problem. In Chapter 4, we make use of a special form of hazard function, known as the proportional hazards model (Cox 1972), where the hazard rate is expressed as the product of two factors, one being dependent on the characteristics

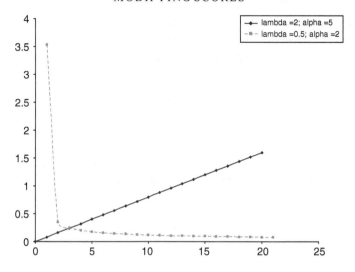

FIG. 1.6.2. Hazard functions for Weibull distributions.

$\mathbf{x}$ of the individual borrower and the other on the age, t, of the loan. This gives a hazard function of the form:

$$h(t, \mathbf{x}) = g(\mathbf{x})h_0(t) = e^{\mathbf{w} \cdot \mathbf{x}}h_0(t) \qquad (1.6.23)$$

where one writes $g(\mathbf{x})$ in exponential form to ensure that it is non-negative since all rates must be non-negative. $h_0(t)$ is the baseline hazard function which describes the impact of the age of the loan on the default rate of all borrowers. If $H(t)$ and $H_0(t)$ are the corresponding cumulative hazard functions, Eq. (1.6.23) leads to the relationship in (1.6.24) between them.

$$\exp(-H(t)) = \exp -\left\{ \int_0^t e^{\mathbf{w} \cdot \mathbf{x}}h_0(u)du \right\} = \left(\exp -\left\{ \int_0^t h_0(u)du \right\} \right)^{e^{\mathbf{w} \cdot \mathbf{x}}}$$

$$= \left(\exp -H_0(t) \right)^{e^{\mathbf{w} \cdot \mathbf{x}}}. \qquad (1.6.24)$$

Discrete time hazard probabilities

In the equivalent discrete time notation, $P_B(n) = \Pr\{T < n\}$ and $P_G(n) = \Pr\{T \geq n\}$ can have the same interpretation as in continuous time model. The hazard rate $h(t)$ becomes the hazard probability, $h(n)$ namely the conditional probability of default in period n given no default up to that time.

$$h(n) = \Pr\{T = n | T \geq n\} \qquad (1.6.25)$$

The probability of defaulting before period n, $P_B(n)$ can be calculated by recognizing that not defaulting by that time must be the product of the probabilities of not defaulting at any of the periods up to then. This leads to

$$P_B(n) = 1 - \prod_{j=1}^{n-1} (1 - h(j)). \tag{1.6.26}$$

The equivalent of the cumulative hazard function, now though is no longer the sum of the hazard functions but rather is defined as

$$H(n) = -\sum_{j=1}^{n-1} \ln(1 - h(j))$$

Since $P_G(n) = 1 - P_B(n) = \Pr\{T \geq n\} = \prod_{j=1}^{n-1}(1 - h(j)) \tag{1.6.27}$

$$= e^{\sum_{j=1}^{n-1} \ln(1-h(j))} = e^{-H(n)}.$$

We would have expected that the hazard function would be $H(n) = \sum_{j=1}^{n-1} h(j))$ but that is only approximately correct when the hazard probability is small. This can be seen by using the following approximation which holds when x is small:

$$-\ln(1 - x) = x + \tfrac{1}{2}x^2 + \tfrac{1}{3}x^3 + \cdots$$

This leads to $H(n) = -\sum_{j=1}^{n-1} \ln(1 - h(j)) = \sum_{j=1}^{n-1} h(j) + o(h^2) \ldots$
and if $h(i)$ is small one can ignore the second-order terms. We will use this discrete version of the hazard probabilities in the next section when we look at models over more than one time period.

Notice we have not specified what clock is measuring the time T. In fact this idea of hazard rates and hazard function can be used in two different ways. In the first – the one that is used most in this area – the clock starts when the loan starts and so one is measuring the maturity of the loan. This is important because it is recognized the chance of defaulting on a loan changes with the maturity of the loan. There is a saying 'If they go bad, they go bad fast'. This would be one way of trying to deal with that effect. The alternative is that the clock measures calendar time and in this case the time dependence is allowing for changes in the economic conditions in the credit market. This is something that is used quite a lot in corporate credit risk modelling but has not yet been widely used in consumer credit risk.

1.7 Lending returns and costs

In Section 1.4, the models for consumer lending depended on estimating the risk of the borrower defaulting and the return obtained by the lender. In the last two sections, we introduced ways of estimating the risk of lending to a single borrower: probability of default, and risk score, among others. In this section we look at the return to the lender in more detail. First, we suggest a 'cleaner' formulation of the basic problem by concentrating on the returns on the lending rather than the actual amount of profit or loss. These rate models are the ones we will use predominately in the rest of the book.

We point out that in other types of lending like a corporate bond portfolio, lenders measure the rate of return of their investment rather than the profit and we compare these two ways of measuring the outcome for our simple one period consumer loan model. Most lending though is over several periods with partial repayments being made each period. We show how the rate of return extends in such cases in two different ways – the short rate and the spot rates – by looking at the two period cases. Finally we discuss the types of repayments that occur in a multi-period loan and how the expressions for the profitability of a loan and rate of return on the loan extend to the multi-period case.

Rate of return model for one period loan

In the decision tree-based lending models, introduced in Section 1.4, the outcomes were given in terms of profit and loss on the loan. These did not involve how much was the original loan. Banks though are interested in the return on the loan – how much is the revenue or the profit on the loan as a ratio of the amount loaned. It is clear that a bank would rather make two loans of $100 each, each of which gives profits of $20, rather than one loan of $200 which gives a profit of $30 even though the profit on the latter is greater than that on each of the individual loans in the former case.

The relationships between risk and return are much clearer if the outcomes are expressed as the return on 1 unit of money ($, £, €, ¥) loaned. To translate the results of the return models back to total amounts we just need to multiply by the total amount loaned (or in later portfolio models in the book, the total amount that would have been loaned if every applicant had been accepted and taken the loan).

Assume that a loan of 1 unit results in a pay-off of 0 if the borrower defaults, and has a return of $1 + r_L$, where r_L is the lending rate charged, if the borrower repays. If the probability of default is p_B, the return of $(1 + r_L)$ is obtained with probability $p_G = 1 - p_B$. If on the other hand the loan is not made then the 1 unit can be put into non-defaultable loans like treasury bonds or cash savings account, where the return is the risk-free rate, r_F and so the pay-off is $1 + r_F$. This leads to the decision tree in Fig. 1.7.1 which is identical with the simple consumer lending

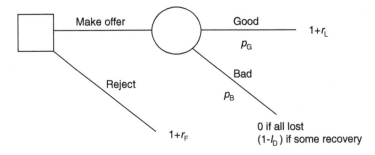

FIG. 1.7.1. Decision tree of simple consumer lending decision with rate of return pay-offs.

tree displayed in Fig. 1.4.5 except the pay-offs are given in terms of the return on the loan.

If the bank is risk-neutral, that is, its utility or satisfaction is linear in the profit or loss it makes, then it will decide to offer the loan if the expected return on the loan is greater than not offering the loan, that is if

$$p_G(1 + r_L) > 1 + r_F \Rightarrow r_L > \frac{1 + r_F}{p_G} - 1 \Rightarrow r_L > \frac{r_F + p_B}{p_G}. \quad (1.7.1)$$

If when the borrower defaults, the bank is still able to recover some of the loan – which might be the whole amount in the case of mortgages for example – then the pay-off at the end of the bad arc has to be changed. If we assume that a fraction l_D of the loan is actually lost when the borrower defaults then the pay-off is $(1 - l_D)$. The loan should then be offered provided:

$$p_G(1 + r_L) + p_B(1 - l_D) > 1 + r_F \Rightarrow r_L > \frac{r_F + p_B l_D}{p_G} \quad \text{or} \quad p_G > \frac{r_F + l_D}{r_L + l_D}. \quad (1.7.2)$$

From now on we shall use this model with lending and risk-free rate as our standard model rather than the model with pay-offs of g and $-l$.

What is meant by loss given default and how one calculates the recovery rate $(1 - l_D)$ are not straightforward. One of the outcomes of the new Basel banking regulations, discussed in more detail in Chapter 5, has been to require banks to address the way of modelling loss given default more fully. It is recognized that loss given default is a random variable, but in this book we will always use its expected value and so it can be considered as a constant. That still leaves open the question of what the denominator is in the fraction l_D. Normally, as in a one-period loan, we define l_D as the fraction of the original loan that is lost, and so in Fig. 1.7.1, the amount recovered on a loan of 1 is $1 - l_D$. In other circumstances, including the Basel banking regulations alluded to above and the case of multi-period loans, the loss is considered as a fraction of the balance at default, and so in Fig. 1.7.1 one would assume that it is a fraction of $1 + r_L$ that is lost since the loan has accrued interest. On the few occasions we use this definition we will denote the loss given default as l_D^B as the 'loss given default on the outstanding balance'. Since the amount recovered is the same whichever way we define l_D the two definitions are connected in the problem described in Fig. 1.7.1 by

$$(1 - l_D)1 = (1 - l_D^B)(1 + r_L) \text{ or}$$

$$l_D^B = \frac{l_D + r_L}{1 + r_L} = l_D + \frac{r_L(1 - l_D)}{1 + r_L}. \tag{1.7.3}$$

In most cases we will use l_D since it leads to simpler expressions and shows more clearly why loss given default acts as if it were adjusting the interest rates being charged as is shown in Eq. (1.7.2).

Calculating risk rates using one period rate of return model on corporate bonds

The simple rate of return model introduced earlier also describes the loan decisions for corporate bonds but these are continuously traded thereafter. This means there is a market in these bonds and their price keeps changing until risk-neutral investors are indifferent between buying such a bond or putting their money in a risk-free investment, that is indifference between 'offering' or 'not offering' the loan. So for bonds the lending rate r_L (often called the coupon) of the bond is not the return on the bond, since the cost c of buying the bond keeps varying. Thus the return if the bond does not default is $1 + r_R = (1 + r_L)/c$ which the investor will expect with probability p_G. If the bond defaults, which we assume happens with probability p_B, then the return on the money the investor paid for the bond is $1 - l_D$. This means the return is 0 if the loss given default on the defaulted bond is 1, and so no money is returned. The return is 1 if the loss given default on the bond is 0 and so the money paid for the bond is recovered completely. Note here for simplicity we take loss given default to be based on the price paid for the bond not its face value, whereas in bond pricing models the latter definition of loss given default is taken. So at the market price of the bond an investor is indifferent between buying the bond and putting the money into a risk-free opportunity with a risk-free rate of r_F. This means that for a risk neutral investor the no arbitrage equation says:

$$p_G(1 + r_R) + p_B(1 - l_D) = 1 + r_F$$

or

$$r_R = \frac{r_F + l_D p_B}{p_G} = r_F + \frac{(r_F + l_D)p_B}{p_G}. \tag{1.7.4}$$

Note that, if we know the risk-free rate, then observing the bond prices in the market means we can calculate the implicit default probability the market puts on the bond, provided the loss given default is known by rearranging Eq. (1.7.4) to get:

$$p_B = \frac{r_R - r_F}{r_R + l_D}. \tag{1.7.5}$$

Alternatively if the probability of default is known (through the rating the bond is given), one can determine what the market believes the loss given default to be by solving for the default rate to obtain

$$l_D = \frac{(1 - p_B)r_R - r_F}{p_B}. \tag{1.7.6}$$

Two ways of measuring consumer lending – profitability and rate of return

Although there is no continuous market trading consumer debt as there is trading corporate debt bonds, one can measure the rate of return on the loans in the same way as described earlier. Thus we have already identified two ways of measuring the financial outcomes of consumer loans. First we can calculate the extra expected profit or return the bank will make on the loan, compared with investing the money in a risk-free asset, which from (1.7.2) is

$$p_G(1 + r_L) + p_B(1 - l_D) - (1 + r_F) = p_G r_L - p_B l_D - r_F. \tag{1.7.7}$$

Another way of thinking of this is to say that the lender borrows the money at the risk-free rate and then lends it at the rate r_L. If the lender has to pay more to borrow the money than the risk-free rate, say a borrowing rate r_B then the expected profit is again given by Eq. (1.7.7) but with r_F replaced by r_B.

The second way of measuring the outcome of the consumer loans is to evaluate the rate of return, r_R, on the loan as defined in (1.7.4). This says how much the loan would be worth if there was a market in which to trade such loans. The bank can then compare investing in the loan with other investments where there is a market and hence a rate of return that can be calculated from the price. Note in this case the rate of return on the loan is only a function of the risk-free rate r_F, the default probability of the loan p_B, and the loss given default l_D. The lending rate r_L does not come into the rate of return r_R because Eq. (1.7.4) assumes the market is full of risk-neutral investors who price the loan simply on its default characteristics. The profit criterion is important in the relationship between the bank and the borrower; the rate of return criteria is important in the relationship between the bank and its investors.

Two period rate of return model with spot and short rates

We described the model earlier in this section as a one period model because there was no need to distinguish the maturity (months on books) of the loan. This is the case provided there are no partial repayments of the loan during its term, and that the market and economic conditions do not change. If any of these events occur then it is more sensible to model the loan as extending over several time periods. A time period is usually taken to be a month in the consumer context because repayments usually occur monthly but any appropriate time interval can be used. The question then is how the rate of return definition changes when we have a multi-time period loan and how these new variants of rate of return relate to each other and to the default hazard rates introduced in Section 1.6. We do this initially by looking at a loan or a bond that repays at the end of two time periods.

Suppose one has a loan which must be repaid at the end of two time periods and let the risk-free rate in period 1 be r_F^1 and in period 2, r_F^2. Recall that in Section 1.6 we defined $h(i)$ to be the probability of the loan defaulting in period i given that it has not defaulted up to that period. So here we are interested in $h(1)$ and $h(2)$, the default hazard rates in the two periods. One may ask how a loan can go bad if there is no repayment in the period. This occurs when the borrower defaults on other loans in that period, but also corporate loans (bonds) have coupons and so the interest rate at least has to be paid in each period and the borrower can default on that payment. If the loan or bond is to be sold at the end of the first period to some other lender, then the rate of return in that period r_R^1 must satisfy the same relationship as that for a one period bond in (1.7.4) namely:

$$(1 - h(1))(1 + r_R^1) + h(1)(1 - l_D) = 1 + r_F^1. \tag{1.7.8}$$

Similarly, in period 2, define r_R^2 to be the rate of return in that period. Assuming the borrower has not defaulted in the first period, the relationship between the return on the bond in this period and investing in a risk-free opportunity in this second period must again satisfy the no arbitrage equation namely:

$$(1 - h(2))(1 + r_R^2) + h(2)(1 - l_D) = 1 + r_F^2. \tag{1.7.9}$$

The two Eqs. (1.7.8) and (1.7.9) can only be verified if the lender can sell the loan at the end of the first period and someone else can then buy it. This is obviously true for corporate bonds and can be done for consumer loans by securitizing the loan into an asset-backed security. Since the value of the loan is varying between the two periods, it may be easier to write these equations in terms of the loss given default on outstanding balances, in which case they become

$$(1 - h(1))(1 + r_R^1) + h(1)(1 + r_R^1)(1 - l_D^B) = 1 + r_F^1$$
$$(1 - h(2))(1 + r_R^2) + h(2)(1 + r_R^2)(1 - l_D^B) = 1 + r_F^2 \tag{1.7.10}$$

r_R^1 and r_R^2 with called the short rates for periods 1 and 2. They describe the one period interest rates that should be charged at the start of the loan for loans with default hazard rates of $h(1)$ and $h(2)$ in periods 1 and 2, respectively. So r_R^2 reflects the estimates at the start of period 1 of the likely risk-free rate in period 2 together with the risk of this type of loan defaulting in period 2. At the start of period 1, one should also be interested in estimating what the average return per period is likely to be over the two periods of the loan. This is the two-period spot rate r_{SP} and it reflects the return the lender will get by lending at a rate r_R^1 in period 1 and a rate r_R^2 in period 2 so

$$(1 + r_{SP})^2 = (1 + r_R^1)(1 + r_R^2). \tag{1.7.11}$$

If the bank does not expect to make any more profit from the loan beyond that which can be obtained in the general market for such a loan, then the spot rate is the rate at which the bank should lend. Substituting the expressions of the short rates from Eqs. (1.7.8) and (1.7.9) gives the expression for the spot rate of

$$(1 + r_{SP})^2 = \frac{(1 + r_F^1 - (1 - l_D)h(1))(1 + r_F^2 - (1 - l_D)h(2))}{(1 - h(1))(1 - h(2))}. \tag{1.7.12}$$

If the bank actually charged a lending rate of r_L per period on the two period loan where the loan is repaid at the end of the second period, one can calculate the profit of the loan. However, one needs to deal with the time value of money and discount the future payments because they are not worth as much as having those payments today. One way of doing this is to assume the discount rate is the risk-free rate, which is equivalent to assuming that the money used to fund the loan would be put in a risk-free investment if not used in this way. Discounting the repayment stream from the loan in this way allows one to calculate the present worth W_P of the loan. Subtracting the amount of money loaned from this gives the net present value (NPV) of the loan.

In the case of the two period loan described earlier one has

$$W_P = \frac{(1 + r_L)^2(1 - h(1))(1 - h(2))}{(1 + r_F^1)(1 + r_F^2)} + \frac{(1 + r_L)^2(1 - l_D^B)(1 - h(1))h(2)}{(1 + r_F^1)(1 + r_F^2)}$$

$$+ \frac{(1 - l_D^B)(1 + r_L)^2 h(1)}{(1 + r_F^1)(1 + r_R^2)}$$

$$\text{NPV} = W_P - 1. \tag{1.7.13}$$

The first term in W_P corresponds to the repayment of the loan at the end of the second period, provided there has been no default multiplied by the probability $(1 - h(1))(1 - h(2))$ that there was no default. This is discounted back two periods. The second term is the cash recovered if the loan defaults at the end of the second period when it is worth $(1 + r_L)^2$ multiplied by the chance of this default which is $(1 - h(1))h(2)$. The third term is the most difficult to understand in that it corresponds to the cash recovered if the loan defaults at the end of period 1, multiplied by $h(1)$ the chance of such a default. It would appear that the balance of the loan at the end of period 1 is $(1 + r_L)$ but this is not really the case as one cannot stop the loan at this point. What the market knows is that the balance of the loan at the end of the second period is $(1 + r_L)^2$ and that the market thinks of the interest rate that is appropriate to charge for loans of such risk in the second period is r_R^2. Thus the market value of the loan at the end of the first period is $(1 + r_L)^2/(1 + r_R^2)$ and this is the amount of which we assume we recover a fraction $(1 - l_D^B)$. The NPV is the net worth less the 1 unit which was loaned initially.

So the present worth net worth can be calculated by discounting each element of the cash flow by the risk-free rate and multiplying each element by the chance that amount will actually be paid. It is interesting to note that one can use Eq. (1.7.10) to rewrite (1.7.13) as follows.

$$
\begin{aligned}
W_P &= \frac{(1 + r_L)^2(1 - h(1))(1 - h(2))}{(1 + r_F^1)(1 + r_F^2)} + \frac{(1 + r_L)^2(1 - l_D^B)(1 - h(1))h(2)}{(1 + r_F^1)(1 + r_F^2)} \\
&\quad + \frac{(1 - l_D^B)(1 + r_L)^2 h(1)}{(1 + r_F^1)(1 + r_R^2)} \\
&= \frac{(1 + r_L)^2(1 - h(1))}{(1 + r_F^1)(1 + r_F^2)}(1 - h(2) + h(2)(1 - l_D^B)) + \frac{(1 - l_D^B)(1 + r_L)^2 h(1)}{(1 + r_F^1)(1 + r_R^2)} \\
&= \frac{(1 + r_L)^2(1 - h(1))}{(1 + r_F^1)(1 + r_R^2)} + \frac{(1 - l_D^B)(1 + r_L)^2 h(1)}{(1 + r_F^1)(1 + r_R^2)} = \frac{(1 + r_L)^2}{(1 + r_R^1)(1 + r_R^2)}.
\end{aligned}
$$
$$(1.7.14)$$

So the present worth is not just the expected cash flow discounted by the risk-free rate but also the assumed cash flow, ignoring the possibility of default discounted by the short rates.

Multi-period loans

Most loans are repaid over many time periods, not just one or two. For such loans the repayment patterns are calculated assuming that there will be no defaulting. The balance equations are use to keep track of how much is owed at the end of each period. Suppose a bank gives a loan L_0 and charges an interest rate of r_L per period on the loan. The repayment schedule is such that the borrower should repay a_i in period $i, i = 1, \ldots, N$. Then if L_i is the amount of the loan still to be repaid at the end of period i one must have

$$L_1 = (1 + r_L)L_0 - a_1 \quad L_0: \text{the original loan size}$$

$$\vdots$$

$$L_i = (1 + r_L)L_{i-1} - a_i, i = 2, \ldots, N - 1 \tag{1.7.15}$$

$$\vdots$$

$$L_N = (1 + r_L)L_{N-1} - a_N,$$

$$0 = L_N.$$

Multiplying the balance equation for L_i by $(1 + r_L)^{N-i}$ and summing over all the equations gives

$$\sum_{i=1}^{N}(1 + r_L)^{N-i}L_i = (1 + r_L)^N L_0 + \sum_{i=1}^{N}(1 + r_L)^{N-i}L_i - \sum_{i=1}^{N}(1 + r_L)^{N-i}a_i$$

$$\Rightarrow L_0 = \frac{\sum_{i=1}^{N}(1 + r_L)^{N-i}a_i}{(1 + r_L)^N}. \tag{1.7.16}$$

The usual choice of repayment schedule is to make the repayments constant so that $a_i = a$. In that case the repayment amount must satisfy:

$$(1 + r_L)^N L_0 - \sum_{i=1}^{N}(1 + r_L)^{N-i}a = 0 \Rightarrow a\left(\sum_{i=1}^{N}(1 + r_L)^{N-i}\right)$$

$$= (1 + r_L)^N L_0 \Rightarrow a = L_0 \frac{r_L}{1 - (1 + r_L)^{-N}}. \tag{1.7.17}$$

In that case, the bank, if it ignores defaults, and believes the risk-free rate will remain r_F throughout the duration of the loan, expects the present worth of the loan and the NPV of the lending opportunity to be

$$W_P = \sum_{i=1}^{N}\frac{a}{(1 + r_F)^i} = a\left(\frac{1 - (1 + r_F)^{-N}}{r_F}\right)$$

$$= L_0\left(\frac{r_L}{r_F}\frac{1 - (1 + r_F)^{-N}}{1 - (1 + r_L)^{-N}}\right) > L_0 \quad r_L > r_F \tag{1.7.18}$$

$$\text{NPV} = W_P - L_0 = L_0\left(\frac{r_L}{r_F}\frac{1 - (1 + r_F)^{-N}}{1 - (1 + r_L)^{-N}} - 1\right),$$

which, in the limit of a very long-term structure (mortgage over 50 years say) converges to a present worth of $L_0(r_L/r_F)$. and a NPV of $L_0((r_L - r_F)/r_F)$.

Other repayment schedules are sometimes used. For example, the bank may be willing to accept a contract where only interest payments are made during the life of the loan but the final payment includes a 'balloon' payment for the value of the original loan. In this case we would have

$$a_n = r_L L_0; \qquad a_N = (1 + r_L)L_0 \qquad 1 \le n \le N - 1. \qquad (1.7.19)$$

A third way of paying for an instalment loan is popular amongst car finance companies that provide financing to their customers when they purchase cars. The proposed repayment schedule has constant instalment payment, $a = a(N)$, but these include two components: interest on the original face value of the loan and a pay-off of $1/N$th of the loan in each period:

$$a = (r_L + (1/N))L_0. \qquad (1.7.20)$$

This is also how endowment mortgages work where $a = r_L L_0 + E$ so that the interest on the full loan is paid each month while E is invested in an investment trust with the hope that it will grow sufficiently to cover the principle L_0 at the maturity of the mortgage. If it does then the borrower will receive a bonus at the end of the loan but if it does not, as has been the case for some time, then the borrower is faced with very large final payments.

In the first and second examples (1.7.18) and (1.7.19) the quoted lending rate is the actual yield or return on investment to the bank, if there were no defaults. The third method of paying for an instalment loan in N periods, (1.7.20) has the 'hidden' feature that the effective lending rate is not the quoted rate r_L but rather a much larger quantity. When there is uncertainty in default or prepayment, the analysis becomes even more difficult and there are increased opportunities for misrepresentation of returns such as yields, annual percentage rate (APR) rates, effective interest rates, nominal interest rates, and many others.

When one allows for the chance of default in these multi-period loans then the rate of return on the loan, the current worth of the loan and the expected profit or NPV will change from these calculations. One can extend the analysis of the two period case in the obvious way though the resulting expressions can become quite complicated.

Consider a loan with a repayment schedule $\mathbf{a} = (a_0, a_1, a_2, \ldots, a_N)$ with the first cash payment a_0 at time 0, at the time the loan is taken out (often a fee of some sort). Assume the default risk of the loan is given by the set of hazard functions $h(i)$, $i = 1, 2, \ldots, N$ which are the probabilities the borrower will default in period i given that no default has occurred before then. Assume that the repayments are made at the end of each period and that the vector of one period short interest rates is given by $r = (r_R^1, r_R^2, \ldots, r_R^N)$ with equivalent risk-free rates r_F^i. If l_D^B is the loss given default as a fraction of the amount outstanding at default, then the arbitrage equation for a risk-neutral investor will require that for all periods i

$$(1 - h(i))(1 + r_R^i) + h(i)(1 + r_R^i)(1 - l_D^B) = 1 + r_F^i. \tag{1.7.21}$$

Note that the definition of r_R^i does not depend on the repayment pattern but only on the default hazard probability, the risk-free rate and the loss given default in any period. Moreover if r_{SP} is the spot rate for such a N-period loan one can define it by

$$(1 + r_{SP})^N = (1 + r_R^1)(1 + r_R^2) \ldots (1 + r_R^N) = \prod_{i=1}^{N} (1 + r_R^i). \tag{1.7.22}$$

Assume for simplicity of expression that $l_D^B = 1$, then we can write the expected profit or rather the expected current worth of the loan by discounting the actual cash flow by the risk-free rate, weighting each repayment by how likely it is to occur. This gives

$$W_P \overset{\Delta}{=} a_0 + \frac{(1 - h(1))a_1}{1 + r_F^1} + \frac{(1 - h(1))(1 - h(2))a_2}{(1 + r_F^1)(1 + r_F^2)} + \cdots$$

$$+ \frac{(1 - h(1))(1 - h(2)) \ldots (1 - h(N))a_N}{(1 + r_F^1)(1 + r_F^2) \ldots (1 + r_F^N)}. \tag{1.7.23}$$

Applying the relationship between the risk-free rates and the short rates described in Eq. (1.7.21), one can rewrite (1.7.23) as

$$W_P = a_0 + \frac{a_1}{1 + r_R^1} + \frac{a_2}{(1 + r_R^1)(1 + r_R^2)} + \cdots + \frac{a_N}{(1 + r_R^1)(1 + r_R^2) \cdots (1 + r_R^N)}, \tag{1.7.24}$$

which is the anticipated cash flow discounted using the short rates. Note that in the present worth and hence NPV measures the repayment schedules are essential to finding the profit values.

A similar analysis can be performed in the case when $l_D^B < 1$, but it is a lot messier since at any default one needs to be careful when calculating the amount outstanding on the loan in terms of the subsequent repayments which will now not be made.

1.8   Fundamentals of scorecard building

Basic approach to scorecard development

In Sections 1.5 and 1.6, we discussed the idea of scores as a way of forecasting the default probability of new customers. In the next three sections we return to the idea of scores and examine how such scores can be derived. This sections looks at the basic preparation needed to build a scorecard whatever approach is used. In the next section we discuss how one uses logistic regression, the most common way of deriving a scorecard, while in Section 1.10 we look at alternative methods that are used.

Whatever methods are used, the objective of deriving a score is to use the large data set of information on previous would-be and actual borrowers to classify them into those whom the bank would have wished to accept and those whom the bank would have wanted to reject if it had known their subsequent behaviour. In application scoring, the bank takes a sample of applicants over some time period in the recent past, their application form data and the credit bureau information obtained on them at application. These often add up to 50 to 100 character-istics. The bank also defines a binary variable value for each applicant in the sample that indicates whether the borrower's performance over the first year (or possibly some other time period) was satisfactory or not. The definition of satis-factory and not satisfactory or 'good' and 'bad', which is the terminology we use throughout this book, is at the discretion of the bank. Most lenders have tended to choose unsatisfactory to mean 90 days overdue (3 months missed payments) in the first 12 months. Even with this there is a choice of time or money. Is it 90 days since the last payment of any sort or a balance which is 90 days of pay-ment below what it should be The regulations of the Basel Accord introduced in 2007 specify default as the loan being 90 days overdue or the lender having reason to believe it will not be repaid. Even then some regulators, the FSA in the UK for example, take other definitions such as 180 days overdue, which is a more common definition of default in mortgage loans. Moreover while some banks equate 'bad' with default, others take a weaker condition for 'bad' than for default.

There is also the problem of whether 'bads' can become 'goods' again if the underpayments on the loan are made up or the credit card balance is cleared. It is almost universal to classify such 'cured' loans as bads (or defaults) and then set $l_D = 0$. There are also customers in the sample being analysed whose status is not clear at the end of the 12-month outcome period – ones who are 30 or 60 days overdue for example. These are classified as indeterminates and removed from any subsequent analysis, but are then scored to get the distribution of scores on the full accepted population.

Reject inference

There is another difficulty in analysing a sample of past applicants to build an application scorecard in that for those applicants who were rejected one does not have their good/bad status. Techniques that go under the name of 'reject inference', as the name suggests, try to infer what this status would have been. This is done for two reasons. One is to try and improve the discrimination of the scorecard and the second is to give an accurate estimate of how the scorecard will perform on the application population which is what it will be applied to and not just on the accepted population. It appears to be quite difficult to improve the scorecard discrimination in this way but the second objective is a sensible and easy thing to achieve.

A number of methods have been used to deal with this problem (see Thomas et al. 2002), but there is some confusion in the names given to the different approaches with augmentation, extrapolation, parcelling, reweighting, and reclassification used differently by different authors for overlapping or interconnected approaches. Essentially each approach consists of giving a 'value' or determining the status of each reject or segment of rejects and then using this 'value' or status to increase the size of the sample population with an extra case representing this rejected applicant.

Reclassification is when a reject is classified as a bad because it has some negative characteristics – defaulted in the last 3 months say – which the bank will always consider as unacceptable. Parcelling is when the rejects are given good or bad status depending on the 'value' the first part of the process has given then. This could be done randomly so if the 'value' is $P(G)$, the estimate of the probability of the reject being good, then if $P(G) = 0.9$ a random experiment is performed which gives the reject a good status with 0.9 probability and a bad status with 0.1 probability. Alternatively it could be that two copies of each reject are added to the sample one with a good status and the other with a bad status and if $P(G) = 0.9$ then the one with the good status is given a 0.9 weight while the one with the bad status is given a 0.1 weight. Another approach is that all the rejects with 'values' below a certain level are determined to be bads and all those with 'values' above this level are determined to be goods. Reweighting is when no rejects are added to the sample but the existing goods and bads in the sample with the same 'value' as a certain band of rejects are increased in weight in the sample proportionally to the number of rejects in the band. So if there were 90 goods, 10 bads, and 50 rejects in the same band, each of the goods and the bads is given a weight of $150/100 = 1.5$ so it would appear as if there were 135 goods and 15 bads in that band. Note however that the characteristics of the extra-weighted cases in a reweighting are those of the original sample while in parcelling and reclassification the extra cases added to the sample have the characteristics of the rejected applicants.

Augmentation and extrapolation are ways of calculating this 'value' – normally the probability of being a good – for each of the rejects. In augmentation, one seeks to identify groups of rejects and groups of accepts who will have the same probabilities of being good. Suppose there is some statistic Z which means that accepts and rejects with the same value of this statistic will have similar probabilities of being good. Thus the assumption is that

$$P(G|A, z) = P(G|R, z) \tag{1.8.1}$$

where A is the group who are accepted and R the group who are rejected. One common choice of Z is the score obtained by building a scorecard to differentiate who in a sample was accepted and who was rejected – the accept/reject scorecard. Sometimes it is assumed that the rejected group has a good rate which is only a certain fraction of the accepted good rate and even that this fraction can vary with z, namely

$$P(G|R, z) = k(z)P(G|A, z). \tag{1.8.2}$$

Having got these probabilities of being good, one can use parcelling or reweighting to increase the sample size. Sometimes a scorecard builder uses the known good–bad cases to build the score statistic Z (the KGB scorecard). If one then uses the assumption in Eq. (1.8.1) and then uses reweighting to change the sample size, one will not change the scorecard at all. All this will do is change the size of the sample to reflect more the applicant population rather than the accepted population.

In extrapolation, the idea is that there are certain characteristics X where there is no overlap between the accepted and rejected groups. One then constructs a function, g, which relates the good rate to the values of x for those values in the region where everyone is being accepted, which we denote as X_A, that is

$$g(x) = P(G|A, x) = P(G|x) \ x \in \mathcal{X}_A.$$

Then extrapolate this function to $\tilde{g}$ on the values of X where there were only rejects namely X_R so

$$\tilde{g}(x) = P(G|R, x) = P(G|x) \ x \in \mathcal{X}_R.$$

There continue to be other methods and variants of these approaches suggested as ways of dealing with reject inference but as Hand and Henley (1993) pointed out that they all depend on making some assumption about the relationship between the good rate for the accepted applicants and that for the rejected applicants, which cannot be tested without taking some of the 'rejects'. More recently authors such as Crook and Banasik (2004) and Feelders (2000) have pointed out that the standard techniques for dealing with missing data cannot be used in this context because the data is 'missing not at random' (MNR). This means that the rejects, who are the applicants on which one has missing data – namely their subsequent status – are not chosen at random, but because of certain uncreditworthy properties they may be perceived to have. Further discussion of these techniques can be found in Hand and Henley (1993) and Thomas et al. (2002).

The most satisfactory way to overcome this problem, in statistical if not in economic terms, would be to accept a random sample of all applicants just to

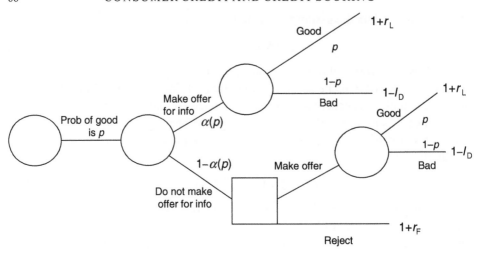

FIG. 1.8.1. Decision tree of randomly accepting borrowers to overcome reject inference.

acquire information on their subsequent status. The probability of being chosen in such a way would be known but very small. This is what retail stores and mail order companies do with their customers but banks rarely follow this strategy. This strategy is shown in the decision tree in Fig. 1.8.1 where for an applicant with probability p of being good there is a chance $\alpha(p)$ that the applicant will be chosen just to acquire extra data, but for those not so chosen the normal acceptance decision process is then applied. In essence one is running what may be a costly experiment to gather information for the underlying decision problem. This means that there may now be two separate but linked decision variables: the performance maximizing cut-off decision and the fraction of applicants who are admitted to gather information and learn how best to discriminate 'goods' from 'bads'. The first is straightforward and was already calculated in Eq. (1.7.2), where it says one should make the offer if

$$p(1 + r_L) + (1 - p)(1 - l_D) > 1 + r_F$$

or

$$p > \frac{r_F + l_D}{r_L + l_D}. \tag{1.8.3}$$

For the second, one might put a limit on the extra costs one will pay for the extra information. This cost is

$$C = \int_0^{\frac{r_F + l_D}{r_L + l_D}} ((r_F + l_D) - p(r_L + l_D))\alpha(p)f(p)dp \tag{1.8.4}$$

where $f(p)$ is the density function of the distribution of the probability of being good over the population. Reasonable requirements on the choice of $\alpha(p)$ are that $\alpha(0) = 0$, and $\alpha(r_F + l_D)/(r_L + l_D) = 1$. If one takes $f(p) = 1$ and $\alpha(p) = (r_L + l_D)/(r_F + l_D p)$ then this extra cost is $C = (r_F + l_D)^2/6(r_L + l_D)$.

Accepting applicants who are highly likely to default can become an informative but very expensive business so one has to proceed with great care in measuring the expected marginal cost of new information.

There are other ways some banks are able to get information on the good/bad status of rejected applicants. The first is to use the overrides, those whom the system would have rejected on risk grounds, but who for commercial non-risk reasons were accepted. These though tend to be from a special group – employees of the firm or relations of those who are important to the bank because they are major borrowers in other contexts and so will not span the whole rejected population. The second way a bank gets information on rejects is to check with the credit bureaus how rejected applicants have subsequently performed with other banks. This though assumes that the applicants were able to get further loans and these were of the type they were requesting from the first lender.

Behaviour scoring

Reject inference is only a problem for application scoring. In behavioural scoring, the data on all borrowers is available. For it the problem in deciding on the sample is over what time period should one consider the characteristics. For behaviour scoring, we choose some date in the past and look at the customers who have performance data throughout some *performance period* preceding this time (often 1 year) and through some *outcome period* which follows this time (again often 1 year) (see Fig. 1.8.2).

Taking a sample of such customers, one chooses a large number of characteristics to describe the customer's behaviour during the performance period. These

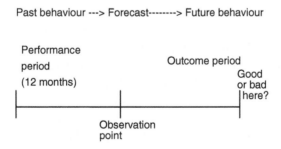

FIG. 1.8.2. Performance period and outcome period in behavioural scoring.

characteristics could include average balance, ratio of balance at end of period to start of period, number of credit transaction and debit transactions, times overdrawn or payments missed, and so on, together with the initial application data (though usually the latter is far less powerful than the former). One can easily construct up to a 1000 variables. Moreover, both in application scorecard and in behavioural scorecards one can construct new variables which are combinations of the original ones. For example, one might choose a usage variable which would be the current balance on the card as a ratio of the credit limit or take current balance divided by disposable income (income less repayment commitments) which gives a measure of the repayment ability of the borrower. The strongest information though is whether the borrower is or has recently been in arrears and the current credit bureau information. The latter is often given in terms of a generic credit bureau score.

These characteristics are used to classify the status of the borrower at the end of the outcome period where again one would have a binary variable classifying the performance as good or bad. In this case rejection inference is not a problem, but a much more insidious bias and one which, at present, banks do not deal with satisfactorily is *policy inference*. This bias arises because the behaviour and hence the final status of the borrower depends partly on the operational policy in place. For example, if the borrowers are given an enormous credit limit and lots of other products are marketed to them and their balance allowed to rise without any comment from the lender, the chance of default may be higher than if they were given a very low credit limit and warning letters sent every time they approach the limit. How can one decide what would have happened to the customer if the credit limit and operating policy was a standard *vanilla* one? This bias is likely to increase with the advent of customized credit products and individual customer relationship management policies.

Data sample

In both application and behavioural scoring, one starts with a data set of applicants/borrowers which includes a large number of characteristics on each together with their outcome status. In many situations, such as major credit card organizations the number of borrowers in the set could be more than a million and one would then need to select a sample from the data set. The main decision is either to take a random sample so that the number of goods and bads in the sample reflects the population odds, or to use a stratified sample so as to increase the number of bads in the sample compared with their usually very small proportion in the original population. There are scorecard builders who choose an equal numbers of goods and bads in the sample, while others choose their samples so the ratio of goods to bads is a fixed ratio somewhere between 1:1 and the actual population odds. The number of bads in the population is usually so small that one takes every one of these in the original data set so the sampling is usually applied to the good population.

Having settled on the data set, including any augmentation needed to deal with reject inference, one has then to go through four steps – data validation, cutting the number of characteristics, coarse classifying, and creating new variables from the coarse classes – before applying any of the scorecard-building methodologies.

Data validation and cleaning

This means checking that the data entries are valid (no one aged 150 or no one who is 21 and has been with the bank for more than 30 years). Special codes like 9999 should not be misinterpreted, and if there are missing values, the norm is to code them as missing and not to seek to use estimation algorithms to enter a value. Although it is only a few lines in this book to state this, the work involved can be the most time consuming of the scorecard-building steps. A data dictionary or data log, which records the information learnt about the data set, is a great help for future scorecard development on this data set, but is something that is rarely given the importance it deserves in practice.

Segmentation

Once a clean sample has been constructed, one can start building a scoring system and the first decision is whether to segment the population and build different scorecards for each segment. For example one might build a scorecard for those under 25 in age and a different one for those 25 or over, or one might build a scorecard for those with high incomes and another for those with low incomes. Building several scorecards rather than just one is a lot of extra work so it should only be done if it results in improved predictions.

Segmentation is undertaken for several reasons:

1. There are differences in the information available for the different segments.
2. There are interactions between one characteristic and several other characteristics.
3. It supports a policy decision by the lender.

The difference in information between segments can be due to the amount of data available. For example, the data on young people is usually very limited as they are unlikely to have many loans apart from a student loan and an overdraft, and are highly unlikely to own property. Thus the data on them is limited (a 'thin' file) while there may be a lot more data (a 'thick' file) on previous borrowings for older people and a much more diverse set of residential status attributes. In other cases, there is no data available on some characteristics of some people. For example in behavioural scoring on credit cards, there are usually lots of characteristics requiring information on the last 12 months performance like the average balance, the maximum credit, or the number of debits. These would not be available for those who have had the credit card for less than 12 months, and so one would segment the population into those who have had cards for more or less than 12 months. Another example is when characteristics concerning a borrower's current or checking account are used in building a score to be used for loans or mortgages. Then one has to have different scorecards for those who have current accounts with the bank and those who do not.

If there are characteristics which both interact strongly with each other and are also highly predictive one might want to segment on one of the characteristics. This avoids having lots of interaction characteristics in the one scorecard and instead has several scorecards each of which will have more straightforward characteristics. This rarely happens in practice because usually the interactions are not strong or numerous enough to necessitate that. One way of checking for such interactions is to build a classification tree and look at the characteristics, whose splits appear at the top of the tree. We will discuss this further in Section 1.10.

The bank might also decide to segment the population since it wants to treat the different segments in different ways. So for example it may want to be more generous to those with high incomes than those with low incomes. Other lenders are motivated by the customer's lifetime value (CLV) and so may want to deal more positively with younger borrowers than older ones since they are likely to have higher CLVs. Having different scorecards make it a lot easier to set different cut-offs or to have different promotional policies for cross-selling or up-selling.

Development and validation samples

When one has agreed how many scorecards are being built and one has a 'clean' set of data for each segment, the data for that segment should be split into two portions: build the scorecard on one (the development or training sample) and keep the other (the validation or hold-out or testing sample) to estimate how good is the performance of the scorecard. The distribution between the two depends on the size of the original sample but if there is plenty of data scorecard builders tend to go for a 70:30 split between the size of the development and validation samples. The rest of the steps in building the scorecard use only the data in the development sample.

Cutting down the number of characteristics considered

Robust scorecards tend to have between 10 and 20 characteristics in them and so there are usually far more characteristics available than needed for such a robust scorecard. So the next task is to cut down the characteristics to be considered.

One removes characteristics because they give little discrimination between the goods and the bads; they are strongly correlated or even collinear with other characteristics already being considered; or their values are not robust over time. One can check for the first two difficulties by performing a linear regression of the good/bad status variable on subsets of the characteristics. Using forward introduction or backward removal of characteristics in the regression equation gives an indication of which are the important characteristics, namely those that enter the regression first in the forward approach or are the last to leave in the backward approach. Another way of gauging the strength of the relationship between a characteristic and the status variable would be to use univariate relationship measurements like chi-square (CS) and information statistics. One might think of using the correlation R^2 between the characteristic value and the good:bad status variable, but since the latter is binary, the R^2 values are always poor. Moreover many characteristics are categorical and even for the continuous ones the relationship between the characteristic and the good:bad status may not be monotone let alone linear. These problems of categorical variables and non-monotone continuous characteristics also mean if one thinks of such characteristics as simple scorecards then the scorecard discrimination measures, such as area under the receiver operating characteristic (AUROC) curve and Gini coefficient which will be discussed in the next chapter, are not appropriate. One does not know what is the best ordering of the attributes of the characteristic. This can be addressed by coarse classifying the characteristics. However, if there are hundreds of variables one cannot coarse classify them all so one tends to use the linear regression approach to get rid of some of the variables so one is left with a manageable group to coarse classify.

Robustness over time can be checked by analysing the values of the characteristics over the performance period (behavioural scoring) or when applications were made (application scoring). If there is no significant trend in the attribute values and no great change in the good–bad classification power between the start and end of these time periods, it would suggest the characteristic is fairly stable over the time periods involved in building and running a scorecard.

Coarse classifying characteristics

Once the number of characteristics has been reduced to a manageable set, each remaining characteristic is coarse classified so as to increase its robustness and to cope with any non-monotonicity in the relationship between the default risk and that characteristic. When coarse classifying a categorical characteristic, one tries to group the attributes into a number of bins so that attributes with roughly the same good:bad ratio are in the same bin. The number of bins is such that each has a reasonable percentage of the population in it – certainly at least 5% of the population. This avoids there being too much sample variation involved in calculating the score for that set of attributes. Coarse classifying is an art as much as a science and so whether it seems reasonable on common sense grounds to put certain attributes in the same bin is as important as them having similar good:bad odds. For ordinal variables one tries to ensure that the bins are in fact bands with adjacent attributes put together. For continuous characteristics like age, one splits the values of the characteristic into 10 to 20 quantiles initially, and then works as if it were an ordinal variable with these attributes, in deciding whether adjacent attributes should be combined in the same band.

Example 1.8.1 Coarse classifying using the Bank of Southampton data

Looking at the Bank of Southampton example of Appendix B, there is no need to coarse classify the *credit card* characteristic as it is already binary. For *residential status* one looks at the good:bad odds for *owners* which is $570/30 = 19:1$, for *renters* which is $150/50 = 3:1$, and *others* which is $180/20 = 9:1$. These are fairly widely separated and the numbers in each attribute (outcomes of the characteristic) are fairly large percentages of the underlying population (owners are $600/1000 = 60\%$ of the population, renters are $200/1000 = 20\%$ of the population, and others also $200/1000 = 20\%$ of the population). So there is no reason to group any two of them together. *Age* is an example of a continuous variable and in reality one would probably split this initially into 10 to 20 groups with roughly equal numbers in each and consider banding adjacent ones of those together. For simplicity we start with just four groups and the good:bad odds for each group is as follows – *under 30* has odds of $175/26 = 6.73:1$, 30–39 has odds $175/30 = 5.83:1$, *40–49* has odds $175/15 = 11.67:1$, and *over 50* has odds $375/29 = 12.9:1$. There is no need to put these groups together on percentage of the population grounds (under 30s are $201/1000 = 20.1\%$ of the population, *30–39* are $205/1000 = 20.5\%$ of the population, 40–49 are $190/1000 = 19\%$ of the population, and over 50 is $404/1000 = 40.4\%$ of the population). However, the good:bad odds for the *under 30* and the *30–39* are sufficiently close that one might want to group those together. Similarly one might feel the *40–49* and the *over 50s* are sufficiently close to put those together but they would then lead to a group which is 59.4% of the population. Also in both case when one looks at the interactions between age and residential status the case for putting these groups together is less clear. There is quite a difference for example between the good:bad odds for the *40–49s* who have *other* residential status (13 goods and 3 bads so odds of 4.33:1) and the *over 50s* who have the same status (80 goods and 4 bads with odds of 20.0:1). In real examples, these second-order interactions tend to be less marked but still need consideration during coarse classifying. Notice that one does not consider banding together non-adjacent groups like the *under 30s* and the *40–49* for continuous or ordinal characteristics whereas for categorical ones it is reasonable to consider most combinations of attributes.

One can also use the chi-square (CS) statistic and the information value statistic to estimate how strong is the relationship between the binned characteristics and the good:bad status variable. These are useful both for deciding between different binnings of the same characteristic and then finally to rank the binned characteristics to help decide which ones should be considered when the scorecard is finally constructed.

Chi-square and information value statistics

In the CS statistic, one takes the hypothesis that the good:bad ratio is the same in each of the bins or bands and then uses the CS statistic to check this hypothesis. Usually one hopes the value is low so that the hypothesis is true but here we look for binnings with large values of the CS statistic since in that case there will be significant differences in the good:bad ratio between different bins. Suppose there are K bins and there are n_k borrowers in bin k and g_k of these are goods (and hence $b_k = n_k - g_k$ are bads). When we are using several characteristics at the same time, we will define the characteristics by $j = 1, 2, \ldots, J$ and the attributes of characteristic j are indexed by $i = 1, 2, \ldots, m_j$. Define

$$g_{i,j} \triangleq \text{number of Goods in attribute i of characteristic j}$$

$$b_{i,j} \triangleq \text{number of Bads in attribute i of characteristic j}$$

$$n_{i,j} \triangleq \text{total number of cases in attribute i of characteristic j.}$$

The hypothesis that the distribution of goods (and bads) in each bin is the same as that in the whole population odds p_G (p_B) and would suggest the expected number of goods (and bads) in the bin is $n_k p_G$ ($n_k p_B$). The CS statistic for the goodness of this fit is the sum of the squares of the differences in the forecast and observed numbers, normalized by dividing by the theoretical variance, and summed over all the bins. Since the number of goods in a bin has a binomial distribution $B(n_k, p_G)$ with mean $n_k p_G$ and variance $n_k p_G (1 - p_G)$. Hence the CS statistic is

$$CS = \sum_{k=1}^{K} \frac{(n_k p_G - g_k)^2}{n_k p_G (1 - p_G)}. \tag{1.8.5}$$

In fact, one normally calculates this by summing over all the bins the difference between the actual and expected numbers of goods in that bin divided by the expected number of goods plus the difference between the expected and actual number of bads in the bin divided by the expected number of bads. This is the same as (1.8.5) since

$$CS = \sum_{k=1}^{K} \frac{\text{(expected number of goods in interval } k - \text{observed number of goods in interval } k)^2}{\text{expected number of goods in interval } k} +$$

$$\sum_{k=1}^{K} \frac{\text{(expected number of bads in interval } k - \text{observed number of bads in interval } k)^2}{\text{expected number of bads in interval } k}$$

$$= \sum_{k=1}^{K} \left(\frac{(n_k p_G - g_k)^2}{n_k p_G} + \frac{(n_k p_B - b_k)^2}{n_k p_B} \right) \qquad (1.8.6)$$

$$= \sum_{k=1}^{K} \left(\frac{(n_k p_G - g_k)^2}{n_k p_G} + \frac{(g_k - n_k p_G)^2}{n_k p_B} \right)$$

$$= \sum_{k=1}^{K} (n_k p_G - g_k)^2 \left(\frac{1}{n_k p_G} + \frac{1}{n_k (1 - p_G)} \right)$$

$$= \sum_{k=1}^{K} \left(\frac{(n_k p_G - g_k)^2}{n_k p_G (1 - p_G)} \right).$$

The CS test then calculates for each cell the square of the difference between the actual and expected numbers in that cell divided by the expected numbers.

Example 1.8.2 Chi-square calculations on age from Bank of Southampton data (Appendix B)

Suppose instead of the four age bands created in Appendix B, one only wanted two bands. So there are three possibilities; split into under and over 30, under and over 40, or under and over 50. In the split at 30 there are 175 goods and 26 bads below 30, and 725 goods and 74 bads above 30. The numbers for the other splits are 350 goods, 56 bads below 40; 550 goods, 44 bads above 40; 535 goods, 71 bads below 50; and 375 goods, 29 bads above 50. The whole population of 1000 has 900 goods and 100 bads so $p_G = 0.9$ and $p_B = 0.1$. So the chi-square calculation is as shown in Table 1.8.1.

Since the CS value for the middle binning – under and over 40 is the largest we would probably decide to choose this split as the best among those three.

One has to be a little more careful if one is comparing splits where the number of bins in each split is different since one really has a chi-square statistic with $K - 1$ degrees of freedom if there are K bins. If one checks the tables for chi-square

TABLE 1.8.1. Chi-square calculations for coarse classifying in Example 1.8.2.

Age bands	Actual no. goods	Expected no. goods	Actual no. bads	Expected no. bads	(Act − Exp)²/ Exp goods	(Act − Exp)²/ Exp bads	CS = sum of 4 terms
Under 30	175	180.9	26	20.1	0.19	1.73	
Over 30	725	719.1	74	79.9	0.05	0.44	2.41
Under 40	350	365.4	56	40.6	0.65	5.84	
Over 40	550	534.6	44	59.4	0.44	3.99	10.93
Under 50	525	536.4	71	59.6	0.24	2.18	
Over 50	375	363.6	29	40.4	0.36	3.22	6.00

values with different degrees of freedom the chi-square values obviously increase with the number of degrees of freedom and so having more bins would tend to give a higher value. One could try to use the chi-square tables to translate the value into the probability of such an outcome occurring if the assumption of constant population odds in each bin were true. This would be one way of comparing splits with different numbers of bins but in reality scorecard builders tend to look at whether there was a big increase in the CS value when one introduced another bin. They then subjectively make their decision of which is better using this comparison.

The idea of weights of evidence $w(\mathbf{x}) = \ln\left(f(\mathbf{x}|G))/(f(\mathbf{x}|B)\right)$ has already been introduced in Section 1.5, where it indicated how much information on a borrower being good or bad was in a piece of data, $\mathbf{x}$. If one was interested in measuring how well the characteristic x was at separating the goods from the bads one might think of using the difference in the mean values $\int \mathbf{x}(f(\mathbf{x}|G) - f(\mathbf{x}|B))d\mathbf{x}$ of the characteristics. However, this difference does not recognize that the information value for some x values is much higher than others and only works for continuous characteristics. This leads to taking the differences in the expected weights of evidence between the good and bad populations:

$$\int (f(\mathbf{x}|G) - f(\mathbf{x}|B))w(\mathbf{x})d\mathbf{x} \tag{1.8.7}$$

which is called the *divergence*. This can also be written as the sum of the expected weight of evidence of good to bad for the good population plus the expected weight of evidence of bad to good for the bad population, namely:

$$\int f(\mathbf{x}|G) \ln\left(\frac{f(\mathbf{x}|G)}{f(\mathbf{x}|B)}\right) d\mathbf{x} + \int f(\mathbf{x}|B) \ln\left(\frac{f(\mathbf{x}|B)}{f(\mathbf{x}|G)}\right) d\mathbf{x}.$$

We examine this important measure in more detail in Section 1.10 where one builds a scorecard by seeking to maximize it and in Section 2.2 where we use it as a way of measuring the quality of a scorecard. The discrete equivalent of divergence is called the *information value*. The information value for a particular binning of a characteristic is given as follows. If there are K bins with n_k borrowers in bin k of which g_k are goods (and hence $b_k = n_k - g_k$ are bads), then the information value (IV) is calculated by

$$\text{Information value} = \text{IV} = \sum_{k=1}^{K} (g_k/n_G - b_k/n_B) \ln\left(\frac{g_k/n_G}{b_k/n_B}\right)$$

$$= \sum_{k=1}^{K} (g_k/n_G - b_k/n_B) \ln\left(\frac{g_k n_B}{b_k n_G}\right). \qquad (1.8.8)$$

Example 1.8.3 Information value using age from the Bank of Southampton data

We take the same data as in Example 1.8.3 based on the age split in Appendix B data. So again we are trying to decide between three splits; in the split at 30 there are 175 goods and 26 bads below 30, and 725 goods and 74 bads above 30; in the split at 40 there are 350 goods, 56 bads below 40 and 550 goods, 44 bads above 40; in the split at 50 there are 535 goods, 71 bads below 50 and 375 goods, 29 bads above 50. Calculating the information value for these splits gives the values as shown in Table 1.8.2.

In this case one again would choose the split at 40 as the best of the three because its information value of 0.119 is higher than those of the other two splits, namely 0.025 and 0.071.

Having used the information value and chi-square to get the best splits in each characteristic, one could also compare the values of the different characteristics, each with their best split. This is one way of identifying which of the characteristics are most discriminating in differentiating the goods from the bads. If one coarse classifies a characteristic and then applies these measures to the resulting binnings,

TABLE 1.8.2. Information value for coarse classifying in Example 1.8.4.

Age bands	Actual no. goods	Actual no. bads	% Goods −% bads	ln(% goods/% bads)	IV contribution	IV
Under 30	175	26	−0.066	−0.291	0.019	
Over 30	725	74	0.066	0.085	0.006	0.025
Under 40	350	56	−0.171	−0.365	0.062	
Over 40	550	44	0.171	0.329	0.056	0.119
Under 50	525	71	−0.127	−0.197	0.025	
Over 50	375	29	0.127	0.362	0.046	0.071

the coarse classification overcomes the problems one has with categorical attributes and non-monotonicity of continuous characteristics which were mentioned earlier. So these statistics are then measuring the discrimination of the 'most discriminating' versions of the characteristics.

Transforming coarse classified characteristics into new variables

Having split the characteristic X, which has attributes x, into bins $C_1, \ldots, C_K$ one converts X into a quantitative variable in one of two ways, either by binary variables or using weights of evidence. In the binary case one defines $K - 1$ binary variables $X_1, \ldots, X_{K-1}$ with $X_i(x) = 1$ if $x \in C_i$, and 0 otherwise. One should not include X_K as this would force co-linearity between the variables in that $\sum_{i=1}^{K} X_i = 1$. C_K is then the 'base' class or bin against which the others are compared. Of course one can choose any of the classes to be the base class. So for the Bank of Southampton example, residential status would lead to two new variables X_{owner} and X_{renter} where $X_{owner}(x) = 1$ if x is an owner and 0 otherwise; and $X_{renter}(x) = 1$ if x is a renter and 0 otherwise. Thus a borrow who has 'other' residential status is recognized as one who is both $X_{owner}(x) = 0$ and $X_{renter}(x) = 0$.

The weights of evidence approach builds on Eq. (1.5.18) in Section 1.5 where we show that if one has a log score built on only one characteristic, X, then the score given to attribute x of that characteristic is

$$w(x) = \log \left(\frac{p(G|x)}{p(B|x)} \Big/ \frac{p_G}{p_B} \right). \tag{1.8.9}$$

So define a new variable X^{woe} using weights of evidence as follows. If g_i, b_i, are the numbers of goods (bads) in bin C_i and $n_G = \sum_{i=1}^{K} g_i$; $n_B = \sum_{i=1}^{K} b_i$. are the total number of goods (bads) in the population, then define:

$$X^{woe}(x) = \log \left(\frac{g_i/b_i}{n_G/n_B} \right) = \log \left(g_i n_B / b_i n_G \right) \quad \text{if } x \in C_i. \tag{1.8.10}$$

The ratios in Eq. (1.8.10) are estimates of the ratios of probabilities in Eq. (1.8.9), namely:

$$n_G/n_B = p_G/p_B \quad \text{and} \quad g_i/b_i = P(G|x \in C_i)/P(B|x \in C_i).$$

The values in (1.8.10) are estimates of the weights of evidence for the attributes of the characteristic X. This ensures that the values given to the bins in X^{woe} have the same ordering as the empirical odds in each class. The disadvantage is that if there is a strong interaction with other characteristics, this ordering may not reflect the impact of just this characteristic's attributes.

Note that if we take a sub-sample of the original data set, say we only sampled 1 in 10 goods, then the new g_i is approximately 0.1 of the original g_i and the new n_G is 0.1 of the original n_G. So there will be no change in the weights of evidence values, and this emphasizes that weights of evidence is part of the information score s_{inf} and does not require the 'true' population odds which make up s_{pop}

**Example 1.8.4 Constructing weights of evidence variables
on Bank of Southampton data**

If we consider the Southampton Bank example then using the weights of evidence which we calculated in Example 1.5.2, we would transform residential status and age into two new weights of evidence variables with values as follows.

Residential status:

- Owner: value $= \log((570/30)/(900/100)) = \log(19/9) = 0.747$.
- Renter: value $= \log((150/50)/(900/100)) = \log(1/3) = -1.099$.
- Other: value $= \log((180/20)/(900/100)) = \log(1) = 0.000$.

Age:

- Under 30: value $= \log((175/26)/(900/100)) = \log(6.73/9) = -0.291$.
- 30–39: value $= \log((175/30)/(900/100)) = \log(5.833/9) = -0.434$.
- 40–49: value $= \log((175/15)/(900/100)) = \log(11.67/9) = 0.259$.
- Over 50 value $= \log(375/29)/(900/100)) = \log(12.93/9) = 0.362$.

Notice though, from the data in Appendix B, for those who do have a credit card and 'other' residential status, the odds ratio for the 30–39-year olds $(15/1) = 15:1$ is better than that for the 40–49s $(10/2) = 5:1$, even though the weights of evidence scores will require those groups to have scores in the opposite order. This is because these weights of evidence approach does not allow for interactions between the variables.

The advantage of the weights of evidence is that the number of characteristics does not increase and so there is less chance of correlation between the variables and more robustness in the statistical estimation but there is a disadvantage in that one can only keep all the attributes of the characteristic in the scorecard or none of them. Using binary variables it is quite common for some of the attributes of a characteristic to be left in the scorecard but for others to drop out. This is very useful in focusing on the vital attributes which affect default.

Building final scorecard and validating it

Now that the ground has been prepared, one is in a position to build the scoring system. In the next section we discuss the most common approach to doing this – logistic regression – while in the section after that we look at other approaches that have been used in practice to build scoring systems.

Building the scorecard is not the end of the story, however. We then have to test how good it is. In Chapter 2, we look at the different ways the quality of a scorecard can be measured. There we will discuss why, to ensure unbiased estimates of the quality of the scorecard, we will need to perform these measurements on the hold-out sample which we constructed early in the scorecard-building process. The data in this sample has not been used in any of the steps involved in building the actual scorecard, and so the performance of the scorecard on this data should be an unbiased estimate of how it will perform on the new data it will subsequently be used on.

1.9 Using logistic regression to build scorecards

Logistic regression is the most commonly used method for building scorecards, and it also has a strong theoretical underpinning in that it gives rise directly to an additive log odds score which is a weighted linear sum of attribute values. Thus there is no need to calibrate scores obtained from logistic regression as they have the properties of log odds scores described in Section 1.5 (unless of course one wants the scores to have suitable anchor point and scaling properties as discussed in Section 1.6). Logistic regression assumes that the relationship between the good–bad status and the attributes of the characteristics $\mathbf{x} = (x_1, x_2, \ldots, x_m)$ is given by

$$s(\mathbf{x}) = \log\left(\frac{p(G|\mathbf{x})}{p(B|\mathbf{x})}\right) = \log\left(\frac{p(\mathbf{x})}{1 - p(\mathbf{x})}\right) = \mathbf{c} \cdot \mathbf{x} = c_0 + c_1 x_1 + \cdots + c_m x_m$$

$$\Rightarrow p(\mathbf{x}) = \frac{e^{s(\mathbf{x})}}{1 + e^{s(\mathbf{x})}} = \frac{e^{\mathbf{c} \cdot \mathbf{x}}}{1 + e^{\mathbf{c} \cdot \mathbf{x}}}. \tag{1.9.1}$$

To obtain this relationship one takes a sample of n previous borrowers, and undertakes all the tasks outlined in the previous section, of cleaning the data, removing unimportant characteristics, and coarse classifying the others. One ends up with a set of $(\mathbf{x}^i, y^i)\ i = 1, 2, \ldots, n$ consisting of the attributes of the 'important' characteristics $\mathbf{x}^i = (x_1^i, x_2^i, \ldots, x_m^i)$ of each borrower and the good–bad status of the borrower which is $y^i = 1$ if the borrower was a good, and 0 if they were a bad. One can use maximum likelihood estimation (MLE) to find the estimates $\hat{\mathbf{c}}$ of the parameters $\mathbf{c}$ in Eq. (1.9.1). With MLE one calculates the probability that one gets the correct status for each customer given a particular choice of $\mathbf{c}$ (the likelihood of getting the correct outcome) and then finding the $\mathbf{c}$ that maximizes this probability or likelihood. The maximization is as follows in this case:

$$\text{Maximize L}(\mathbf{c}) = \prod_{i=1}^{n} \left(\frac{e^{\mathbf{c} \cdot \mathbf{x}^i}}{1 + e^{\mathbf{c} \cdot \mathbf{x}^i}}\right)^{y_i} \left(\frac{1}{1 + e^{\mathbf{c} \cdot \mathbf{x}^i}}\right)^{(1-y_i)}, \tag{1.9.2}$$

which by taking logs is equivalent to

$$\text{Maximize } LL(\mathbf{c}) = \text{Maximize } \ln L(\mathbf{c})$$

$$= \text{Maximize } \sum_{i=1}^{n} y_i \log \left(\frac{e^{\mathbf{c} \cdot \mathbf{x}^i}}{1 + e^{\mathbf{c} \cdot \mathbf{x}^i}} \right) \quad (1.9.3)$$

$$+ \sum_{i=1}^{n} (1 - y_i) \log \left(\frac{1}{1 + e^{\mathbf{c} \cdot \mathbf{x}^i}} \right)$$

since it is easier to deal with log likelihoods than likelihoods. Differentiating Eq. (1.9.3) with respect to the c_j, $j = 1, \ldots m$ and setting the derivatives equal to zero means the maximization occurs when

$$\sum_{i=1}^{n} \left(y_i - \left(\frac{e^{\mathbf{c} \cdot \mathbf{x}^i}}{1 + e^{\mathbf{c} \cdot \mathbf{x}^i}} \right) \right) = 0$$

and

$$\sum_{i=1}^{n} x_j^i \left(y_i - \left(\frac{e^{\mathbf{c} \cdot \mathbf{x}^i}}{1 + e^{\mathbf{c} \cdot \mathbf{x}^i}} \right) \right) = 0 \quad \text{for each } j = 1, \ldots m. \quad (1.9.4)$$

These are non-linear equations and so solving them needs an iterative approach like the Newton–Raphson method, which can be computationally intensive. This is why logistic regression only started being used for scorecard building in the 1980s when computers were powerful enough to do this on very large data sets. Nowadays of course there is no problem in carrying out the computation even on the smallest computer, and it is standard in most statistical packages.

Most of the statistical packages will report the coefficient values $\hat{c}_i$, the standard errors on the $\hat{c}_i$, the Wald CS test statistic, and maybe the degrees of freedom and the p-value of the test $H_0:c_i = 0$ against $H_a:c_i \neq 0$ together with the log likelihood value and possibly the divergence. These statistics are useful in determining whether this is a statistically sensible model and whether some of the variables can be removed. So it is worth briefly outlining their role. An excellent and very readable more detailed account of understanding the output from logistic regression is to be found in Hosmer and Lemeshow (1989).

Clearly the coefficient values $\hat{c}_i$ are the most important outputs. If one has only binary variables to describe the attribute classes (possibly after coarse classification) of the characteristics, then the coefficients of the binary variables are the scores for each attribute. If one has built a logistic regression using characteristics transformed using the weights of evidence approach, then the score for attribute x_i of characteristic i is the coefficient $\hat{c}_i$ multiplied by the weights of evidence, namely $\hat{c}_i w_i(x_i)$. One might wonder why the coefficients $\hat{c}_i$ are not all 1 since in Section 1.5 we derived scorecards which were just linear sums of the population scores and the weights of evidence for each variable. There it was assumed that the characteristics were all independent and were all in the scorecard. The coefficients $\hat{c}_i$ try to deal with the interdependence between the characteristics and the fact some of the characteristics have been left out during the variable selection phase.

One obvious question is whether a variable really adds anything to the discrimination between the goods and the bads. One can assume the coefficient $\hat{c}_i$ is normally distributed if the data set is large enough and so the standard deviation $\hat{\sigma}_i$ gives an indication of the confidence interval in this value. For example, if Z is the standard normal distribution, then one can use tables to find the value $z(\alpha)$ where

$$P\{Z > z(\alpha)\} = 1 - \alpha.$$

In that case, one can be $(100 - 200\alpha)\%$ confident that the coefficient lies in the interval $\hat{c}_i \pm \hat{\sigma}_i z(\alpha)$. The Wald test builds on this by calculating the Wald statistic:

$$W = \hat{c}_i / \hat{\sigma}_i.$$

W^2 has asymptotically a χ^2 distribution with one degree of freedom and if one wants to test the hypothesis $H_0 : c_i = 0$ against $H_1 : c_i \neq 0$ one can use this test to find the significance probability that the coefficient could be zero and so the variable could be left out. One has to be careful in that the Wald tests can sometimes be unreliable if one of the characteristics has a very large impact on the good:bad status but since most packages report its results, it still remains the most used univariate test.

Another way of examining whether a variable should be in the scorecard or not is to look at how well the two models – with and without the variable – fit the data. This also gives an indication of how well the overall model fits the data. The standard statistic that is used is the log likelihood ratio statistic, 2LL (since it is twice the log likelihood ratio) which looks at how well the current model fits the data compared with a saturated one which had so many parameters that one can fit the data exactly. If there are $j = 1, \ldots, J$ different combinations of attribute values $\mathbf{x} = (x_1, x_2, \ldots, x_m)$ and among the sample there are n_j cases which have combination j of the attribute values and g_j of these are goods and b_j are bad 2LL becomes

$$2LL = -2 \log \left(\frac{\text{likelihood of the current model}}{\text{likelihood of the saturated model}} \right)$$

$$= -2 \sum_{j=1}^{J} \left[g_j \log \left(\frac{\left(\frac{e^{c \cdot x^j}}{1 + e^{c \cdot x^j}} \right)}{g_j / n_j} \right) + b_j \log \left(\frac{\left(\frac{1}{1 + e^{c \cdot x^j}} \right)}{b_j / n_j} \right) \right]. \tag{1.9.5}$$

This statistic, sometimes called the deviance has a χ^2 distribution with $J - m$ degrees of freedom. An obvious extension is then to measure the advantage of having a characteristic in the model by calculating:

$$G = -2 \log \left(\frac{\text{likelihood of model without the characteristic}}{\text{likelihood of model with the characteristic}} \right)$$

$$= 2LL(\text{model without the characteristic}) - 2LL(\text{model with the characteristic}).$$

This also has a χ^2 distribution but with 1 degree of freedom and so one can use this to decide whether there is a statistically better fit to the data of the model with the extra characteristic compared with the model without this characteristic. This helps decide whether to keep the characteristic in or not. From this one could develop forward methods of building a logistic regression model where at each step one introduces an extra characteristic into the regression – the one which has the most statistical difference. One can continue this until introducing a new characteristic makes so small a change it is below some predefined level. Similarly in a backward approach one can begin with all the characteristics in the regression and drop out one by one the characteristics whose exclusion makes the least difference to this statistic. One keeps doing this until dropping the next characteristic would mean there is too great a change in the statistic.

Example 1.9.1 Building a logistic regression scorecard using the Bank of Southampton Bank data of Appendix B

The data constructed in Appendix B (Bank of Southampton) represents a much simplified version of the type of data a bank would use to build an application scorecard. There are 1000 cases in the sample and for each case we have the age of the applicant, their residential status, whether they have a credit card, and whether or not they were subsequently good or bad. Age has already been coarse classified into four bands and there are three categories of residential status – owner, renter, or others. Thus there are 24 different combinations of characteristics in the data set, and Appendix B gives the numbers in each grouping.

To produce the scorecard, we build a logistic regression model, where the dependent (target variable) is the binary variable of whether the applicant in the sample was subsequently good or not. We estimate this using the binary variables age 30–39, age 40–49, age over 50, owner, renter, and 'has credit card'. We leave out one of possible attributes from each characteristic – age 30 – from age, 'others' from residential status and 'no credit card' to avoid co-linearity between the variables. The output from a statistical package of applying the logistic regression module is given in Table 1.9.1. This corresponds to saying that $p(G|\mathbf{x})$ is the probability of

TABLE 1.9.1. Output of logistic regression module using data in Appendix B.
The logistic procedure
Analysis of maximum likelihood estimates

Parameter	DF	Estimate	Standard error	Wald chi-square	Pr > chi-square
Intercept	1	1.5866	0.3429	21.4105	< 0.0001
Age 30–39	1	−0.4628	0.3165	2.1381	0.1437
Age 40–49	1	−0.0932	0.3710	0.0631	0.8017
Age 50+	1	0.1765	0.3031	0.3390	0.5604
Owner	1	0.7363	0.3129	5.5361	0.0186
Renter	1	−1.1090	0.2951	14.1221	0.0002
cc	1	0.9430	0.2422	15.1616	< 0.0001

an applicant with attributes **x** being good satisfies

$$\ln\left(\frac{p(G|\mathbf{x})}{1-p(G|\mathbf{x})}\right) = 1.5866 - 0.4628(\text{age }30-39) - 0.0932(\text{age }40-49)$$

$$+ 0.1765(\text{age over }50) + 0.7363(\text{owner}) - 1.1090(\text{renter})$$

$$+ 0.9430(\text{has credit card}). \tag{1.9.6}$$

This implies that for age, the over 50s have the best chance of being good, then those under 30 (who essentially have a coefficient of 0 since that variable is not in the expression), closely followed by those in their 40s, and the worst age group is those between 30 and 39. For residential status, owners are estimated to have the best chance of being good, followed by 'others' (not in the equation) and finally renters, while having a credit card increases the chance of someone being a good. However, a number of these coefficients are sufficiently small that the Wald test suggests the hypothesis that they are zero cannot be rejected. If one was to use this then the only variables apart from the intercept that should be left in, are owner, renter and 'has a credit card'.

If we keep with Eq. (1.9.6) for now, it can be translated into a scorecard by taking the coefficients of (1.9.6) as the scores but usually they are multiplied by a suitable constant and rounded off so that it is easier to understand at a glance. In Table 1.9.2 we produce two scorecards – one where the coefficients in Eq. (1.9.6) are multiplied by 100 (Scorecard 1) and the second where the constant term is spread over the attributes to avoid any negative scores (Scorecard 2). In that case one adds 48 points to all the age scores, 111 to all the residential status scores, but leaves the credit card scores as they are. Both scorecards give the same result in that a 43-year-old owner with a credit card has a score of 318.

TABLE 1.9.2. Scorecard obtained using logistic regression in Example 1.9.1.

Attributes	Age 30–	Age 30– 39	Age 40– 49	Age 50+	Owner	Renter	Other	Has credit card	No Credit card	Constant
Scorecard 1	0	−46	−9	18	74	−111	0	94	0	159
Scorecard 2	48	2	39	66	185	0	111	94	0	0
Scorecard 3	0	−13	−3	5	21	−32	0	27	0	146

The standard transformation though as outlined in Section 1.6 is to choose one reference or anchor score where the odds are of a particular value and to ensure that adding a fixed amount to a score doubles the good:bad odds. Assume we want a score of 100 to represent good:bad odds of 1:1 and that adding 20 points to the score doubles the odds (so that a score of 120 should give odds of 2:1). The way to translate from the original score s to the score s_{Scaled} with these properties was calculated in Eq. (1.6.4). Repeating that idea here gives

$s_{Scaled} = a + bs$ with the properties

$s_{Scaled} = 100 = a + b \ln 1 = a \quad 20 = (a + b(h + \ln 2)) - (a + bh) = b \ln 2$

$$\Rightarrow b = \frac{20}{\ln 2} = \frac{20}{0.693} = 28.860 \quad a = 100. \tag{1.9.7}$$

Scorecard 3 in Table 1.9.2 gives the scores obtained by scaling Eq. (1.9.6) to have these properties.

1.10 Other scorecard-building approaches

In this section we outline four other methods – linear regression, linear programming, maximizing divergence, and classification trees – which have been used in practice to build scoring systems. There are other classification methods, several of which have been developed since the 1990s, such as neural nets, support vector machines, genetic algorithms, and nearest neighbour models. These have been tested and compared on consumer credit data and on many other classification problems, but they have not been widely used in developing operational credit scorecards. The reasons are twofold – robustness and transparency. These methods may lead to slightly better classifiers on a set of data, but the complexity of the interactions they use make them more vulnerable as the population characteristics change. More importantly, many regulators now require that lenders give reasons for rejecting an applicant for credit. Scorecards make this relatively easy to do because one can compare the score an applicants received for their attributes of a characteristic in the scorecard with the mean score for that characteristic. This identifies which attributes contribute to the applicant's score being below the cut-off. 'Black box' approaches like neural nets do not allow one to make such comparisons, though research is being undertaken to give them such a facility.

Linear regression

Linear regression was the first approach used to build scorecards and can be explained in three different ways. The first idea, developed by Fisher (1936) was to find the linear combination of the $\mathbf{x} = (x_1, x_2, \ldots, x_P)$, namely $\mathbf{c} \cdot \mathbf{x} = c_0 + c_1 x_1 + \cdots + c_m x_m$ which maximizes the distance between the mean of the goods $\boldsymbol{\mu}_{\mathbf{G}} = \int \mathbf{x} f(\mathbf{x}|G) d\mathbf{x}$ and the mean of the bads $\boldsymbol{\mu}_{\mathbf{B}} = \int \mathbf{x} f(\mathbf{x}|B) d\mathbf{x}$. In order to keep this distance invariant when linear transformations are applied to the variables we need to normalize by the square root of the variance. If this variance is the same for the goods as the bads, one is led to the Mahalanobis distance, D_M as a measure of separation where

$$D_M = \sqrt{\frac{(\text{mean of goods}-\text{mean of bads})^2}{(\text{variance within a class})}} = \left| \frac{\mathbf{c}^T \cdot (\boldsymbol{\mu}_{\mathbf{G}} - \boldsymbol{\mu}_{\mathbf{B}})}{(\mathbf{c}^T \cdot \boldsymbol{\Sigma} \mathbf{c})^{1/2}} \right| \quad (1.10.1)$$

where $\boldsymbol{\Sigma} = \boldsymbol{\Sigma}_{\mathbf{G}} = \boldsymbol{\Sigma}_{\mathbf{B}}$ is the common variance-covariance matrix for the goods and for the bads:

This is maximized when

$$\mathbf{c} = k\boldsymbol{\Sigma}^{-1}(\boldsymbol{\mu}_{\mathbf{G}} - \boldsymbol{\mu}_{\mathbf{B}}) \text{ where } k = (\mathbf{c}^T \cdot \boldsymbol{\Sigma} \mathbf{c}). \quad (1.10.2)$$

In practice, the true means and variances of the population are not known but one can replace them by the sample means and variances and hence obtain a maximizing direction. The result is a score that is additive but not necessarily a log odds score.

The reason for doing this maximization to get Eq. (1.10.2) is that if the mean values of the two groups are well separated in a certain direction then there will be less misclassification errors if the score is measured in this direction. So one is trying to find what is the linear combination of the variables that gives a score

$$s = \mathbf{c} \cdot \mathbf{x} = c_0 + c_1 x_1 + \cdots + c_m x_m$$

so that the mean score of the goods $\bar{s}_G = \int sf(s|G) ds = \int \mathbf{c}.\mathbf{x} f(\mathbf{x}|G) d\mathbf{x}$ and the mean score of the bads $\bar{s}_B = \int sf(s|B) ds = \int \mathbf{c} \cdot \mathbf{x} f(\mathbf{x}|B) d\mathbf{x}$ are separated as much as possible given the variance normalization.

The second way of explaining the linear regression approach is called discriminant analysis. It assumes the conditional distributions of the characteristics are multi-variate normal both for the goods and for the bads. One then calculates for each new borrower with characteristic $\mathbf{x}$ the conditional probabilities $p(G|\mathbf{x})$ and $p(B|\mathbf{x})$ and defines the new borrower as good or bad depending which of these is the higher. So one assumes the distribution of the attribute values for the goods is

$$f(\mathbf{x}|G) = (2\pi)^{-m/2} |\mathbf{\Sigma_G}|^{-1/2} \exp\left\{-\frac{1}{2}(\mathbf{x} - \mu_G)^T \mathbf{\Sigma_G}^{-1}(\mathbf{x} - \mu_G)\right\} \quad (1.10.3)$$

where $|A|$ is the determinant of the matrix A. A similar expression holds for $f(\mathbf{x}|B)$. One can then use Bayes' theorem to compute the posterior probabilities:

$$p(G|\mathbf{x}) = \frac{f(\mathbf{x}|G)p_G}{f(\mathbf{x})}; \quad p(B|\mathbf{x}) = \frac{f(\mathbf{x}|B)p_B}{f(\mathbf{x})}$$

and so the classification rule becomes, classify $\mathbf{x}$ as good if

$$p(G|\mathbf{x}) > p(B|\mathbf{x}) \Rightarrow f(\mathbf{x}|G)p_G > f(\mathbf{x}|B)p_B$$

$$\Rightarrow p_G |\mathbf{\Sigma_G}|^{-1/2} \exp\left\{-\frac{1}{2}(\mathbf{x} - \mu_G)^T \mathbf{\Sigma_G}^{-1}(\mathbf{x} - \mu_G)\right\}$$

$$> p_B |\mathbf{\Sigma_B}|^{-1/2} \times \exp\left\{-\frac{1}{2}(\mathbf{x} - \mu_B)^T \mathbf{\Sigma_B}^{-1}(\mathbf{x} - \mu_B)\right\}$$

$$\Rightarrow \ln(p_G) - \frac{1}{2}\ln(|\mathbf{\Sigma_G}|) - \left\{\frac{1}{2}(\mathbf{x} - \mu_G)^T \mathbf{\Sigma_B}^{-1}(\mathbf{x} - \mu_G)\right\}$$

$$> \ln(p_B) - \frac{1}{2}\ln(|\mathbf{\Sigma_B}|) - \left\{\frac{1}{2}(\mathbf{x} - \mu_B)^T \mathbf{\Sigma_B}^{-1}(\mathbf{x} - \mu_B)\right\}$$

$$\Rightarrow (\mathbf{x} - \mu_G)^T \mathbf{\Sigma_G}^{-1}(\mathbf{x} - \mu_G) - (\mathbf{x} - \mu_B)^T \mathbf{\Sigma_B}^{-1}(\mathbf{x} - \mu_B)$$

$$< 2\ln(p_G/p_B) + \ln(|\mathbf{\Sigma_B}| / |\mathbf{\Sigma_G}|)$$

$$(1.10.4)$$

If $\Sigma = \Sigma_G = \Sigma_B$ this reduces to the linear rule

$$-2\mathbf{x}^T \mathbf{\Sigma}^{-1}(\mu_G - \mu_B) + \mu_G^T \mathbf{\Sigma}^{-1}\mu_G - \mu_B^T \mathbf{\Sigma}^{-1}\mu_B < 2\ln(p_G/p_B)$$

$$\Rightarrow \mathbf{x}^T \mathbf{\Sigma}^{-1}(\mu_G - \mu_B) > \frac{1}{2}(\mu_G^T \mathbf{\Sigma}^{-1}\mu_G - \mu_B^T \mathbf{\Sigma}^{-1}\mu_B) - \ln(p_G/p_B) \quad (1.10.5)$$

$$\Rightarrow \mathbf{x} \cdot \mathbf{\Sigma}(\mu_G - \mu_B) > s_c$$

where the left-hand side (LHS) is the linear expression that maximizes the Mahalanobis distance under the Fisher approach in (1.10.2). Again one does not know the true means and variances of the populations but replacing them by the sample means and variances gives a viable way of deriving a scorecard.

If the covariances were different for the two groups, which is normally the case then this would lead to a quadratic decision rule. However, the robustness of the coefficients in the linear rule more than compensates for the advantage of a curved separation surface, and so the linear rule is usually used. This discriminant approach emphasizes that the linear regression approach estimates $f(\mathbf{x}|G)$ and from this gets an indirect estimate of $p(G|\mathbf{x})$, while the logistic regression approach estimates $p(G|\mathbf{x})$ directly.

Perhaps the easiest way to think about this approach, though statistically not quite accurate, is to think that one is trying to fit

$$p(G|\mathbf{x}) = p(\mathbf{x}) = \mathbf{c} \cdot \mathbf{x} = c_0 + c_1 x_1 + \cdots + c_m x_m \qquad (1.10.6)$$

For each borrower, in the sample used to estimate this regression for $p(G|\mathbf{x})$, we have the data $(y,\mathbf{x})$ where $y^i = 1$ if the borrower is good and 0 if the borrower is bad, then $p(G|\mathbf{x}) = 1$ and if $y^i = 0$ then $p(G|\mathbf{x}) = 0$. So one seems to find the coefficients $\mathbf{c}$ that give the best fit for the equation $y = \mathbf{c} \cdot \mathbf{x}$. If the error when trying to fit the data was normal, which is not the case, then the MLE of the c_i would give the same formulae as (1.10.2) from the other two approaches. Thinking of the formulae as derived in this way, one can calculate σ_i^2, the variance in estimating c_i, Wald's statistic W and $P\{\chi^2 > W\}$, which have the same interpretation as in the logistic regression approach. The R^2-statistic which explains how much of the relationship in regression is explained by the linear relationship calculated is usually much poorer than one would normally expect but that is because the dependent variable only takes values 0 or 1.

Notice that thinking of the linear regression in terms of (1.10.6) produces a score which is the probability of a good not the log odds of the probability of being good. If one wants to produce a log odds score s from this linear regression score $\tilde{s}(\mathbf{x}) = p(G|\mathbf{x})$ one would expect that the transformation will be close to $s = \ln(\tilde{s}/1 - \tilde{s})$ which would be the one if there were no errors in the linear regression. This transformation is shown by Fig. 1.10.1 and it is clear the transformation is monotonic and in fact is almost linear over the interval where the probability of being good is between 0.15 and 0.90. If one applied a scalar transformation to this linear regression score, it would have the log odds property over that range. However, for scores corresponding to high probabilities of being good there is little chance of the log odds property holding.

So far we have not discussed whether the variables in the regression should be the binary ones describing the different attribute groups of a characteristic obtained from coarse classification, the weights of evidence transformation of the characteristics, or the original characteristics themselves. The binary variable approach cannot hope to satisfy the normality assumption that motivates the discriminant analysis view of using linear regression to build a scorecard, whereas the actual characteristics for some of the continuous variables may have close to a normality distribution. However, the flexibility of the binary variable approach to deal

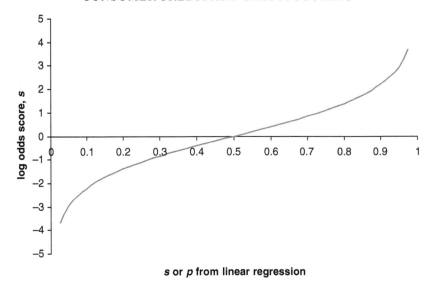

FIG. 1.10.1. Transformation from linear regression to log odds score.

with characteristics which are non-monotonic in default risk means that one almost always coarse classifies variables even if one is going to use linear regression. Some scorecard developers use the idea of linear least squares using weights of evidence (LLSWOE). This is another name for building a linear regression model using the weights of evidence transformation of the original variables as the predictive variables. Since linear regression is obtained by minimizing the mean square errors, this explains the 'linear least square' description of the approach.

Example 1.10.1 Using linear regression to build a scorecard using Appendix B data

Using the data from the Bank of Southampton in Appendix B, it is straightforward to build a scorecard using linear regression. As with logistic regression, one wants to avoid co-linearity between the variables. Thus having coarse classified a characteristic into n attributes, we should only include $n - 1$ of the binary variables, each obtained from one of the attributes, in the regression since the sum of all n attributes is always 1. So in this case we ignore age 'under 30', residential status 'other', and 'no credit card'. Using the binary variable 'good' as the target variable gives the results in Table 1.10.1 from a statistical package.

Again the Wald test suggests that the significant variables are owner, renter, and 'has credit card', and that age is less important. However, if we keep all the variables in at present, this leads to the equation that if $p(G|\mathbf{x})$, the probability of

TABLE 1.10.1. Output of linear regression using data in Appendix B.

Root MSE	0.28637	R^2	0.0952			
Dependent mean	0.90000	Adj R^2	0.0897			
Coefficient variance	31.81934					

Parameter estimates

Variable	Label	DF	Parameter estimate	Standard error	t-value	$Pr > |t|$
Intercept	Intercept	1	0.82185	0.03159	26.02	< 0.0001
Age 30–39	Age 30–39	1	−0.05090	0.02909	−1.75	0.0805
Age 40–49	Age 40–49	1	−0.00533	0.03031	−0.18	0.8604
Age 59	Age 50+	1	0.01157	0.02530	0.46	0.6475
Owner	Owner	1	0.05096	0.02406	2.12	0.0344
Renter	Renter	1	−0.14521	0.02868	−5.06	< 0.0001
cc	cc	1	0.10423	0.02302	4.53	< 0.0001

TABLE 1.10.2. Scorecards obtained from linear regression in Example 1.10.1.

Attributes	Age 30–	Age 30–39	Age 40–49	Age 50+	Owner	Renter	Other	Has credit card	No Credit card	Constant
Scorecard 1	0	−5	1	1	5	−15	0	10	0	82
Scorecard 2	0	0	0	0	5	−15	0	10	0	82

an applicant with characteristics **x** being good satisfies

$$p(G|\mathbf{x}) = 0.82185 - 0.0509(\text{age } 30\text{–}39) - 0.00533(\text{age } 40\text{–}49)$$
$$+ 0.01157(\text{age over } 50) + 0.05096(\text{owner})$$
$$- 0.14521(\text{renter}) + 0.10423(\text{credit card}) \qquad (1.10.7)$$

Multiplying by 100 and rounding off the numbers just for convenience gives the scorecard 1 in Table 1.10.2, which of course does not have the log odds property defined in Section 1.5. If one only used the attributes that were significant one would end up with the even simpler Scorecard 2.

Maximizing the divergence

The Fisher approach to classification, which led to the linear regression approach, looked for a measure that described how well the goods and the bads are separated. This equation used the Mahalanobis distance, Eq. (1.10.1) but there are other measures. What one requires is that if the distribution of attributes among the goods is $f(\mathbf{x}|G)$ and among the bads is $f(\mathbf{x}|B)$, then one would look for a measure $d(G,B)$

so that

$$d(G,B) = 0 \quad \text{if } f(\mathbf{x}|G) = f(\mathbf{x}|B)$$
$$d(G,B) \geq 0 \quad \text{otherwise.}$$

One such measure called the divergence was introduced by Kullback and Leibler (1951). It was introduced as a way of measuring the difference between two probability distributions. Then it was realized how closely it was related to measures in information theory like entropy. In the credit scoring context it is a good way of measuring how different is the distribution of scores among the good and the bad populations because it is essentially the continuous version of the information value. We introduced divergence and information statistic in Section 1.8 as a way of selecting characteristics and determining the best way of coarse classifying a characteristic. As in Eq. (1.8.7) we define the divergence between $f(\mathbf{x}|G)$ and $f(\mathbf{x}|B)$ as

$$\int (f(\mathbf{x}|G) - f(\mathbf{x}|B)) \ln \left(\frac{f(\mathbf{x}|G)}{f(\mathbf{x}|B)} \right) d\mathbf{x} = \int (f(\mathbf{x}|G) - f(\mathbf{x}|B)) w(\mathbf{x}) d\mathbf{x}.$$

$$(1.10.8)$$

In the same way if we already have a scorecard $s(\mathbf{x}) = s$, we can define the divergence between the score distribution for the goods and the bads, $f(s|G)$ and $f(s|B)$, respectively, by

$$\text{Divergence} = D = \int (f(s|G) - f(s|B)) \log \left(\frac{f(s|G)}{f(s|B)} \right) ds$$
$$= \int (f(s|G) - f(s|B)) w(s) ds \qquad (1.10.9)$$

where $w(s)$ is the weights of evidence defined in Section 1.5.

Divergence becomes infinite when there are scores where the density for bads is zero and for goods is positive or vice versa but when this arises there are numerous practical procedures for preserving finite results (that is replacing the zero entry of numbers of goods or bads by a minimum number of say 0.5 or 0.0005). When the conditional distributions are identical, and there is no difference between the score distribution of the goods and the bads, the divergence is zero. When the frequency of goods becomes much larger than the frequency of bads, divergence becomes very large and it is easy to discriminate and distinguish goods from bads; the same argument applies when the frequency of goods is much smaller than that of bads, the only difference being that the weight of evidence in favour of a good is a negative number. If we exclude the case where $f(s|B)$ is zero and $f(s|G)$ is not, score divergence is non-negative because each term in the integrand is either zero or the product of two negative or two positive factors, so:

$$(f(s|G) - f(s|B)) \ln\left(\frac{f(s|G)}{f(s|B)}\right) \geq 0.$$

When using divergence to build rather than just to measure a scorecard, the first task is again to coarse classify the attributes $\mathbf{x} = (x_1, x_s, \ldots x_m)$ of the characteristics into appropriate bins. The aim is then to find a weight or score for each attribute bin so that the resulting additive score maximizes divergence. If one thinks of the bins of the characteristic x_i as being represented by binary variables which take the value 1 if the borrower has an attribute in that bin and 0 if not, one is trying to find attribute scores c_i so that the resulting scorecard:

$$s = s(\mathbf{x}) = \mathbf{c} \cdot \mathbf{x} = c_0 + c_1 x_1 + \cdots + c_m x_m \qquad (1.10.10)$$

maximizes this divergence where the likelihood functions $f(\mathbf{x}|G)$ and $f(\mathbf{x}|B)$ are obtained empirically from the sample of past borrowers being used.

For any choice of attribute scores $\mathbf{c}$ we define the corresponding score distributions $f(s|G, \mathbf{c}) = \sum_{\mathbf{x}:\mathbf{c}\cdot\mathbf{x}=s} f(\mathbf{x}|G)$; $f(s|B, \mathbf{c}) = \sum_{\mathbf{x}:\mathbf{c}\cdot\mathbf{x}=s} f(\mathbf{x}|B)$ and then find the maximum divergence value as $\mathbf{c}$ varies, namely,

$$\underset{\mathbf{c}}{\mathrm{Max}}\, D = \underset{\mathbf{c}}{\mathrm{Max}} \int (f(s|G, \mathbf{c}) - f(s|B, \mathbf{c})) \log\left(\frac{f(s|G, \mathbf{c})}{f(s|B, \mathbf{c})}\right) ds. \qquad (1.10.11)$$

This is a non-linear maximization problem and so one uses iterative procedures to improve the divergence from one iteration to the next. Like all non-linear problems there is no guarantee that the final solution is the global optimal but only that it is a local optimal. That means one might not have found the scorecard that actually maximizes the divergence but only one which has a larger divergence than any other scorecard obtained by a slight modification of it. Often this means there are lots of quite different scorecards with very similar almost optimal divergence values.

If the score likelihood functions $f(s|G)$ (and $f(s|B)$) are in fact normally distributed with means $\mu_G(\mu_B)$ and variance σ_G^2 (σ_B^2), one has the moment relationships

$$\int f(s|G)ds = 1; \quad \int sf(s|G)ds = \mu_G; \quad \int s^2 f(s|G)ds = \sigma_G^2 + \mu_G^2;$$

$$\int f(s|B)ds = 1; \quad \int sf(s|B)ds = \mu_B; \quad \int s^2 f(s|G)ds = \sigma_B^2 + \mu_B^2, \qquad (1.10.12)$$

where the first term is just integrating the density function, the second term is the mean value, and the third term is the second moment which is the variance plus the mean squared. In Eq. (1.6.6) we showed that with such normal distributions the weights of evidence reduced to a quadratic in the score, namely

$$\ln\frac{f(s|G)}{f(s|B)} = \left(\ln\frac{\sigma_B}{\sigma_G} - \frac{1}{2}\left(\frac{s-\mu_G}{\sigma_G}\right)^2 + \frac{1}{2}\left(\frac{s-\mu_B}{\sigma_B}\right)^2\right). \tag{1.10.13}$$

Putting (1.10.12) and (1.10.13) together means that the divergence if the score distributions are normally distributed can be expressed as follows:

$$\text{Divergence} = D = \int (f(s|G) - f(s|B)) \log\left(\frac{f(s|G)}{f(s|B)}\right) ds$$

$$= \int (f(s|G) - f(s|B))\left(\ln\frac{\sigma_B}{\sigma_G} - \frac{1}{2}\left(\frac{s-\mu_G}{\sigma_G}\right)^2 + \frac{1}{2}\left(\frac{s-\mu_B}{\sigma_B}\right)^2\right) ds$$

$$= \left(\frac{1}{2\sigma_B^2} - \frac{1}{2\sigma_G^2}\right)\int s^2 (f(s|G) - f(s|B)) ds$$

$$+ \left(\frac{\mu_G}{\sigma_G^2} - \frac{\mu_B}{\sigma_B^2}\right)\int s (f(s|G) - f(s|B)) ds$$

$$+ \left(\ln\frac{\sigma_B}{\sigma_G} - \frac{\mu_G}{2\sigma_G^2} + \frac{\mu_B}{2\sigma_B^2}\right)\int (f(s|G) - f(s|B)) ds$$

$$= \left(\frac{1}{2\sigma_B^2} - \frac{1}{2\sigma_G^2}\right)((\mu_G^2 + \sigma_G^2) - (\mu_B^2 + \sigma_B^2)) + \left(\frac{\mu_G}{\sigma_G^2} - \frac{\mu_B}{\sigma_B^2}\right)(\mu_G - \mu_B)$$

$$+ \left(\ln\frac{\sigma_B}{\sigma_G} - \frac{\mu_G}{2\sigma_G^2} + \frac{\mu_B}{2\sigma_B^2}\right)(1 - 1)$$

$$= \frac{1}{2}\left(\frac{1}{\sigma_G^2} + \frac{1}{\sigma_B^2}\right)(\mu_G - \mu_B)^2 + \frac{(\sigma_G^2 - \sigma_B^2)^2}{2\sigma_G^2\sigma_B^2}. \tag{1.10.14}$$

In the special case when the variances of the goods and the bads are equal, $\sigma_G^2 = \sigma_B^2 = \sigma^2$, then this reduces further to the square of the Mahalanobis distance function namely:

$$D = \left(\frac{(\mu_G - \mu_B)^2}{\sigma^2}\right) = D_M^2. \tag{1.10.15}$$

Thus, in the case of normally distributed scores with equal variance among the goods and the bads, maximizing divergence has the same objective as the linear regression approach. So it can be considered as an extension of the linear regression approach which does not assume normality of the score distributions. However, note that like logistic regression it is a direct approach in that it is based on estimating $f(x|G)$ directly without recourse to estimating $p(G|x)$ and then using Bayes's theorem to convert it into $f(x|G)$ which is what the linear regression approach does. Although the scorecard obtained by maximizing divergence is additive it is not a log odds one.

Example 1.10.2 Maximizing divergence using Bank of Southampton data (Appendix B)

When calculating divergence one has to split the score range into bands and calculate what is then the information value given those bands, or else to find a smooth approximation of the density functions. However, if one take the simplified expression in Eq. (1.10.14), which follows from the normality assumption, maximizing the divergence becomes easier. One could for example use the non-linear optimizer in the Solver add-on in Excel to find a local maximum.

Note that, if we add a constant to all the attribute scores of a characteristics everyone's score goes up by that value and hence there is no change in the divergence as both the distributions of the goods' scores and the bads' scores go up by that constant. So to try and cut down the number of optimal solutions we again leave one attribute of each characteristic out of the calculation (which is equivalent to giving that attribute a score of zero). If again we set under 30 in the age characteristic to have a zero score, 'others' in the residential characteristic to have zero score and 'no credit card' to be a zero score, one local maximization, obtained by using Solver (Table 1.10.3).

There are though a number of solutions all of which have a maximizing divergence of 1.145146. Note that, though the scores are different from the logistic and the linear regression based scorecards, the relative ordering of the attributes is the same. For age, the least risky group is the over 50s, followed by the under 30s, the 40 to 49 class, with the 30–39 class being the most risky. For residential status being an owner is the best risk, followed by 'others' with the renters having the least risk score, while having a credit card is better than not having one.

Linear programming

Linear programming can also be used for classification as was shown initially by Freed and Glover (1981a,b, 1986a,b), and gives rise to an additive scorecard . It

TABLE 1.10.3. Scorecard using divergence criteria on Example 1.10.2.

Attributes	Age 30–	Age 30–39	Age 40–49	Age 50+	Owner	Renter	Other	Has credit card	No credit card	Divergence
Values	0	−2.607	−0.240	0.052	1.524	−6.318	0	4.390	0	1.145146

is not based on the probabilities of belonging to one or other of the classes being classified but simply on how wrong is the scorecard when it assigns a data point incorrectly. So in the credit scoring context it assumes there is a scorecard and a cut-off values s_c, and those with scores above this cut-off will be classified as good and those below it as bad. If a borrower is misclassified, the misclassification error is how far the wrong way from the cut-off point is the score of the borrower who is misclassified. Linear programming seeks to minimize the sum of such misclassification errors.

Assume the data set is of n previous borrowers and the characteristics have already been coarse classified so that one end up with m attribute classes in total over all the characteristics. Thus the data for borrower i in the sample consists of $(x_j^i, y^i) j = 1, 2, \ldots, m$, where x_j^i are the attribute values for borrower i and $y^i = 1$ if borrower i is good, and 0 if bad. For ease of notation let us assume that the first n_G borrowers are the goods and the remaining borrowers from $n_G + 1$ to $n_G + n_B$ are the bads. This then leads to the linear programme:

$$\text{Minimize } a_1 + a_2 + \cdots + a_{n_G+n_B}$$
$$\text{subject to}$$
$$\begin{aligned} c_1 x_1^i + c_2 x_2^i + \cdots + c_m x_m^i &\geq s_c - a_i & 1 \leq i \leq n_G & \quad (1.10.16)\\ c_1 x_1^i + c_2 x_2^i + \cdots + c_m x_m^i &\leq s_c + a_i & n_G+1 \leq i \leq n &\\ a_i &\geq 0 & 1 \leq i \leq n. & \end{aligned}$$

For the goods, the first type of constraint says that their score should be above the cut-off s_c and there is only an error if their score (the LHS) is below the cut-off. In this case the error a_i comes into play to reduce the RHS so that the constraint is satisfied. For a bad, the constraint says that the score should be below the cut-off score s_c and there is only an error if the score is above the cut-off score in which case the error will increase the RHS until the constraint is satisfied. The objective function is to minimize the sum of the errors, but there are easy extensions that ensure one minimizes the maximum error or minimizes the number of misclassifications (though that will require some of the variables to be integer).

One might be tempted to make the cut-odds score a variable but this will lead to the trivial solution where all the coefficients are zero so all the scores are zero. Then with a cut-off score of zero, no point is wrongly classified. This occurs because there should be a strict inequality in the constraints rather than the greater and equal inequality that linear programming requires. So one normally takes the cut-off score to be a suitable value like 200 or 400. If the cut-off is positive this implies that the scores are such that the goods are getting higher scores than the bads. So it is also useful to test the linear programme with a negative cut-off. If the resultant linear programme has a lower error than with a positive cut-off, then it means the goods are only getting higher scores than the bads if most of the scores are negative. If we multiply all the scores by -1 to make most of them positive then the bads would be having higher scores than the goods and the scorecard is the 'wrong way around'.

Another way to experiment with cut-offs is to require that the goods have a score which is at least s_1 but that the bads have a score no more than s_2 with $s_1 > s_2$. This tries to ensure there is a gap in the scores between the goods and the bads and though in practice there rarely is such a gap, it does often lead to more robust scorecards than those with just one cut-off score.

In linear programming one needs to keep all the attributes of a characteristic in the calculation, unlike in the previous approaches. Adding a constant to all the attributes of a characteristic makes no difference only if the cut-off score is also increased by that constant value. Since the cut-off score is fixed one cannot therefore drop an attribute (which is equivalent to subtracting its score from every other attribute of that characteristic) without it affecting the resultant scorecard.

Notice that this scorecard is obtained from the classification problem directly and does not have any underlying probability assumptions. This is clear because one can only construct the scores if a cut-off value is given. Without choosing a cut-off value one cannot define a score. What is happening is that one is trying to find a score so that the scores for the bads above the cut-off are not too high and similarly that the score for the goods below the cut-off are not too low. This does imply that the number of bads with high scores should be low and getting smaller as the score increases and vice versa for the goods. So it seems reasonable that if one then takes the empirical probability and odds estimates that these scores give they will prove to be mostly monotonic in the underlying scores, but that property is not guaranteed.

There are two significant advantages of the linear programming approach. One is that it deals with large numbers of variables very well. The second is that if one wants to ensure certain relationships between the attribute scores – for example that under 30s get a score more than the over 30s or that owning a home has the highest component in the score – this is very easy to do by adding extra constraints in the linear programme which ensure these requirements between the coefficients are met.

Example 1.10.3 Building a scorecard by linear programming using the Bank of Southampton data in Appendix B

Applying the linear programming optimization in Eq. (1.10.16) to the Southampton Bank data shows some of the difficulties with this approach. There are only nine different attributes after the coarse classifying (unless we allow for interactions between the attributes) – four attributes in the age, three in residential status, and two in credit card ownership. Thus there are only $4 \times 3 \times 2 = 24$ different attribute combinations that are being considered and hence really only 24 different good constraints and 24 bad constraints. One can multiply the error by the number of such cases with each combination in the objective function. Thus the linear programming only has 48 constraints and 9 attribute score variables (and 48 error variables). Define the attribute score as $c(30-)$, and so on, and order the 48 combination beginning with age under 30, owner with credit card and ending with age over

50, other residential status, and no credit cards. If we require the goods to have scores of at least 200 and the bads to have scores less than 150, we get the linear programme formulation:

$Minimize$: $50a_1 + 110a_2 + \cdots + 5a_{24} + 3a_{25} + 5a_{26} + \cdots + 1a_{48}$

subject to

$1.c(30-)+0.c(30-39)+0.c(40-49)+0.c(50+)+1.c(\text{owner})$
$\quad + 0.c(\text{renter})+0.c(\text{other})+1.c(\text{credit card})+0.c(\text{no cc}) \geqslant 200-a_1$

$0.c(30-)+1.c(30-39)+0.c(40-49)+0.c(50+)+1.c(\text{owner})$
$\quad + 0.c(\text{renter})+0.c(\text{other})+1.c(\text{credit card})+0.c(\text{no cc}) \geqslant 200-a_2$

$\cdots$

$0.c(30-)+0.c(30-39)+0.c(40-49)+1.c(50+)+0.c(\text{owner})$
$\quad + 0.c(\text{renter})+1.c(\text{other})+0.c(\text{credit card})+1.c(\text{no cc}) \geqslant 200-a_{24}$

$1.c(30-)+0.c(30-39)+0.c(40-49)+0.c(50+)+1.c(\text{owner})$
$\quad + 0.c(\text{renter})+0.c(\text{other})+1.c(\text{credit card})+0.c(\text{no cc}) \leqslant 150+a_{25}$

$0.c(30-)+1.c(30-39)+0.c(40-49)+0.c(50+)+1.c(\text{owner})$
$\quad + 0.c(\text{renter})+0.c(\text{other})+1.c(\text{credit card})+0.c(\text{no cc}) \leqslant 150 + a_{26}$

$\cdots$

$0.c(30-)+0.c(30-39)+0.c(40-49)+1.c(50+)+0.c(\text{owner})$
$\quad + 0.c(\text{renter})+1.c(\text{other})+0.c(\text{credit card})+1.c(\text{no cc}) \leqslant 150 + a_{48}$

$a_i \geqslant 0 \qquad \forall i.$

$$(1.10.17)$$

The solutions are given in Table 1.10.4 where the first row represents the solution if good and bad errors are weighed the same and in the second we increase the weighting of the errors in the bads ($a_{25}, \ldots, a_{48}$) fivefold so that the objective

TABLE 1.10.4. Scorecards built using linear programming on Appendix B data.

Attributes	Age 30–	Age 30–39	Age 40–49	Age 50+	Owner	Renter	Other	Has credit card	No Credit card
Equal errors	200	200	200	200	0	0	0	0	0
Bad errors = 5 × good errors	200	200	200	200	0	−50	0	0	0

function becomes $\ldots + 15a_{25} + 25a_{26} + \ldots 5a_{48}$. The resulting scorecards do not have many different scores – one in the first cases and two in the second. So linear programming requires a lot more different combinations of attributes in order to give meaningful results.

Classification trees (recursive partitioning algorithms)

The result of this classification approach is not really a scorecard but rather a set of rules which enable one to classify new applicants by looking at what combination of characteristics they have. However, one can reinterpret the results so that one arrives at a score for each consumer, albeit a highly non-additive one. Thus, unlike linear programming, one can give a probability interpretation to the scores from the data itself though really what one is doing is the log odds calibration discussed earlier. So if pushed one would say classification trees lead to a non-additive log odds score.

Classification trees, sometimes called recursive partitioning algorithms (RPA) classify the consumers into groups, each group being homogeneous in its default risk and as different from the default risks of other groups as is possible. This tree approach has been developed in statistics (Breiman et al. 1984), in artificial intelligence (Safavain and Landgrebe 1991), and in machine learning (Quinlan 1993) but though the definitions vary the basic idea is the same in all cases. In classification trees one starts by splitting the attributes of one characteristic into two subsets. One then chooses the split where some measure of the difference in the default risk between the two subsets is as large as possible. Other less myopic criteria can be used where the measure of a split is calculated by looking ahead to the situation after several more levels of splits. Having found the best split for a specific characteristic, the process is repeated for all the characteristics. One chooses the characteristic and the binary split of that characteristic that maximizes the measures of the difference in default risk between the two subsets created. This process is then repeated on each of the two subsets created in turn. One keeps on splitting subsets of the borrowers until either one ends up with groups which are so small that it is not statistically sensible to split anymore or that the best split produces two new sub-groups which are not statistically significantly different. When one has stopped splitting the tree, one classifies each remaining group as good or bad depending on the numbers of goods and bads in that group. Figure 1.10.2 gives an example of such a tree using the data from Appendix B.

One can convert the tree into a score by using the numbers of goods and bads in these final nodes. Suppose in Fig. 1.10.2 one looked at the final group, two in from the left of the tree who are renters who have a credit card. There are 120

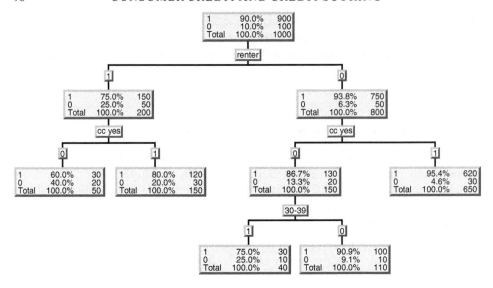

Fɪɢ. 1.10.2. Classification tree using Southampton Bank Appendix B data.

goods and 30 bads in that group and so one would give the group the score of
$s = \log(120/30) = 1.386$ and similarly for the other groups.

The most important thing to realize in classification trees is that one is bound
to be over-fitting the data. If one keeps on going and arrives at a tree with only
one data point in each final node then the tree will be a perfect classifier for that
data sample, and likely to be a useless one on any other sample. Thus, usually in
building trees, one divides the data set not just into the two of training sample and
validation/holdout sample (for assessing the classification ability of the scorecard)
but into three – the training sample, the hold-out sample and a testing sample which
can be used to prune back the tree by seeing how it is performing on a different
data set than the one it was created on. Since the nuances in this second set will
affect the classification ability of the tree because it is being used to decide how far
to prune the tree one has to then check its accuracy on the third hold-out sample.

Even so, over-fitting is a real problem and an alternative way is now being
used. This is the idea of a random forest (Breiman 2001), which builds a number of
different trees. For each tree the data used to build the tree and the characteristics
that can be used to create the splits are chosen randomly from the original data
set so the different trees involve different characteristics and are built on different
sub-samples of the borrower data set. When one wants to classify a new applicant
one looks at which good/bad status the majority of the trees ascribe to the applicant.

In normal classification trees and in random forests, the trees built depend
critically on the choice of splitting measure, which decides into which two subsets
to divide any node of the tree, when one is considering one specific characteristic.

One can think of this as coarse classifying the characteristic into two attribute groups and hence one can use the chi-square value and information value statistics which we introduced when discussing course classifying in Section 1.8. For continuous characteristics, one might want to split into two intervals – one above and one below the split. Again, information value or chi-square statistics can be used to decide but one can also look for the split where there is the maximum difference in the proportions of the goods in the set as a ratio of the whole good population and the whole bad population. This is the Kolmogorov Smirnov distance, which we look at in more detail in Section 2.2 when we discuss how to measure the discriminating ability of the bads in the set as a ratio of a scorecard.

2

Measurement of scoring systems

2.1 Measuring scorecard quality

Having constructed a scorecard and having a set of data consisting of the scores of individuals and their subsequent good/bad status, one would like to know how good is the scorecard. As Professor Joad (a 1950s UK TV philosopher) would say, 'it all depends on what you mean by good'. There are at least three ways of measuring the effectiveness of a scoring system:

- The discriminatory ability of the scorecard
- The calibration accuracy of the scorecard probability predictions
- The correctness of the categorical prediction decisions made by the scoring system.

Each of these reflects different features of the scorecard system.

The first of these – *the ability of the scorecard to separate the Goods from the Bads* – is the traditional way scorecards have been assessed. Most measures of discrimination depend only on the scorecard itself and are independent of the good:bad odds in the population. This means that one can take a sample of the population which is weighted differently to the population's good:bad odds and the discrimination measure will be the same as that for the original population. There are some discrimination measures though, which do depend on the good:bad odds in the sample of the population on which the scorecard is being measured.

The second, calibration accuracy of the probability prediction, requires knowledge of the function that transforms score into the probability of an event. We recall from Section 1.5 that if the scorecard is a log odds one, then the probability of being good is

$$p(s) = \frac{1}{1 + e^{-s}}$$

If it is a scaled log odds score, say $s = a + b s_{\text{log odds}}$ where $s_{\text{log odds}}$ is a log odds score, then the transformation is

$$p(s) = \frac{1}{1 + e^{-(s-a)/b}}$$

since $(s - a)/b$ is a log odds score. For other scores, the transformation from score to probability of Good (or equivalently to probability of bad or default, which is widely used in the Basel Accord discussed in Chapter 5) can be obtained by comparing the score with the empirical odds or percentage defaulting on the training set. This data is part of what is called the run book. Thus measuring the calibration of the probabilities predicted is really a comparison of how robust is this transformation. The transformation is obtained by looking at the odds in different score bands on the development sample and then measuring what the score band to odds results on an out-of-sample, or even an out-of-time, population were.

The third way of measuring effectiveness – *the accuracy of the classification of borrowers into good and bad classes* – depends not just on the scorecard but also on the cut-off score chosen, and so can be different for the same scorecard system if different cut-offs are used.

In Section 2.2 we look at discrimination measures, before concentrating in Section 2.3 on the receiver operating characteristic (ROC) curve and its Gini coefficient, which are the most widely used discrimination measures. It is usual to measure the discrimination of a specific scorecard but in reality a scoring system can consist of several scorecards, each being applied to a different segment of the population. Section 2.4 shows how in these cases some of the discrimination is due to the segmentation, no matter how good or bad is the discrimination of the individual scorecards. Section 2.5 discusses the measures used to estimate the probability forecasting ability of a scorecard, which has only become important with the introduction of the Basel Accord. Lastly, in Section 2.6 we discuss how one measures how good are the categorical predictions made by the scoring system consisting of the scorecards and their cut-off values. This was the original purpose of building a scorecard, and as can be seen from the decision tree models in Section 1.4, these types of measures translate immediately into actual profits and losses.

Whichever aspect of the scorecard is being investigated, it is important that the measurement should be carried out on a different set of data from that on which it was built. When one builds a scorecard on a development or training data set $\mathcal{D}$, one can think of the scorecard as a map from the data set to the reals, $s : \mathcal{D} \to \mathcal{R}$ and we define $\mathcal{S}_\mathcal{D}$ as the set of all possible such functions

$$\mathcal{S}_\mathcal{D} = \{f \mid f : \mathcal{D} \to \mathcal{R}\}. \tag{2.1.1}$$

If one chooses the function which optimizes some criterion $\mathcal{L}$ (which could be likelihood if the scorecard is built using logistic regression, least square error if built using linear regression, divergence or one of the discrimination measures described hereafter), one chooses a scoring function s_D (.) so that

$$\underset{s \in S_D}{\text{Max}}\, \mathcal{L}(s|\mathcal{D}) = \mathcal{L}(s_D|\mathcal{D}) \qquad (2.1.2)$$

where $\mathcal{L}(s|\mathcal{D})$ is the value of the measure given by the scoring function $s(.)$ over the data set $\mathcal{D}$. One finds the scorecard that maximizes the measure being used on the development sample.

Since $\mathcal{D}$ is an integral part of obtaining $s_D(.)$, then it is likely to lead to a scorecard that performs better on that data sets than on other data sets. This is true for all measures not just the one it was optimized on. So to get an unbiased estimate of any measure of the scorecard, one has to look at its performance on a hold-out or validation sample $\mathcal{V}$ where $\mathcal{V} \cap \mathcal{D} = \{\phi\}$. The measure $\mathcal{L}(s_D|\mathcal{V})$ is then an unbiased estimator of the scorecard performance and one almost always finds that the scorecard performance on $\mathcal{V}$ is worse than the performance on the development sample $\mathcal{D}$.

$$\mathcal{L}(s_D|\mathcal{D}) \geq \mathcal{L}(s_D|\mathcal{V}) \qquad (2.1.3)$$

Usually in credit scoring there is sufficient data available when building a score-card that it is possible to obtain a completely separate hold-out sample from the training (development) sample and the test sample when that is required. If that is not the case, one can use standard statistical approaches such as *cross-validation* or *bootstrapping* to obtain unbiased estimates without losing too much information.

Cross-validation

In cross-validation, one builds a scorecard on $\mathcal{D}_r$, a subset of the data and then tests it on the remaining data. $\mathcal{D}_r^c$, the complement of $\mathcal{D}_r$. By repeating this process and choosing the subsets $\mathcal{D}_r$ to cover the whole of $\mathcal{D}$ one gets a series of scorecards s_{D_r} and unbiased measures $\mathcal{L}(s_{D_r}|\mathcal{D}_r^c)$ of their performance. One needs to amalgamate the resultant scorecards into one by, for example, taking the scores for each attribute to be the mean of the scores from the various scorecards. This seems sensible, provided there is not too much variation in these scores.

There are two ways of implementing cross-validation. One is the rotation method where one splits $\mathcal{D}$ into N non-intersecting subsets $\mathcal{D}_1, \mathcal{D}_2, \ldots, \mathcal{D}_N$ and then builds N scorecards $s_{D_r^c}(.)$, $r = 1, \ldots, N$. So each scorecard is built on a fraction $((N-1)/N)$ of the total data set and then tested on the remaining $1/N$. In each case, one is testing the measure on data that was not used to build the scorecard. Then one defines a scorecard where the value for a particular attribute is the average of the values of that attribute on the N scorecards developed. An unbiased estimate of the value of the measurement for this scorecard is then the average value of the measure over the N scorecards used to build it, tested on the complement of the data used to build each one, namely:

$$\frac{\sum_{r=1}^{N} \mathcal{L}(s_{\mathcal{D}_r^c} | \mathcal{D}_r)}{N}.$$

(2.1.4)

The other way of implementing cross-validation is the leave-one-out approach where for each data point $d \in \mathcal{D}$ one looks at the split $\{d, \mathcal{D} - \{d\}\}$ and constructs the scorecard $s_{\mathcal{D}_{-\{d\}}}$. Repeating this by leaving each point out in turn and taking the final scorecard to have attribute values which are the average of those obtained in each of the N scorecards developed leads to an unbiased measurement of this final scorecard of

$$\sum_{d \in \mathcal{D}} \mathcal{L}(s_{\mathcal{D}-\{d\}} | \{d\}) / |\mathcal{D}|$$

(2.1.5)

where $|\mathcal{D}|$ is the number of data points in $\mathcal{D}$. Although this means developing a large number of scorecards, they are all very similar and one can exploit this similarity when calculating the next scorecard in the sequence since it has only two data points different from the set used for the previous scorecard. Most statistical software packages can do this automatically.

Bootstrapping

Bootstrapping is slightly different in that if $\mathcal{D}$ is a data set of $|\mathcal{D}|$ data points one constructs a new data set $\mathcal{B}_r$ by sampling from $\mathcal{D}$, $|\mathcal{D}|$ times with replacement so that the same data point can be chosen several times. This sampling with replacement is repeated N times to obtain samples $\mathcal{B}_1, \mathcal{B}_2, \ldots, \mathcal{B}_N$. One uses the data in each such sample $\mathcal{B}_r$ to create a scorecard $s_{\mathcal{B}_r}$ which is then tested on the sample $\mathcal{B}_r^c$. Thus one obtains measure estimates $\mathcal{L}(s_{\mathcal{B}_r} | \mathcal{B}_r^c)$ for the scorecards and the assumption is that the mean of errors $\mathcal{L}(s_{\mathcal{B}_r} | \mathcal{B}_r) - \mathcal{L}(s_{\mathcal{B}_r} | \mathcal{B}_r^c)$ where $\mathcal{B}_r \cap \mathcal{B}_r^c = \{\phi\}$ is a good estimate for the error $\mathcal{L}(s_{\mathcal{D}} | \mathcal{D}) - \mathcal{L}(s_{\mathcal{D}} | \mathcal{V})$ where $\mathcal{D} \cap \mathcal{V} = \{\phi\}$.

Thus one has that

$$\mathcal{L}(s_{\mathcal{D}} | \mathcal{V}) = \mathcal{L}(s_{\mathcal{D}} | \mathcal{D}) - (\mathcal{L}(s_{\mathcal{D}} | \mathcal{D}) - \mathcal{L}(s_{\mathcal{D}} | \mathcal{V}))$$

$$\approx \mathcal{L}(s_{\mathcal{D}} | \mathcal{D}) - \left(\frac{\sum_{r=1}^{N} \left(\mathcal{L}(s_{\mathcal{B}_r} | \mathcal{B}_r) - \mathcal{L}(s_{\mathcal{B}_r} | \mathcal{B}_r^c) \right)}{N} \right).$$

(2.1.6)

In fact, one can be a little more sophisticated by realizing that the set $\mathcal{D}$ will split into those points which are in $\mathcal{B}_r$ and those which are not. The chance an element of $\mathcal{D}$ is not in $\mathcal{B}_r$ is $\left(1 - \frac{1}{|\mathcal{D}|}\right)^{|\mathcal{D}|}$ and as $|\mathcal{D}| \to \infty$ this converges to $1/e = 0.368$

using the approximation $\ln |(1 - x)| \to -x$ as $x \to 0$ in the following way.

$$\ln\left(\left(1 - \frac{1}{|\mathcal{D}|}\right)^{|\mathcal{D}|}\right) = |\mathcal{D}| \ln\left(1 - \frac{1}{|\mathcal{D}|}\right) \approx |\mathcal{D}| \frac{-1}{|\mathcal{D}|} = -1$$

$$\Rightarrow \left(1 - \frac{1}{|\mathcal{D}|}\right)^{|\mathcal{D}|} \approx e^{-1}. \tag{2.1.7}$$

Thus there is a 0.368 chance the data point is not in $\mathcal{B}_r$ and a 0.632 chance it is in $\mathcal{B}_r$. Thus $\mathcal{B}_r$ can be considered to have less information in it than $\mathcal{D}$ because it only has 63% of the data that makes up $\mathcal{D}$. So assuming $\mathcal{L}(s_{\mathcal{B}_r}|\mathcal{B}_r^c)$ is a good estimate of $\mathcal{L}(s_{\mathcal{D}}|\mathcal{V})$ is too pessimistic as the $s_{\mathcal{B}_r}(.)$ scorecard has only 63% of the information that helped build $s_{\mathcal{D}}(.)$. Thus a better approximation turns out to be

$$\mathcal{L}(s_{\mathcal{D}}|\mathcal{V}) \approx \sum_{r=1} \left(0.632 \mathcal{L}\left(s_{\mathcal{B}_r}|\mathcal{B}_r^c\right) + 0.368 \mathcal{L}\left(s_{\mathcal{B}_r}|\mathcal{B}_r\right)\right). \tag{2.1.8}$$

This gives more stable estimates than the boot strap approximation of (2.1.6). It is important to stress again though that for the vast majority of scorecard measurements there is enough data to construct a hold-out sample and hence to calculate $\mathcal{L}(s_{\mathcal{D}}|\mathcal{V})$ directly.

2.2   Discrimination measures: divergence, Kolmogorov–Smirnov statistic, and D-concordance statistic

Having identified there are different ways one can measure the quality of a scorecard, let us begin by looking at the ways one can measure its discriminating ability, that is, how effective it is at separating the goods and the bads. This is the most basic of the ways one can measure a scorecard's quality because to do so one only needs the scorecard itself. One does not need to know about the population odds for the population it will be applied to nor the cut-off score that will be used, which one would need to measure the quality of the probabilistic forecasts and categorical forecasts.

There is a plethora of ways of measuring the discriminating ability of a scorecard. We leave discussion of the most commonly used of these – ROC curve and the associated Gini coefficient – to the next section since it deserves a section to itself. In this section we investigate other well-known discrimination measures – divergence and information value (IV), Kolmogorov–Smirnov (KS) statistic, and the concordance statistic – that are used.

Divergence and information value

In Section 1.10, we described a method of estimating a score by maximizing a statistical measure called divergence. Given a score s, let $f(s|G), f(s|B)$ be the resulting conditional density functions of the scores of good and bad subpopulations, respectively. Divergence is defined by

$$D \triangleq \int \left(f(s|G) - f(s|B) \right) \ln \left(\frac{f(s|G)}{f(s|B)} \right) ds$$

$$= \int \left(f(s|G) - f(s|B) \right) w(s) ds \qquad (2.2.1)$$

where $w(s)$ is the weight of evidence of a good at score s.

Divergence is a continuous analogue to information value (first introduced and described in Section 1.8) and measures the discriminatory power of a scorecard. Even if the scorecard is not built by maximizing divergence, it can be used to measure the discriminatory power of a scorecard.

As mentioned in Section 1.10, divergence was originally suggested by Kullback and Leibler (1951) as a way of measuring the relative distance between a 'true' probability distribution and another one obtained from a model. If $p(x)$ is the density function of the true distribution and $q(x)$ that of the alternative distribution, they defined the K–L divergence as

$$D_{K-L}(q|p) = Exp \left\{ \ln \left(\frac{p}{q} \right) \right\} = \int p(x) \ln \left(\frac{p(x)}{q(x)} \right) dx. \qquad (2.2.2)$$

If the two distributions are the same, then $\ln \left(p(x)/q(x) \right) = 0$ everywhere and so the divergence is 0. The divergence will be large when $p(x) \gg q(x)$ or $p(x) \ll q(x)$ for some x, though since both $p(x)$ and $q(x)$ integrate to 1, this can only happen in certain regions. The $D_{K-L}(q|p)$ measure is not symmetric in p and q and so its value depends on which is the true probability. Divergence as defined in Eq. (2.2.1) for the consumer credit context satisfies

$$D \triangleq \int \left(f(s|G) \right) \ln \left(\frac{f(s|G)}{f(s|B)} \right) ds + \int \left(f(s|B) \right) \ln \left(\frac{f(s|B)}{f(s|G)} \right) ds$$

$$= D_{K-L}(f(s|B)|f(s|G)) + D_{K-L}(f(s|G)|f(s|B)). \qquad (2.2.3)$$

So it is the sum of the 'distance' between the score distribution of the bads and the score distribution of the goods given that the score distribution of the goods is the true one plus the distance between the score distribution of the goods and that of the bads if it is the bads which is the true one. The larger the sum of these differences, the more separate are the two distributions, which is why it can be used as a measure of discrimination. Since nowhere in the definition of divergence do we have to use the probabilities of the goods or the bads in the whole sample, divergence does not depend on the population odds and so will give the same answer on a weighted sample of the population as on the original population itself.

If the score distributions are described by continuous functions, then one can calculate the divergence from the integral in Eq. (2.2.1). However, score distributions are usually calculated on a finite population, the sample of past borrowers on which the scorecard was created. In that case, one can either estimate the density function by a continuous curve and use that in the integration or make a discrete approximation to the density function. This is done by splitting the scores into bins (there may be many of these) and taking the summation over the bins rather than the integral over the continuous score. This is the information value of the score bands. Suppose there are I bands $i = 1, 2, \ldots, I$, then one can use the conditional likelihoods $f(s_i|G), f(s_i|B)$ produced by the original scorecards or one can count the number of goods g_i and the number of bads b_i in band i, where $\sum_{i=1}^{I} g_i = n_G$ and $\sum_{i=1}^{I} b_i = n_B$. In the former case one calculates the information value by

$$\text{IV} = \sum_{i=1}^{I} (f(s_i|G) - f(s_i|B)) \ln \left(\frac{f(s_i|G)}{f(s_i|B)} \right) \qquad (2.2.4)$$

while in the latter case one calculates it through the computation

$$\text{Information value} = \text{IV} = \sum_{i=1}^{I} (g_i/n_G - b_i/n_B) \ln \left(\frac{g_i/n_G}{b_i/n_B} \right)$$

$$= \sum_{i=1}^{I} (g_i/n_G - b_i/n_B) \ln \left(\frac{g_i n_B}{b_i n_G} \right). \qquad (2.2.5)$$

Example 2.2.1 Information value calculation using Appendix A data

Consider the validation results for a scorecard given in Appendix A where the scorecard has been tested on a hold-out sample of 19,117 (18,234 goods and 883 bads).

The density function of the scores of the goods and the bads using the data in Appendix A is given in Fig. 2.2.1, where one can see the scores for the bads peak around 240 while those for the goods peak around 350. If one uses Eq. (2.2.4) to try and calculate the weights of evidence using each score as a separate bin, then the weights of evidence for some bins will be infinity or minus infinity because there are no goods or no bads in the bin. So our approximation is to assume for the weights of evidence calculations that the density functions must be at least 0.0001. In that case the information value at each score $\text{IV}(s_i) = (f(s_i|G) - f(s_i|B)) \ln \left(\frac{f(s_i|G)}{f(s_i|B)} \right)$ is given by Fig. 2.2.2 and summing these terms gives a divergence of 3.294. Again

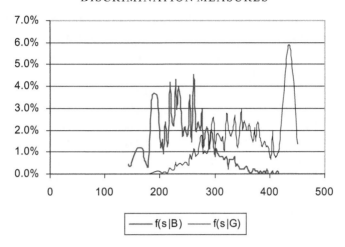

FIG. 2.2.1. Density functions of scores for goods and bads in Example 2.2.1.

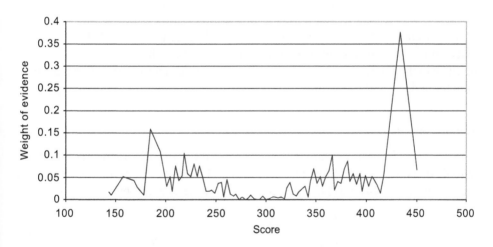

FIG. 2.2.2. IV(*s*) for data in Example 2.2.1.

notice the information value terms are large both around scores of 220 where there is a high proportion of the bads but few goods and then again above scores of 350 where there are a high proportion of the goods but few of the bads.

Alternatively the scorecard can be split into 10 roughly equal score bands and the results of the IV calculation of Eq. (2.2.5) are given in Table 2.2.1.

The information value of the scorecard with this approximation is 2.81. Taking more bins will raise the approximation to close to 3.29. These results show that the calculation of the divergence is not necessarily straightforward and one needs to

TABLE 2.2.1. Information value for Appendix A scorecard with 10 bins.

Scoreband	No. of goods	No. of bads	% of goods	% of bads	IV contribution
253–	1026	481	0.056	0.545	1.109
254–277	1588	186	0.087	0.211	0.109
278–298	1822	98	0.100	0.111	0.001
299–319	1938	52	0.106	0.059	0.028
320–334	1936	27	0.106	0.031	0.094
335–349	2002	18	0.110	0.020	0.151
350–364	1942	9	0.107	0.010	0.226
365–382	2010	6	0.110	0.007	0.288
383–406	1946	5	0.107	0.006	0.297
407+	2024	1	0.111	0.001	0.504
Totals	18234	883	1	1	2.807

be careful in striking a balance between two few bins and having bins with none of one class of borrower in them.

Experience suggests that a scorecard with divergence value of 0.5 or more is discriminating well, though the divergence for some behavioural scorecards can often be in the range from 1.5 to 5. Obviously the information value depends on the number and content of the bins, and is only an approximation to the divergence.

Mahalanobis distance

A measure which can be thought of as a special case of divergence is the Mahalanobis distance. If the scores for the goods and the bads are normally distributed, then in Eq. (1.10.14) we showed that the divergence is given by

$$D = \frac{1}{2}\left(\frac{1}{\sigma_G^2} + \frac{1}{\sigma_B^2}\right)(\mu_G - \mu_B)^2 + \frac{(\sigma_G^2 - \sigma_B^2)^2}{2\sigma_G^2\sigma_B^2} \tag{2.2.6}$$

and in the special case where the variances of the goods and bads are identical this reduces to the simpler expression:

$$D = D_M^2 \quad \text{where } D_M = \left|\frac{\mu_G - \mu_B}{\sigma}\right| \tag{2.2.7}$$

and $||$ is the absolute value. In this form D_M is known as the Mahalanobis distance. It is the one-dimensional case of an n-dimension distance measure introduced by P.C. Mahalanobis in 1936 to measure the 'distance' of a new data point away from another set of data and is essentially equivalent to the test statistic used in t-tests.

Although the normality assumption does not usually hold for conditional score distributions, and the assumption of equal variance is dubious, the Mahalanobis distance has some appealing properties. First, it is easy to calculate the means and variances of the scores of the goods and bads in a sample and so it can be used with very large data sets. Second, it is an easy way to visualize the differences between a good and a bad scorecard. The scorecard whose joint probability densities of the scores for the goods ($p_G f$ (s|G)) and the scores for the bads ($p_B f$ (s|B) is given in Fig. 2.2.3a is obviously a better discriminator than the one that gives the joint probability distribution of the scores in Fig. 2.2.3b because the difference between the means of the good and bad distributions are further apart. We have drawn the graphs in Fig. 2.2.3 so the area under each distribution represents the percentage population who are in that class so the maximum height in the density function of the bads is less than that in the density function of the goods.

The Mahalanobis distance is the distance between the means of the two curves, which since they are normal is also the mode (the highest value of the density function) divided by the standard deviation. Provided one can accept that the standard deviation is the same for both goods and bads, then again this calculation does not depend on the population odds of the underlying population and so can be calculated without knowing this.

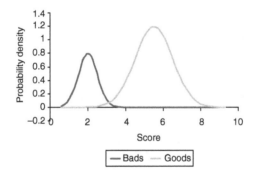

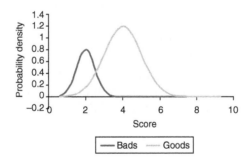

FIG. 2.2.3. (a) Means of goods and bads apart; and (b) Means of goods and bads close.

Let us calculate D_M for the data in Appendix A though it is clear from the density function graphs in Fig. 2.2.1 the score distributions are not normal.

Example 2.2.2 Mahalanobis distance for Appendix A scorecard data

One can calculate μ_G the mean score for the goods, μ_B the mean score for the bads, and σ^2 the variance which is assumed to be the same for both the good and bad population from the cumulative data in Appendix A. Looking at the cumulative numbers of goods we can identify there are two goods with scores of 69, one with score of 72, one with a score of 78, and so on. Similarly we can identify the scores of the bads to get the following estimates:

$$\mu_G = \left(\frac{4}{18234}\right) 169 + \left(\frac{2}{18234}\right) 172 + \left(\frac{2}{18234}\right) 178 + \cdots$$

$$+ \left(\frac{252}{18234}\right) 450 = 339.27$$

$$\mu_B = \left(\frac{8}{883}\right) 143 + \left(\frac{6}{883}\right) 146 + \cdots = 250.26$$

so that

$$\sigma^2 = \left(\frac{4}{19113}\right)(169 - 339.27)^2 + \left(\frac{2}{19113}\right)(172 - 339.27)^2 + \cdots$$

$$+ \left(\frac{4}{19113}\right)(144 - 250.26)^2 + \left(\frac{3}{19113}\right)(146 - 250.26)^2 + \cdots$$

$$= 2842.8$$

$$D_M = \sqrt{\frac{(\mu_G - \mu_B)^2}{\sigma^2}} = \sqrt{\frac{(339.27 - 250.26)^2}{2842.8}} = 1.669.$$

Notice this looks as if it is in close agreement with the divergence results calculated in Example 2.2.1, since $D_M^2 = (1.669)^2 = 2.79$. However, that was when the 10 band approximation was used and for the finer approximations the result there was 3.29. The reason for the difference between the fine divergence calculation and the Mahalanobis distance calculation is that the score distributions are not normal and so the simplification of the divergence in Eq. (2.2.7) which reduces it to the square of the Mahalanobis distance is not valid for this data set.

Kolmogorov–Smirnov statistic

Divergence and related statistics are differences in expectations of functions of the scores of the goods and bads. A second group of measures of discrimination concentrates on the difference in the distribution functions of the scores of the two groups. Foremost among these is the ROC curve and the Gini coefficient which is the area under the ROC curve (AUROC curve). These are important enough to deserve discussion in the following section (Section 2.3). However, there are two other discriminating measures which also use the conditional score distributions and are widely used in credit scoring – the KS statistic and the Somers D-concordance statistic.

To calculate the KS statistic, one makes use of the conditional distribution functions $F(s|G)$ for goods and $F(s|B)$ for bads. If the minimum and maximum scores possible are s_{min} and s_{max}, then trivially $F(s_{min}|G) = F(s_{min}|B) = 0$ and $F(s_{max}|G) = F(s_{max}|B) = 1$, so that the probability distribution functions agree at the extreme scores. However if the distribution functions are very different at the other scores, the scorecard is likely to be discriminating well. Define the KS statistic as

$$\text{KS} \overset{\Delta}{=} \max_{s} \left(F(s|B) - F(s|G) \right) \tag{2.2.8}$$

In Fig. 2.2.4 the KS statistic is the length of the dotted line that maximizes the distance between the distribution functions $F(s|B)$ and $F(s|G)$. In terms of the density function of the scores then this maximum separation occurs when the density functions of the goods and the bads cross, which can be seen by remembering that at the maximum of a function the derivative of the function is zero. Applying that to Eq. (2.2.8) says that $f(s^*|B) - f(s^*|G) = 0$ at the maximizing score s^*.

The disadvantage of using the KS statistic is that it describes the situation at an 'optimal separating score' and this is seldom if ever a relevant or appropriate cut-off score for making a business decision. In general all one can say is that the distance separating the conditional score distributions at an actual cut-off used will be less than the KS statistic; alternatively think of the KS statistic as the upper bound on a measure of distance or separation.

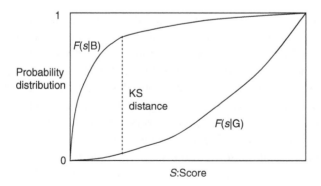

FIG. 2.2.4. Kolmogorov–Smirnov statistic.

Suppose one uses the categorical forecasts at a cut-off score of s_c and classifies all those with higher scores as 'goods' and all those with lower scores as 'bads'. In Section 2.6 we consider how to measure how good such categorical forecasts are when one has a specific cut-off as well as the scorecard. Among the measures considered are sensitivity and specificity where

$$\text{Sensitivity at } s_c \triangleq F(s_c|B) \quad \text{Specificity at } s_c \triangleq F^{(C)}(s_c|G) \qquad (2.2.9)$$

so sensitivity is what fraction of the bads would have scores below the cut-off and so rightly would be rejected, while specificity is what fraction of the goods have score above the cut-off and so are rightly accepted. We can rewrite the KS statistic as the cut-off score that maximizes the sum of sensitivity and specificity measures:

$$\underset{s}{\text{Max}} |F(s|B) - F(s|G)| = \underset{s}{\text{Max}} |\text{sensitivity} - (1 - \text{specificity})|$$

$$= \underset{s}{\text{Max}} |(\text{sensitivity} + \text{specificity})| - 1 \qquad (2.2.10)$$

Example 2.2.3 Kolmogorov–Smirnov statistic from Appendix A data

Note that in Appendix A we are given $F^c(s|G)$ and $F^c(s|B)$, the percentage of the goods and the bads above each score, but $F(s|B) - F(s|G) = F^c(s|G) = F^c(s|B)$ and so it is enough to identify when the latter is a maximum. By inspection of the data in Appendix A we see that it occurs in the score band 287–289, when this difference is 0.638. So the KS statistic value is 0.638. It is difficult to give limits on what are acceptable levels of discrimination because the discrimination depends on the population of borrowers, the lending product, and the definition of bad. However, a useful rule of thumb is that KS statistics of 0.4 suggest good discrimination.

Somers D-concordance statistic and the Wilcoxon Mann-Whitney U statistic

These statistics compare whether, if one has the values of a particular variable from two different data sets, could these two sets of values have come from the same underlying distribution? However, the statistics use only the relative rankings of the values of the data sets and not the values themselves, and so are examples of non-parametric or distribution-free statistical tests. In our context the variable is the credit score and the two sets are the good and the bad populations. One only looks at the ordering of whether the borrowers were good or bad as they are written in decreasing order of score. The scores themselves are not used at all and so there is no assumption about the form of the score distribution.

The U statistic is the statistic calculated in the Wilcoxon Mann-Whitney test, which does this non-parametric comparison between the two data sets. The Somers D-concordance statistic though can be defined in a more general context, where it measures the regression of the sign of $(Y_2 - Y_1)$ on the sign of $(X_2 - X_1)$ where (X_i, Y_i) are sampled from a bivariate distribution. However when X is a binary variable (that is $X = 1$ if a borrower was good and 0 if the borrower was bad) it reduces to the Mann-Whitney U-statistic needed for that test, and it is this name that has stuck in the consumer credit context.

In this context, if one picked a good at random from the goods and a bad at random from the bads the Somers D-concordance statistic calculates the difference between the probability that the score of the good will be higher than that of the bad and the probability that the bad's score will be higher than the good's score. Formally D_S (Somers D-concordance statistic) is the expected payoff of a variable which is 1 if the good's score is above the bad's score; -1 if it is below it, and 0 if they are the same, so if S_G is the random variable of the score of a good chosen at random and S_B is the random variable of the score of a bad chosen at random then,

$$D_S = 1 \times \Pr\{S_G > S_B\} + 0 \times \Pr\{S_G = S_B\} - 1 \times \Pr\{S_G < S_B\}$$

$$= \int F(s|B) f(s|G) ds - \int F^c(s|B) f(s|G) ds. \qquad (2.2.11)$$

If one has divided the scores into bins with g_i goods and b_i bads in bin i, then one can calculate the concordance statistic for that score using that validation set by

$$D_S = 1 \times \Pr\{S_G > S_B\} - 1 \times \Pr\{S_G < S_B\}$$

$$= (n_G n_B)^{-1} \left(\sum_i g_i \sum_{j<i} b_j - \sum_i g_i \sum_{j>i} b_j \right) \quad n_G = \sum_i g_i \text{ and } n_B = \sum_i b_i.$$

$$(2.2.12)$$

In fact one can choose the bands so each consists of an individual score and this gives an easy way of calculating D_S. Order the sample in increasing order of score and sum the ranks of the bads in that sequence. Let this be R_B. Note that if there are $n = n_G + n_B$ in the sample then if R_G is the sum of the ranks of the goods then $R_G + R_B = 1/2\, n(n + 1)$. The Mann-Whitney U-statistic in such a context is defined as

$$U \triangleq n_G n_B + \frac{1}{2} n_B (n_B + 1) - R_B = R_G - \frac{1}{2} n_G (n_G + 1) \qquad (2.2.13)$$

The Somer's statistic can be expressed in terms of U as

$$D_S = 2 \frac{U}{n_G n_B} - 1. \qquad (2.2.14)$$

One way of seeing that Eq. (2.2.14) is correct is to consider the ith good in this increasing score sequence. If $R(i)$ is the rank of that good, the number of bads with lower scores will be $(R(i) - i)$ and the number of bads with higher scores will be

$(n_B - (R(i) - i))$. Summing overall the goods as in (2.2.12) gives

$$D_S = 1 \times \Pr\{s_G > s_B\} - 1 \times \Pr\{s_G < s_B\}$$

$$= \frac{1}{n_G n_B} \left(\sum_i (R(i) - i) - \sum_i (n_B - (R(i) - i)) \right)$$

$$= \frac{1}{n_G n_B} \sum_i (2R(i) - n_B - 2i) = \frac{1}{n_G n_B} (2R_G - n_B n_G - 2(n_G(n_G + 1)/2))$$

$$= \frac{2U}{n_G n_B} - 1. \tag{2.2.15}$$

Statistical tables exist for the U values which determine the validity of the hypothesis that the goods and bads have the same score distribution. In scoring applications one just uses the D_S value as a measure – the higher the value the more discriminating the scorecard. Note that if $D_S < 0$, then the interpretation would be that the higher the score the more likely the borrower is to default. It is important to remember that these calculations do not depend on the particular value of individual scores, only on their relative rank. Although one might think these calculations depend on the population odds, the way D_S is defined in Eq. (2.2.11) shows that it does not depend on p_G or p_B in the original population.

Example 2.2.4 Concordance statistic, D_S, for simple scorecard

The size of the data in Appendix A makes the calculations of D_S quite tedious and so instead we show how the calculations are made using the following validation sample of 10 scores and their status:

Scores of bads:	150	190	200	250		
Scores of goods:	180	205	230	260	280	300

So $n_B = 4, n_G = 6$ and the sequence in increasing score is

$$\text{B \quad G \quad B \quad B \quad G \quad G \quad B \quad G \quad G \quad G.}$$

Hence $R_B = 1 + 3 + 4 + 7 = 15$ and $R_G = 2 + 5 + 6 + 8 + 9 + 10 = 40$.

From Eq. (2.2.13) with $n_B = 4, n_G = 6$ we get

$$U/gb = \frac{40 - \frac{1}{2}(6)(7)}{4.6} = \frac{40 - 21}{24} = 0.79 \text{ or}$$

$$U/gb = \frac{(4)(6) + \frac{1}{2}(4)(5) - 15}{4.6} = \frac{24 + 10 - 15}{24} = \frac{19}{24} = 0.79 \tag{2.2.16}$$

$$D_S = 2U/gb - 1 = 2\left(\frac{19}{24}\right) - 1 = \frac{7}{12} = 0.583.$$

Example 2.2.5 D_s concordance statistic for the data in Appendix A

For those who like to do spreadsheet calculations obtaining D_S from the data in Appendix A is not too difficult if one uses formula Eq. (2.2.12). The result is that $D_S = 0.788$.

2.3   ROC curve and Gini coefficient

The most widely used measures of discrimination in credit scoring are the Receiver Operating Characteristic (ROC) curve and the almost equivalent cumulative accuracy profile (CAP) curve. The areas under these curves lead to two more measures of discrimination – the Gini coefficient (GINI) and the accuracy ratio (AR) which turn out to be identical.

As its name suggests the ROC curve originated in estimating the errors in transmitting and receiving message. In the credit scoring context it is an alternative way of expressing the relationship between the cumulative score distribution functions of the goods and the bads to that which is shown in the graphs that give the KS calculations. Those graphs plot the cumulative distribution of the scores of the goods and the bads, $F(s|G)$ and $F(s|B)$ against the score. The ROC curve is constructed by plotting the cumulative distribution of the conditional scores of the goods and the bads against one another:

$F(s|G) = \Pr\{\text{score} \leq s|G\}$ on the x-axis versus $F(s|B) = \Pr\{\text{score} \leq s|B\}$ on the y-axis. An example of the resultant curve is shown in Fig. 2.3.1, though some users do swap the axes around.

If one had perfect discrimination then there would be a score value, s_B so all the bads had scores below this value and all the goods had scores above this value. In that case, the ROC curve would go through B, the point (0,1) in Fig. 2.3.1 which corresponds to the score s_B with the property $F(s_B|G) = 0$ and $F(s_B|B) = 1$. Such a curve consists of the two straight line sections AB and BC. At the other extreme, a scorecard which discriminates no better than random (that is where the ratio of goods to goods below the score is the same no matter what the score) and so $F(s|G) = F(s|B)$) will give rise to the diagonal line AC.

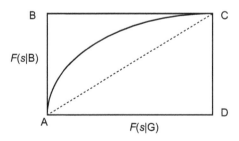

FIG. 2.3.1. ROC curve.

So the nearer the curve is to the point (0,1), the better the discrimination of the scorecard. If one has two ROC curves R_1 and R_2 corresponding to two scorecards then if R_1 is always above R_2 as in Fig. 2.3.2a the first scorecard discriminates between the goods and the bads better than the second scorecard at all scores, that is the difference $F(s|B) - F(s|G)$ is always greater. If the curves of the two scorecards overlap as in Fig. 2.3.2b, then one scorecard is better in one region of scores and the other in another region of scores. At low scores in Fig. 2.3.2b (so $F(s|G)$ and $F(s|B)$ are small) R_2 is a better discriminator but at high cut-off scores R_1 is the better one. Normally one is anxious to accept a large proportion of the goods and so the cut-off scores would tend to be in the area nearer the left of the graph.

We define a score to be odds monotonic if the posterior odds of a good is a strictly increasing function of the score so that

$$o(G|s) = \frac{p(G|s)}{p(B|s)} = o_{Pop}\frac{f(s|G)}{f(s|B)} \quad \uparrow s. \qquad (2.3.1)$$

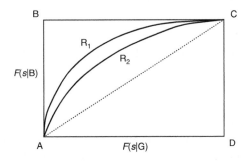

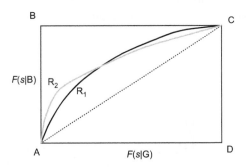

FIG. 2.3.2. (a) Non-intersecting ROC curves; and (b) Intersecting ROC curves.

For such monotone scores we have that the slope of the ROC curve:

$$\frac{dF(s|B)}{dF(s|G)} = \frac{f(s|B)}{f(s|G)} = \alpha(s)$$

is a strictly decreasing function of s. If the slope of a function is decreasing the function is concave (that is any line joining two points on the curve lies below the curve or $f(\lambda s_1 + (1-\lambda)s_2) \geq \lambda f(s_1) + (1-\lambda)f(s_2)$). Thus for odds monotonic scores the ROC curve will be concave. Moreover the tangent of any ROC curve coming from an odds monotonic score (which most reasonable scores are) will start with a very positive slope at low scores and should then be flattening out as the score increases. With real data, the score distribution may not always satisfy the concavity requirement because of noisy data and difficulties inherent in estimating ratios of likelihood density functions.

Gini coefficient and AUROC curve

The idea that the 'fatter' the ROC curve or the nearer it gets to the point (0,1) then the better it discriminates can be used to define a measurement which describes the discrimination. Consider the area under the ROC curve (AUROC), which is the area ACD in Fig. 2.3.1. The larger this value the better the discrimination because the 'fatter' the curve is. For perfect discrimination this area is 1, since both AB and AD are of length 1 as they go from A(0,0) to B(0,1), and then to D(1,1). For a scorecard which has purely random discrimination as described earlier, the area under the curve is the area of the triangle ACD which is $1/2 \times 1 \times 1 = 0.5$. For any other scorecard, the AUROC curve will be between 0.5 and 1 and the larger the area the better the discrimination.

In terms of the distribution functions $F(s|G)$ and $F(s|B)$, the AUROC curve is defined by

$$\text{AUROC} = \int F(s|B)dF(s|G) = \int F(s|B)f(s|G)ds \qquad (2.3.2)$$

One might prefer a measure where useless (equivalent to random) discrimination is 0 and perfect discrimination is 1. One can transform AUROC so that this property holds. This is the Gini coefficient which corresponds to twice the area between the ROC curve and the diagonal.

$$\begin{aligned}
\text{GINI} &= 2\text{AUROC} - 1 \\
&= 2\int F(s|B)f(s|G)\,ds - 1 \\
&= \int F(s|B)f(s|G)\,ds - 2\int F(s|G)f(s|G)\,ds \\
&= 2\int (f(s|B) - F(s|G))f(s|G)\,ds
\end{aligned} \qquad (2.3.3)$$

where the second equality in Eq. (2.3.3) follows from integration by parts since

$$\int_{-\infty}^{\infty} F(s|G)f(s|G)\,ds = \left[F(s|G)^2\right]_{-\infty}^{\infty} - \int_{-\infty}^{\infty} f(s|G)f(s|G)\,ds$$

$$\Rightarrow 2\int_{-\infty}^{\infty} F(s|G)f(s|G)\,ds = 1.$$

The final line of Eq. (2.3.3) shows that the Gini coefficient is twice the area between the ROC curve and the diagonal since the height of the diagonal at the point where the ROC curve has coordinates $(F(s|G), (F(s|B))$ is the same as the distance along the horizontal axis, namely $F(s|G)$.

Since the area of ACD in Fig. 2.3.1 is 0.5 and the area between the ROC curve and the diagonal is (AUROC − 0.5), another way of thinking of the Gini coefficient is as the improvement in the area under the scorecard when compared with the area under the random discrimination curve. One can compare this improvement in area with the improvement in the area under the perfect discriminator over the area under the random discriminating curve, which is $1 - 0.5 = 0.5$. The ration of these two improvements is then

$$\frac{\text{AUROC} - 0.5}{0.5} = 2(\text{AUROC}) - 1 = \text{GINI}.$$

The data needed to draw the ROC curve and to calculate the AUROC and Gini coefficients does not include anything about the population odds. So all these measures are independent of the population odds or the way the sample on which the scorecard was built was chosen from the original population. They depend only on the properties of the scorecard.

Example 2.3.1 ROC curve and Gini coefficient for simple example

Suppose as in Example 2.2.4, the scorecard is validated on a population of 10 borrowers, consisting of four bads with scores 150, 190, 200, and 250, and six goods with scores 180, 205, 230, 260, 280, and 300. The actual values of the scores do not matter when drawing the ROC curve and calculating the Gini coefficient. What does matter is the position of the goods and the bads in the ranking given by the scores. In this case as the scores increase, the ranking is BGBBGGBGGG. If one takes a score below all those in the ranking, say 140, the fraction of goods and bads below this score is 0 and so the ROC curve goes through the point (0,0). For a score of 160 say, which is above the lowest bad but below all the others, we have 1/4 of the bads will score below this value and none of the goods. So the point (0,1/4) must be on the ROC curve. Moving up the scores and in each case increasing by one the number of cases below the score being considered shows that the ROC curve will go through the points (1/6,1/4) (when there is one bad and one good

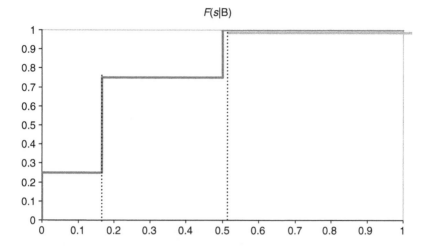

FIG. 2.3.3. ROC curve for Example 2.3.1.

below the score), then $(1/6,2/4)$, $(1/6,3/4)$, $(2/6,3/4)$, $(3/6,3/4)$, $(3/6,4/4)$, $(4/6,4/4)$, $(5/6,4/4)$, and $(6/6,4/4)$, respectively. This gives the ROC curve in Fig. 2.3.3.

For a finite population, the ROC curve will always consist of piecewise linear horizontal and vertical sections, and unless there are goods and bads with the same score will have this stepwise form. To calculate AUROC we recognize that the area under the curve consists of three rectangles (given by the dotted lines) and so

$$AUROC = 1/4 \times 1/6 + 3/4 \times 1/3 + 1 \times 1/2 = 19/24 = 0.79$$

and the Gini coefficient is given by

$$G = 2AUROC - 1 = 2(19/24) - 1 = 7/12 = 0.583 \qquad (2.3.4)$$

Note that the Gini coefficient for this example is the same as the D-concordance statistic, D_S, in Example 2.2.4, which uses the same data set.

Example 2.3.2 ROC curve using validation data in Appendix A

For the 19,117 validation sample in Appendix A, the ROC curve looks almost continuous as is shown in Fig. 2.3.4.

To calculate AUROC and Gini coefficients from the ROC curves requires software packages that can calculate areas under numerically derived curves. However, we can prove that the equivalence of the Gini coefficient in Example 2.3.1 and the D_S concordance statistic in Example 2.2.4 is no fluke and so we can use the formulae Eq. (2.2.12) or those in Eqs. (2.2.13) and (2.2.14) to calculate D_S and hence GINI and then AUROC. Using the definition of D_S in Eq. (2.2.11) as the expectation of the variable which is $+1$ if a good chosen at random has a higher score than

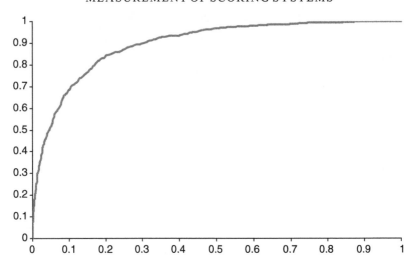

FIG. 2.3.4. ROC curve for Example 2.3.2.

a bad chose at random and -1 if the ranking is the other way around gives, in the case of a continuous score distribution that as $F^c(s|B) = 1 - F(s|B)$,

$$D_S = 1 \left(\int_{-\infty}^{\infty} F(s|B)f(s|G)ds \right) - 1 \cdot \left(\int_{-\infty}^{\infty} F^c(s|B)f(s|G)ds \right)$$

$$= 2 \int_{-\infty}^{\infty} F(s|B)f(s|G)ds - 1 \cdot \int_{-\infty}^{\infty} f(s|G)ds$$

$$= 2\text{AUROC} - 1 = \text{GINI} \tag{2.3.5}$$

Thus, instead of calculating the Gini coefficient by integrating the area between the ROC curve and the diagonal, one can use the ranking calculations in Eq. (2.2.13) and (2.2.14) to get D_S and hence GINI.

Example 2.3.3 Calculating AUROC and GINI from Appendix A data

In the case of the data in Appendix A, the result of Example 2.2.5 at the end of Section 2.2 gives the D-concordance statistic, D_S was 0.788 and so this is also the value of the Gini coefficient. Hence the AUROC value is $0.5(1 + G) = 0.894$.

Usually one hopes that application scorecards give Gini coefficients of at least 0.4 while behavioural scorecards because of the extra power of some of the characteristics, particularly those about recent arrears, usually have Ginis of 0.6 and above. If the Gini coefficient is in the 0.4 to 0.8 range, the AUROC value will be in the range of 0.7 to 0.9. Hosmer and Lemeshow (2000) describe AUROC values in the range 0.7 to 0.8 (hence Ginis of 0.4 to 0.6) as acceptable, those in the range 0.8 to 0.9 (and hence Ginis of 0.6 to 0.8) as excellent, and AUROCs of over 0.9 or Ginis of over 0.8 as outstanding. As mentioned earlier, behavioural scorecards

TABLE 2.3.1. Five-point approximation to AUROC.

Score band	No. of goods	No. of goods	% of goods	Cumulative % of goods	Area of trapezium
143–277	2614	667	0.143	0.755	$.143(0 + .755)/2 = 0.054$
278–319	3760	150	0.206	0.925	$.206(.755 + .925)/2 = 0.173$
320–349	3938	45	0.216	0.976	$.216(.925 + .976)/2 = 0.2053$
350–382	3952	15	0.217	0.993	$.217(.976 + .993)/2 = 0.2134$
383+	3970	6	0.218	1.000	$.218(.993 + 1)/2 = 0.2170$
Totals	18234	883	1	1	0.8631

have higher discrimination than application scorecards but even for behavioural scorecards there are very few that would merit the outstanding accolade.

If one wants to calculate AUROC and GINI by estimating the areas of the curve, then one can get good approximations to it by using the trapezium rule.

Example 2.3.4 Approximate AUROC for Appendix A data

One can get a good approximation to this area AUROC by looking at the set of trapeziums which are obtained by connecting a few points on the curve. If for example we just take the four scores 278, 319, 349, and 382, then we get a subset of the numbers that appeared in Table 2.2.1 namely those in Table 2.3.1. The results of Table 2.3.1 lead to an approximate AUROC value of 0.8631 and hence an approximate value for the Gini coefficient of $G = 2(0.8631) - 1 = 0.726$. These are reasonable approximations to the true values of 0.894 and 0.788 obtained in Example 2.3.3.

This approach of using trapeziums is equivalent to Simpson's rule for calculating the area under a curve. Provided the ROC curve is concave which is what one would expect of a reasonable scorecard, these approximations will always under estimate the AUROC and Gini values.

ROC curve and its relationship with the Somers D-concordance and the KS statistic

One reason why the ROC curve is more important than the KS statistic and the D-concordance statistic is that one can recover both these measures from the curve. We have already shown in Eq. (2.3.5) that the value of the Gini coefficient is the same as the Somers D-concordance statistic D_S. This connection between GINI and D_S can be exploited to get statistical tests concerning the value of the Gini coefficient and the AUROC value. So for example one could derive confidence intervals for the Gini coefficient given a particular data set on which to validate the scorecard. Alternatively one can evaluate hypothesis tests on whether the Gini coefficient has a particular value or whether the Gini coefficients of two different scorecards are really the same.

These tests and confidence intervals use the results of Bamber (1975) who considered the random variable $\tilde{D}$ which is essentially the experiment that underlies the concordance statistic where one picks a good at random and a bad at random. If the score of the good is above that of the bad $\tilde{D} = 1$; if the scores are the same, $\tilde{D} = 0$; and if the score of the good is below that of the bad $\tilde{D} = -1$. Then clearly $\text{Exp}(\tilde{D}) = D_S$ and what Bamber did was to get an unbiased estimator $\hat{\sigma}^2$ for $\text{Var}(\tilde{D})$ calculated from empirical data in a sample as follows. Suppose in the sample there are n_G goods and n_B bads, and the value of D_S from this sample is d. One needs to calculate two estimators $\hat{P}(B,B,G)$ and $\hat{P}(G,G,B)$ of two different probabilities $P(B,B,G)$ and $P(G,G,B)$. The first $P(B,B,G)$ is obtained by randomly choosing two bads and one good from the sample, supposing their scores to be $s(B_1)$ and $s(B_2)$ and $s(G)$, respectively. One then defines

$$P(B,B,G) = \text{Prob}\{s(B_1), s(B_2) < s(G)\} + \text{Prob}\{s(G) < s(B_1), s(B_2)\}$$
$$- \text{Prob}\{s(B_1) < s(G) < s(B_2)\} - \text{Prob}\{s(B_2) < s(G) < s(B_1)\}$$
$$(2.3.6)$$

which is the difference in the chance that the good has one of the extreme scores compared with the chance it has the middle of the three scores. The second probability $P(G,G,B)$ is estimated by randomly choosing two good cases and one bad case from the sample, assuming the scores are $s(G_1)$, $s(G_2)$, and $s(B)$, respectively. The probability $P(B,B,G)$ is then defined as

$$P(G,G,B) = \text{Prob}\{s(G_1), s(G_2) < s(B)\} + \text{Prob}\{s(B) < s(G_1), s(G_2)\}$$
$$- \text{Prob}\{s(G_1) < s(B) < s(G_2)\} - \text{Prob}\{s(G_2) < s(B) < s(G_1)\}$$
$$(2.3.7)$$

Bamber proved that an unbiased estimator of the variance is then given by

$$\hat{\sigma}^2 = \frac{1}{(n_G - 1)(n_B - 1)}\left[1 + (n_B - 1)\hat{P}(B,B,G) + (n_G - 1)\hat{P}(G,G,B)\right.$$
$$\left. - (n_G + n_B - 1)d^2\right]$$
$$(2.3.8)$$

The estimators $\hat{P}(G,G,B)$, $\hat{P}(B,B,G)$ in Eq. (2.3.8) are calculated by repeatedly sampling appropriate triples and counting the number of times the different score combinations occurred. One can use the estimate (2.3.8) of the standard deviation of $\tilde{D}$ to get confidence intervals and test hypotheses.

As n_G and $n_B \to \infty, (\tilde{D} - d)/\hat{\sigma}$ converges to a normal distribution with mean 0 and variance 1. So in this case the confidence interval at confidence level α can be calculated for $\tilde{D}$ and hence for D_S and GINI by using the relationship:

$$P\left(d - \hat{\sigma}N^{-1}\left(\tfrac{1+\alpha}{2}\right) \leq \tilde{D} \leq d + \hat{\sigma}N^{-1}\left(\tfrac{1+\alpha}{2}\right)\right) = \alpha \qquad (2.3.9)$$

where N^{-1} is the inverse normal distribution.

The KS statistic can also be obtained from the ROC curve. Recall from Eq. (2.2.8) that

$$KS = \max_{s}(f(s|B) - F(s|G)). \qquad (2.3.10)$$

Every score s in the scorecard gives a point on the ROC curve with coordinates $(F(s|G), F(s|B))$. Thus if we consider the vertical distance from any point to the diagonal this must be $|F(s|B) - F(s|G)|$ since the diagonal will have height $F(s|B)$ at that point. Now it is obvious to see that KS is the maximum vertical distance between the curve and the diagonal. Since the Gini coefficient is twice the integral of this vertical distance over the whole graph, then $G < 2KS$.

An easy bound on the Gini coefficient

We showed earlier in this section that an odds monotonic score will give rise to a concave ROC curve. If we assume the scorecard is concave, then one can get a very simple lower bound on the Gini coefficient.

In the concave ROC curve of Fig. 2.3.5 take any point E and assume it has coordinates (b, g). The Gini coefficient GINI is twice the area between the curve AEC and the diagonal AC. If we connect E to A and C by straight lines then the concavity of the curve will mean these are below the curve. Hence the area between the curve and the diagonal is greater than the sum of the areas of the two triangles AEF and CEF. Thus

$$G > 2\,(\text{area}\,\triangle AEF + \text{area}\,\triangle EFC)$$
$$= 2(g(b-g)/2 + (1-g)(b-g)/2) = b - g. \qquad (2.3.11)$$

This is a very simple lower bound on the Gini coefficient, which says that the Gini coefficient is greater than the difference between the fraction of the bads below any cut-off score and the fraction of the goods below that score. A commonly used

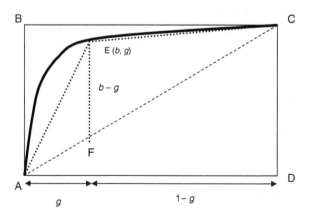

FIG. 2.3.5. Approximation to Gini on concave ROC curve.

rule of thumb for a scorecard is the 50–10 rule, which says that the scorecard will have rejected 50% of the goods by the time the cut-off score rejects 10% of the goods. This bound says the Gini coefficient for such a scorecard must be at least 0.4 (that is 0.5–0.1).

Moreover, since the bound holds at all scores, it will hold for the score which maximizes the difference between $F(s|G)$ and $F(s|B)$ in which case $(b-g)$ becomes the KS statistic. So an immediate corollary to this bound is that for odds monotonic scores, which includes most scores, then

$$G > \text{KS}. \tag{2.3.12}$$

Moreover, for such odds monotonic scores, the tangent to the ROC curve at the KS point will be parallel to the 45 degree diagonal and all the ROC curve will lie between these parallel lines. Since the area of the corresponding paralellogram is KS.1 and the area between the ROC curve and the diagonal is 1/2.G this gives the bound $G < 2\text{KS}$. In fact one can also subtract the part of the parallelogram that lies above the horizontal line $F(s|B) = 1$ and the bound still holds as the ROC curve cannot exceed $F(s|B) = 1$. This would give a bound $G/2 < \text{KS} - 1/2(\text{KS})^2$ (i.e. $G < \text{KS}(2 - \text{KS})$) or $\text{KS} > 1 - \sqrt{1 - G}$.

ROC curve and business measures

Not only does the ROC curve contain most of the other discrimination measures, except divergence and Mahalanobis distance, but also it can be used to see the impact of changes in cut-off levels on various business measures of the loan portfolio. In Section 1.3 we discussed three of these – profit, loss, and market share – which corresponds to the volume of the loans accepted.

Suppose we have applicants for a loan product where we assume the total amount lent if we loan to everyone is 1 (as in the rate models of Section 1.7). The lending decision is governed by a scorecard where the conditional distributions of the scores among the goods and the bads are $F(s|G)$ and $F(s|B)$, respectively and the distribution function for the whole application population is $F(s)$. The proportion of goods (and bads) in the applicant population is p_G (p_B). It is assumed that the loss given default for this product is l_D, while the return on those who repay the loan is r. If the lender decides to accept all those with scores above s_c and reject those with scores below s_c, then the resulting expected profit from the portfolio is defined as $E[P(s_c)]$, the expected losses incurred by the portfolio is defined as $E[L(s_c)]$, and the volume of loans in the portfolio as a fraction of the potential maximum volumes is defined as $E[V(s_c)]$. The values of these business measures are then given by

$$E[V(s_c)] = \int_{s_c}^{\infty} dF(s) = F^{(C)}(s_c) = p_G F^{(C)}(s_c|G) + p_B F^{(C)}(s_c|B)$$

$$= 1 - p_G F(s_c|G) - p_B F(s_c|B)$$

$$E[L(s_c)] = \int\limits_{s_c}^{\infty} l_D p(B|s) dF(s) = l_D p_B F^{(C)}(s_c|B) = l_D p_B (1 - F(s_c|B))$$

$$E[P(s_c)] = r p_G F^{(C)}(s_c|G) - l_D p_B F^{(C)}(s_c|B). \qquad (2.3.13)$$

In the ROC curve, one can see how these business measures change as the cut-off value changes. Since the expressions in Eq. (2.3.13) are $F(s|G)$, $F(s|B)$, or $F(s)$ one can plot these changes in the ROC curve which plots these conditional distributions.

In a ROC curve the bottom left of the curve corresponds to a very low cut-off where no goods or bads are rejected. As one moves clockwise around the curve, this corresponds to higher and higher cut-offs until one ends up with everyone below the cut-off and no one accepted. Thus the volume in the portfolio increases as we move anti-clockwise around the curve. The expected losses are proportional to $F^c(s_c|B) = 1 - F(s|B)$ and so the losses increase as we go lower down the y-axis. So we can end up at A by accepting everyone and so having maximum expected losses.

In the case of expected profit, one can rewrite Eq. (2.3.13) as

$$E[P(s_c)] = r p_G F^{(C)}(s_c|G) - l_D p_B F^{(C)}(s_c|B)$$

$$= r p_G \left(1 - \frac{l_D p_B}{r p_G} + \frac{l_D p_B}{r p_G} F(s_c|B) - F(s_c|G) \right) \qquad (2.3.14)$$

$$= r p_G \left(1 - \frac{1}{o_w} + \frac{1}{o_w} F(s_c|B) - F(s_c|G) \right)$$

where $o_w = {}^{p_G r}\!/_{p_B l_D}$ is the population odds weighted by the relative returns and losses on the loans. So one can see the isobars of constant profit in the ROC curve are when

$$\frac{F(s_c|B)}{F(s_c|G)} = o_w$$

which are lines with slope o_w. The expected profit increases as these lines move nearer to the point B where $F(s|B)$ increase more than $F(s|G)$. These movements are shown in the ROC curve in Fig. 2.3.6.

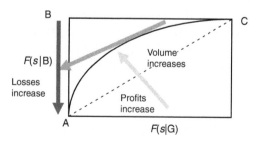

FIG. 2.3.6. Direction of business measures change in the ROC curve.

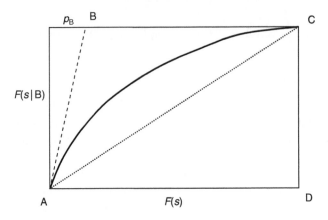

FIG. 2.3.7. Cumulative accuracy profile or lift curve.

Cumulative accuracy profiles and accuracy ratios

A very similar approach to ROC curves was developed in the marketing literature where it is known as the Cumulative accuracy profile (CAP) or the lift curve. The difference is that instead of plotting $F(s|B)$ against $F(s|G)$ for each score s, one plots $F(s|B)$ against $F(s)$ for each score. So the horizontal direction gives what percentage of the population one rejects (which is 100% minus what is accepted) and the vertical axis gives the proportion of the goods one rejects. A typical CAP curve looks like Fig. 2.3.7.

A scorecard that discriminates perfectly would have a CAP curve that goes through B which is the point $(p_B,1)$ where p_B is the proportion of the population which is good. The curve will consist of the segment AB, in which one is rejecting only bads as one moves the cut-off score higher, followed by the segment BC, where one is removing only goods as the cut-off score increased. A scorecard which is equivalent to randomly guessing and in which the score gives no information would give rise to the diagonal line AC since at any score the proportion of the goods below that score equals the proportion of the population below that score, that is, $F(s) = F(s|B)$.

As with the ROC curve and the Gini coefficient, one way of combining all the information in the CAP curve into one number is to calculate the ratio of the area between the curve and the diagonal compared with the area between the perfect discriminator and the diagonal (which is a non-discriminating scorecard). This ratio is called the Accuracy Rate (AR) where,

$$AR = \frac{\text{Area between CAP curve and diagonal}}{\text{Area between perfect discriminator and diagonal}}$$

$$= \frac{\text{Area between CAP curve and diagonal}}{0.5(1 - p_B)}$$

$$= \frac{2}{1 - p_B} \left(\int (F(s|B)f(s)ds - 0.5) \right) \qquad (2.3.15)$$

Although the ROC curve and the CAP curve for a scorecard are not the same, it is true that the Gini coefficient GINI and the AR of a scorecard are always the same. We show this assuming a continuous score distribution but the identical proof will hold for discrete score distributions replacing integrals by sums:

$$AR = \frac{2}{1 - p_B} \left(\int_{-\infty}^{\infty} F(s|B)f(s)ds - 0.5 \right)$$

$$= \frac{2}{1 - p_B} \left(\int_{-\infty}^{\infty} F(s|B) \left(p_B f(s|B) + p_G f(s|G) \right) ds - 0.5 \right)$$

$$= \frac{2}{1 - p_B} \left(p_B \int_{-\infty}^{\infty} F(s|B)f(s|B)ds + p_G AUROC - 0.5 \right). \qquad (2.3.16)$$

Integrating by parts gives

$$\int_{-\infty}^{\infty} F(s|B)f(s|B)ds = \left[F(s|B)^2 \right]_{-\infty}^{+\infty} - \int_{-\infty}^{\infty} f(s|B)f(s|B)ds \text{ or}$$

$$2 \int_{-\infty}^{\infty} F(s|B)f(s|B)ds = 1.$$

So,

$$AR = \frac{2}{1 - p_B} \left(0.5 p_B + (1 - p_B)AUROC - 0.5 \right)$$

$$= \frac{2}{1 - p_B} (1 - p_B) (AUROC - 0.5) = 2AUROC - 1 = GINI. \qquad (2.3.17)$$

This result might suggest that the CAP and ROC curves are completely interchangeable. This is not the case because the ROC curve is a more fundamental description of a scorecard's discrimination power than the CAP curve. One can construct the ROC curve for a scorecard on any sample of data irrespective of what are the proportions of goods and bads in the sample. One does not need to know anything about the distribution of the original population to derive a ROC curve. It is all about the scorecard itself. The CAP curve on the other hand, does need to know about the population on which one is using the scorecard and the curve will be different for different populations. This is most obviously seen in that to draw the perfect discriminator ABC one needs to know p_B the correct proportions of bads in the original population. Thus the ROC curve, the Gini coefficient GINI, and surprisingly the AR are functions of the scorecard only, while the CAP curve has in it information on the population being scored and will vary for the same scorecard, depending on which population is being scored.

2.4   Scorecard segmentation and measuring its impact on discrimination

The discrimination measures described in the previous two sections have tradi-tionally been used to look at the power of one individual scorecard. Most scoring systems though consist of a suite of scorecards, each built on a different segment of the population. As outlined in Section 1.8 there are a number of reasons why banks will build a suite of scorecards on different segments of the population to assess the borrowers' credit risks on the same product. It may be because of absence of data for some of the segments (recently opened loan accounts as opposed to established accounts in behavioural scoring); it may be the difference in the quantity of the data, (there will be less information on students' past repayment performance on loans compared with that for adult wage earners); it may make it easier for the lender to implement a policy of targeting one group by taking riskier borrowers (younger borrowers or those with higher income levels are possible targets); or it may be that a characteristic that discriminates well between the goods and the bads also has strong interactions with several other characteristics. In that case instead of having a number of interaction characteristics in the scorecard, different scorecards are built segmented by the attributes of the original characteristic.

What is surprising is that scorecard builders tend only to measure the discrim-ination of each scorecard in the suite separately and do not look at the overall discrimination of the whole system, even though that is what is most important. So this section seeks to emphasize that one should look at the discrimination of the whole system as well as the individual scorecards and that in fact some of the discrimination of the system comes from the segmentation itself and not just from the individual scorecards that are built. For some suites of scorecards, it turns out that 'the whole is better than the sum of its parts', that is, that there is more discrim-ination in the whole system than would appear by just looking at each scorecard separately.

Given a suite of scorecards one could always construct a single scorecard that gives the same scores as the suite of segmented scorecards, but although its con-struction is straightforward, the relationship between the discrimination measure for the overall scorecard and the segmented ones is more complex. Consider the situation where the population is split into just two segments on the characteristic

x_0, which may be age. The first segment $x_0 = 1$ corresponds to those under 25 and gives rise to a score $s_1(x_1, \ldots, x_m, y_1, \ldots, y_k)$ which depends on the attributes $(x_1, \ldots, x_m, y_1, \ldots, y_k)$ and is given by a scorecard S_1, while the second segment $x_0 = 2$ corresponds to those over 25 and the scorecard S_2 gives rise to a score $s_2(x_1, \ldots, x_m, z_1, \ldots, z_l)$ which depends on the attributes $(x_1, \ldots, x_m, z_1, \ldots, z_l)$, where some attributes will be common between the two scorecards and others different. One can define a score s for the whole population by defining a scorecard S as follows:

$$s(x_0, x_1, \ldots, x_m, y_1, \ldots, y_k, z_1, \ldots, z_l) = \begin{cases} s_1(x_1, \ldots, x_m, y_1, \ldots, y_k) & \text{if } x_0 = 1. \\ s_2(x_1, \ldots, x_m, z_1, \ldots, z_l) & \text{if } x_0 = 2. \end{cases}$$

If each of the individual scores is additive, then the resultant score is additive on attributes which are interactions of x_0 with the other attributes. However even if both s_i are log odds score, then the resulting score s will not necessarily be a log odds score.

To derive the ROC curve for the scorecard S from those of S_1 and S_2 we need to know the probabilities:

$$p_1^G = \Pr\{x_0 = 1|G\}, p_2^G = \Pr\{x_0 = 2|G\}, p_1^B = \Pr\{x_0 = 1|B\}, p_2^B = \Pr\{x_0 = 2|B\}. \tag{2.4.1}$$

Then if $F_i(s|G)$ and $F_i(s|B)$ are the conditional score distributions of the goods and the bads for the scorecards $S_i, i = 1, 2$, these give the ROC curves for those two scorecards. The ROC curve for S depends on $F(s|G)$ and $F(s|B)$ where

$$F(s|G) = p_1^G F_1(s|G) + p_2^G F_2(s|G); F(s|B) = p_1^B F_1(s|B) + p_2^B F_2(s|B). \tag{2.4.2}$$

In Fig. 2.4.1 we show the possible results that can be obtained. Consider the very special case when $p_i^G = p_i^B = 0.5$ then the ROC curve for the whole system passes through the midpoint of the line joining the points on the two segment ROC curves which have the same scores. As these scores move so does the point on each of the curves and hence the midpoint. However, there is no reason for them to move at the same rate. It could be that the scores in one segment will all be above a large fraction of the scores in the other segment so the end point of the line whose midpoint traces out the overall scorecards ROC curve will stay at $(0,0)$ while the other end point moves along the other segment's ROC curve. Thus it is quite possible for the ROC curve of the overall scorecard to be below both segment ROC curves in some regions, and above both ROC curves in other regions (see Fig. 2.4.1a and b). It is also quite clear that the resultant ROC curve need not be concave and so the overall score is not monotonic even if the scores in the different segments are monotonic.

In the more general case where $p_i^G \neq p_i^B$ the ROC curve for the total system is not going through any point on this line joining the points with the same score on the

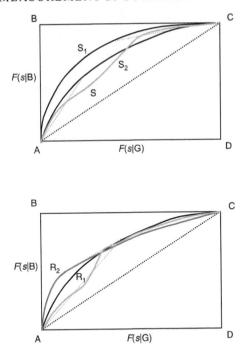

FIG. 2.4.1. (a) Overall ROC curve with non-intersecting ROC curves in each segment; and (b) Overall ROC curve with intersecting ROC curves in each segment.

two segment curves, because the averaging of the two end points in the horizontal direction is not the same as the averaging in the vertical direction. Thus it is even more likely that the total curve will be above or below the two ROC curves for the two segment scorecards.

One of the reasons for the total ROC curve being so different from those in the segments is that the discrimination of the whole system does not just come from the discrimination in each of the segment scorecards but also depends on the way the segmentation has split the good and bad population. So one obvious question is how much of the discrimination comes from the segmentation itself?

Impact of segmentation on Gini coefficient

Consider again the case where one splits the population into two segments and builds separate scorecards on each segment. Assume when one analyses the data in the segments, the first segment has g_1 goods and b_1 bads in its sample and the second segment has g_2 goods and b_2 bads in its sample. We will always order the samples so $g_1/b_1 \leq g_2/b_2$, that is, the first segment has lower good:bad odds than the second segment. Building scorecards for each segment and putting the scores together would lead to a ROC curve R.

If only the segmentation had been created and there were no subsequent scorecards built on each segment, this is equivalent to having a purely random scorecard on each segment but with the caveat that all the scores in the first segment (the one with lower good:bad odds) are below any in the second segment. Essentially one is giving everyone in the same segment the same score, but this would produce lots of ties. If one wants to avoid ties then give borrower j in segment i a score of $s_i + \varepsilon u_j$ where u_j has uniform distribution on $[0,1]$ and $s_{i+1} > s_i + \varepsilon$.

The ROC curve one gets based on this scoring system that only uses the segmentation and has no information in the scorecard is given by S in Fig. 2.4.2. It is a straight line from $A(0,0)$ to $E\big(g_1/(g_1 + g_2), b_1/(b_1 + b_2)\big)$ describing the random scorecard on the first segment and then the straight line EC from $\big(g_1/(g_1 + g_2), b_1/(b_1 + b_2)\big)$ to $(1,1)$ describing the random scorecard on the second segment. The Gini coefficient for this scorecard which is purely the segmentation is defined as GINI$_S$. It is exactly the same as that for the bound in Eq. (2.3.1), namely,

$$\text{GINI}_S = \left(\frac{b_1}{b_1 + b_2} - \frac{g_1}{g_1 + g_2} \right). \tag{2.4.3}$$

GINI$_S$ is the amount of the original Gini coefficient that is due to the segmentation and the remainder GINI$_S - \big(b_1/(b_1 + b_2) - g_1/(g_1 + g_2)\big)$ is due to the scorecards built.

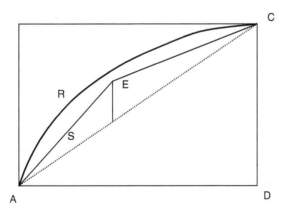

FIG. 2.4.2. ROC curve if two segments.

Example 2.4.1 Segmented Gini coefficient for behavioural scorecard with two segments

An important characteristic for behavioural scoring systems is whether the borrower has previously been in arrears or not. Two scorecards were built segmenting on this characteristic and the overall system had a Gini coefficient of 0.88. In the population sample, there were 990 borrowers who had been in arrears and 830 of these were subsequently good and 160 became bads. There were 7210 borrowers who had never been in arrears and of these 40 subsequently became bad but the remaining 7170 were goods. In this case GINI$_S$ the Gini due to segmentation only is

$$\frac{160}{200} - \frac{830}{8000} = 0.8 - 0.104 = 0.696.$$

So just segmenting on arrears ensures that one would have a Gini coefficient of 0.69 even if the actual scorecards were not better than random. In this case a high proportion of the discrimination measured in the Gini coefficient is due to this one divide in the population. This is one of the reasons why behavioural scores tend to have higher Gini coefficients than application scores.

If the population is split into more than two segments, the same approach can be used to calculate the power of the segmentation as part of the overall Gini coefficient of the system. Assume that the population is split into N segments and segment i has g_i goods and b_i bads where again we will assume the segments are ordered so that the good:bad odds g_i/b_i is increasing in i. If we define the cumulative numbers of goods and bads by

$$B_j = \sum_{i=1}^{j} b_i \text{ with } B_0 = 0 \quad \text{and} \quad B_N = n_B = \sum_{i=1}^{N} b_i :$$

$$G_j = \sum_{i=1}^{j} g_i \text{ with } G_0 = 0 \quad \text{and} \quad G_N = n_G = \sum_{i=1}^{N} g_i$$

then the first segment has a proportion b_1/n_B of the bads and g_1/n_G of the goods.

The first two segments have a proportion B_2/n_B of the bads and G_2/n_G of the goods and the first i segments have B_i/n_B of the bads and G_i/n_G of the goods. Thus following the argument in the two segment case if we choose a random scorecard in each segment but make sure that any score in one segment is below any score in the segment above, the corresponding ROC curve is given in Fig. 2.4.3. The area under that ROC curve with just this segmentation, AUROC$_S$, is given by the

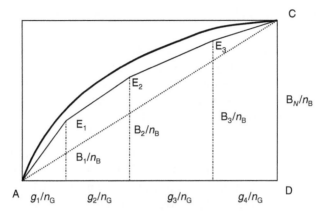

FIG. 2.4.3. ROC curve with several segments.

trapezium rule as was used in Example 2.3.4, and is

$$\text{AUROC}_S = \frac{1}{n_G n_B} \sum_{i=1}^{N} g_i \left(\frac{B_i + B_{i-1}}{2} \right)$$

$$G_S = 2(\text{AUROC}_S) - 1. \qquad (2.4.4)$$

Example 2.4.2 Discrimination due to segmentation with three segments

Assume one has a suite of scorecards where the population has been segmented into three segments. In the data, the first segment has 100 bads and 400 goods; the second has 50 bads and 400 goods; and the third 50 bads and 1200 goods (so the good:bad odds increase from segment to segment). The AUROC and the GINI due just to the segmentation is

$$\text{AUROC}_S = \frac{1}{200.2000} \left(400 \left(\frac{0 + 100}{2} \right) + 400 \left(\frac{100 + 150}{2} \right) \right.$$
$$\left. + 1200 \left(\frac{150 + 200}{2} \right) \right) = 0.7$$

$$\text{GINI}_S = 2(0.7) - 1 = 0.4.$$

Having determined how to measure the discrimination in a suite of scorecards due just to the segmentation, one could ask whether this information is of any use. One thing it does is to give another reason for segmenting. If one has a characteristic where the Gini coefficient when just segmenting on that characteristic is high, it may be worthwhile segmenting to 'lock in' the discrimination one is getting. That does not preclude segmenting on other characteristics whose GINI_S is low, because of the reasons outlined at the start of this section. It could be that segmenting improves the discrimination in the individual scorecards compared with the one based on the whole population.

When one segments on a characteristic and then calculates the $GINI_S$ for the segmentation this is essentially equivalent to coarse classifying the characteristic and using the Somer's D-concordance statistic to measure the discriminatory power of the characteristic with those specific splits. In Section 1.8, we discussed the use of the chi-square statistic and information value as ways of determining what are the best ways to coarse classify a characteristic. They could then be used with the 'best' classification splits as univariate tests to determine which characteristics should be considered for inclusion in the final scorecard. The D-concordance statistic could play exactly the same role although in practice it is not as widely used as the other two statistics. So even if these calculations are not used for determining how strong a particular segmentation is, perhaps because no segmentation will be undertaken, they can be used as a way of determining what is an appropriate coarse classification of the characteristic.

Having calculated how much of the Gini coefficient in a suite of scorecards is due to the segmentation, we can ask the same question of the other discrimination measures.

Impact of segmentation on KS statistic

The same idea, to use scorecards which are completely random in each of the segments of the population, can be used to calculate how much of the other discrimination measures like KS are due to the segmentation.

Again assume there are only two segments with the first segment having g_1 goods and b_1 bads in its sample and the second segment having g_2 goods and b_2 bads in its sample and $g_1/b_1 \leq g_2/b_2$. Again assume the scores in the first segment are chosen from a uniform distribution which is the same for both goods and bads so the curves of $F(s|B)$ and $F(s|G)$ against the score s will be straight lines. The scores in the second segment are chosen in exactly the same way except they are all higher than those in the first segment, and again $F(s|G)$ and $F(s|B)$ are straight lines as functions of the score. The curves of $F(s|G)$ and $F(s|B)$ plotted against the scores for the whole population are given by Fig. 2.4.4. The upper curve is the distribution of $F(s|B)$ and the lower curve gives that of $F(s|G)$. Both curves change their slope at the end of the first segment, when $F(s|B)$ has value $b_1/(b_1 + b_2)$ and $F(s|G)$ has value $g_1/(g_1 + g_2)$. It is obvious from the figure that this is the score which maximizes $(F(s|B) - F(s|G))$. So if KS_S is the value of the KS statistic if one had segmentation and only random scorecards in each segment, one gets

$$KS_S = \frac{b_1}{b_1 + b_2} - \frac{g_1}{g_1 + g_2}. \tag{2.4.5}$$

This is exactly the same expression as in Eq. (2.4.3) and so we have $GINI_S = KS_S$.

Example 2.4.3 KS for behavioural score Example 2.4.1

In the behavioural scoring example (Example 2.4.1), the actual KS that was obtained in that scorecard was 0.75. If we had split on whether people were in arrears or not, and do nothing more than segment on this we would get $g_1 = 830, b_1 = 160, g_2 = 7170, b_2 = 40$ and so $KS_S = GINI_S = 0.696$. Thus almost all of the KS statistic can be explained by the arrears segmentation.

If one assumed again that there were N segments in the hold-out sample, and segment i has g_i goods and b_i bads where again we will assume the segments are ordered so that the good:bad odds g_i/b_i is increasing. Define the cumulative numbers of goods and bads by

$$B_j = \sum_{i=1}^{j} b_i \text{ with } B_0 = 0 \quad \text{and} \quad B_N = n_B = \sum_{i=1}^{N} b_i :$$

$$G_j = \sum_{i=1}^{j} g_i \text{ with } G_0 = 0 \quad \text{and} \quad G_N = n_G = \sum_{i=1}^{N} g_i.$$

It is clear the maximum difference between $F(s|B)$ and $F(s|G)$ must be at one of the segment ends, since the difference between the two curves changes linearly in each segment. Hence KS_S, the maximum value of this difference between the two curves when only segmentation occurs, is at the end of segment j where

$$j = \max\{i | g_i/b_i \le n_G/n_B\}. \tag{2.4.6}$$

This follows because if we call the KS value at the end of segment i, KS_i then:

$$KS_i = \frac{B_i}{n_B} - \frac{G_i}{n_G} = \frac{B_{i-1} + b_i}{n_B} - \frac{G_{i-1} + g_i}{n_G} = KS_{i-1} + \frac{b_i}{n_B}\left(1 - \frac{g_i/b_i}{n_G/n_B}\right)$$

and the last term in this expression is positive provided $g_i/b_i \le n_G/n_B$.

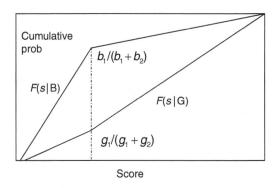

FIG. 2.4.4. KS for two segments with random scorecard in each.

Example 2.4.4 KS segmentation for the three-segment Example 2.4.2

In Example 2.4.2 the data is $g_1 = 400; b_1 = 100; g_2 = 400; b_2 = 50; g_3 = 1200;$ $b_3 = 50$ and hence $n_G = 2000; n_B = 200$. Then the KS_S value occurs after the second segment since $g_1/b_1 = 4; g_2/b_2 = 8; g_3/b_3 = 24$ and its value is

$$KS_S = \left| \frac{100 + 50}{200} - \frac{400 + 400}{2000} \right| = 0.75 - 0.4 = 0.35.$$

Note in this case this is not equivalent to $GINI_S$.

Impact of segmentation on divergence

The effect of segmentation on divergence is in fact even more straightforward because now in the approach of ascribing random scorecards to each segment, we can assume all the borrowers in one segment have the same score since we do not have to worry about ties. Thus there are only a finite number of scores in the scorecard and the divergence reduces to the information value. Then with N segments and g_i, b_i being the numbers of goods and bads in each segment, the information value IV_S when applied just to a scorecard with N such scores s_i becomes

$$IV_S = \sum_{i \in I} \left(g_i/n_G - b_i/n_B \right) \ln \left(\frac{g_i/n_G}{b_i/n_B} \right). \qquad (2.4.7)$$

Example 2.4.5 Impact of segmentation on divergence on behavioural score example

Using the data of the behavioural example on Example 2.4.1, we have $g_1 = 830, b_1 = 160, g_2 = 7170, b_2 = 40$ and hence

$$IV_S = \sum_{i \in I} \left(g_i/n_G - b_i/n_B \right) \ln \left(\frac{g_i/n_G}{b_i/n_B} \right)$$

$$= (830/8000 - 160/200) \ln \left(\frac{830/8000}{160/200} \right) + (7170/8000 - 40/200)$$

$$\ln \left(\frac{7170/8000}{40/200} \right)$$

$$= 1.422 + 0.825 = 2.247.$$

This compares with the actual divergence D of 2.400 in this case.

2.5 Calibration measures of scorecard probability predictions

As scorecards were originally developed to support acceptance and operating decisions in consumer lending by differentiating who would or would not default, it
was the discrimination of the scorecards (and the categorical forecasts) that were
pre-eminent. What was important was that the scorecard correctly ordered the borrowers in terms of default risk. Correctly estimating the value of that default risk
was less important. The decision on what score to choose for the cut-off between
those accepted and those rejected was guided by business considerations such as
acceptance rate and used empirically derived estimates of the good:bad rate at the
cut-off score. The fact that the score – especially if it were a log odds score – could
be considered to give a prediction of the proportion of borrowers who would be
good was ignored as was whether the actual prediction was accurate. In order to
make a probability prediction one needs one more piece of information on top of
the likelihoods $f(s|G)$ and $f(s|B)$ that are all that is required for the discrimination
measures. One needs to have the population odds so one can translate $f(s|G)$ and
$f(s|B)$ into the probabilities $p(G|s)$ and $p(B|s)$.

The New Basel Accord introduced in 2007 has changed all that. Under it, a
portfolio of loans has to be segmented into score bands and a probability of default
(PD) given for the borrowers in each band. Some regulators have defined default
as 90 days overdue which is the standard definition of bad used in consumer credit.
Other regulators though have defined default as 180 days overdue. In the Basel
context, we use the PD notation to cover both these cases and will call defaulters
the bads and non-defaulters the goods. So with our normal notation that a borrower
with score s has probability $p(s) = P(G|s)$ of being Good, then that borrower
has probability of default given by $PD = 1 - p(s) = P(B|s)$. We will use both our
standard notation and the PD notation in this section since measures of a scorecard's
probability prediction are used almost exclusively in the Basel Capital Accord
context. There it is assumed that a scorecard is predicting PD. The amount of
regulatory capital that has to be set aside to cover unexpected losses from the
borrowers in any segment of the loan portfolio is dependent on this probability
of default value as we shall see in Chapter 5. Moreover this PD value has to be
validated by comparing predicted values with the actual ones that subsequently
occurred. Hence there is a need for tests to validate the accuracy of the predictions
of default probabilities which the scores give.

In Section 1.5 we introduced the idea of a log odds score where the relationship
between the score and the probability of being good is that given by logistic regres-
sion, namely $s = \log\left(\frac{P(G|s)}{P(B|s)}\right)$. In such cases the relationship between the score
and the predicted probability of bad ($PD = P(B|s)$) is immediate. Other methods
of building scorecards lead to scores which do not have the log odds property.
One could then use historical data to create a score to PD transformation function

(equivalent to a score to probability of good transformation) or use the ideas in Section 1.6 on scaling scores to recover the log odds property. Whichever approach is taken – developing log odds score, creating a score to probability of default transformation function, or scaling the score to recover the log odds property – one ends up with a system which identifies a probability of default with each score. Calibration measures seek to test how good the predictions of these default probabilities are.

To measure the calibration of a score, the score is split into bands and a probability of default (PD) or a probability of being good attached to each band. If the scores are split so the ith band is the interval of scores $[s_i, s_{i+1}]$, then the probability of default PD $_i$ for this band is defined as

$$\text{PD}_i = \frac{\int_{s_i}^{s_{i+1}} p(\text{B}|s)f(s)ds}{\int_{s_i}^{s_{i+1}} f(s)ds} = \frac{\int s_{s_i}^{s_{i+1}} p_\text{B}f(s|\text{B})ds}{\int_{s_i}^{s_{i+1}} f(s)ds}. \tag{2.5.1}$$

Alternatively one can translate the scores to probability of default, PD(s), for each borrower and then choose PD bands. So band i contains all the borrowers with scores s where

$$\{s|\text{PD}_i \leq \text{PD}(s) < \text{PD}_{i+1}\} = \{s|\text{PD}_i \leq P(\text{B}|s) < \text{PD}_{i+1}\}$$

and the PD of such an interval is usually taken as the midpoint $(\text{PD}_i + \text{PD}_{i+1})/2$.

The need to calibrate the accuracy of predictions has been very important in areas like economic forecasts, sales forecasts, and even weather forecasts for many years, so the measures of the accuracy of the forecasts used in these contexts can be used for the default risk forecasts. Since this aspect of scorecards has only become important in the last few years, the number of tests used or suggested to be used in the retail credit risk area is surprisingly small. There is the binomial test and its normal approximation when there are large numbers in the samples. There is also the chi-square goodness-of-fit test sometimes called the Hosmer–Lemeshow test (Hosmer Lemeshow 1980) which has proved a good way of assessing the accuracy of forecasts given by logistic regression models. In all these tests the population scored is first segmented into groups depending on their scores or their PD values, as this is what is needed in validating the scorecard for the Basel New Accord. These tests all assume the probability of a borrower being bad (defaulting) is independent of whether another borrower in the same defaults or not. Another test suggested is the normal test which uses the PD rate in different periods to give a measure of the prediction. This does not require the independence of defaults between borrowers in a given period but does assume independence of defaults in different time periods. We will concentrate on the first two approaches – the binomial test and the chi-square statistic.

Binomial test

This test is an obvious way of checking the validity of a PD estimate for a particular score band but as we said it assumes the chance each individual in the band will go bad (default) is independent of the chance of any other borrower in the band going bad. With this assumption, the number of bads in band i containing n_i borrowers has a binomial distribution. One assumes that the probability of each individual going bad is $\text{PD}_i = 1 - p_i$ where PD_i is the probability of default for that score band and p_i the probability of a borrower in that band being good. So the binomial test compares the two hypotheses:

- Null hypothesis H_0: the PD_i rating of score band i is correct
- Alternative hypothesis H_1: the PD_i of score band i is underestimated.

If the null hypothesis is true the chance that there will be b_i bads in the n_i borrowers is $b_i!(n_i - b_i)!/n_i!(\text{PD})^{b_i}(1 - \text{PD})^{n_i - b_i}$. Hence the null hypothesis will be rejected at the α-confidence level if the number of bads k in the score band is greater than or equal to k^* where

$$k^* = \min\left\{ k \mid \sum_{j=k}^{n_i} \frac{n_i!}{j!(n_i - j)!}\text{PD}^j(1 - \text{PD})^{n_i - j} \leq 1 - \alpha \right\}$$

$$= \min\left\{ k \mid \sum_{j=k}^{n_i} \frac{n_i!}{j!(n_i - j)!}(1 - p_i)^j(p_i)^{n_i - j} \leq 1 - \alpha \right\}. \qquad (2.5.2)$$

Example 2.5.1 Binomial test on band with three borrowers

Suppose there is a score band with estimated PD of 0.1. In the subsequent period it is found that three borrowers fall into this score band, two of whom turn out to be good and one to be bad. Can we reject at the 95% level the hypothesis that the PD is 0.1?

If H_0 is correct, so that PD $= 0.1$ for this score band, then:

- the chance of getting 3 bads is $(0.1)^3 = 0.001$
- the chance of getting 2 bads and 1 good is $(3!/2! \times 1!)(0.1)^2 (0.9) = 0.027$
- the chance of getting 2 or more bads is 0.0028 which is below 0.05
- the chance of getting 1 bad and 2 goods is $(3!/2! \times 1!)(0.9)^2 (0.1) = 0.243$
- the chance of getting 1 or more bad is 0.271 which is higher than 5%.

Thus one cannot reject the null hypothesis at the 95% level.

Substituting in (2.5.2) gives that at $\alpha = 0.99, k^* = 3$; at $\alpha = 0.95, k^* = 2$; at $\alpha = 0.5, k^* = 1$, for the values in Example 2.5.1 which confirms that one cannot reject the assumption that PD $= 0.01$ at the 95% level.

Normal approximation to binomial test

If the number of borrowers in a particular score band of the validation sample is large, then the calculations involved in estimating the binomial probabilities become too complex to undertake. Instead one can assume that the distribution of the number of defaulters is almost normal. If there are n_i borrowers in band *i*of the sample and the hypothesis H_0 is that the probability of default is PD_i, then the standard binomial results give that the expected number of defaulters is $n_i PD_i$ and the variance of the number of defaulters is $n_i PD_i(1-PD_i)$. The number of defaulters can be thought to have the normal distribution $N(n_i PD_i, n_i PD_i(1-PD_i))$. Thus the critical k^* of defaulters at or above which the null hypothesis can be rejected at the α-confidence level is given by

$$k^* = N^{-1}(\alpha)\sqrt{n_i PD_i(1-PD_i)} + n_i PD_i = N^{-1}(\alpha)\sqrt{n_i p_i(1-p_i)} + n_i(1-p_i)$$

where N^{-1} is the inverse of the cumulative normal distribution.

Example 2.5.2

Suppose the PD $= 0.1$ band has 85 goods and 15 bads in its validation sample, should the hypothesis that PD $= 0.1$ be rejected at the 95% level.

The number of defaulters has approximately the normal distribution $N(100(0.1),100(0.9)(0.1)) = N(10,9)$. So 15 defaulters is 5/3 standard deviations above the mean. There is a 4.9% chance of getting a value higher than this. So one should reject the hypothesis that the probability of default is 0.1 at the 95% level (just). In fact the critical number of defaults $k*$ at which one should reject the hypothesis is given by

$$k^* = N^{-1}(0.95)\sqrt{100(0.1)(0.9)} + 100(0.1) = 1.645(3) + 10 = 14.935. \quad (2.5.3)$$

Chi-square test (Hosmer–Lemeshow test)

Another way of validating the calibration of a scorecard is to use the chi-square goodness-of-fit tests which were introduced into statistics by Karl Pearson. This is a general test which assesses how well data fits a specific statistical model by comparing the actual results with those which the model predicted. It looks at the sum of the squares of the errors in the prediction, weighted by the inverse of the variance in the prediction. So this is just what is required to test a scorecard's predictive capability by using a hold-out sample. The idea is exactly the same as was suggested in Section 1.8 to measure how good is a coarse classification of a characteristic. The difference was that there the hypothesis was that the odds in every bin was the PopOdds. Here it is that the probabilities of default in each band $i, i = 1, 2, \ldots, N$ have specific values PD_i or equivalently that the probabilities of being good p_i have values $1 - PD_i$.

Assuming the scorecard is split into N intervals or rating grades where the scorecard prediction of the good rate in interval i ($i = 1, 2, \ldots, N$) is p_i (and hence the predicted bad rate is $1 - p_i = PD_i$). If there are n_i borrowers in interval i and g_i of these are goods (and hence $b_i = n_i - g_i$ are bads), then the chi-square statistic for how good this fit is the sum of the squares of the differences between the forecast number of goods (or defaults) and the observed numbers, normalized by dividing by the theoretical variance. So in interval i, the expected number of goods is $n_i p_i$ and the variance in the number of goods, assuming a binomial distribution is $n_i p_i (1 - p_i)$. Then the chi-square statistic (also called in this context the Hosmer–Lemeshow statistic) is

$$HL = \sum_{i=1}^{N} \frac{(n_i p_i - g_i)^2}{n_i p_i (1 - p_i)}. \tag{2.5.4}$$

In fact one usually expresses the data by using a contingency table with N rows corresponding to each interval and two columns which are the two outcomes (good and bad) of the target variable. The entries in each cell then correspond to the actual numbers in the data sample that are in that interval. The table is then repeated with the expected numbers in each cell if the hypothesis being tested were true. Sometimes the two sets of numbers – actual and expected – are put into one N by two tables with the expected numbers in parenthesis in the relevant cell. In this case the expected numbers are the predicted good and bads if the predictions $p_i(1 - p_i) = PD_i$ are correct. The chi-square test then calculates for each cell the square of the difference between the actual and expected numbers in that cell divided by the expected numbers. In fact this is the same as (2.5.4) as the calculation in (2.5.5) shows:

$$HL = \sum_{i=1}^{N} \frac{\begin{pmatrix} \text{Expected number of goods in interval } i - \\ \text{observed number of goods in interval } i \end{pmatrix}^2}{\text{Expected number of goods in interval } i}$$

$$+ \sum_{i=1}^{N} \frac{\begin{pmatrix} \text{Expected number of bads in interval } i - \\ \text{observed number of bads in interval } i \end{pmatrix}^2}{\text{Expected number of bads in interval } i}$$

$$= \sum_{k=1}^{N} \left(\frac{(n_i p_i - g_i)^2}{n_i p_i} + \frac{(n_i(1 - p_i) - b_i)^2}{n_i(1 - p_i)} \right)$$

$$= \sum_{i=1}^{N} \left(\frac{(n_i p_i - g_i)^2}{n_i p_i} + \frac{(g_i - n_i p_i)^2}{n_i (1 - p_i)} \right) = \sum_{i=1}^{N} (n_i p_i - g_i)^2 \left(\frac{1}{n_i p_i} + \frac{1}{n_i (1 - p_i)} \right)$$

$$= \sum_{i=1}^{N} \left(\frac{(n_i p_i - g_i)^2}{n_i p_i (1 - p_i)} \right). \tag{2.5.5}$$

The chi-square statistic has a χ^2 distribution with N-2 degrees of freedom provided the expected numbers in each cell are large enough and the number of segments N is fixed. The normal rule of thumb is that these expected numbers should be at least 5 (otherwise a correction needs to be applied) but some statisticians feel this is too restrictive and require only that the expected numbers in all the cells be at least 1 with no more than 20% of them being less than 5. In this way one can test the hypothesis that the predictions p_i for all the bands are correct in one test.

This still leaves the question of how to choose the intervals and how many intervals N to have. In some cases, particularly when using the scorecards in the Basel New Accord modelling, these are already predefined as lenders have decided into which probability of default intervals they want to segment their portfolio. Hosmer and Lemeshow suggest two methods of deciding the intervals. First, they suggest choosing fixed cut-off points in the probability of being good. For example one interval might be those with probabilities of being good of between 0 and 0.5; another is the group from 0.5 to 0.8; and so on. In credit scoring it is common to implement this approach by splitting the population into score bands, so that one segment will be the scores between 200 and 250, a second those between 250 and 280. Since there is a monotone relationship between score and probability of being good, these are essentially the same approach. The alternative is to split the population ordered by probability of being good into intervals which have equal numbers of observations, that is, split the population into percentiles of risk, and it is normal to take $N = 10$. Research has shown that splitting the population by using percentiles rather than the pre-assigned groups gives a statistic which has closer adherence to the χ^2 distribution but in the Basel Accord context the groups to be used have already been chosen in terms of default probabilities.

There is one other query to be resolved. Given a specific score band what is the probability of being good that one should ascribe to that band. Suppose one has a log odds scorecard so that the relationship between score s and probability of being good p is $\log(p/_{1-p}) = s$ or $p(s) = 1/_{1+e^{-s}}$, and hence $PD(s) = 1 - p(s) = 1/_{1+e^{s}}$. Ideally one should calculate the average $p(s)$ for the band but this is a lot of extra work and has to be repeated each time one wants to use a specific band. So instead if one has a score band $[s_1, s_2]$, lenders choose between taking the probability of being good of the midpoint of the score band $p = 1/_{1+e^{-(s_1+s_2)/2}}$ or the midpoint of the probabilities in the score band, that is, $p = (p_1 + p_2)/2 = \left(1/_{1+e^{-s_1}} + 1/_{1+e^{-s_2}} \right) /2$. If the bands have been chosen by first considering the probabilities, the second approach seems more appropriate but if one is unsure about the score to probability

TABLE 2.5.1. Comparison of ways of assessing probability of bands.

End points of probability band	Midpoint of probability band	Equivalent score of end points of bands	Midpoint score of bands	Probability of midpoint score of band
1E-10	0.05	−23.02585093	−12.61153775	3.33332E-06
0.1	0.15	−2.197224577	−1.791759469	0.142857143
0.2	0.25	−1.386294361	−1.116796111	0.246606056
0.3	0.35	−0.84729786	−0.626381484	0.348331477
0.4	0.45	−0.405465108	−0.202732554	0.449489473
0.5	0.55	0	0.202732554	0.550510257
0.6	0.65	0.405465108	0.626381484	0.651668523
0.7	0.75	0.84729786	1.116796111	0.753393944
0.8	0.85	1.386294361	1.791759469	0.857142857
0.9	0.95	2.197224577	12.61153771	0.999996667
1		23.02585085	11.51292542	0.99999

calibration then lenders have been taking the first approach. The differences are usually quite small but as Table 2.5.1 shows it can be quite considerable at the extreme bands (though normally one would have limits on the probabilities because one would reject accounts where the score is too low and there must be an upper limit on what an account can score on any given scorecard).

The Basel New Accord regulations stress the need for conservatism, so one might consider taking the lowest good rate (highest PD rate) in the band as its value. However, this means the calibration measures might suggest the PD value is overestimated. This is not a problem with the binomial test since the alternative hypothesis is that the PD value is underestimated.

Example 2.5.3 Hosmer–Lemeshow applied to three-band case

Consider a segmentation for the Basel Accord of a portfolio split into three bands with probabilities of default (PD) of 0.02, 0.05, and 0.1, respectively (that is probability of being good of $p = 0.98$, 0.95, and 0.9, respectively). If there were 1000 in the first band of which 25 were defaulter (bad); 600 in the second of which 35 were bads; and 100 in the third group of whom 15 were bads, the calculation of the chi-square values are given in Table 2.5.2. In Table 2.5.2 we calculate using Eq. (2.5.4) rather than the contingency table approach of Eq. (2.5.5). The chi-squares statistic for the three groups sums up to 4.931, which with one degree of freedom corresponds to a p-value of 0.026. So the chance of getting a more extreme result if the given PD values are correct is between 2 and 3 in 100.

We repeat the calculation in Table 2.5.3 using the contingency approach to confirm that they give the same results. Since of the six cells – estimated number of defaults (bads) and non-defaults (goods) in the three bands – were all more than 5 it is reasonable to assume this statistic has a chi-square distribution with 1(3−2)

TABLE 2.5.2. Chi-square calculations for Example 2.5.3 using Eq. (2.5.4).

PD band	Number in band	Observed number of default	Estimated number of defaults	Estimate of variance in number of defaults	(actual default − estimated defaults)^2/ variance
0.02	1000	25	20	19.6	1.278
0.05	600	35	30	28.5	0.877
0.1	100	15	10	9.0	2.777
					4.931
				p-value	0.026

degrees of freedom. The chance of such a distribution having a value of 4.931 or higher is 0.026. Thus at the 95% confidence level one cannot be confident the PD estimates are correct, but at the 99% level one could not reject the hypothesis that 0.02, 0.05, and 0.1 are the correct values.

TABLE 2.5.3. Chi-square calculations for Example 2.5.3 using equation (2.5.5).

PD band	Observed number of Goods	Observed number of Bads (default)	(actual Goods-estimated Goods)^2/ estimated Goods	(actual Bads-estimated Bads)^2/ estimated Bads
0.02	975(980)	25(20)	0.026	1.250
0.05	565(570)	35(30)	0.044	0.833
0.1	85(90)	15(10)	0.278	2.500
			Total	4.931
			p-value	0.026

Example 2.5.4 Calibration using Appendix A scorecard using splits from Table 2.2.1

Consider the results in Appendix A on the outcome of running a scorecard on validation data. Using Hosmer and Lemeshow's idea of splitting the data into 10 score band with roughly the same number of borrowers in each group gives the splits already used in Table 2.2.1. Appendix A also gives the odds at each score and if we assume the score is a natural log odds one we can get the parameters by linearly regressing the log of the odds on the score. This gives the estimation that

$$\log\left(\frac{p}{1-p}\right) = -5.997 + 0.030588\,s \quad \text{or} \quad p = \frac{1}{1 + e^{5.997 - 0.030588s}} \quad (2.5.6)$$

In Table 2.5.4 we look at the mid point of the scores in each band and take the probability given by the transformation (2.5.6) as the probability of that band. The chi-square value is 182.3 and assuming it is a chi square distribution with 8 degrees of freedom, the chance of the observed numbers of Goods and Bads occurring if

TABLE 2.5.4. Chi-square calculations using probability of midpoint score of score band.

Start score of band	End score of band	Midpoint score of band	Probability of good of midpoint	No. of goods	No. of bads	Total number	Expected number of goods	Variance in number of goods	(Exp−obs) variance	(exp−obs)/ With only 9 bands
142	253	197.5	0.511005	1026	481	1507	770.08	376.57	173.920	With only 9 bands
254	277	265.5	0.893213	1588	186	1774	1584.56	169.21	0.070	
278	298	288	0.943332	1822	98	1920	1811.20	102.64	1.137	
299	319	309	0.969367	1938	52	1990	1929.04	59.09	1.359	
320	334	327	0.982104	1936	27	1963	1927.87	34.50	1.916	
335	349	342	0.988614	2002	18	2020	1997.00	22.74	1.099	
350	364	357	0.992774	1942	9	1951	1936.90	14.00	1.857	
365	382	373.5	0.995625	2010	6	2016	2007.18	8.78	0.906	
383	406	394.5	0.997694	1946	5	1951	1946.50	4.49	0.056	
407	476	441.5	0.999451	2024	1	2025	2023.89	1.11	0.011	
Chi-square									182.330	8.410
p-value									3.34E−35	2.98E−01

these were the true probabilities is minute (10^{-35}). However, it is clear that almost all of the misfitting occurs in the first band (scores 142–253), which has a chi-square value of 173.9. This is where there is the problem of what is a suitable probability of Good for a low score band when the probabilities vary a lot. However, most lenders would reject such applicants anyway and so they would not appear in the portfolio. If we assume that the portfolio consists of only those with scores above 253, so we only have to consider the remaining nine score bands, the chi-square value is 8.41. Assuming this is a chi-square distribution with 7 degrees of freedom the chance of this or a more extreme value occurring is 0.3, which means that the estimated probabilities seem to be justified by the data.

2.6   Measures of the correctness of categorical prediction

Credit scoring systems were first developed to assist decision making for the initial acceptance decision. Therefore one way of measuring their effectiveness is to assess how good are the forecasts used in making these decisions. In these decisions, applicants are either accepted or rejected and as outlined in Section 1.4 the scores are used to classify the applicants into two groups one of which will be the accepts and the other is the rejects. Since returns and profits are maximized when all those who are accepted are good and all those who are rejected are bad, one can rename those who are accepted as the predicted good group, and those who are rejected are renamed the predicted bad group. However this decision process requires not just a risk scorecard but also a cut-off score, so that those with scores above the cut-off will be the predicted goods and so are accepted and those with scores below the cut-off will be the predicted bads and so rejected.

Confusion matrix

This decision problem has thus become analogous to a simple hypothesis testing problem. The applicant population is split into two groups – 'goods' and 'bads' – and the decisions of the scoring system can be reinterpreted as predictions of the group to which an individual belongs. Those who are accepted are chosen because it is predicted that they are good while the others are rejected because they are predicted to be bad. Thus the results of these scorecard decisions applied to a population of n applicants can be represented in a table of predicted class type against actual class type called *the confusion matrix*. With only two classes – goods and bads – the confusion matrix reduces to a 2×2 table of numbers (Table 2.6.1). In the table $n_G = g_G + b_G$ is the actual number of goods in the population or sample of the population considered and $n_B = g_B + b_B$ is the number of bads.

It is illuminating to write the confusion matrix in terms of the underlying score distributions – $F(s|G)$ and $F(s|B)$ – the fractions of the goods and the bads, respectively, who have scores of s or less. One immediately realizes this can only be

TABLE 2.6.1. Confusion matrix.

	Actual goods	Actual bads	Predicted numbers
Predicted goods	g_G	g_B	g
Predicted bads	b_G	b_B	b
Actual numbers	n_G	n_B	

TABLE 2.6.2. Confusion matrix in terms of underlying probabilities.

	Actual goods	Actual bads	Percentage so predicted
Predicted goods	$p_G F^c(s_c|G)$	$p_B F^c(s_c|B)$	$F^c(s_c)$
Predicted bads	$p_G F(s_c|G)$	$p_B F(s_c|B)$	$F(s_c)$
Actual percentage	p_G	p_B	

done if we also define what is the cut-off score s_c and also what are the proportions of goods and bads in the underlying population, which we defined as p_G, p_B, respectively. With this notation the confusion matrix is given by the cell values in Table 2.6.2.

It is then clear that these categorical prediction measures do need knowledge of the cut-off score and the population odds, and cannot be recovered from any of the discrimination measures. The proportion of actual goods and bads are of course those of the underlying probabilities p_G, p_B, while it is the cut-off s_c that determines the numbers of predicted goods and bads $F^c(s_c), F(s_c)$, respectively.

Type I and Type II errors, sensitivity, and specificity

Using the analogy with hypothesis testing (where the null hypothesis would be that the borrower is 'good'), the prediction errors are given by the numbers in the off diagonal cells of the confusion matrix. Thus a Type I error is when the hypothesis is true and the system predicts otherwise. Hence here a Type I error is when the system classifies as bad a good applicant, that is, the bottom left cell. The probability of this error is b_G/n_G, which is the proportion of the actual goods who are predicted as bad. Similarly a Type II error is when the hypothesis is false (that is the applicant is bad) and the system predicts it is true (that is the applicant is good). This corresponds to the top right cell and the chance of this error is g_B/n_B, which is the proportion of the actual bads who are predicted as good.

In any population or population sample n_G and n_B are fixed and so there are only really two variables that can vary in the 2×2 table and these will then fix the others since $g_G/n_G + b_G/n_G = 1$ and $g_B/n_B + b_B/n_B = 1$. The error rates b_G/n_G and g_B/n_B are one way of describing the two variables but in other contexts other terminology has been used to describe these fractions, and other pairs of variables are sometimes used. All have been used in on some occasions in the credit scoring

TABLE 2.6.3. Position of different measures in the confusion matrix.

	Actual goods	Actual bads
Predicted goods	Significance, confidence level, specificity	Type II error
Predicted bads	Type I error	Power, sensitivity

context. A summary of the terms is as follows:

$$\text{Proportion goods predicted as good} \equiv \text{significance} \equiv \text{confidence level}$$
$$\equiv \text{specificity} = g_G/n_G \equiv F^c(s_c|G)$$
$$\text{Proportion of goods predicted as bad} \equiv \text{Type I error} = b_G/n_G \equiv F(s_c|G)$$
$$\text{Proportion of bads predicted as bad} \equiv \text{power} \equiv \text{sensitivity}$$
$$= b_B/n_B \equiv F(s_c|B)$$
$$\text{Proportion of bads predicted as good} \equiv \text{Type II error} = g_B/n_B$$
$$\equiv F^c(s_c|B) \tag{2.6.1}$$

Note that these measurements are not functions of the underlying Population Odds, which was needed to calculate the confusion matrix. These measures do though depend on the cut-off score s_c.

In terms of the confusion matrix, Table 2.6.3 shows which cells are needed to calculate these different measures.

Let us now see these measures applied to a numerical example.

Example 2.6.1 Confusion matrix and error rates using Appendix A data

Taking the data from the scorecard in Appendix A suppose it is decided that a score of 299 is the cut-off point so those on 299 or above will be accepted. The confusion matrix is then that in Table 2.6.4.

This would give the following statistics:

Significance $\equiv$ confidence level $\equiv$ specificity $= 3798/18134 = 75.7\%$.

Type I error $= 4426/18134 = 24.3\%$. $\tag{2.6.2}$

Power $\equiv$ sensitivity $= 765/883 = 86.6\%$.

Type II error $= 118/883 = 13.4\%$.

With a total error of $(4436 + 118)/19117 = 23.82\%$.

To show that these statistics can vary for the same scorecard depending on the cut-off, we repeat the calculation but this time taking a cut-off score of 251. This

TABLE 2.6.4. Confusion Matrix using Appendix A data with 299 cut-off.

	Actual Goods		Number so predicted
Predicted Goods	13798	118	13916
Predicted Bads	4436	765	5201
Actual numbers	18134	883	19117

TABLE 2.6.5. Confusion Matrix using Appendix A data with 251 cut-off.

	Actual Goods	Actual Bads	Number so predicted
Predicted Goods	17282	424	17706
Predicted Bads	952	459	1411
Actual numbers	18234	883	19117

leads to the confusion matrix in Table 2.6.5.

The error and related statistics would then be

Significance $\equiv$ confidence level $\equiv$ specificity $= 17282/18234 = 94.8\%$.

Type I error $= 952/18234 = 5.2\%$. 　　　　　　　　　　　　　　(2.6.3)

Power $\equiv$ sensitivity $= 459/883 = 52.0\%$.

Type II error $= 424/883 = 48.0\%$.

With a total error of $(952+424)/19117 = 7.20\%$.

As we emphasized in Section 2.1 to get unbiased estimators for these error rates the confusion matrix should be built on a holdout sample and not on the training sample. One should find that the errors on the training sample are less than those on the holdout sample and if there is too great a difference in these errors it suggests that the scorecard has been over-fitted. This over optimism if one tests on the development or training sample and the consequent need for a hold out or test sample occurs with all the measures discussed in this chapter.

Swap sets

Comparing the two cut-offs in Example 2.6.1 it is tempting to prefer the 251 cut-off system to the 299 one because the total error rate in Eq. (2.6.3) is so much smaller than that in Eq. (2.6.2). However, it really depends on the importance of the two types of errors. One way of understanding the difference between two predictions is to look at the swap set – how many of the sample are predicted differently by the two systems. Comparing the two predictions in Tables 2.6.4 and 2.6.5 leads to the swap set matrix in Table 2.6.6.

TABLE 2.6.6. Swap set matrix.

	Actual good	Actual bad
Predicted good by 151 cut-off and bad by 199 cut-off	3484	306
Predicted bad by 151 cut-off and good by 199 cut-off	0	0

TABLE 2.6.7. Swap set matrix for comparing two scorecards.

	Actual good	Actual bad
Predicted good by Scorecard A and bad by Scorecard B	400	50
Predicted bad by Scorecard A and good by Scorecard B	130	20

Thus one should prefer the 251 cut-off score, only if one believes the extra 3484 goods in the portfolio compensates for the extra 306 bads, that is, the profit from 11.4 goods is enough compensation for the losses from 1 bad.

If one is only changing cut-offs then the predictions can only go one way in that some predicted goods at the lower cut-off will be predicted bad at the higher one and so the swap sets will not have anything in one of the possible swaps. One can use swap sets to compare different scorecards and then it is usual for changes to go both ways, that is, some predicted goods under scorecard A will be predicted bad by scorecard B and vice versa. A typical swap sets in this case would look like Table 2.6.7.

In this case $400 + 50 - 130 - 20 = 300$ more borrowers are predicted good under scorecard A than B. Of these $400 - 130 = 270$ are good and $50 - 20 = 30$ are bad and so A would be preferred to B if 270 extra goods in the portfolio compensate for the extra 30 bads in the portfolio.

Minimum cost errors

Measuring the categorical predictions by using the confusion matrix leads to reporting two independent values of the matrix, from which the other two values can be calculated. So one can define the categorical prediction by Type I and Type II errors, or by the sensitivity and specificity. However, it is a lot easier to decide on how good something is if one only has one measurement to consider. So is it possible to combine the two measures into one?

Recall that in Section 2.2 the KS statistic was shown to be the maximum value of the sensitivity plus the specificity minus one. Similarly in some hypothesis testing one is interested in the sum of the errors (Type I plus Type II). So here are two examples where one combines two of the measures. Sum of the errors though is an inappropriate measure for consumer risk assessment because the two types of errors are so different in cost. Predicting a bad to be a good means accepting a borrower who will default and so the bank will occur a loss of l. Predicting a good as a bad means rejecting a borrower who would have repaid satisfactorily and so will lose the profit of g which is made on good loans. In terms of the rate models introduced in Section 1.7, if the loan is 1, then the default loss will be $l_D + r_F$ the loss given default on the loan plus the risk-free rate which the money could have earned if it had not been lent to a defaulter. In this rate model, the profit if the loan is repaid is $r_L - r_F$, the extra of the lending rate on this loan compared with using it in a risk-free context. Apart from the psychological effect that one of the errors – rejecting those who would have repaid – cannot be seen by others in the organization, while the other – accepting those who default – will be obvious to everyone, the loss for a default is likely to be much higher than the profit for a repaid loan. So it is sensible to weight the errors and define a weighted cost of errors (WCE(C)) as follows:

$$\text{WCE}(C) = \frac{b_G}{n_G} + C\frac{g_B}{n_B}$$
$$= F(s_c|G) + CF^c(s_c|B) \qquad (2.6.4)$$

Note that this cost varies as the cut-off s_c varies but if one wanted to minimize the cost WCE(C) for a given value of C by choosing the optimal cut-off that would be when the marginal odds are $p_G C/p_B$. This can be seen by differentiating Eq. (2.6.4) with respect to s_c and setting the derivative equal to zero so that

$$f(s_c|G) - Cf(s_c|B) = 0 \Rightarrow o(s_c|G) = \frac{P(s_c|G)}{P(s_c|B)} = \frac{p_G f(s_c|G)}{p_B f(s_c|B)} = \frac{p_G}{p_B}C \quad (2.6.5)$$

Normally one does not know the exact costs of defaults or lost profits and so it pays to calculate WCE(C) for a number of different values of C. If one can choose $C = l p_B/g p_G$ or in the rate models $C = (l_D + r_F) p_B/(r_L - r_F) p_G$ then the resultant WEC for any scorecard and any cut-off is proportional to the drop in the expected profits that will occur under that scorecard with that cut-off score compared with the profits which would accrue with a perfect categorical forecast, $E[P_{\text{perfect}}] - E[P]$.

$$E[P_{\text{perfect}}] - E[P] = g p_G F(s_c|G) + l p_B F^c(s_c|B) = g p_G \times \text{WCE}\left(\frac{l p_B}{g p_G}\right) \qquad (2.6.6)$$

In terms of the rate models, this is

$$E[P_{\text{perfect}}] - E[P] = (r_L - r_F) p_G F(s_c|G) + (l_D + r_F) p_B F^c(s_c|B)$$
$$= (r_L - r_F) p_G \times \text{WCE}\left(\frac{(l_D + r_F) p_B}{(r_L - r_F) p_G}\right) \qquad (2.6.7)$$

3

Risk-based pricing

3.1 Variable pricing in consumer lending

The title of this chapter is a misnomer in that though risk-based pricing is what the strategy of offering varying loan terms to different borrowers is called in the consumer lending industry, this 'price' is rarely set just by the riskiness of the loan. Thus variable pricing is a more appropriate generic description. The riskiness of the loan is usually factored into the cost of the loan and the price is set by the banks with reference to their overall objectives of maximizing expected profit, return on capital, or market share. In consumer lending the 'price' of a loan is taken to be the interest rate charged by the lender to the borrower, though as we will see in Section 3.5 it can also encompass other features of the loan.

In looking at the history of consumer credit, it is surprising for how long there was near unanimity between lenders on the price they charged for a loan or a mortgage or the interest rates they applied to credit cards. Moreover these prices were charged to all the banks' customers, irrespective of their circumstances or credit history. It was as if consumer lending was a commodity. This normally requires that borrowers have full knowledge of all loans, and are indifferent from which lender to borrow, and so always choose the lender with the lowest interest rate. It also requires that each lender is so small relative to the whole market that they could not individually affect the interest rate being charged in the market. Whether these conditions really held is problematic but the result was that there was little variation in interest rates charged. The banks used application scoring to determine the default risk of each applicant and determined whether at the prevailing market 'price' it was profitable to lend to that applicant. If it was, the loan was offered; if not the loan was not offered.

Variable pricing

Since the early 1990s, though, banks have recognized that they can improve their profitability by segmenting the population and offering different loan terms to each segment. More recently the development of the internet and the telephone as channels for loan applications has made that offer process private to each individual. This allows the offers to be customized so that in principle a different offer could

TABLE 3.1.1. Interest rates for £5000 unsecured loan with repayments over 3 years advertised on moneysupermarket.com on 11 September 2007.

Company	APR rate advertised (%)
Yourpersonalloan.co.uk	6.3
Bradford and Bingley	6.7
GE Money	6.9
Sainsbury	7.1
Northern Rock	7.4
Royal Bank of Scotland	7.8
Nat West Bank	8.0
Halifax	8.7
Nationwide Building Society	8.9
Intelligent Finance	9.7
Tesco	9.9
Lloyds TSB	11.4
Autocredit	16.7
Citi Finance	23.1
Provident	177.0

be made by a bank to each borrower who applies for a loan. Thus the move by banks from the objective of minimizing the default risk of a loan portfolio to that of maximizing the profitability of the portfolio has led to much more variety in the loan products being offered and to the interest rate, the 'price', being charged for them. For example Table 3.1.1 shows the rates being advertised on an internet broker for unsecured personal loans of £5000 to be repaid over 3 years.

There are many competitors in the market place ranging from retailers (Tesco, Sainsbury) to specialist internet banks (Intelligent Finance). Provident is a subprime lender whose rates reflect not only the risk of its customer base but also the cost of its weekly door-to-door collection strategy.

Even with one lender and one product, discounting the interest rate depending on the size of the loan, the circumstances of the borrower, and the default risk involved is becoming common. In fact in mortgage lending, UK lenders have got themselves into a position where new customers are offered better rates than existing ones, and so churn is being encouraged. When one of the leading lenders, Nationwide, sought in 2001 to offer the same rate to everyone, it lost market share so rapidly that it gave up the idea. Thus borrowers and banks are locked into a counter-intuitive system of discounting rates initially in the loan, even though default risk goes down as the loan ages, and lenders have started raising the costs of arrangement fees for mortgages to make them profitable. In most consumer lending products, though, the differences in rates charged on the same loan product seem more logical and are based on the apparent default risks involved.

Phillips (2005) in his excellent book on pricing outlines a number of reasons why the same product can be sold at different prices. Channel pricing, group pricing, regional pricing, and product versioning are ways that one can 'price' loans and credit cards at different rates.

In channel pricing, the loan is given a different interest rate depending on whether it is obtained via the internet, the telephone, a branch network of via intermediaries such as independent financial advisors. One reason for this difference would be the cost. For example running a branch network and training all the staff involved in the selling of the loan product is more expensive than supporting an internet or a call centre system. Intermediaries usually receive a commission on the sale of the loan, which has to be factored into the price. The psychology of consumers in buying financial products is fascinating. In the UK consumers using financial advisors are given the choice of paying the advisors who will not then be allowed to take a commission on the sale of any product, or not paying the advisors but allowing them to suggest products on which they get sales commissions. The overwhelming majority of consumers choose the latter course with its obvious conflicts of interest on the advisor. Channel pricing is not all about cost though in that there also occurs self-segmentation. Those who use the internet to apply for loan products are likely to have more knowledge of the other 'prices' in the market and to be more price sensitive than consumers using other application channels.

In group pricing, the same product is offered at different prices to different groups of borrowers. For group pricing to work, the groups must be unambiguously defined, some groups must be more price sensitive than others, and the groupings must be culturally and legally acceptable. The last is a problem in consumer lending where there are legal requirements in many countries on what characteristics can be used to discriminate who gets a loan and by implication the interest rate charged on the loan. However, discriminating in favour of existing customers of a bank is usually acceptable as is lending to students at advantageous rates, because of their expected enhanced customer lifetime value. In the USA where borrowers can easily obtain their generic credit risk score, such as their FICO score, it is becoming common to group according to this score.

Regional pricing occurs when there are legal ceilings on the rates that can be charged on loans, such as occur in some US states, but geographical differences in the rates charged occur mostly between countries and reflect the differences in the underlying risk-free interest rates (Japan) or differences in the default rates in the whole population (Brazil).

Product versioning occurs when extra services are added, or removed, from a loan product. This is clearest in the credit card market, where the basic credit card was enhanced into silver, gold, and platinum cards, by increasing the credit limits allowed, and adding discounts on travel or attendance at prestigious events. Similarly American Express has a range of cards including the Centurion or Black

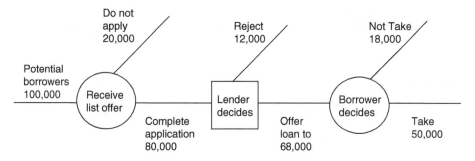

FIG. 3.1.1. Decision tree and volumes of application process with list pricing.

card, with its concierge services, though in their case the price differential is more in the annual fee charged than in the nominal interest rate.

These are examples of variable pricing within a list pricing model. The bank decides what interest rate, and possibly what annual fee to offer on each product to each group of borrowers through each application channel. The prospective borrower comes across the offer and decides whether to apply for it. When the application process has determined whether the borrower's default risk is acceptable to the bank, the bank makes the formal offer of the loan to the borrower, who then decides whether to take or not take the offer. Figure 3.1.1 shows this sequence and a hypothetical example of the numbers of applicants involved at each stage. One problem with quantifying this process is that recording accurately the number of consumers who show any interest in the loan depends on the application channel used. Thus potential borrowers who rung up for an initial 'ballpark figure' quote of the cost of the loan and then do not continue to give their details as part of an application process are probably recorded, while those who ask for similar information at a branch of the bank are probably not recorded. We will define the population of potential borrowers as those who, or whose agents, have interacted with the bank in a way that displays their interest in the loan product.

Figure 3.1.1 can be thought of as a decision tree from the bank's perspective, since whether potential borrowers complete the application process or complete it but then do not take up the offer are chance events as far as the bank is concerned. The numbers in the figure are arbitrary but are closer to those in mortgage offers – where take rates are often below acceptance rates and there are lots of incomplete applications – than of credit cards or personal loans.

Customized pricing

Banks have recognized in the past few years that telephone or internet application channels give the opportunity for customized pricing in that each application process is a private transaction between the bank and the potential borrower. Thus

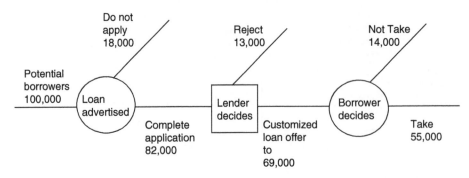

F<small>IG</small>. 3.1.2. Decision tree and volumes of application process with customized pricing.

the bank may be able to increase the take rate by customizing the offer made to each applicant. This customization may involve adjusting the price – a discount on the interest rate originally advertised – or may mean modifying the product some-what – adding the opportunity to collect Air Miles, or removing the usual annual fee charged; whatever is more attractive to that particular applicant. So for customized pricing the application process and the numbers going through the various stages will change from those in Fig. 3.1.1 to those in Fig. 3.1.2.

In Fig. 3.1.2, a few more potential borrowers will complete the application form because there is a promise of a possible discount of the original offer. Some of these extra applicants will be refused on default risk grounds. The real advantage then comes in the increased take rate which becomes 55,000/69,000 = 80% compared with the previous 50,000/69,000 = 73%.

Take probability and response rate

A fundamental quantity in the analysis of what price to set for any product is the price–response function – how much the demand for a product varies as the price varies. In the consumer loan context this can be reinterpreted as the probability $q(r, \mathbf{o}, \mathbf{x})$ that a borrower with characteristics $\mathbf{x}$ will take, that is will accept, the offer of a loan with interest rate r, and other features $\mathbf{o}$ made by a bank. Note we will always define the interest rate r as what the interest paid in the period is as a fraction of the loan so an interest rate of 4% per period will be represented by $r = 0.04$. We distinguish between take and not take, which is the borrower accepting or not accepting the loan from the lender, and accept and reject, which is whether the lender will or will not make the loan offer to the borrower.

In Section 1.5 we mentioned that one could score the likelihood of a con-sumer responding or taking a loan offer in the same way as scoring their chance of subsequently repaying the loan. So a response scores is a 'sufficient statistic' that allowed the lender to estimate $q(r,\mathbf{o},\mathbf{x})$ or in the case of a log odds score $\log\left(q(r,\mathbf{o},\mathbf{x})/1 - q(r,\mathbf{o},\mathbf{x})\right)$ as a function of the borrower's characteristics and possibly the offer characteristics as well. We have to be slightly careful here because the response scores tend to be used in the context of mailing information about the loan products and is often taken as the percentage of those who respond to the mailing. In these cases the vast majority of those who respond and are then made the offer of a loan will in fact take it. Since the response rate of those who fill in the mailed application form is usually so low and the subsequent take rate among those made the offer is really high, one can take the response rate as a good surrogate of the take probability. In Fig. 3.1.3 we look at some typical figures for such a mailing.

The response rate is 2% and if we consider what the take rate would be as a percentage of the mailed population it would be either 1.98% (assuming the take rate among the rejects would be the same as among the accepts) or 1.985% (if we assumed all the rejected applicants would have taken the offer if it had been made to them). Thus the difference in this case between the response rate and the take probability is small.

We will call $q(r,\mathbf{o},\mathbf{x})$ both the take probability and the response rate function interchangeably, using the latter description even in the non-mailing context. This take probability is a function of the interest rate r charged and other offer characteristics $\mathbf{o}$. It is also a function of the characteristics $\mathbf{x}$ of the borrower, particularly the probability p of the borrower being a good as far as default behaviour is concerned. Defining it as the take probability makes it clear what $q(\cdot)$ really is, while describing it as the response rate function reflects its relationship with the price-response functions in general pricing problems. When dealing with customized pricing so that the offer characteristics $\mathbf{o}$ are chosen so as to maximize the take probability, we will refer to $q(r,\mathbf{o},\mathbf{x})$ as the acceptance probability. We will look at this problem in more detail in Section 3.5.

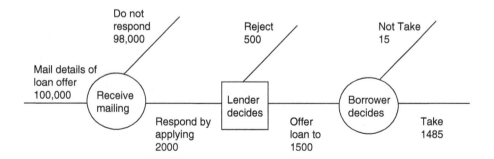

FIG. 3.1.3. Decision tree and volumes of mailing application process.

Two tier pricing

We close this section by looking at the simplest example of variable pricing where the bank will only charge one of two interest rates r_1 or $r_2, r_1 < r_2$ on a loan. Assume $q_1 = q(r_1)$ and $q_2 = q(r_2)$ are the respective response rates to the loans and that $q_1 \geq q_2$. The profit and losses on the loan are given using the rate notation model of Fig. 1.7.1. Assume the risk-free rate at which the money is borrowed is r_F and the loss given default on any loan is l_D irrespective of the rate charged. Consider a potential borrower whose probability of being good is p. The expected pay-offs under the three actions of (a) rejecting the borrower, (b) offering the borrower a loan at a rate r_1, or (c) offering the loan at the rate r_2 are

$$\begin{array}{lll} \text{Reject} & 0 & \\ \text{Offer at } r_1 & q_1(r_1 p - l_D(1-p)) - r_F) & (3.1.1) \\ \text{Offer at } r_2 & q_2(r_2 p - l_D(1-p)) - r_F) & \end{array}$$

where it is assumed the probability of the borrower being good is independent of the loan rate (this is not always true but is a reasonable assumption if r_1 and r_2 are not too different). So the expected profit on such an account $E[P_A]$ satisfies

$$E[P_A] = \max\{0, q_1((r_1 - r_F)p - (l_D + r_F)(1-p)),$$
$$q_2((r_2 - r_F)p - (l_D + r_F)(1-p))\}. \quad (3.1.2)$$

Figure 3.1.4 shows how these three functions vary as p varies. If the bank only made offers at the r_1 rate, the bank would accept the borrower provided:

$$p > p_1 \quad \text{where} \quad \frac{p_1}{1 - p_1} = \frac{r_F + l_D}{r_1 - r_F}. \quad (3.1.3)$$

Similarly, if the bank only made offers at the r_2 rate, the bank would accept the borrower provided:

$$p > p_2 \quad \text{where} \quad \frac{p_2}{1 - p_2} = \frac{r_F + l_D}{r_2 - r_F}. \quad (3.1.4)$$

Since $r_1 < r_2$ the good:bad odds at which the lender would accept borrowers for loans at interest rate r_2 is less than that at which the lender would accept borrowers for the loan at interest rate r_1 and so $p_2 < p_1$. So for any borrower with probability p of being a good where $p_2 \leq p < p_1$ then the bank should offer the loan at rate r_2. In fact, it should keep offering the loan at rate r_2 until the offer at rate r_2 line crosses the offer at rate r_1 line in Fig. 3.1.4 which is at a probability of p_{12} where

$$q_1((r_1 + l_D)p_{12} - (l_D + r_F)) = q_2((r_2 + l_D)p_{12} - (l_D + r_F))$$
$$\Rightarrow p_{12} = \frac{(q_1 - q_2)(l_D + r_F)}{(q_1 - q_2)l_D + q_1 r_1 - q_2 r_2}. \quad (3.1.5)$$

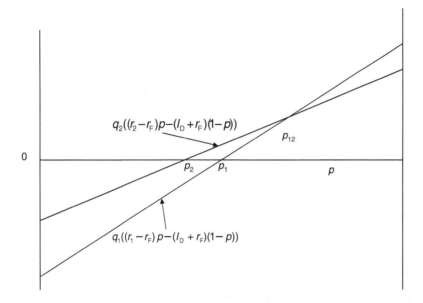

FIG. 3.1.4. Three function in Eq. (3.1.2).

Note that if $q_1(r_1 - r_F) \geq q_2(r_2 - r_F)$ then $p_{12} \leq 1$ and so there will be a group of borrowers whose probability of being good p satisfies $p \geq p_{12}$ who should be offered the loan at rate r_1 because the chance they will accept the loan at rate r_1 is so much more than that of then accepting the loan at rate r_2, that it more than compensates for the drop in the profit if the interest rate is r_1. Notice that the region where the low rate should be offered changes from $p \geq p_1$ to $p \geq p_{12}$. If, on the other hand, $q_1(r_1 - r_F) < q_2(r_2 - r_F)$, all borrowers with probability of being good greater than p_2 should be offered the loan at rate r_2 and no one is offered the loan at the lower rate.

If there were three rates at which the loan could be offered, then the result could be to offer the loan at all three rates to different groups or to offer only two rates (one of which would be the highest rate) or possibly just offer the highest rate to everyone.

Example 3.1.1

Assume the bank is offering a loan at interest rates of 8% and 10% where the interest-free rate is 6% and the losses given default on the loans are $l_D = 0.5$. If 60% of the potential population accepted the offer at an interest rate of 8% and 40% of the population accept the loan offer when it has the 10% interest rate, then as a function of p, the probability of the borrower being good, the expected profits are

$$0 \qquad\qquad \text{if no offer made}$$

$$0.6(0.08p - 0.5(1 - p) - 0.06) \quad \text{if 8\% interest rate was offered}$$

$$0.4(0.1p - 0.5(1 - p) - 0.06) \quad \text{if 10\% interest rate was offered.}$$

Then

$$\frac{p_1}{1 - p_1} = \frac{0.5 + 0.06}{0.08 - 0.06} = \frac{0.56}{0.02} = 28 \Rightarrow p_1 = \frac{28}{29} = 0.97$$

$$\frac{p_2}{1 - p_2} = \frac{0.5 + 0.06}{0.1 - 0.06} = \frac{0.56}{0.04} = 14 \Rightarrow p_2 = \frac{14}{15} = 0.93 \qquad (3.1.6)$$

$$p_{12} = \frac{(0.6 - 0.4)(0.5 + 0.06)}{(0.6 - 0.4)0.5 + 0.6 \times 0.08 - 0.4 \times 0.1} = \frac{0.112}{0.108} > 1.$$

This last result follows since $q_1(r_1 - r_F) = 0.6(0.08 - 0.06) = 0.012 < q_2(r_2 - r_F) = 0.4(0.1 - 0.06) = 0.016$. So the bank should only offer the loan at 10% rate and then to those whose probability of being good exceeds 93%.

If on the other hand, 90% of the potential population would accept the 8% interest rate offer then

$$q_1(r_1 - r_F) = 0.9(0.08 - 0.06) = 0.018 \geq q_2(r_2 - r_F) = 0.4(0.1 - 0.06) = 0.016$$

and so

$$p_{12} = \frac{(0.9 - 0.4)(0.5 + 0.06)}{(0.9 - 0.4)0.5 + 0.9 \times 0.08 - 0.4 \times 0.1} = \frac{0.28}{0.282} = 0.993 \qquad (3.1.7)$$

So in this case the lender should offer the 10% interest rate to those whose probability of being good is between 93% and 99.3% while those who chance of being good is greater than 99.3% should be given the 8% offer.

3.2   Risk-free response rate function and optimal pricing

Risk-free response rate

In this section we concentrate on the situation where the take probability $q(\cdot)$ depends only on the interest rate, r, charged on the loan. Thus the characteristics of the borrower and in particular the chance they will default on the loan does not affect the likelihood they will take a particular loan. We assume the interest rate r charged can be any positive value from 0 to ∞, though we will on occasions add in conditions that $r \geq r_F$ where r_F is the risk-free rate and $r \leq r_M$ where r_M is a maximum allowable rate that some countries impose to avoid usurious rates.

The following assumptions are made about the response rate function (the take probability function):

- $0 \leq q(r) \leq 1$, since $q(.)$ is a probability and we always assume $q(\infty) = 0$, so the lender can always find an interest rate r which no one will accept the loan.

- $q(r)$ is monotonic non-increasing in r so that as the interest rate increases, the take probability, which can be interpreted as the fraction of the population taking the loan, will stay the same or decrease.

- $q(r)$ is continuous in r, if r is continuous, though in many cases the bank will only set a finite number of possible interest rates for a given loan product. However, this assumption makes the analysis of the models easier as does the last assumption.

- $q(r)$ is differentiable in r. This has the same caveats as requiring $q(r)$ to be continuous but means one can use calculus in the models. In particular the monotone non-increasing property means that

$$\frac{dq(r)}{dr} = q'(r) \leq 0 \tag{3.2.1}$$

Elasticity

The elasticity of the response rate function or take probability to interest rate measures the sensitivity if the fraction of the takes to changes in the interest rate. The take elasticity is the ratio of the percentage change in the take probability to the percentage change in the interest rate charged:

$$\varepsilon(r_1) = - \lim_{r_2 \to r_1} \frac{q(r_2) - q(r_1)/q(r_1)}{(r_2 - r_1)/r_1} = \frac{-q'(r_1)r_1}{q(r_1)} \tag{3.2.2}$$

where the minus sign is there because the change in the take probability goes in the opposite direction to the change in the interest rate. $\varepsilon(r)$ gives the relative percentage drop in the current chance of a borrower taking a loan if the relative interest rate on the loan goes up by 1%.

Example 3.2.1

If the current interest rate on a loan is 5% and 60% of the applicants take the loan, then if the elasticity of the take rate is $\varepsilon(0.05) = 4$, then changing the interest rate to 5.05% (a 1% relative increase in the rate 0 the fraction taking the loan will drop to 57.6% (that is a drop of 2.4% which is a relative drop of 4% = 4 × 1% of the current take fraction of 60%).

Maximum willingness to pay

An alternative way of thinking of the take probability is to describe what fraction of the interest population (the potential borrowers) would accept the loan at various interest rates. Inherent in this idea is that each potential borrower has a maximum rate at which they are willing to take the loan (their reservation price). So a borrower with a maximum willingness to pay of 8% would accept a loan if the interest rate was 7.5% but would not take the loan of the interest rate was 10%. Someone with a willingness to pay of 0% is not interested in borrowing at any interest rate level (despite some lenders advertising 0% interest rate loans). Let $w(r)$ be the density function of this maximum willingness to pay across the population of potential borrowers, then

$$\int_{r_1}^{\infty} w(r)dr \equiv \text{Fraction of population willing to pay } r_1 \text{ or more} \equiv q(r_1). \quad (3.2.3)$$

Note that $q'(r) = -w(r)$ since only those with a maximum willingness to pay of exactly r will turn down the loan if the interest rate goes up by an infinitesimal amount above r.

Common response rate functions

Banks can estimate response rate functions if they are willing to experiment with different interest rates and record whether potential borrowers did take the loan at the offered rate. Experience suggests that the resultant function will have a reverse S-shape, as in Fig. 3.2.1, which is an example of a particular type of response rate function. There is a high probability of a borrower taking the loan offer if the interest rate on the loan is very low; only a slight probability of the borrower taking the offer if the interest rate is high; and in between an interval of rates where the elasticity of the response rate function is very high. The simplest response rate function with some of these properties is the linear response rate

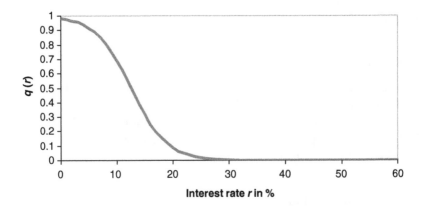

FIG. 3.2.1. Logistic response rate function with $a = 4, b = 32$.

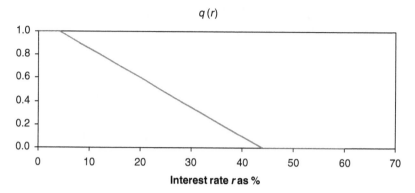

FIG. 3.2.2. Linear response rate function with $r_L = 0.04$ and $b = 2.5$.

function:

$$q(r) = \max\{0, 1 - b(r - r_L)\} \text{ for } r \geq r_L > 0 \qquad (3.2.4)$$

where the interest rates that can be charged can be bounded above by $r_M = r_L + 1/b$ since $q(r_M) = 0$ and no borrower will take the loan. This is an easy response rate function to work with and vaguely resembles the reverse S-shape as Fig. 3.2.2 shows but is not very realistic because of the form of the elasticity.

The elasticity of the linear response rate function is

$$\varepsilon(r) = \frac{-q'(r)r}{q(r)} = \frac{-br}{1 - b(r - r_L)} = 1 - \frac{1}{1 - \dfrac{br}{1 + br_L}} \quad \text{for } r_L \leq r \leq r_M; \text{ 0 elsewhere} \quad (3.2.5)$$

and so there are discontinuities in the elasticity at rates r_L and r_M.

The maximum willingness to pay of the linear response rate function is a uniform distribution on $[r_L, r_M]$ since $w(r) = -q'(r) = b$ for $r_L \leq r \leq r_M$; 0 elsewhere.

We found in Sections 1.5 and 1.9 that the logistic function played a vital role in estimating the default risk of a borrower and led to the idea of a log odds score. Exactly the same function can be used to estimate the response rate of potential borrowers as a function of the interest rate charged.

The logit (or logistic) response rate function satisfies:

$$q(r) = \frac{e^{a-br}}{1 + e^{a-br}} \Leftrightarrow \ln\left(\frac{q(r)}{1 - q(r)}\right) = a - br \equiv s_{\text{response}}. \qquad (3.2.6)$$

This shows that the log odds of take:not take are linear in the interest rate charged. If we think of this as a response score, then this response score is just a linear function of the response rate. We take the gradient to be $-b$ since the take probability will go down as the interest rate charged goes up. The logit response rate function has the reverse S-shape which is considered the appropriate shape.

Figure 3.2.1 is an example of Eq. (3.2.6) with $a = 4$ and $b = 32$. The corresponding elasticity and willingness to pay are

$$\varepsilon(r) = \frac{-q'(r)r}{q(r)} = \frac{br}{1 + e^{a-br}} = br(1 - q(r))$$

$$w(r) = -q'(r) = \frac{be^{a-br}}{(1 + e^{a-br})^2} = bq(r)(1 - q(r)). \tag{3.2.7}$$

This makes it clear that the parameter b is very closely related to price sensitivity and the larger it is the more sensitive to the interest rate is the population. The a parameter describes how likely the population is to take the loans at any price since the fraction who take a loan with interest rate 0% would be $1/1 + e^{-a}$. The willingness to pay distribution has a bell-shaped curve which is similar to a normal distribution but has fatter 'tails'. It is called the logistic distribution. The maximum of the willingness to pay distribution occurs at the rate $r = a/b$. Since $w(r) = -q'(r)$ this will also be the point at which the slope of the response rate function is greatest, whereas the linear response rate function has the same slope throughout.

Thus, the logit response rate function has more realistic properties than the linear one and so is used more frequently. The only disadvantage is that it means the acceptance rate is never quite 1 even if the interest rate charged is 0% and on the other hand never falls exactly to 0, even when the rate being charged is very high. If one wanted to ensure that the take probability is in fact 1 when the interest rate is at some given rate r_L one can always used a translated logistic response function. This is defined as follows:

$$q(r) = (1 + e^{-a})\left(\frac{e^{a-b(r-r_L)}}{1 + e^{a-b(r-r_L)}}\right) = \frac{e^{-b(r-r_L)} + e^{a-b(r-r_L)}}{1 + e^{a-b(r-r_L)}}$$

$$= \frac{1 + e^{-a}}{1 + e^{-a+b(r-r_L)}} \quad \text{for } r \geq r_L; 1 \text{ otherwise.} \tag{3.2.8}$$

This has the property that $q(r_L) = 1$ but the shape of response rate function is the same as the logistic response rate in the region above r_L apart from the multiplicative factor (see Fig. 3.2.3). The elasticity is that of the ordinary logistic response rate function case with the obvious translation from 0 to r_L, though this does mean it is not continuous at that rate. The maximum willingness to pay function

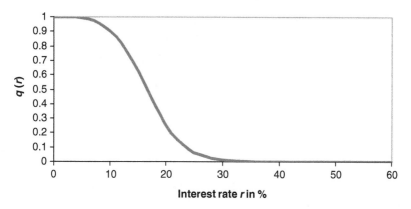

FIG. 3.2.3. Translated logit response rate function with $a = 4, b = 32, r_L = 0.04$.

has the distribution of a truncation logistic function as follows:

$$w(r) = -q'(r) = \frac{(1+e^{-a})be^{a-b(r-r_L)}}{(1+e^{a-b(r-r_L)})^2} = bq(r)\left(1 - \frac{q(r)}{1+e^{-a}}\right) \text{ for } r \geq r_L$$

$$\varepsilon(r) = \frac{-q'(r)r}{q(r)} = \frac{br}{1+e^{a-b(r-r_L)}} = br\left(1 - \frac{q(r)}{1+e^{-a}}\right). \qquad (3.2.9)$$

Optimal pricing

Having discussed the take probability or response rate function, we are in a position to find what is the optimal interest rate r that should be charged if the take probability is $q(r)$ which is assumed the same for all potential borrowers independent of their default risk. Again we use the rate model of Section 1.7. Assume the risk-free rate at which the money is borrowed is r_F and the loss given default on any loan is l_D irrespective of the rate charged. Consider a potential borrower or a segment of the population of potential borrowers whose credit scores suggest that their probability of being good is p, then as Fig. 3.2.4 suggests if they pay back the loan of one unit the profit from them is $(r - r_F)$ while if they default the losses including the loss of interest on the money lent is $(l_D + r_F)$. If the interest rate is r then the probability of take is $q(r)$, so one should choose the interest rate to charge to optimize the following expression for the expected profit:

$$\text{Max}_r E[P_A(r)] = (q(r)((r - r_F)p - (l_D + r_F)(1 - p))). \qquad (3.2.10)$$

This is the fraction, $q(r)$ of those taking the loan (or the probability of the one potential applicant) if the interest rate is r times the expected profit on each loan

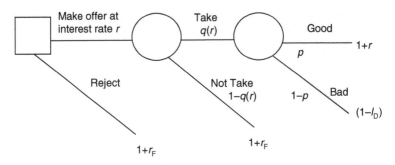

FIG. 3.2.4. Decision tree of variable rate lending decision with rate of return pay-offs.

taken. Differentiating (3.2.10) and setting the derivative to zero gives

$$q'(r)\left((r - r_F)p - (l_D + r_F)(1 - p)\right) + q(r)p = 0$$

$$\Rightarrow r = r_F - \frac{q(r)}{q'(r)} + \frac{(l_D + r_F)(1 - p)}{p} \tag{3.2.11}$$

$$\Rightarrow r = r_F - \frac{q(r)}{q'(r)} + (l_D + r_F)e^{-s}$$

where we assume that s is a log odds risk score such as those defined in Section 1.5 and so

$$s = \ln\left(\frac{p}{1 - p}\right).$$

Note that we can rewrite (3.2.11) as

$$q'(r)\left(rp - l_D(1 - p)\right) + q(r)p = r_F q'(r). \tag{3.2.12}$$

The left-hand side of Eq. (3.2.12) is the marginal decrease in the revenue if the interest rate is increased fractionally from r. The first term is the decrease in revenue because of the drop in the number who will take the loan as the interest rate increases while the second term is the increase in revenue because the interest rate is higher from those who will still take the loan. The right-hand side of Eq. (3.2.12) is the decrease in the cost of funding the loans because less will take the loan. Thus (3.2.12) says that at the optimal interest rate, the change in marginal revenue is equal to the change in marginal cost – a result which occurs in many contexts in pricing.

In terms of elasticity, we can rewrite the derivative of the profit, Eq. (3.2.11), as

$$q(r)\left[p + \frac{q'(r)}{q(r)}(rp - l_D(1-p))\right] - q'(r)r_F$$

$$= \frac{q(r)}{r}[pr - \varepsilon(r)(rp - l_D(1-p))] - q'(r)r_F. \qquad (3.2.13)$$

The last term here is always positive since $q'(r) < 0$, and so one should keep increasing the interest rate charged because it will keep increasing the profit, provided

$$\varepsilon(r) < \frac{pr}{pr - l_D(1-p)}. \qquad (3.2.14)$$

Thus provided the elasticity is below the ratio of the expected revenue ($pr - (1-p)l_D$) plus the expected losses ($l_D(1-p)$) to the expected profit, one can always keep increasing the interest rate charged and the expected revenue will increase.

Example 3.2.1 Optimal interest rate with linear response rate function

Consider the situation where the risk-free rate is 5% and the loss given default is 50%, so $l_D = 0.5$.

Assume the response function is linear with $r_L = 0.04, b = 2.5$, so $q(r) = \max\{0, 1 - 2.5(r - 0.04)\}$. This means that if the interest rate charged is 4% or less everyone will accept the loan; but if the interest rate is 44% then the take probability is zero. We can substitute these values into Eq. (3.2.11) so that the optimal rate r should satisfy

$$r = r_F - \frac{q(r)}{q'(r)} + \frac{(l_D + r_F)(1-p)}{p} = 0.05 + \frac{(1 - 2.5(r - 0.04))}{2.5} + \frac{0.55(1-p)}{p}$$

$$\Rightarrow 2r = 0.49 + \frac{0.55(1-p)}{p} \qquad (3.2.15)$$

provided r is in the range $0.04 \le r \le 0.44$. Solving this for different values of p gives the results in Table 3.2.1.

So the interest rate charged goes from 44% for those whose probability of being good is 58.5% (when $r = 0.44$ in Eq. (3.2.15)) down to 24.5% for those whose probability of being good is 1. The interest rate charged those with a lower than 58.5% chance of being good is above 44% and so deters all of them from taking the loan offered. The 24.5% interest rate charged to those who are bound to be good ($p = 1$) still means that only 48.8% of them will take the offer.

TABLE 3.2.1. Optimal interest rate for the linear response rate of Example 3.2.1.

Probability of being good, p	Optimal interest rate r as %	Take probability $q(r)$ as %
0.5	52.0	0
0.6	42.8	2.9
0.7	36.3	19.3
0.8	31.4	31.6
0.9	27.6	41.1
0.94	26.3	44.4
0.96	25.6	45.9
0.98	25.1	47.3
0.99	24.8	48.1
1.00	24.5	48.8

Example 3.2.2 Optimal interest rate with logit response rate function

Let us assume the same cost structure as in Example 3.2.1 with the risk-free rate being 5% and the loss given default l_D being 0.5. However, suppose the take probability or response rate function has the logistic form this time with $a = 4$ and $b = 32$ so

$$q(r) = \frac{e^{a-br}}{1 + e^{a-br}} = \frac{e^{4-32r}}{1 + e^{4-32r}} \Leftrightarrow \ln\left(\frac{q(r)}{1 - q(r)}\right) = 4 - 32r.$$

Thus the maximum willingness to pay is at $r = 4/32 = 0.125$ or a rate of 12.5%, while the fraction of the population who will accept a loan at 0% interest rate is $1/1 + e^{-4} = 0.982$. With this response rate function the optimal rate as a function of the probability p of the borrower being good is

$$r = r_F - \frac{q(r)}{q'(r)} + \frac{(l_D + r_F)(1 - p)}{p} = 0.05 + \frac{1 + e^{4-32r}}{32} + \frac{0.55(1 - p)}{p}.$$

$$(3.2.16)$$

The optimal interest rate appears on both sides of Eq. (3.2.16) and so one can find the value by using the methods for solving a non-linear equation such as the bisection or Newton–Raphson methods. The easiest way of solving non-linear equations is to use the Solver tool in Excel and this leads to the results in Table 3.2.2.

Now there is no upper limit on the interest rate charged but once it reaches 63% which is what is being charged to those with only a 0.5 chance of being good, the take rate is infinitesimally small. The logistic form of the response rate means the interest rate charged drops more quickly as the quality of the borrowers improves

TABLE 3.2.2. Optimal interest rate for the logistic response
rate of Example 3.2.2.

Probability of being good, p	Optimal interest rate r as %	Take probability $q(r)$ as %
0.5	63.1	0.000009
0.6	44.8	0.003
0.7	31.7	0.2
0.8	22.0	4.5
0.9	15.5	28.0
0.94	13.7	40.2
0.96	13.0	45.7
0.98	12.4	50.5
0.99	12.2	52.7
1.00	11.9	54.7

so that a rate of 11.9% is charged to those who are certain of being good ($p = 1$). That still means that only 54.7% of those borrowers will decide to take the loan at this rate.

These results make it clear that with variable pricing although there is no such thing as a cut-off score below which applicants are rejected, the effect of charging really high interest rates for those with low probabilities of being good, means that none or hardly any of them will actually take the loan. So de facto there is a cut-off. However, one has to be careful with this analysis because when a lender charges very high rates in reality there can sometimes be a surprise in that more borrowers accept the loan than might be anticipated. However, these are likely to be those borrowers who cannot get such a loan from any other lender and so are likely to be more risky than was expected. This is the phenomenon of adverse selection and we look at this in more detail in the next section.

3.3 Risk response relationship, adverse selection, and affordability

Risk response relationship

Assuming that the take probability $q(\cdot)$ is only a function of the interest rate r charged implies that the potential application population is essentially homogeneous in their response. This is not the case as those with high credit scores and so high probabilities p of being good are likely to be targeted by many more lenders than those with lower credit scores and so worse probabilities of being good. Hence the chance of the former taking a particular loan is likely to be lower.

To model this, assume an applicant with characteristics $\mathbf{x}$, has an application credit score of $s(\mathbf{x})$, which relates to the probability, p, of that applicant being a good. If the score is a log odds score, this relationship is $\ln\left(p/(1-p)\right) = s(\mathbf{x})$. To deal with the heterogeneity of the population define the take probability $q(r,p)$ as a function of the interest rate, r, charged and of the applicant's probability p of being good. This is equivalent to saying that the take probability $q(r,s)$ is a function of r and of s the credit score of the individual, which is how this probability of being good is really expressed in practice. We will normally express the take probability/response rate function as a function of r and p but in this section we also need to concentrate on $q(\cdot)$ as a function of interest rate r and credit score s as well so that we can point out where there are difficulties in moving from $q(r,p)$ to $q(r,s)$ and vice versa.

As in Section 3.2, it is reasonable to assume that $q(r,p)$ is monotonic non-increasing in the interest rate r, and differentiable in r if this condition is needed for analytic purposes. It is also reasonable to assume that $q(r,p)$ is also monotonic non-increasing in p. This reflects the idea that the better the quality of the potential borrowers (in terms of lower default risk), the less likely they are to take a loan at a given interest rate. This decrease in the response rate as p increases reflects the idea that the better the borrower, the more loan offers they will receive and the better the terms of these loans offered to them. Thus the better the borrower the more choosy they can be about whether to accept a particular loan and hence the lower the take probability. We will call this the risk response relationship.

Adverse selection

If one assumes that the take probability is a function of the quality of the applicant, then there is a second interaction between the quality of the applicant and the chance of them taking the loan, namely adverse selection. Adverse selection occurs when there is asymmetric information between the buyer and seller of a contract. The most obvious example is in insurance where a life insurance company knows about the mortality statistics for the whole population and so can price its insurance product using that information. However, the individuals who want to buy the life insurance know more about themselves and their individual health circumstance and can decide whether or not they are at greater risk than the general population. If they feel they are at more risk than the general population, they will buy the insurance while if they feel they are at less risk they will not. Smoking or not smoking is a good example of this and when life insurance companies did not ask questions about whether the individual smoked, this adverse selection meant the take up rate for life insurance should have been higher among smokers than non-smokers. Of course, the effect was mitigated because many of the smokers did not believe the impact of smoking on life expectation or did not wish to take out life insurance. A similar analysis was done for other products such as buying second-hand cars, where there are lemons (bad cars) and cherries (good cars). The sellers know the status of their car but the buyers do not, while the price in the market initially seeks to reflect the mix in the market between the two types. If this market price is above the worth of the lemon to a seller but below the worth of a cherry to the seller, then only lemons will be offered for sale and the 'bad' cars drive out the 'good' cars from the market. This is called Gresham's law.

In the personal loan context, the lender can estimate the probability p of the individual borrower being good, but this is done by using data on previous borrowers with similar characteristics and translates into the credit score s for that applicant. The potential borrowers know more about their particular circumstances – how likely are they to be made redundant in the immediate future, their general health and that of their family – and their attitudes to defaulting on a loan – how important is it to their self-esteem to avoid bankruptcy, or repossession of house or effects. What this means is that if one offers a loan at a particular rate, r, then using information from previous borrowers one might expect, the bad rate in the whole population for someone with credit score s to be $p(B|s)$. What adverse selection says is that if T is the event that a borrower actually takes a loan with interest rate r, then the bad rate among those taking the loan who have credit scores of s is $p(B|r,s,T)$.

$$p(B|r, s, T) > p(B|s). \tag{3.3.1}$$

This says that the bad rate among those taking the loan at rate r is likely to be worse than that among the whole population at the same credit score. Of course

$$p(B|s) = p(B|r, s, T)p(T|r, s) + p(B|r, s, N)p(N|r, s)$$
$$= p(B|r, s, T)q(r, s) + p(B|r, s, N)(1 - q(r, s)) \tag{3.3.2}$$

where N is the event that the borrower does not take the loan. From (3.3.2) one can see that $p(B|r, s, N) < p(B|s) < p(B|r, s, T)$. Since

$$p(G|s) = 1 - p(B|s); p(G|r, s, T) = 1 - p(B|r, s, T)$$

then $p(B|r, s, T) > p(B|s) \Rightarrow \ln \dfrac{p(G|r, s, T)}{p(B|r, s, T)} < \ln \dfrac{p(G|s)}{p(B|s)} = s.$ \hfill (3.3.3)

Thus the log odds at score s among the population who took the loan would be lower than that among the total population. How to deal with this is only now being considered by lenders and is sometimes called withdrawal inference. It seems a similar problem to the reject inference problem considered in Section 1.8 but in some ways it is more difficult to deal with. In reject inference one tried to estimate whether the applicants one rejected would have been good or bad. Here the difference between the two log ratios in Eq. (3.3.3) is because one does not know which of the not takes would have been good and which would have been bad. Whereas one can take some or all of the rejects and so solve the reject inference problem at a cost, how does one get the 'not takes' to accept a loan so one can see how they would have performed? Certainly one has to make the loan terms more attractive but even then the lender cannot force the borrower to take the loan.

Of course there is an argument that it does not matter, because for a specific loan product what one is interested in is the good:bad odds among the take population and that is what one can get data on. However that presupposes that the loan product used to build the scorecard has similar characteristics and hence a similar take population as the one on which the score is being applied. Moreover if one wants to apply variable interest rates on the same loan to different customers, it is highly unlikely that one had the same relationship of loan rate charged to credit score in the previous loans as that which one wants to apply now.

As Eq. (3.3.1) suggests, the bad rate among those who take the loan depends on the interest rate charged. What adverse selection suggests is that the higher the interest rate the more marked is the increase in the bad rate among those who take the loan. Increasing the interest rate is like dropping the market price in the second-hand car example and so less and less sellers with 'cherries' are willing to sell their car at that price. Here less and less of the people who, because of the stability of their circumstances and their aversion to being defaulters, recognize that they are highly likely to be goods will take a loan as the interest rate goes up. Thus we can extend the definition of adverse selection in (3.3.1) by saying that if there were two loans at interest rates $r_1, r_2, r_2 > r_1$ then

$$p(B|r_2, s, T) > p(B|r_1, s, T). \tag{3.3.4}$$

Equation (3.3.1) can be thought of as a special case of this if we assumed that everyone would take a loan where the interest rate is 0%. From Eq. (3.3.4) it immediately follows that the risk score obtained by using the take population on a loan depends on the interest rate being charged on the loan:

$$p(B|r_2, s, T) > p(B|r_1, s, T) \Rightarrow s(r_2) = \ln\frac{p(G|r_2, s, T)}{p(B|r_2, s, T)} < \ln\frac{p(G|r_1, s, T)}{p(B|r_1, s, T)} = s(r_1). \tag{3.3.5}$$

This suggests that in future the risk scores may need to include the interest rates of the credit cards or loans as a characteristic as these affect the performance of those in the sample used to build the risk scoring system. If one has a standard interest rate r_0 and one anchors the credit risk to the score $s_0(\mathbf{x})$ describing the performance of those with characteristics $\mathbf{x}$ on such a loan, then the simplest modification would be to define the score for the good:bad performance on a loan with interest rate r as

$$s(\mathbf{x}, r) = s_0(\mathbf{x}) - a(r - r_0), \quad a > 0. \tag{3.3.6}$$

So the score drops as the interest rate rises. Whether this is a major or minor and unimportant effect, time will tell as variable pricing becomes more established, and scorecards are built which recognize the different interest rates being charged.

Difference between risk response relationship and adverse selection

It is important to recognize that when one introduces a loan with a higher interest rate, both the risk response relationship and adverse selection work to increase the bad rate over that which might have been expected. However one should recognize and try to separate the two effects because often all the impact is put down to adverse selection, whereas the risk response relationship is making a significant change in the bad rate. We use a simple example to try and illustrate this.

Example 3.3.1 Impact of risk response and adverse selection on bad rates

Table 3.3.1 gives the number of potential borrowers in two different score bands 100–200 and 200–300 together with the numbers who take two different loans – one at 5% where there is no adverse selection and one at 10% where adverse selection does occur.

In the original population the good:bad odds are $100/40 = 2.5{:}1$ in 100–200 band and $300/60 = 5{:}1$ in the 200–300 band with overall population odds of $400/100 = 4{:}1$. With the 5% interest rate loan all that happens is that 90% of the lower band takes the loan and only 50% of the higher band does. The good:bad odds in each band stay as they were in the original population. The good:bad odds for the take population though have reduced to $250/66 = 3.64{:}1$. This decrease is purely down to the risk response relationship, in that a smaller fraction of higher band borrowers take the offer than lower band borrowers. It translates into the bad rate moving from $100/500 = 20\%$ in the original population to $66/306 = 21.6\%$ in the take population.

In the case of the 10% offer, adverse selection does take place. The good:bad odds in the 100–200 band is now $77/35 = 2.2{:}1$ rather than 2.5:1 in the original population. Similarly the good:bad odds in the 200–300 band is $117/27 = 4.3{:}1$ rather than 5:1 in the original population.

TABLE 3.3.1. Data for population in Example 3.3.1.

Score band	Original population		Take probabil- ity 5% rate	Take population at 5% interest rate		Take prob- ability 10% rate	Take population at 10% interest rate	
	Goods	Bads		Goods	Bads		Goods	Bads
100–200	100	40	0.9	90	36	0.8	77	35
200–300	300	60	0.5	150	30	0.4	117	27

Now the overall good:bad odds are $194/62 = 3.13:1$ down from both 4:1 and 3.64:1. Note that if there had been no adverse selection then with a 80% response rate function in the 100–200 score band, there would have been 80 goods and 32 bads who took the loan while with a 40% response rate in the 200–300 band there would have been 120 goods who took the loan and 24 bads who took the loan from this score band. Thus the overall good:bad odds would have been $(80 + 120)/(32 + 24) = 200/56 = 3.57:1$. So the bad rate of $100/500 = 20\%$ in the original population rose to one of $62/256 = 24.2\%$ for those taking the 10% loan but if there had only been the variation in response from the different risk groups and no adverse selection, this bad rate would have still risen to $56/256 = 21.9\%$.

Affordability

The third type of interaction between risk and response rate is where the interest rate charged on the loan impacts on whether the borrower can afford to pay back the loan and hence on the bad rate. If this were the case then the probability of being good p is a function of the interest rate charged, r, that is $p(r)$. The argument is that a borrower with limited resources might be able to service the interest rate payments of a 5% loan quite easily, and so the probability of a good outcome would be high. However, if the rate were 20% then the borrower's available income might not be enough to cover the interest rate payments and so the probability of a good outcome would drop substantially. It could be argued that this was one of the causes of the sub-prime mortgage crisis in 2007. The mortgages offered to credit-impaired borrowers were at very favourable interest rates for an initial period, but at the end of this period when the rated reverted to much higher levels, the default rate increased considerably.

The view that the probability of a borrower being bad is related to what fraction of the borrower's disposable income is needed to cover the repayments on the loan underpins the emphasis put on affordability by various regulators in the last decade. In some countries, like Australia, it is mandatory to check whether the borrower can afford to repay the loan, while in other countries, lenders are increasingly adding in checks of this form as well as the normal risk scoring as part of the application procedure. These tests are currently mainly used to determine the maximum size of the loan or mortgage that will be offered but with variable pricing it is clear that it is the size of the repayments that is critical. Thus these tests will be ways of assessing whether the interest rate r is such that the probability of being a good repayer $p(r)$ is high enough to warrant the loan being offered.

This section has pointed out that estimating the relationship between the interest rate r charged on a loan or credit card, the probability of the Borrower being good, p, the credit score s of that borrower, and the probability the borrower will take the loan being offered, $q(r,p)$ or $q(r,s)$ is not straightforward. The interactions between default risk and response to offers means one will need to be very careful in getting accurate estimates of risk and response through the use of risk and response scores. However, these estimates are needed to build the models to find the optimal risk-based pricing function, as we see in the next section.

3.4   Risk-based response function and risk-based pricing

Rate-based probabilities of being good

The most obvious form of variable pricing in consumer lending is risk-based pricing where the interest rate r charged on a loan to a potential borrower is a function of the risk of the borrower defaulting. In the previous section we noticed that adverse selection and affordability issues means that the probability p of the borrower being a good (or $1 - p$, the probability of being a bad) can depend on the interest rate of the loan, that is $p(r)$ and so we need to be very careful about our definition of p to avoid having r as a function of p which is in turn a function of r. In this section we define p to be the probability of the borrower being a good if the loan has a specific interest rate which we will take to be 0%. Then we define the probability that a borrower with such a probability p in terms of the interest-free loan will have a probability $\tilde{p}(r,p)$ of being a good if they take a loan with interest rate r. So the adverse selection condition in Eq. (3.3.4) implies

$$p(B|r, s(p), T) > p(B|0, s(p), T) \Rightarrow 1 - \tilde{p}(r,p) > 1 - p \Rightarrow \tilde{p}(r,p) < p.$$
$$(3.4.1)$$

In Eq. (3.4.1) we are assuming that p and $s(p)$ are the probability of being good and the corresponding score which gives that probability $(s(p) = \ln(p/(1-p))$ for a log odds score) for the whole of the potential population. We assume that the potential population are those who would take the loan if it were offered at 0% interest rate. Note that if there were no adverse selection nor any problem with affordability of loans then $\tilde{p}(r,p) = p$ for all interest rates r.

With this definition of p relating to a 0% loan, we can define the take probability of a loan with interest rate r among borrowers with that risk characteristic as

$$q(r,p) = p(T|r,p)$$

even though the actual good rate for such a loan among such borrowers is $\tilde{p}(r,p)$. Similarly we will define the risk-based interest rate charged to be $r(p)$ so that it is a function of the good rate when the loan has the standard 0% interest rate. If necessary this can then be translated into representing the interest rate as a function $\tilde{r}(\tilde{p})$ of the good rate on the current loan by defining $\tilde{r}$ as

$$\tilde{r}(\tilde{p}(r,p)) = r(p).$$
$$(3.4.2)$$

Optimal risk-based interest rate

One objective for a lender is to determine the risk-based interest rate which maximize the expected profit over a portfolio of potential borrowers. Assume that the distribution of risk among this population is given by the distribution of the probability p of them being good when the standard 0% interest rate loans are given. We assume this has distribution function $F(p)$ (with density function $f(p)$). Following the rate models of earlier in this chapter, assume the total amount that could potentially be lent to the whole population is 1 unit, and if the money is not lent it can be invested to give a risk-free return of r_F. On any loan that defaults the loss given default is the fraction l_D. Those in the portfolio with probability p of not defaulting on the standard loan will be offered the loan at a rate $r(p)$ and the probability of them taking such a loan is $q(r(p),p)$. Recall that the probability they will be a good on such a loan is $\tilde{p}(r,p)$. Then as in the model in Section 3.2, the potential profit $E[P_A(r,p)]$ on offering a loan at rate r to an account whose probability of being a good on the 0% interest rate loan is p is

$$E[P_A(r,p)] = q(r,p)((r(p) - r_F)\tilde{p}(r,p) - (l_D + r_F)(1 - \tilde{p}(r,p))). \quad (3.4.3)$$

So to find the risk-based interest rate $r(p)$ that maximizes the expected profit over the whole portfolio is equivalent to

$$\underset{r(p)}{\text{Max}} \int_0^1 (E[P_A(r,p)]) \, dF(p) = \underset{r(p)}{\text{Max}} \int_0^1 ((r(p) - r_F)\tilde{p}(r,p) \quad (3.4.4)$$

$$- (l_D + r_F)(1 - \tilde{p}(r,p))) \, q(r,p)dF(p).$$

Initially this looks like a calculus of variation problem (Gelfand and Fomin 2000) where one seeks to find the function $r(p)$ that maximizes the integral $\int_0^1 L(r,r',p)dp$. The Euler–Lagrange equation gives a necessary condition for the solution of such calculus of variation problems. It states that the optimizing function must satisfy

$$\frac{\partial L}{\partial r} - \frac{d}{dp}\left[\frac{\partial L}{\partial r'}\right] = 0. \quad (3.4.5)$$

However, in Eq. (3.4.4), the profit depends only on $r(p)$ and not on its derivative so the necessary condition reduces to

$$\frac{\partial (E[P_A(r,p)]f(p))}{\partial r} = 0 \Rightarrow \frac{\partial (E[P_A(r,p)])}{\partial r} = 0. \quad (3.4.6)$$

This is the obvious condition that given accounts whose 'standard loan' probability of being good is p one chooses the interest rate $r(p)$ so as to maximize the expected profit on each potential account. Differentiating Eq. (3.4.3) with respect to r to get Eq. (3.4.6) leads to

$$\left((r(p) - r_F)\tilde{p}(r,p) - (l_D + r_F)(1 - \tilde{p}(r,p))\right)\frac{\partial q(r,p)}{\partial r}$$

$$+ q(r,p)\left(\tilde{p}(r,p) + (r(p) + l_D)\frac{\partial \tilde{p}(r,p)}{\partial r}\right) = 0$$

$$\Rightarrow (r(p) - r_F)\left(\tilde{p}(r,p)\frac{\partial q(r,p)}{\partial r} + q(r,p)\frac{\partial \tilde{p}(r,p)}{\partial r}\right)$$

$$= (l_D + r_F)\left((1 - \tilde{p}(r,p))\frac{\partial q(r,p)}{\partial r} - q(r,p)\frac{\partial \tilde{p}(r,p)}{\partial r}\right) - q(r,p)\tilde{p}(r,p)$$

$$\Rightarrow r(p) = r_F + (l_D + r_F)\frac{\frac{\partial}{\partial r}\left((1 - \tilde{p}(r,p))q(r,p)\right)}{\frac{\partial}{\partial r}\left(\tilde{p}(r,p)q(r,p)\right)} - \frac{\tilde{p}(r,p)q(r,p)}{\frac{\partial}{\partial r}\left(\tilde{p}(r,p)q(r,p)\right)}$$

$$\Rightarrow r(p) = -l_D + \frac{(l_D + r_F)\frac{\partial q(r,p)}{\partial r} - \tilde{p}(r,p)q(r,p)}{\frac{\partial}{\partial r}\left(\tilde{p}(r,p)q(r,p)\right)}. \tag{3.4.7}$$

In the case where there is no adverse selection or affordability problems so that $\tilde{p}(r,p) = p$, Eq. (3.4.7) reduces to

$$r(p) = r_F + (l_D + r_F)\frac{1 - p}{p} - \frac{q(r, p)}{\partial/\partial r\left(q(r,p)\right)}, \tag{3.4.8}$$

which is essentially the solution in Eq. (3.2.11) of the risk-free response case. Another way of expressing Eq. (3.4.3) is

$$E[P_A(r,p)] = (r(p) + l_D)\tilde{p}(r,p)q(r,p) - (l_D + r_F)q(r,p) \tag{3.4.9}$$

and so the derivative can also be expressed as

$$\frac{\partial E[P_A(r,p)]}{\partial r} = (r(p) + sl_D)\frac{\partial\left(\tilde{p}(r, p)q(r, p)\right)}{\partial r} - (l_D + r_F)\frac{\partial q(r,p)}{\partial r} + \tilde{p}(r,p)q(r,p). \tag{3.4.10}$$

The first term is negative and the second and third terms are positive because of the signs of the derivatives. In terms of elasticity, we can extend the definition of elasticity of the response rate function which appeared in Eq. (3.2.2) to allow for risk-dependent response rate functions as follows:

$$\varepsilon(r_1,p) = -\lim_{r_2 \to r_1}\frac{q(r_2,p) - q(r_1,p)q(r_1,p)}{(r_2 - r_1)/r_1} = \frac{-\partial q(r_1,p)/\partial r r_1}{q(r_1,p)}. \tag{3.4.11}$$

In a similar way, we can define the elasticity of the response rate among the goods, ε_G as the ratio of the percentage change in the goods who take the offer compared to the percentage change in the interest rate charged as follows:

$$\varepsilon_G(r_1,p) = -\lim_{r_2 \to r_1} \frac{\tilde{p}(r_2,p)q(r_2,p) - \tilde{p}(r_1,p)q(r_1,p)/\tilde{p}(r_1,p)q(r_1,p)}{(r_2 - r_1)/r_1}$$

$$= \frac{-\partial(\tilde{p}(r_1,p)q(r_1,p))/\partial r r_1}{q(r_1,p)}. \tag{3.4.12}$$

So the derivative of the profit as a function of the interest rate in Eq. (3.4.10) can be written as

$$\frac{\partial E[P_A(r,p)]}{\partial r} = \frac{q(r,p)}{r(p)}\left[-(r(p) + l_D)\tilde{p}(r,p)\varepsilon_G(r,p) + (l_D + r_F)\varepsilon + r(p)\right]. \tag{3.4.13}$$

The optimal interest rate function is found when this derivative is zero and so is

$$r(p) = \frac{(r_F + l_D)\varepsilon - l_D\tilde{p}(r,p)\varepsilon_G}{\tilde{p}(r,p)(\varepsilon_G - 1)}. \tag{3.4.14}$$

In the case of constant elasticity ε and ε_G are both constant and so the denominator of this expression is increasing in p while the numerator is decreasing in p. Thus $r(p)$, the interest rate charges decreases as p, the probability of the borrower being a good under the standard offer, increases.

If there is no adverse selection then it follows that $\varepsilon_G = \varepsilon$ and Eq. (3.4.14) reduces so that the optimal interest rate to charge becomes

$$r(p) = \frac{\varepsilon}{p(\varepsilon-1)}(r_F + l_D(1 - p)). \tag{3.4.15}$$

Examples with no adverse selection

If there is no adverse selection or affordability issue, the interest rate charged on the loan does not affect the probability of the borrower being a good, and so $\tilde{p}(r_p) = p$. Assuming this is the case we only need to define the response rate function $q(r, p)$. We will consider two examples of this function both of which are extensions of the response rate function described in Section 3.2.

For a linear response rate function we define

$$q(r,p) = \min\{\max(0, 1 - b(r - r_L) + c(1 - p)), 1\}\ 0 \le p \le 1, \tag{3.4.16}$$

which is anchored so that for those who are definitely good, all of them will accept a loan at interest rate r_L. In that case, Eq. (3.4.8), which give the optimal interest rate to charge reduces in the region where $0 \le 1 - b(r - r_L) + c(1 - p) \le 1$ to the expression:

$$r(p) = r_F + (l_D + r_F)\frac{1-p}{p} + \frac{1 - b(r - r_L) + c(1 - p)}{b}. \qquad (3.4.17)$$

Example 3.4.1 Optimal interest rate with linear risk-dependent response rate function and no adverse selection

Extend Example 3.2.1 by again considering the situation where the risk-free rate is 5% and the loss given default is 50% so $l_D = 0.5$. We assume the linear response rate function in Eq. (3.4.16) with $r_L = 0.04, b = 2.5, c = 2$. This means that if the interest rate charged is 4% or less everyone will accept the loan. For those who are definitely good, some will accept the loan offer until the interest rate reaches 44%, while for those with $p = 0.9$ so the good:bad odds are 9:1, everyone will accept the loan if the interest rate is 12% or less, while no one will accept it once the interest rate exceeds 52%.

The optimal risk-based interest rate function is obtained by substituting these values into Eq. (3.4.17) to get

$$r(p) = 0.05 + (0.5 + .05)\frac{1-p}{p} + \frac{1 - 2.5(r - 0.04) + 2(1 - p)}{2.5}$$

$$\Rightarrow r(p) = 0.245 + 0.275\frac{1-p}{p} + 0.4(1 - p). \qquad (3.4.18)$$

This leads to the numerical results in Table 3.4.1.

Notice that whereas the optimal lending rate increases as the risk increases that is, as the probability of being good decreases, it is no longer the case as in Example 3.2.1 that the take probability decreases as the probability of being good

TABLE 3.4.1. Optimal interest rate and take probability for Example 3.4.1.

Probability of being good, p	Optimal interest rate r as %	Take probability $q(r)$ as %
0.5	72.0	30.0
0.6	58.8	42.9
0.7	48.3	49.3
0.8	39.4	51.6
0.9	31.6	51.1
0.94	28.7	50.4
0.96	27.2	49.9
0.98	25.9	49.3
0.99	25.2	49.1
1.00	24.5	48.8

decreases. For good risks, there is such a small change in the interest rate being charged as they get worse that this is more than compensated for by them being more eager to accept a loan. However for the bad risks where the probability of being good is below 0.8, the optimal interest rate starts increasing so much that their extra eagerness to have a loan does not compensate for them being turned off by the high rates being charged. Once the probability of being good drops below 0.383, then the optimal interest rate of 93% will mean no one will take the loan.

The second example is the logistic or logit response rate function, which was introduced in Eq. (3.2.6). Since one expects the take probability to decrease as the probability of being a good increases the obvious simplest extension of the logit response function to make it risk-dependent is to define

$$q(r,p) = \frac{e^{a-br-cp}}{1 + e^{a-br-cp}} \Leftrightarrow \ln\left(\frac{q(r)}{1 - q(r)}\right)$$

$$= a - br - cp = (a - c) - br + c(1 - p) \equiv s_{\text{response}}, \qquad (3.4.19)$$

which suggests that for those who are definitely good ($p = 1$) this response is like that in Eq. (3.2.6) but with a different constant. In this case the maximum willingness to pay occurs at the rate $r = a/b - (c/b)p$ which shows how the riskier the borrower is, the higher rate they are willing to pay.

Substituting this risk-based logistic response rate function into the Eq. (3.4.8) which gives the optimal interest rate to charge if there is no adverse selection leads to the following calculation:

$$q(r,p) = \frac{e^{a-br-cp}}{1 + e^{a-br-cp}} \Rightarrow \frac{\partial q(r,p)}{\partial r} = \frac{-be^{a-br-cp}}{(1 + e^{a-br-cp})^2} = \frac{-bq(r,p)}{1 + e^{a-br-cp}}$$

So

$$r(p) = r_F + (l_D + r_F)\frac{1-p}{p} - \frac{q(r,p)}{\frac{\partial}{\partial r}(q(r,p))}$$

$$\Rightarrow r(p) = r_F + (l_D + r_F)\frac{1-p}{p} + \frac{1 + e^{a-br-cp}}{b}. \qquad (3.4.20)$$

Let us now extend the numerical results in Example 3.2.2 to allow for this risk-based response function.

Example 3.4.2 Optimal interest rate for logistic risk-dependent response rate function

Using the cost structure of the previous example with risk-free rate of 5% and loss given default of 0.5, assume the parameters for the logistic response rate function are $a = 54, b = 32, c = 50$. This means that for those who are definitely good the response rate function reduces to that in Example 3.2.2, but for the riskier customers

TABLE 3.4.2. Optimal interest rate and take probability for Example 3.4.2.

Probability of being good, p	Optimal interest rate r as %	Take probability $q(r)$ as %	Take probability from Example 3.2.2 with risk-free logit response rate function
0.5	84.6	87.3	0.000009
0.6	68.6	88.4	0.003
0.7	53.3	87.4	0.2
0.8	38.5	84.2	4.5
0.9	24.4	76.5	28.0
0.94	19.1	70.6	40.2
0.96	16.6	66.5	45.7
0.98	14.2	61.3	50.5
0.99	13.0	58.2	52.7
1.00	11.9	54.7	54.7

the take probabilities will be higher than in that example. Substituting these values into Eq. (3.4.20) gives that the optimal interest rate function $r(p)$ should satisfy

$$r = 0.05 + (0.55)\frac{1-p}{p} + \frac{1 + e^{54-32r-50p}}{32}. \qquad (3.4.21)$$

The solution of this for different values of p is given in Table 3.4.2.

   The optimal interest rate to charge drops as the borrowers become less risky but unlike the linear risk-based response rate case, the take probability is also monotonically decreasing as the quality of the borrowers increases. So the fact that risky borrowers are much more anxious to get loans than higher quality borrowers completely swamps the impact of the higher interest rates they will be charged on the take probability. In the linear risk-based response function example this happened only with borrowers whose probability of being good was above 0.9. This impact of risk on the take rates of the borrowers is clear if one compares the take rates in column three of Table 3.4.2, with those in the last column which are the take rates obtained in Example 3.2.2 where the risk-independent response rate function is used. This is the response rate function which applies to those with $p = 1$ in this example (Example 3.4.2). In the risk-independent case the take rates decrease as the borrower quality decreases, because the risky borrowers are put off by the high rates charged. In this risk-dependent case, the take rates are highest for these risky borrowers because they are so anxious to get a loan, they are not put off by the even higher rates charged, which are shown in column two of Table 3.4.2.

Examples with adverse selection

If there is adverse selection then $\tilde{p}(r, p)$ should decrease as the interest rate r increases and so two obvious models is to let the probability of being good be a decreasing linear function of the interest rate or let the log odds score be a linear function of the interest rate. We call the first of these a linear probability adverse selection function and define

$$\tilde{p}(r,p) = p - dr; \quad d > 0. \tag{3.4.22}$$

We call the second a linear log odds adverse selection function and define it by

$$\ln\left(\frac{\tilde{p}(r,p)}{1 - \tilde{p}(r,p)}\right) = \ln\left(\frac{p}{1-p}\right) - dr; \quad d > 0$$

$$\Rightarrow \tilde{p}(r,p) = \frac{p}{(1-p)\mathrm{e}^{dr} + p} \leq p. \tag{3.4.23}$$

Note that whatever the choice of d then $\tilde{p}(r,0) = 0$ and $\tilde{p}(r,1) = 1$ but at other values the good rate is slightly below what it would be for the standard 0% interest rate loan. This is the form of adverse selection discussed in Eq. (3.3.6) where one is assuming the rate has a linear effect on the score if one takes the anchor rate to be $r_0 = 0$. Figure 3.4.1 shows what the curve $\tilde{p}(r,p)$ looks like as a function of p when $d = 4, r = 0.1$.

If we take a model with the linear probability adverse selection function and the linear response rate function that is, $\tilde{p}(r,p) = p - dr$ and $q(r,p) = \min\{\max(0, 1 - b(r - r_L) + c(1 - p)), 1\}$ $0 \leq p \leq 1$, then substituting these

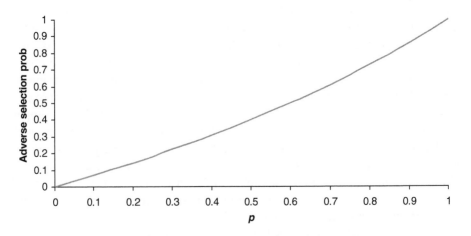

FIG. 3.4.1. Example of a log odds adverse selection function.

expression into Eq. (3.4.7) gives that the optimal interest rate function should be

$$r(p) = r_F + (l_D + r_F)\frac{d\left(1 - b(r - r_L) + c(1 - p)\right) - b(1 - p + dr)}{-d\left(1 - b(r - r_L) + c(1 - p)\right) - b(p - dr)}$$

$$- \frac{(p - dr)\left(1 - b(r - r_L) + c(1 - p)\right)}{-d\left(1 - b(r - r_L) + c(1 - p)\right) - b(p - dr)}$$

$$\Rightarrow r(p) = -l_D + \frac{b(r_F + l_D) + (p - dr)\left(1 - b(r - r_L) + c(1 - p)\right)}{d\left(1 - b(r - r_L) + c(1 - p)\right) + b(p - dr)}.$$

$$(3.4.24)$$

Example 3.4.3 Optimal interest rate for model with linear probability adverse selection function and linear response rate function

We take the same values as in Example 3.4.1 so that the risk-free rate is 5% and the loss given default is 50% so $l_D = 0.5$. The response rate function is also the same as in that example with $r_L = 0.04$, $b = 2.5$, $c = 2$ and we take the linear probability adverse selection function to be $\tilde{p}(r, p) = p - 0.6r$ where $d = 0.15$. Substituting these values into Eq. (3.4.24) gives a non-linear equation that the optimal interest rate should satisfy for each probability p of being good, namely,

$$r = -0.5 + \frac{0.15(0.55) + (p - 0.15r)\left(1 - 2.5(r - 0.04) + 2(1 - p)\right)}{0.15\left(1 - 2.5(r - 0.04) + 2(1 - p)\right) + 2.5(p - 0.15r)}. \quad (3.4.25)$$

This can be solved using the iterative methods for solving non-linear equations such as the Newton–Raphson approach and which are found in the Solver tool in Excel. Solving using these methods gives the results in Table 3.4.3.

TABLE 3.4.3. Optimal interest rate and take probability for Example 3.4.3.

Probability of being good, p	Optimal interest rate r as %	Take probability $q(r, p)$ as %	Rate adjusted probability of being good $\tilde{p}(r, p)$	Optimal interest rate r if no adverse selection
0.5	102.6	0.0	0.346	72.0
0.6	66.2	24.4	0.501	58.8
0.7	51.1	42.4	0.623	48.3
0.8	40.4	49.0	0.739	39.4
0.9	31.8	50.5	0.852	31.6
0.94	28.7	50.1	0.897	28.7
0.96	27.3	49.8	0.919	27.2
0.98	25.8	49.4	0.941	25.9
0.99	25.1	49.2	0.952	25.2
1.00	24.4	49.0	0.963	24.5

The interest rate if the probability is 0.5 need not be 102.6% as suggested, which is the solution of Eq. (3.4.25), since any interest rate above 84% will mean no one takes the offer and so any rate above 84% is optimal for that probability band. Again one sees that though the interest rate that should be charged does go down as the riskiness of the borrower decreases, there is no such monotone relationship of the take probability with the probability of being good in the group. Initially as the quality of the borrower increases the drop in the interest rate offered overcomes the fact that better groups are being made more offers. Once the probability of being good exceeds 0.9 though there is little change in the interest rate and the take rate drops because of the impact of the quality of the borrowers in the response rate function. The fourth column shows the impact of the adverse selection in this example where in all cases the quality of those who take the offer is below those who might have been expected to take the standard interest-free loan. It shows there is an impact even on those who initially were assumed to have probability of being good of 1. If one did not accept, this was the case one could use other adverse selection function such as $\tilde{p}(r, p) = p - dr(1 - p)$.

The last column shows the results in Table 3.4.1 of what the interest rate was for this example with no adverse selection. For risky borrowers, adverse selection has increased the rate that should be charged but for high-quality borrowers it seems as if the rate has been lowered. This is not really accurate because the rate is taking into account the fact the probability of being good for a group is $\tilde{p}$ rather than p. Thus in the final row it looks as if the interest rate charged drops from 24.5% without adverse selection to 24.4% if adverse selection is considered. However, it is recognized that because of adverse selection this group really has a probability of being good of $\tilde{p} = 0.963$ and for those, the result from Example 3.4.1 – the model without adverse selection – which is shown in the last column suggests the optimal rate is 27.2%.

Finally consider the situation where one has a linear log odds adverse selection function and a logistic form of the response rate function. Of course one can have any combination of forms of the response rate function and the adverse selection function but these both have a log odds feel about them. So for this situation, $q(r, p) = e^{a-br-cp}/1 + e^{a-br-cp}$ and $\tilde{p}(r, p) = p/(1 - p)e^{dr} + p$ Substituting these expressions into Eq. (3.4.7) which gives the optimal interest rate gives the following calculations:

$$q(r,p) = \frac{e^{a-br-cp}}{1 + e^{a-br-cp}} \Rightarrow \frac{\partial q(r,p)}{\partial r} = \frac{-be^{a-br-cp}}{(1 + e^{a-br-cp})^2} = \frac{-bq(r,p)}{1 + e^{a-br-cp}}$$

$$\tilde{p}(r,p) = \frac{p}{(1-p)e^{dr} + p} \Rightarrow \frac{\partial \tilde{p}(r,p)}{\partial r} = \frac{-p(1-p)e^{dr}}{((1-p)e^{dr} + p)^2} = \frac{-(1-p)e^{dr}}{(1-p)e^{dr} + p}\tilde{p}(r,p)$$

$$\Rightarrow \frac{\partial q(r,p)\tilde{p}(r,p)}{\partial r} = -q(r,p)\tilde{p}(r,p)g(r,p)$$

$$\text{where } g(r, p) = \frac{(1-p)de^{dr}}{(1-p)e^{dr}+p} + \frac{b}{1+e^{a-br-cp}}$$

$$r(p) = -l_D + \frac{(l_D + r_F)\partial q(r, p)/\partial r - \tilde{p}(r, p)q(r, p)}{\partial/\partial r\left(\tilde{p}(r, p)q(r, p)\right)}$$

$$\Rightarrow r(p) = -l_D + \frac{\left((l_D + r_F)b/(1+e^{a-br-cp})\tilde{p}(r,p)\right)+1}{g(r,p)}. \tag{3.4.26}$$

Example 3.4.4 Optimal interest rate for logistic risk-dependent response rate function with linear log odds adverse selection function

Using the cost structure of all the previous examples in this section and the risk-dependent logistic response rate function of Example 3.4.2, we have parameters $r_F = 0.05, l_D = 0.5, a = 54, b = 32, c = 50$. We assume the adverse selection function is the one portrayed in Fig. 3.4.1 with parameter $d = 4$. The optimal interest rate function with these forms of response rate function and adverse selection function satisfy Eq. (3.4.26). Substituting in the parameters gives us that the optimal interest rate satisfies

$$r = -0.5 + \frac{\left(\dfrac{(0.55) \times 32((1-p)e^{4r}+p)}{p(1+e^{54-32r-50p})}\right)+1}{g(r,p)}$$

$$\text{where } g(r,p) = \frac{4e^{4r}(1-p)}{(1-p)e^{4r}+p} + \frac{32}{1+e^{54-32r-50p}}. \tag{3.4.27}$$

Solving this for different values of p using Solver in Excel gives the results in Table 3.4.4.

TABLE 3.4.4. Optimal interest rate and take probabilities for Example 3.4.4.

Probability of being good, p	Optimal interest rate r as %	Take probability $q(r,p)$ as %	Rate adjusted probability of being good $\tilde{p}(r,p)$
0.5	76.5	98.9	0.045
0.6	63.4	97.6	0.106
0.7	50.1	95.1	0.239
0.8	36.5	91.0	0.482
0.9	25.1	72.5	0.767
0.94	19.3	69.2	0.878
0.96	16.7	65.6	0.925
0.98	14.2	60.8	0.965
0.99	13.1	58.0	0.983
1.00	11.9	54.7	1.000

There is more consistency in this result than with the linear response functions and adverse selection of Example 3.4.3. The optimal interest rate decreases, the 'better' the riskiness of the borrower but this does not compensate for the desire of the risky borrowers for a loan and so the take probability keeps dropping as the quality of the borrowers improves. The impact of adverse selection (the difference in the probability of being good between columns one and four) is quite small for the very good customers but is very marked for those whose probability of being good when given the 0% loan is 0.8 nor less, that is, the first four rows of Table 3.4.4.

3.5 Acceptance scoring for multi-feature offers

Multi-feature loan offers

Previously we have concentrated on 'interest rate' (the price) as the aspect of a loan offer that a bank may vary. There are though many features of a generic loan that a bank could vary. Table 3.5.1 gives examples of the different features that can be part of an offer of a credit card, mortgage loan, or bank account.

So a bank might decide to vary these other features as well as the interest rate or annual percentage rate (APR) charged. For a credit card, the bank has to decide what credit limit to offer, and what, if any, initial discount offer to make – 0% on balance transferred, for example. For some borrowers, the travel-related features like collecting air miles on all purchases made with the credit card or free or discounted travel insurance might be what is important.

With so many combination of features to offer a bank does not want to create a new loan product for each combination of features, because the potential borrower would be overloaded with choices trying to consider them all. Instead as we discussed in Section 3.1, the banks seek to customize the offer made to each applicant during the application process. As was pointed out there, especially with telephone and internet application channels, the application process is essentially a private transaction between the lender and the applicant. Thus the lender can advertise a generic product and customize it for each applicant without applicants being aware of how the offer they received compared with that given to

TABLE 3.5.1. Features of loan products that can be varied.

Product	Features
Credit card	Credit limit, APR, annual fee, points scheme, initial discount offer, travel insurance
Bank account	Overdraft limit, ATM card, credit card, interest when in credit, no fee foreign exchange
Mortgage	Loan amount, APR, duration, fixed/variable/capped/tracking interest, initial discount, cashback, mortgage indemnity guarantee

others. This is akin to what happens with airline flights where passengers in the same cabin class may be paying quite different fares, maybe because of different restrictions on the use of the tickets, but are not aware of what their neighbours have paid.

Unlike when only the interest rate is being varied, it is quite difficult for a bank to build a model to estimate the profitability or the cost of some of the other features. For example how much more will a customer use a credit card because it has an Air Miles feature attached to it than if the card did not have that feature, and how profitable is this then to the bank. Suppose one has a loan where the interest rate charged is r and the other offer characteristics are described by a vector $\mathbf{o}$. If this offer is made to a potential borrower whose individual characteristics – age, residential status, and so on – are $\mathbf{x}$, then the chance they will take the offer (their response rate function) is $q(r, \mathbf{o}, \mathbf{x})$ and the profit to the bank if the applicant takes the offer is $P_A(r, \mathbf{o}, \mathbf{x})$. Ideally the bank wants to choose $r, \mathbf{o}$ as functions of $\mathbf{x}$ so as to maximize the expected profit, that is,

$$\underset{r,\mathbf{o}}{\text{Max}}\, P_A(r, \mathbf{o}, \mathbf{x})q(r, \mathbf{o}, \mathbf{x}). \tag{3.5.1}$$

The problem is that it is so hard to get accurate estimates of the profit $P_A(r, \mathbf{o}, \mathbf{x})$ and anyway the difference in the profitability of loans with or without certain features is small compared with the profitability from the basic loan itself. So instead a bank will seek to maximize the chance of the applicant accepting the offer, that is,

$$\underset{r,\mathbf{o}}{\text{Max}}\, q(r, \mathbf{o}, \mathbf{x}), \tag{3.5.2}$$

which is equivalent to Eq. (3.5.1) if the profitability on all loans accepted is the same. For multi-features offers this is a more realistic objective for a lender. The lender is customizing the offer, that is, choosing the features of the product to offer to that applicant, so as to maximize the probability that the applicant will take the loan offered. Methods that help to do this by estimating the chance any particular applicant takes any specific offer are called acceptance scoring. With such an acceptance score available, the lender can decide which acceptable combination of features is optimal to offer the applicant, where an acceptable combination of features is one that is judged profitable to the lender, and optimality means maximizing the chance that particular applicant will accept the loan with these features. So during an interactive application process, the lender must be able to calculate both a risk score to estimate whether the chance of the applicant defaulting is acceptable and also an acceptance score for several different versions of the product to identify which one an applicant, acceptable on risk grounds, should be offered to maximize the chance of the loan being taken.

An alternative approach is for the lenders to offer all the variants of the product to the applicants and let them choose which one they want. In many retail environments, for example, clothing, furniture, this is a standard strategy but in the financial sector some lenders prefer the customizing approach. They argue that otherwise the applicant is most likely to choose the most unprofitable product as far as the lender is concerned and that there is still a feeling among consumers that banks and other financial institutions have expert knowledge and should be able to advise on what is the most suitable product for each individual. Moreover, as mentioned earlier, too much choice unsettles some consumers especially when it comes to financial products.

Logit or logistic acceptance probability function

The logit or logistic take probability function was introduced in Eq. (3.2.6) to describe the effect of the interest rate on the probability of an applicant accepting a loan with that interest rate. There is an obvious extension of this function which makes it a function of both the other features $\mathbf{o}$ of the offer and the characteristics $\mathbf{x}$ of the applicant, namely,

$$q(r, \mathbf{o}, \mathbf{x}) = \frac{e^{a - br + \mathbf{c} \cdot \mathbf{o} + \mathbf{d} \cdot \mathbf{x}}}{1 + e^{a - br + \mathbf{c} \cdot \mathbf{o} + \mathbf{d} \cdot \mathbf{x}}} \Leftrightarrow \ln\left(\frac{q(r, \mathbf{o}, \mathbf{x})}{1 - q(r, \mathbf{o}, \mathbf{x})}\right)$$

$$= a - br + \mathbf{c} \cdot \mathbf{o} + \mathbf{d} \cdot \mathbf{x} \equiv s_{\text{accept}} \qquad (3.5.3)$$

so the response or acceptance score is a linear function of these variables. However with a probability function of this form then the linearity of the score means that the same offer will be the most likely to be accepted by all the applicants, since the characteristics of any individual add the same to the acceptance score of all the possible offers and so cannot change the ranking of the probabilities of acceptance. This is not something one would normally expect to occur in reality and the way around it is to add in interaction terms $\mathbf{i}_{(\mathbf{x},\mathbf{o})} = (i_1, i_2, ..., i_k)$ each of which is a variable combining both offer and borrower characteristics. For example, they could be variables like, free travel insurance and the applicant is between 18 and 30 on a credit card or no mortgage arrangement fee and the applicant is re-mortgaging on a mortgage. This would lead to the acceptance score function in Eq. (3.5.4):

$$q(r, \mathbf{o}, \mathbf{x}) = \frac{e^{a - br + \mathbf{c} \cdot \mathbf{o} + \mathbf{d} \cdot \mathbf{x} + \mathbf{e} \cdot \mathbf{i}_{(\mathbf{o},\mathbf{x})}}}{1 + e^{a - br + \mathbf{c} \cdot \mathbf{o} + \mathbf{d} \cdot \mathbf{x} + \mathbf{e} \cdot \mathbf{i}_{(\mathbf{o},\mathbf{x})}}} \Leftrightarrow \ln\left(\frac{q(r, \mathbf{o}, \mathbf{x})}{1 - q(r, \mathbf{o}, \mathbf{x})}\right) \qquad (3.5.4)$$

$$= a - br + \mathbf{c} \cdot \mathbf{o} + \mathbf{d} \cdot \mathbf{x} + \mathbf{e} \cdot \mathbf{i}_{(\mathbf{o},\mathbf{x})} \equiv s_{\text{accept}}.$$

As with standard risk scoring one can build such a scorecard using information on past applicants the offers that were made to them and whether or not they took the offer. The stages outlined in Section 1.8 of data validation and cleaning, data sampling, coarse classification of the characteristics their transformation into new variables, and the building and validating of the final scorecard are all implemented in building these acceptance scorecards. There are three extra problems when one is trying to build such a scorecard. The first is that one wants a reasonable variety of offers to have been made to the applicants. Otherwise there will be lots of data on some attributes if they are the past offers' characteristics and very little on the others.

Second, there are likely to be strong interactions between the offer characteristics and the take/not take decision, which could give spurious results when one tries to coarse classify the individual's characteristics. Suppose for example the bank had offered very attractive interest rates on their loans to those in the 20–30 age group and so it is likely the acceptance rate among these might be very high. When one coarse classifies on age then it would appear that this group stands out as having a high acceptance rate and the age variable will be split into bands to reflect this. The reality may be that age has little impact on whether an applicant takes a loan and it is the effect of the attractive interest rate which is causing this effect. Further details of this problem may be found in Jung and Thomas (2008).

Third, these acceptance scorecards need to be rebuilt much more frequently than the risk-based scorecards. Whereas the economic environment which affects the risk of borrowers defaulting or not changes relatively slowly and so one normally would expect when monitoring a scorecard that it still is performing relatively satisfactorily 2 or 3 years after it was built, the commercial environment of what other offers are out there in the market will change much more quickly. When competitors introduce new loan offers or withdraw existing successful offers the impact on the acceptance probabilities of applicants for a bank's loan among the potential applicants will be quick. Thus scorecards are likely to age and become unusable in months or weeks rather than years and the bank must be able to rapidly collect the new data and rebuild the scorecard.

So one way of determining what offer to make to a new applicant for a loan is to build such an acceptance scorecard and then use it to score which is the offer such an applicant is most likely to accept. The idea of acceptance scoring together with an example of how to build a scorecard using the logistic acceptance function (and in fact the other two approaches we will discuss in this section) can be found in Thomas et al. (2006).

Estimating maximum willingness to pay value using linear programming

A second approach, to developing a model to determine which offer to make to an applicant, is based on the maximum willingness to pay idea, which was introduced in Section 3.2. There one assumed that only the interest rate affected the take probability and one calculated $w(r)$ the density function of the maximum willingness to pay across the potential borrower population. Thus,

$$\int_{r_1}^{\infty} w(r)\,dr \equiv \text{Fraction of population willing to accept a loan with interest rate } r_1.$$

Here we are dealing with offers with several features or characteristics that might vary not just the interest rate. However, we assume that there is a dominant offer characteristic, where the attractiveness of the offer decreases (or increases) monotonically as this characteristic's value increases. The idea is that, given the other offer and applicant characteristics, one can identify the value of this dominant characteristic at which this applicant would accept the offer. In the credit card context, this dominant characteristic could be the interest rate charged to the borrowers which is less attractive the higher it is or the credit limit which is important for transactors and which is more attractive the higher it is. For student bank accounts in the UK, where usually the overdraft is often interest-free, it is the overdraft limit that is the most important offer feature to students and they are more willing to accept the account (which for many soon becomes a loan) the higher the limit.

So we will not assume the dominant characteristic is the interest rate but instead take a more general model where we assume the offer characteristics are $\mathbf{o} = (o_2, \ldots, o_n)$ with $O = o_1$ being the dominant offer characteristic, the applicant characteristics are $\mathbf{x} = (x_1, x_2, \ldots, x_n)$, and the interaction characteristics $\mathbf{i}_{(\mathbf{o},\mathbf{x})}$. We assume that the dominant characteristic is one where the attractiveness of the offer decreases as its value increases, like interest rate. For this model assume there is a maximum willingness to pay value of the dominant characteristic which is a deterministic function of the other offer, applicant, and interaction characteristics, namely, $W_{o_1}^*(\mathbf{o}, \mathbf{x}, \mathbf{i}_{(\mathbf{o},\mathbf{x})})$. This means that the applicant with characteristics $\mathbf{x}$ will accept the offer with characteristics $\mathbf{o}$ provided the dominant characteristic value is less than or equal to $W_{o_1}^*(\mathbf{o}, \mathbf{x}, \mathbf{i}_{(\mathbf{o},\mathbf{x})})$, that is, $o_1 \leq W_{o_1}^*(\mathbf{o}, \mathbf{x}, \mathbf{i}_{(\mathbf{o},\mathbf{x})})$. The applicant will reject the offer if the dominant characteristic value is above the cut-off point $W_{o_1}^*(\mathbf{o}, \mathbf{x}, \mathbf{i}_{(\mathbf{o},\mathbf{x})})$, that is, $o_1 > W_{o_1}^*(\mathbf{o}, \mathbf{x}, \mathbf{i}_{(\mathbf{o},\mathbf{x})})$. This is equivalent to assuming that the willingness to pay distribution as a function of o_1, $w(o_1)$ is a step function with willingness to pay of 1 if $o_1 \leq W_{o_1}^*(\mathbf{o}, \mathbf{x}, \mathbf{i}_{(\mathbf{o},\mathbf{x})})$ and willingness to pay of 0 if $o_1 > W_{o_1}^*(\mathbf{o}, \mathbf{x}, \mathbf{i}_{(\mathbf{o},\mathbf{x})})$. This is shown in Fig. 3.5.1. It is as if one is calculating the utility value of the other features in the offer and the utility of their interaction with the applicant's characteristics in terms of the impact on how much one needs to change the dominant characteristic's value to get the applicant to take the offer.

The simplest model is to assume this take/not take cut-off point in the dominant characteristic is a linear function of the other characteristics. This assumes that

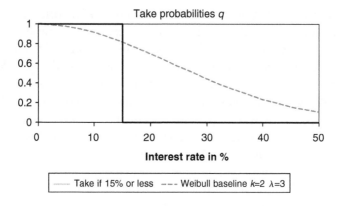

FIG. 3.5.1. Take probability functions.

$W_{o_1}^*(\mathbf{0}, \mathbf{x}, \mathbf{i}_{(\mathbf{x},\mathbf{0})})$ satisfies

$$W_{o_1}^*(\mathbf{0}, \mathbf{x}, \mathbf{i}_{(\mathbf{0},\mathbf{x})}) = c_0 + c_1 \cdot \mathbf{0} + c_2 \cdot \mathbf{x} + c_3 \cdot \mathbf{i}_{(\mathbf{0},\mathbf{x})}$$

$$\equiv W_{o_1}^*(\mathbf{y}) = \mathbf{c} \cdot \mathbf{y} \text{ where } \mathbf{y} = (\mathbf{0}, \mathbf{x}, \mathbf{i}_{(\mathbf{0},\mathbf{x})}) \qquad (3.5.5)$$

To calculate the coefficients in Eq. (3.5.5) take a sample of previous applicants and look at their characteristics, the offer characteristics, and whether they took the offer made. If applicant i (with characteristics $\mathbf{y}^i$) accepted an offer of o_1^i then $o_1^i \leq W_{o_1}^*(\mathbf{y}^i) = \mathbf{c} \cdot \mathbf{y}^i$ while if applicant j (with characteristics $\mathbf{y}^j$) rejected on offer of o_1^j then $o_1^j > W_{o_1}^*(\mathbf{y}^j) = \mathbf{c} \cdot \mathbf{y}^j$, where we are assuming that the likelihood of acceptance increases as o_1 increases. These inequalities are reminiscent of the way linear programming was used in Section 1.10 to obtain a credit scorecard, and we can modify the linear programming approach used there to determine the coefficients needed in Eq. (3.5.5).

Let the sample of previous customers be labelled 1 to n where $i = 1, 2, \ldots, n_T$ accepted the offer and $j = n_T + 1, n_T + 2, \ldots, n$ rejected the offer. Let applicant i have applicant/offer characteristics $\mathbf{y}^i = (y_1^i, \ldots, y_p^i)$ and be made an offer o_1^i. Then to find the coefficients $\mathbf{c}$ that give the best estimate of the take/not take indifference level $W_{o_1}^*(\mathbf{0}, \mathbf{x}, \mathbf{i}_{(\mathbf{0},\mathbf{x})}) \equiv W_{o_1}^*(\mathbf{y})$, we want to solve the following linear programme.

Minimize $e_1 + \cdots + e_n$

subject to

$$o_1^i - e_i \leq c_1 y_1^i + c_2 y_2^i + \cdots + c_p y_p^i \qquad i = 1, 2, \ldots, n_T$$

$$o_1^j + e_j \geq c_1 y_1^j + c_2 y_2^j + \cdots + c_p y_p^j \qquad j = n_T + 1, \ldots, n$$

$$e_i \geq 0 \quad i = 1, \ldots, n. \qquad (3.5.6)$$

The first constraint requires that for those who took the offer, the value of the dominant characteristic o_1^i should be below the take/not take cut-off function. If it is not there is an error of e_i reflecting the amount by which this condition is not satisfied. The second set of constraints applies to those who did not take the offer. In that case, the value of the dominant characteristic in that offer o_1^j should be above the take/not take cut-off function. If it is not the case, then the error e_j describes by how much this condition is not satisfied. Seeking to minimize the sum of all these errors gives the linear take/not take cut-off function that best fits this data. This is not the same formulation as in the use of linear programming to build a credit scorecard but there are strong similarities. Note that if the dominant characteristic is such that the attractiveness of the offer increases as the characteristic value increases (like credit limit) then the constraints in the linear programme Eq. (3.5.6) need to be reversed with the second type of constraint being attached to those who take the offer and the first to those who reject the offer.

Estimating maximum willingness to pay distribution using accelerated life modelling

In the previous approach, we assumed there was an exact value of the dominant characteristic at which an applicant would change from not taking an offer to taking it. A more realistic assumption would be to say there is a probability distribution over the values of the dominant characteristic of the cut-off between not taking and taking the offer. This is equivalent to saying there is a probability distribution, with density function $w(o_1|\mathbf{o}, \mathbf{x})$ over the values of the dominant characteristic, o_1 of the maximum amount an applicant with characteristics $\mathbf{x}$ is willing to pay for an offer whose other characteristics are given by $\mathbf{o}$. Assuming a probability distribution of willingness to take rather than an exact take/not take cut-off point as in the previous section allows for the fact that similar people can make different decisions about the same offer and even the same person may make different decisions at different times. This is because an individual's priorities, and economic circumstances are constantly changing and the environment in which the offer is made can affect the decision.

The question is how to estimate the maximum willing to pay density function $w(o_1|\mathbf{o}, \mathbf{x})$ given a sample of previous applicants, the offers that were made to them, and whether or not they took the offer. This is not as easy as it looks as far as maximum willingness to pay is concerned because all such data is censored in that it only gives a range of values for the maximum willingness to pay for each applicant in the sample. If the dominant characteristic was interest rate and so the higher the rate the less attractive the offer, then for someone who accepted an offer where the interest rate was 10%, all one can say is that their maximum willingness to pay must be greater than 10%. Similarly, for someone who rejected an offer when the interest rate was 15% all that is to know is that the maximum willingness to pay interest rate must be below 15%. However, survival analysis models which are the statistical techniques that seek to measure the time until some event occurs are well used to dealing with censored data. In trying to determine how long some-one will live data on those who are still alive in censored in that all one can say is that their lifetime is longer than their current age. We introduced survival analysis and the idea of the hazard function of default in Section 1.6 when we discussed the extension of time dependency of credit scores. We will look at it again in Section 4.6 when we see how proportional hazard models – one of the most commonly used models in survival analysis – can be used to model the dynamics of the credit risk of borrowers. In this section we show how using accelerated life models, which is one of the techniques used in survival analysis, can help one determine a max-imum willingness to pay distribution, because it can cope with situations where every piece of data is censored. It is a very unusual application of survival analysis because normally in survival analysis one is estimating a distribution over time and here we would be estimating the distribution over the dominant characteristic which could be interest rate, or credit limit.

To estimate this maximum willingness to pay distribution function, assume o_1 is the dominant offer characteristic. If one has applicant characteristics $\mathbf{x}$ and offer characteristic $(r, \mathbf{o})$ where r is the value of the dominant monotone characteristic $\mathbf{o}_1$, then we are interested in the probability of an applicant with characteristics $\mathbf{x}$ accepting offer $(r, \mathbf{o})$. We assume $\mathbf{o}_1$ has the property (like interest rate) that as its value increases the offer becomes less attractive to all potential borrowers. Thus, if R is the maximum value of $\mathbf{o}_1$ at which the offer will be acceptable, then

Prob{individual with characteristic $\mathbf{x}$ will not take the offer$(r, \mathbf{o})$}

$$= \text{Prob}\{R \leq r|(\mathbf{o}, \mathbf{x})\} = F(r|\mathbf{o}, \mathbf{x}). \tag{3.5.7}$$

Hence that the probability of an individual with characteristic $\mathbf{x}$ taking the offer $(r, \mathbf{o})$ is given by

$$= \text{Prob}\{R > r|(\mathbf{o}, \mathbf{x})) = 1 - F(r|\mathbf{o}, \mathbf{x}) = S(r|\mathbf{o}, \mathbf{x}) \equiv q(r, \mathbf{o}, \mathbf{x}) \tag{3.5.8}$$

where $q(r, \mathbf{o}, \mathbf{x})$ was defined in Section 3.1 as the probability such a potential bor-rower will take such an offer. Recall that the maximum willingness to pay density function $w(r|\mathbf{o}, \mathbf{x})$ satisfies

$$\int_{r_1}^{\infty} w(r|\mathbf{o}, \mathbf{x})dr \equiv \text{Fraction of applicants willing to pay } r_1 \text{ or more}$$

$$\equiv q(r_1|\mathbf{o}, \mathbf{x}) = 1 - F(r_1|\mathbf{o}, \mathbf{x}) = \int_{r_1}^{\infty} f(r|\mathbf{o}, \mathbf{x})dr \tag{3.5.9}$$

and so is the density function of the variable R whose distribution function was $F(r|\mathbf{0}, \mathbf{x})$. $S(r|\mathbf{0}, \mathbf{x})$ is called the survival function in survival analysis and corresponds to the chance in mortality that an individual has not yet died at t the given time. Here it is the take probability which can be interpreted as the chance the borrowers have not yet reached their maximum willingness to pay at that value of the dominant characteristic.

In survival analysis, the hazard rate $h(t)$ is defined as $h(t) = f(t)/S(t)$ (see Eq. (1.6.15) for example). In this take probability context, where the hazard rate is $h(r|\mathbf{0}, \mathbf{x}) = f(r|\mathbf{0}, \mathbf{x})/S(r|\mathbf{0}, \mathbf{x})$, the hazard rate is related to the elasticity $\varepsilon(r|\mathbf{0}, \mathbf{x})$ of the take probability as a function of the dominant characteristic since

$$h(r|\mathbf{0}, \mathbf{x}) \equiv \frac{f(r|\mathbf{0}, \mathbf{x})}{S(r|\mathbf{0}, \mathbf{x})} = \frac{-\frac{\partial q(r|\mathbf{0}, \mathbf{x})}{\partial r}}{q(r, \mathbf{0}, \mathbf{x})} = \frac{\varepsilon(r|\mathbf{0}, \mathbf{x})}{r}. \qquad (3.5.10)$$

Assume that the information available to help estimate whether or not a potential borrower with individual characteristics $\mathbf{x}$ takes or does not take an offer with characteristics $(r, \mathbf{o})$ is given by the vector $\mathbf{y} = (\mathbf{o}, \mathbf{x}, \mathbf{i}_{(\mathbf{o}, \mathbf{x})})$, where $\mathbf{i}_{(\mathbf{o}, \mathbf{x})}$ are the characteristics describing the interactions between the offer and applicant characteristics. In the accelerated life model, the take probability is defined by

$$q(r, \mathbf{o}, \mathbf{x}) = q_0(e^{\mathbf{c} \cdot \mathbf{y}} r), \qquad (3.5.11)$$

which in survival analysis notation is $S(r|\mathbf{0}, \mathbf{x}) = S_0(e^{\mathbf{c} \cdot \mathbf{y}} r)$. $q_0(r)$ is the take probability function of the baseline 'applicant' who has no characteristics when offered a 'vanilla' loan (one which has no other characteristics except the dominant one). The risk factor $e^{\mathbf{c} \cdot \mathbf{y}}$ describes the impact the offer and applicant's characteristics have on the take probability. They recalibrate the actual value of the dominant offer characteristic into a 'perceived' value which is then used in the baseline take probability function to get the actual take probability. If for example the dominant characteristic was interest rate and $e^{\mathbf{c} \cdot \mathbf{y}} = 0.5$ for a particular applicant and offer, then if the actual interest rate in this offer was 20%, the take probability of that offer by that applicant would be the same as that for the baseline borrower on a vanilla loan with an interest rate of 10%. The analogy is with accelerated life models in mortality statistics, where the idea is some individuals live their lives at a 'faster' rate than others and so at 50 may have the mortality rate of an 80-year-old.

To complete the accelerated life model one needs to decide on the baseline take probability distribution function $q_0(r)$. The Weibull distribution is one of the most commonly used baseline distributions in accelerated life models and in that case, we define:

$$q_0(r) = \exp\{-(\lambda r)^k\} \qquad (3.5.12)$$

where λ and k are the scale and shape parameters of the Weibull distribution. From Eq. (3.5.12) it follows that if $f_0(\cdot)$, $h_0(\cdot)$, $\varepsilon_0(\cdot)$ are the density function, hazard rate, and elasticity for a baseline hazard function then,

$$f_0(r) = k\lambda^k r^{k-1} e^{-(\lambda r)^k}; \quad h_0(r) = k\lambda^k r^{k-1}; \quad \varepsilon_0(r) = k\lambda^k r^k. \tag{3.5.13}$$

$k = 1$ corresponds to the exponential distribution where the hazard rate is constant, while with $k > 1$ the hazard rate is monotonically increasing, and with $k < 1$ it is monotonically decreasing. In Fig. 3.5.1, the take probability distribution $q_0(r)$ is shown when it is a Weibull distribution with $k = 2, \lambda = 3$.

So putting Eqs. (3.5.11) and (3.5.12) together gives the take probability distribution for an accelerated life model with Weibull baseline function as

$$q(r|\mathbf{o}, \mathbf{x}) = \exp\{-(\lambda \exp(\mathbf{c} \cdot \mathbf{y})r)^k\} = e^{-(e^{\mathbf{c} \cdot \mathbf{y}}\lambda r)^k}. \tag{3.5.14}$$

To calculate the coefficients $\mathbf{c}, \lambda, k$ we use a sample of n past applicants. For applicant i in the sample we have the offer characteristics $(r^i, \mathbf{o}^i)$ and the applicant characteristics $\mathbf{x}^i$. We label the applicants so that $i = 1, \ldots, n_T$ take the offer made to them and the remainder $j = n_T + 1, \ldots, n$ do not take the offer made to them. In every case this data is censored as far as the maximum willingness to pay variable R is concerned, since for those who took the offer all that is known is that $R \geq r^i$, while for those who did not take the offer all that is known is that $R < r^j$. We can though obtain the likelihood function of this doubly censored data as follows:

$$L(\mathbf{c}, \lambda, k) = \prod_{i=1}^{n_T} (q(r^i|\mathbf{o}^i, \mathbf{x}^i) \prod_{j=n_T+1}^{n} (1 - q(r^j|\mathbf{o}^j, \mathbf{x}^j))$$

$$= \prod_{i=1}^{n_T} \exp\left\{-(\lambda \exp(\mathbf{c}.\mathbf{y}^i)r^i)^k\right\} \prod_{j=n_T+1}^{n} \left[1 - \exp\left\{-(\lambda \exp(\mathbf{c}.\mathbf{y}^j)r^j)^k\right\}\right]$$

$$\Rightarrow Ln(L(\mathbf{c}, \lambda, k)) = -\sum_{i=1}^{n_T} (\lambda \exp(\mathbf{c}.\mathbf{y}^i)r^i)^k$$

$$+ \sum_{j=n_T=1}^{n} \ln\left[1 - \exp\left\{-(\lambda \exp(\mathbf{c}.\mathbf{y}^j)r^j)^k\right\}\right] \tag{3.5.15}$$

The maximum likelihood estimates of λ, k, and $\mathbf{c}$ in the Weibull-based accelerated life model are then obtained using Newton–Raphson methods.

One can then estimate the take probability for any new applicant who has characteristics $\mathbf{x}$ for any loan offer with characteristics $(r, \mathbf{o})$ that one wants to make. Hence for individual applicants one can identify the offers that they are most likely to take and for a portfolio of applicants one can identify given a specific set of offers who are the applicants most likely to take at least one of them. Thus these application scorecards, whichever way they are developed, have considerable potential in helping to decide which combination of features to offer an applicant for a loan or credit card product.

These probability of acceptance models will become increasingly important as the consumer lending market matures and it becomes a buyers rather than a sellers market. They are ideally suited to the interactive application processes that modern telecommunication technology is supporting and they also satisfy the customer relationship marketing credo of tailoring the product to the customer.

3.6   A borrower–lender game model for pricing

The previous models in this chapter all consider the pricing problem as one where there is only one decision maker, the lender (the bank), who has to decide what price to set. The borrowers are represented by the take probability function (the response rate function), which describes what percentage of borrowers will take the loan offered. This function is a representation of the historical responses by the borrowers but the reality is that each borrower is a decision maker and each one makes the take/not take decision in the light of their own preferences. Modelling a problem with two or more decision makers, the lender and the borrower in this case, can be done using game theory. The only researchers who have used game theory to model the variable pricing problem in consumer lending are Keeney and Oliver (2005) and the rest of this section follows closely their analysis.

In Section 1.3, we suggested that the main objective of the lender was to maximize profit or alternatively to maximize return on capital. However, it was pointed out that lenders are also very interested in maximizing their market share since this gives them more opportunities for increasing their profits in the future. In this section we assume the lenders are interested in the profit they make from their lending portfolio and the size of their portfolio, which is equivalent to their share of the market. Throughout this chapter we have assumed that the critical feature for the borrower is the interest rate being charged on the loan and for revolving credit products like credit cards the borrower will also be very interested in the credit limit offered. So in this game, both borrower and lender measure their outcome from the game in two dimensions, but they are not the same two for each though they are strongly related.

The bank decides what interest rate and credit limit to offer on its loan product to all prospective borrowers. These are the two features that are most important to the borrowers and each borrower in turn considers the combination offered and compares it with the other combinations being offered in the marketplace. Their collective decisions give the probability of take by the borrowers of this offer, and from this the bank will find out what percentage of the potential borrower market will take this offer. Moreover the interest rate charged and the credit limit offered are the key features in determining how profitable each loan will be to the bank.

Thus it is able to calculate the two measures that are paramount to the bank – the profitability of the portfolio of borrowers who took its offer and the size of its portfolio.

There are strong similarities between the lender–borrower game which we detail in this section and a market game introduced more than 125 years ago by Edgeworth (1881). In that game two traders come to a market, the one with apples and the other with pears. Each has a preference function which means they would like to have a mix of fruit rather than just all of one kind and Edgeworth was able to construct a simple diagram – the Edgeworth box – using only the indifference contours of their preferences which showed which trades would be Pareto optimal. Pareto optimal means that there is no other trade where one trader could do better and the other no worse than they are doing under the trade being considered. What is surprising about this result is that this corresponds to the equilibrium solutions one can get in this market game but 60 years before the foundations of game theory including the equilibrium solution concept were first formally laid out (Von Neumann and Morgernstern 1944). The equilibrium solution for a game is a set of strategies for each player so that no players can improve their pay-off by changing their strategy if the other players do not change their strategies.

Returning to the game itself where the bank is offering a revolving loan product. The borrowers are interested in two features of the loan – the interest rate r being charged and the credit limit L – and so their preferences are given by a utility function $u(r, L)$. One does not know what other offers are available to the potential borrower or how much effort the borrower is willing to put into finding and comparing loan offers, but whatever these are for a particular borrower, it is reasonable to assume that if $q(r, L)$ is the probability of the potential borrower taking offer (r, L), then the relative ordering of $q(r, L)$ over the different (r, L) combinations is the same as the relative ordering of $u(r, L)$ over those values. All this says is that the borrowers are more likely to take the offer they prefer when confronted with two loan offers. We assume that this preference ordering is the same for all borrowers even if the corresponding take probability is not necessarily the same.

We assume the utility function $u(r, L)$ is monotonically decreasing in r and monotonically increasing in L (though there may be some borrower who do not like large credit limits because it is too tempting to spend it). One possibility would be $u(r, L) = a - br + cL$, with $b, c > 0$, which would mean the isopreference curves (the offers which have the same utility value to the borrower) are straight lines in the (r, L) plane with a positive slope so L goes up as r goes up. A more realistic set of isopreference curves are given in Fig. 3.6.1 where the curve AA$'$ describes equally preferred offers all of which are preferred to the offers on the curve BB$'$ where again the borrower is indifferent to the offers on this latter curve. Given the assumption that the ordering of $u(r, L)$ and the ordering of $q(r, L)$ is the same over the offers (r, L), then all the offers on an isopreference curve have the same take probability.

The profitability to the bank of the different offers on an isopreference curve is quite different though. Initially when both the rate and the credit limit is very low, there is hardly any revenue and so there is not much profit and the chance of a borrower defaulting is low. As one moves up the curve, three changes occur. If the borrower does not default, then the revenue increases because of the higher rate charged and the higher credit limit allowed; if the borrower does default the losses are likely to be higher because the credit limit has increased; and the chance of defaulting is likely to increase because of the higher rates and higher credit limits as was discussed in Section 3.3. Moving up the curve, initially the increase in interest rate and credit limit increases the revenue considerably with little impact on the default risk, and so profit increases. There comes a point though where the increase in credit limit means the default losses would start increasing much more than the revenue and this together with the increase in the chance of defaulting will mean profits start to drop. So for each isopreference curve, there is some point, A* or B* of maximum profitability.

If we express the results of this analysis of Fig. 3.6.1 in terms of the banks objectives we get Fig. 3.6.2. Here we plot Exp{profit|take}, the expected profitability of those who take the offer against Pr{take}. The isopreference curves in Fig. 3.6.1 correspond to vertical lines in this figure since all the loans on them have the same take probability. On each vertical line there is some loan with maximum expected profitability given that the loan was taken. Finding the optimal Exp{profit|take} offer for each different isopreference curve allows us to plot the graph of maximum Exp{profit|take} against Pr{take}. Moving across the isopreference curves in Fig. 3.6.1 from left to right, one starts with offers where the interest rates are so low that one is not making any money on any loan, even the optimal profit one.

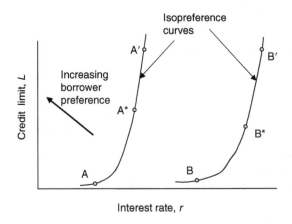

FIG. 3.6.1. Isopreference curves of a borrower over the interest rate and credit limit of offers.

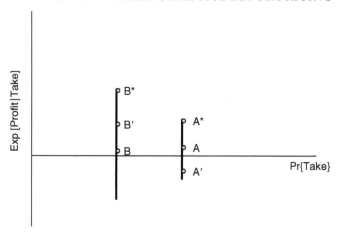

FIG. 3.6.2. Outcome of loans in Fig. 3.6.1 using bank's objectives.

As one moves to the right, the interest rates increase and so the profitability on the loans take increases. So this optimal profitability becomes positive and keeps increasing. However, the take probability is dropping all the time and because of adverse selection those who take the loan are more likely to be bads and so contribute losses rather than profits. Hence for some isopreference curve the optimal expected profit on those who take the loans starts to drop and it will keep dropping on the curves to its right until one arrives at a curve where even the optimal loan is no longer profitable for those who take it. This is shown in Fig. 3.6.3 where maximum Exp{profit|take} is plotted against Pr{take}. Recall that the points on the right of Fig. 3.6.3 with high take probabilities correspond to the isopreference curves on the left of Fig. 3.6.1 where the interest rate is low.

It is now a simple matter to plot Exp{Profit} against Pr{take} since:

$$\text{Exp\{profit\}} = \text{Exp\{profit}|\text{ take\}Pr\{take\}} + 0(1 - \text{Pr\{take\}}).   (3.6.1)$$

Thus Fig. 3.6.4 shows the optimal profit to the bank for each potential borrower as a function of the bank's market share (or rather as a function of the proportion of the potential borrowers who take the loan, that is the probability of take). Notice that the only offers the bank should be interested in making are the Pareto optimal ones, which correspond to the thicker part of the curve in Fig. 3.6.4. These are the ones where there is no other offer which gives better profitability and as good a probability of take or vice versa.

What we need to do now is to translate the offers which the bank finds attractive in terms of profitability and market share into what were the interest rates and credit limits that make up these offers. In Fig. 3.6.1 the preferences for the borrower are obvious as they depend on interest rate and credit limit. A borrower's preference increases with increasing credit limit and increases with decreasing interest rate

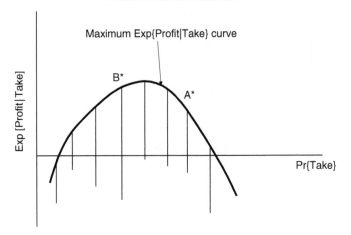

FIG. 3.6.3. Maximum Exp{profit | take} versus Pr{take}.

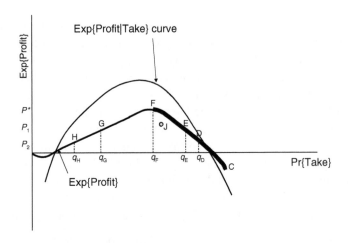

FIG. 3.6.4. Plot of expected profit against market share for the bank.

and so the borrower looks for offers to the northwest of Fig. 3.6.1. The curves of constant interest rate are just the vertical lines and those of constant credit limit are the horizontal lines. The bank's preferences depend on expected profit and probability of take which translates into market share. The curves of constant take probability are of course those of constant utility of the borrower, namely the isopreference curves AA′ and BB′. So all we need to do is to identify the curves of constant profit for the bank in Fig. 3.6.1 and we will have mapped the preferences of both players – borrower and lender onto that diagram.

To do this consider a few specific points on the curves in Fig. 3.6.4 and then we map them onto the corresponding points in Fig. 3.6.5, which is an extension of

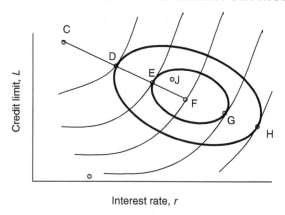

FIG. 3.6.5. The constant profit and take curves for the bank mapped onto Fig. 3.6.1.

Fig. 3.6.1. F is the point of maximum profit and let us suppose it corresponds to a profit of $P*$ and a take probability of q_F. So in Fig. 3.6.5, F sits on the isopreference curve corresponding to a take probability of q_F. A slightly lower profit is $P_1 < P*$ and this is achieved by the points $G(q_G, P_1)$ and $E(q_E, P_1)$ in Fig. 3.6.4. These in turn correspond to points on the isopreference curves corresponding to take probabilities q_G and q_E in Fig. 3.6.5. There are other combinations of interest rate and credit limit which also give a profit of P_1. For example there must be two such points on the isopreference curve q_F either side of the point F, since that gives a higher profit than P_1. This happens at all the other isopreference curves corresponding to values of q between q_E and q_G and so the curve of constant profit will be an oval going through E and G in Fig. 3.6.5. Similarly, if we take a lower profit P_2 (which could be zero profit), we identify two points D and H on the curve in Fig. 3.6.5 which have this profit. The corresponding take probabilities are q_D and q_H and there will be unique points on the isopreference curves q_D and q_H in Fig. 3.6.5 which have the credit limit and the interest rate that give the take probabilities and expected profits (q_D, P_2) and (q_H, P_2), respectively. On the isopreference curves which have take probabilities between q_D and q_H, there will be two combinations of credit limits and interest rate which give a profit of P_2. These points will be further apart than those which give the profit $P_1, P_1 > P_2$ and so the curve of constant profit with profit P_2 will lie outside the curve of constant profit with profit P_1. This mapping from Fig. 3.6.4 to Fig. 3.6.5 can be made even if the profit is negative. Point C for example corresponds to negative profit but a very large take probability and the bank could decide to operate at this point if it felt that market share was much more important than profitability. This point is then mapped onto the point C in the interest rate–credit limit space displayed in Fig. 3.6.5.

The points D and E are rather special points in their respective constant profit contours in Fig. 3.6.5. At these points the tangent to the constant take curve (the borrower's utility isopreference curve) coincides with the tangent to the constant profit curve. This means if one moves to the northwest of this tangent line, the profit will start to decrease, while if one moves to the southeast of the tangent line, the take probability will start to decrease. If one moves along the tangent line, one starts moving down the profit 'hill' and the profitability will again decrease. So there is no other combination of interest rate and credit limit which gives as high a probability of take and better profitability or vice versa. So D and E are Pareto optimal points, while F with its maximum expected profit must also be Pareto optimal. The same argument does not work for G and H because now both expected profitability and the probability of take will increase if one moves to the northwest of the common tangent line.

Note that for a point like J where the tangents to the constant profit and constant take curves going through that point are different, we can find points which are within the constant profitability curve though J and to the northwest of the tangent to the isopreference curve through J. Such points correspond to loans which have a combination of interest rate and credit limit which give a higher expected profit and a higher take probability to the bank. Hence J cannot be Pareto optimal.

Thus the Pareto optimal points for the bank in Fig. 3.6.4, namely those on the curve F, E, D, C translate into the points F, E, D, C in Fig. 3.6.5 where the tangent to the constant expected profit oval and the tangent to the constant take probability curve coincide. These Pareto optimal solutions start at the profit maximizing point F and draw out a curve of points with this common tangent property until it reaches the boundary where the interest rate is zero (this could correspond to all potential borrowers taking the loan offer though it is unlikely that a bank would keep offering loans where the expected profit is negative for very long).

So these are the offers that are the bank's part of an equilibrium solution to the borrow–lender game. They correspond to offers of interest rate and credit limit which give expected portfolio profit and probabilities of take which are Pareto optimal; that is, there is no other offer which can give higher portfolio profit and higher take rates. When the bank has made such an offer all a borrower can do is either take or not take the offer. So to complete the equilibrium solution to the game we need to know when the borrower should take the loan offered. The bank may decide only to offer one combination of interest rate and credit limit in its loan portfolio, in which case borrowers should accept the offer provided their isopreference curve going through that loan combination is further to the northwest (a higher take probability) than one going through the best alternative offer the borrowers have. That might be the offer (0,0) – with 0 credit limit and 0 interest rate if there is no other offer available. For some borrowers it will be best to accept the offer and for others it will not be. The proportion for whom it is worthwhile is the probability of take used by the bank in its offer calculations. So it does not pay anyone to change what they do.

If the bank decides to offer loans with a number of different interest rate–credit limit combinations along the Pareto optimal curve CDEF in Fig. 3.6.5, then the borrowers should choose the one furthest to the northwest in Fig. 3.6.1 given their monotonic preferences in credit limit and interest rate. So the equilibrium points in the game correspond to the Pareto optimal offers by the bank, and whether it is optimal for the borrowers to accept a particular offer depends on their own personal circumstances. The critical point is that all borrowers have the same ordering of their utility function $u(r, L)$ over the different offers (r, L) made by the lender even if the functions themselves are different and so they all have the same ordering over (r, L) of their take probabilities $q(r, L)$.

The bank chooses the offer to make by deciding on its profit-market share trade-off. How much less profit per potential borrower is the bank willing to accept in order to increase the proportion of the population who take its offer by 1% say? This trade-off gives the slope of a curve in Fig. 3.6.4 – the market share–profit graph – and the bank should chose the point on the Pareto optimal boundary where the tangent has this slope.

This is a more abstract model than the others considered in this chapter. To make it concrete, banks would need to undertake market research on their customers to estimate the utility function $u(r, L)$ for different classes of borrowers, as well as building models of how the expected profitability of a borrower depends on the interest rate charged and the credit limit chosen. In the next chapter we recognize that determining profitability and how it depends on credit limits requires modelling the dynamics of customer behaviour rather than the static, application decision-oriented models looked at so far in this book.

4

Profit scoring and dynamic models

4.1 Behavioural scoring and dynamic account management

Account management and profitability

For the last decade, most lenders have been interested in moving from assessing the default risk of a customer to estimating the profitability of the customer. This was implicit in the problems addressed in Chapters 1 and 3, which concentrated on the one-off decisions, made at the beginning of the relationship between the bank and the borrower on who should be offered loans and at what price. Although the decisions were made based on the default score of the borrower, the models sought to calculate the optimal expected profit or at least the optimal rate of return when these decisions are made.

In reality the initial decisions on offering and pricing loans is only the start of the relationship between borrower and bank and the subsequent profitability of the borrower to the bank depends on much more than these initial decisions. How the account is subsequently managed, what changes in credit limits and other terms are made during the period of the loan or credit card, whether the borrowers will pay-off their loan or mortgage early (prepayment) or switch to using another lender's credit card (attrition), all have major impacts on the profit of the borrowers to the bank. It is not just the decisions and performance of the borrower on that product that matters but the bank also has to consider how likely it is that it can cross-sell other products to the borrower or get the borrower to upgrade to a more profitable product.

Thus, optimizing the profitability of a borrower to a bank involves not just the credit risk assessment department of the bank but also the operations management and marketing functions of the organization. Developing a model of profitability that is a holistic view of the borrower's relationship with the bank helps all the different groups within the bank make coherent and sensibly interlinked decisions. This, though, is difficult to implement in practice as is most change that involves removing departmental boundaries within an organization. How often does the student section of an bank offer products on special terms to students because of the enhanced long-term customer value of graduates only for these terms to be withdrawn the moment the student graduates and their accounts are transferred to the general section of the bank? How often are particular segments of the borrower population targeted by marketing departments because of their excellent response rates only for the majority of the responders to fall foul of the credit departments risk requirements? So a major problem in the move from default scoring systems to profit-based systems is that the latter will need to be used by the whole retail bank and not just the credit risk section. The reason why the whole bank needs to be involved is that the profit the bank derives from a borrower depends on the sequence of credit assessment, operating and marketing decisions that will be made about the borrower in the future by the various departments of the bank. So the effectiveness of a current decision concerning the borrowers will depend on what the subsequent decisions are made about them. Moreover the profitability of the borrowers also depend on their current status and also on what their status in the future will be. Currently, the commonest way a bank describes the status of the borrowers are via their behavioural scores.

Behavioural score as a measure of the borrower's condition

In Section 1.8, when we discussed how behavioural scores could be calculated, we pointed out that they describe the probability that an existing borrower will default within a given time horizon, which is usually taken as 12 months. So like application scores, they are a measure of default risk but unlike application scores, they do not appear to be directly related to any immediate decision concerning the borrowers, especially if they have a non-revolving loan. The bank cannot call in an existing loan, if the borrower's behavioural score drops but the borrow is still repaying according to the terms of the loan. If, however, the borrower applied for a further advance on the loan or the mortgage, then the bank can then use the behavioural score to help decide what to do. With a revolving loan, like a credit card, the bank can adjust the borrower's credit limit in the light of changes in the borrower's behavioural score (though many banks are loath to lower the credit limit already communicated to the borrower, even if they lower the 'shadow' limit they calculate internally on the credit card). However if the behavioural score is used for this credit limit decision, one has to take care that the changes in credit limit are not too extreme. A high behavioural score means the borrower's chance of defaulting is low given the current loan level or credit limit, but that does not necessarily mean it will remain low if the credit limit is vastly increased.

The other point to make is that a borrower's behavioural score will change from month to month. So a credit limit rise which the bank might think is sensible now may look less sensible in the future if the borrower's default risk has gone up. Thus it is important to model the dynamics of the borrower's behavioural score if one wants to develop sensible credit limit policies.

There are some decisions which a bank has to make about existing customers where other information about the state of the borrower is needed rather than just the behavioural score. The bank may want to adjust the interest rate being charged on a loan or make it more attractive in some other way so as to stop a borrower paying off the loan early (prepayment). Similarly the bank may want to take preemptive measures so as to stop the borrowers closing or at least cutting down the usage of their credit cards. An attrition scorecard, which relates the borrower's recent transactional behaviour to the chance of prepaying a loan or closing a credit card, would be more useful than a behavioural score in this context. Some banks do develop such scores but others have behavioural score as the only measure of a borrower's current condition. If they use only the behavioural score in such contexts, then they cannot hope to have as successful outcomes as if they had more detailed descriptions of the borrower's situation.

Example 4.1.1 (Reprise of Example 1.4.1) Behavioural score and the credit limit increase decision

In Example 1.4.1 based on Fig. 1.4.8 we looked at a credit limit increase problem where the time horizon was one period, which is the simplest of the credit limit increase problems. We recall that problem because we want to consider what happens when we make the problem more realistic by increasing the time horizon. In this problem, the behavioural score, S, only takes one of two values, high (H) or low (L) and if the behavioural score take value S (S is H or L), then the probability of the borrower being good in the next time period is $p(S)$. The current credit limit is L_0 and the option is to increase to a credit limit of L_1. In Example 1.4.1 the one period pay-off if the credit limit is L_i is g_i if the borrower stays good and is $-l_i$ if the borrower becomes bad and so defaults. All this data is shown in Fig. 4.1.1 which is the decision tree of whether to raise the credit limit. The decision is to increase the credit limit if the behavioural score was S provided,

$$g_1 p(S) + (1 - p(S))(-l_1) > g_0 p(S) + (1 - p(S))(-l_0)$$

or

$$\frac{p(S)}{1 - p(S)} > \frac{l_1 - l_0}{g_1 - g_0}. \tag{4.1.1}$$

Example 4.1.2 Credit limit increase with infinite horizon and no change in borrower's behavioural score

It is more reasonable to consider the profitability of a revolving loan, over a time of several periods, even possibly an infinite number of periods rather than just one period. So consider the credit limit problem under these time horizons. The profit obtained each period is r_i if the borrower is good during the period and the credit limit is L_i. The cost if the borrower is bad and defaults is a one-off cost of $-l_i$. Suppose one is making the credit limit decision when there are n more periods to the end of the horizon, and let $v_n(S)$ be the present value of the total remaining

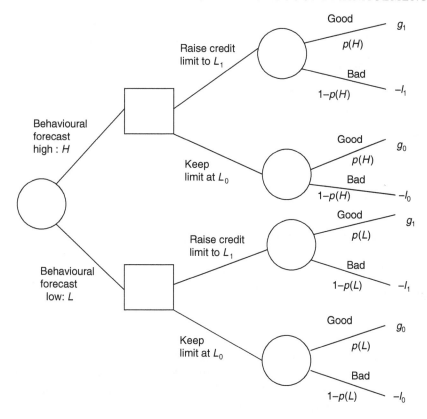

FIG. 4.1.1. Decision tree for increase in credit limit decision.

profit the bank will get from the loan if the optimal set of credit limit decisions is made over these remaining n periods and the current state of the borrower is S.

We make one simplifying assumption which is that the behavioural score of the borrower will stay in state S (either H or L) through all the remaining n periods. This is unrealistic but will help illustrate how important it is to include the dynamics of the behavioural score in calculating the profitability of the borrower. In that case, the total pay-off over the n periods if the borrower who has behavioural score S, stays good in the first period when the credit limit is L_i is $r_i + v_{n-1}(S)$. The first term r_i is the profit in this period while the second term $v_{n-1}(S)$ is the profit over the remaining $(n-1)$ periods of the time horizon given the behavioural score is S.

Often one will want to discount this future reward, which corresponds to saying a pound next year is not worth a pound this year. This discounting reflects the time value of money in that if the risk-free interest rate is i (that is $100\,i\%$), one can get £1 next year by putting £$1/_{1+i}$ in the bank this year. Discounting could also reflect a possible uncertainty in the time horizon. If there is a chance, a, each period that the borrower will stop using the credit card then the expected value of getting £1

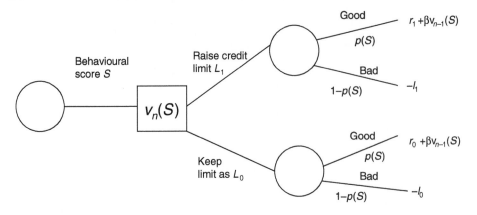

FIG. 4.1.2. Decision tree for first period of n-period credit limit increase problem.

next period is $(1 - a) \times £1 + a \times £0 = £(1 - a)$. Both these effects can be included by defining the discount factor as

$$\beta = \frac{1 - a}{1 + i} \qquad (4.1.2)$$

In such a case the profit if the borrower remains good under the credit limit L_i is $r_i + \beta v_{n-1}(S)$. Since all the rewards and costs in $v_{n-1}(S)$ are one period later than if one was starting a $(n - 1)$ period problem at the current period, one has to discount the future reward $v_{n-1}(S)$ by β in this case.

With these adjustments the decision tree for the first period of the problem when the initial behavioural score is given in Fig. 4.1.2. One should choose to increase the credit limit in this first period provided:

$$
\begin{aligned}
&p(S)(r_1 + \beta v_{n-1}(S)) + (1 - p(S))(-l_1) \\
&\quad > p(S)(r_0 + \beta v_{n-1}(S)) + (1 - p(S))(-l_0) \\
\Rightarrow\ &\frac{p(S)}{1 - p(S)} > \frac{l_1 - l_0}{r_1 - r_0}
\end{aligned}
\qquad (4.1.3)
$$

and the expected profit got from the borrower is

$$
\begin{aligned}
v_n(S) &= \max\{p(S)(r_1 + \beta v_{n-1}(S)) \\
&\quad - (1 - p(S))l_1, p(S)(r_0 + \beta v_{n-1}(S)) - (1 - p(S))l_0\} \\
&= \beta p(S)v_{n-1}(S) + \max\{p(S)r_1 - (1 - p(S))l_1, p(S)r_0 - (1 - p(S))l_0\}
\end{aligned}
\qquad (4.1.4)
$$

So the decision on what to do does not depend on the subsequent values $v_{n-1}(S)$ but only on $l_1, l_0, r_1, r_0, p(S)$. This means the optimal decision is the same every period, and so if it is worth increasing the credit limit in the first period, the bank should use this credit limit for this borrower in all the subsequent periods; if it is not worth increasing the credit limit now, then it never will be.

Since the decisions are constant over time, it is easy to calculate the total expected profitability of a borrower with behavioural score S. Define:

$$g_i(S) = p(S)r_i - (1 - p(S))l_i \quad \text{for } S = H, L, \ i = 0, 1, \text{ then}$$

$$v_n(S) = \max \begin{cases} g_1(S) + \beta p(S)[g_1(S) + \beta p(S)[g_1(S) + \beta p(S) \ldots, \\ g_0(S) + \beta p(S)[g_0(S) + \beta p(S)[g_0(S) + \beta p(S) \ldots, \end{cases}$$

$$= \max \begin{cases} g_1(S)(1 + \beta p(S) + (\beta p(S))^2 + \cdots + (\beta p(S))^{n-1}) \\ g_0(S)(1 + \beta p(S) + (\beta p(S))^2 + \cdots + (\beta p(S))^{n-1}) \end{cases} \quad (4.1.5)$$

$$= \max\{g_1(S), g_0(S)\} \times \frac{1 - (\beta p(S))^n}{1 - \beta p(S)}$$

If one extends the time horizon to be infinite, the same results hold. It is worth using the increased credit limit L_1 in every period if

$$\frac{p(S)}{1 - p(S)} > \frac{l_1 - l_0}{r_1 - r_0} \quad (4.1.6)$$

Otherwise one should never increase the limit. Define $v_\infty(S) = \lim\limits_{n \to \infty} v_n(S)$, then since $\beta p(S) < 1$ the limit of Eq. (4.1.6) becomes

$$v_\infty(S) = \frac{\max\{g_1(S), g_0(S)\}}{1 - \beta p(S)} \quad (4.1.7)$$

Notice we did not require in this model that once the bank increased the credit limit for an individual, it would not then decrease the limit. However, if we impose this condition it makes no difference to the results. The optimal sequence of decision in the original problem without this restriction is either to increase the limit immediately and keep it at the higher level or never to increase the credit limit. Both of these policies satisfy the condition, since neither decreases a credit limit and so they must be optimal for the problem where this extra requirement is imposed.

Example 4.1.3 Credit limit increase with two period horizon and change in borrower's behavioural score

Now consider the situation where the behavioural score of a borrower can change from period to period. None of the 'nice' results of Example 4.1.2 will necessarily still hold as we show by considering a two period problem. Such a problem corresponds to the decision tree in Fig. 4.1.3.

Figure 4.1.3a shows the decision tree for the first period while those in Fig. 4.1.3b and 4.1.3c show the decisions in the second period depending on what is the behavioural score of the borrower. Note again that we define $v_n(S)$ to be the future

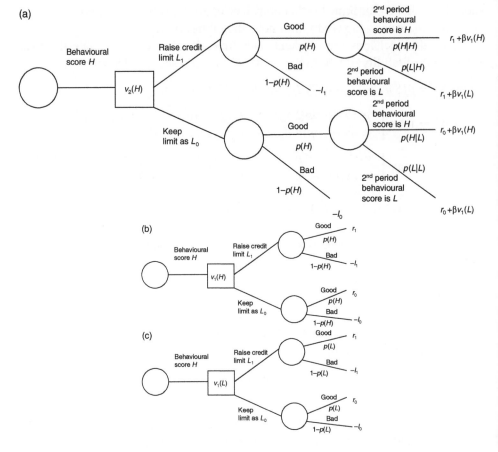

FIG. 4.1.3. Decomposition of two period increase credit limit decision tree.

profit over the next n periods given the borrower's current behavioural score is S. We also have to define $p(H|H), p(L|H), p(H|l), p(L|L)$ where $p(S|S')$ is the probability the behavioural score will be S next period given that it is S' in this period.

Assume the following numerical values:

$$r_1 = 2, l_1 = 20, r_0 = 1, l_0 = 5, p(H) = 0.95, p(L) = 0.9, \beta = 0.9 \qquad (4.1.8)$$

Solving the final period decisions gives

$$v_1(H) = \max\{p(H)(r_1) - (1 - p(H))l_1, p(H)(r_0) - (1 - p(H))l_0\}$$
$$= \max\{0.95(2) - 0.05(20), 0.95(1) - 0.05(5)\}$$
$$= \max\{0.9, 0.7\} = 0.9 \text{ (choose } L_1)$$

$$v_1(L) = \max\{p(L)(r_1) - (1 - p(L))l_1, p(L)(r_0) - (1 - p(L))l_0\}$$
$$= \max\{0.9(2) - 0.1(20), 0.9(1) - 0.1(5)\}$$
$$= \max\{-0.2, 0.4\} = 0.4 \text{ (choose } L_0)$$

$$v_2(H) = \max \begin{cases} p(H)(r_1 + \beta(p(H|H)v_1(H) + p(L|H)v_1(L)) - (1 - p(H))l_1 \\ p(H)(r_0 + \beta(p(H|H)v_1(H) + p(L|H)v_1(L)) - (1 - p(H))l_0 \end{cases}$$

$$= \max \begin{cases} 0.95(2) + 0.9(p(H|H)0.9 + p(L|H)0.4) - 0.05(20) \\ 0.95(1) + 0.9(p(H|H)0.9 + p(L|H)0.4) - 0.05(5). \end{cases} \quad (4.1.9)$$

The first expression here is greater than the second no matter what are the values of $p(H|H), P(L|H)$. So one should increase the credit limit to L_1.

Thus if the borrower has a high behavioural score initially, the bank should increase the credit limit to L_1. If in the next period the behavioural score stays high then the credit limit should be kept at L_1, but if the behavioural score changes to low in the next period then the credit limit should be dropped to L_0.

If we do not allow credit limits to be dropped then if we decided to increase the credit limit to L_1 in the first period, then the total discounted reward over the two periods would be

$$0.95(2 + 0.9(p(H|H)0.9 + p(L|H)(-0.2)) - 0.05(20)$$
$$= 0.9 + p(H|H)(0.7695) - p(L|H)(0.171). \quad (4.1.10)$$

Note that if the behavioural score was low in the second period then the bank has to keep the credit limit at L_1 and so only get a profit of -0.2 rather than the profit of 0.1 that it would get if the credit limit was set at L_0. If the credit limit in the first period is kept at L_0, then it would be possible to raise the credit limit in the second period no matter what the behavioural score was. Then the total discounted reward over the two periods would be

$$0.95(1 + 0.9(p(H|H)0.9 + p(L|H)(0.4)) - 0.05(5)$$
$$= 0.7 + p(H|H)(0.7695) + p(L|H)(0.342). \quad (4.1.11)$$

In the previous example, it was assumed $p(H|H) = 1$ and $p(L|H) = 0$ and so Eq. (4.1.10) is greater than Eq. (4.1.11) and it is best to increase the credit limit in the first period. If one had a very volatile behavioural score so that $p(H|H) = 0$ and $p(L|H) = 1$ then clearly Eq. (4.1.11) is larger than (4.1.10) and it is better not to increase the credit limit in the first period. Even in the case when $p(H|H) = p(L|H) = 0.5$ it turns out that it is better not to increase the credit limit initially. This shows that to identify the policy that optimizes the profitability of a loan over time one needs to model the dynamics of the borrower's risk propensity, which can mean modelling the dynamics of the borrower's behavioural score.

Static versus dynamic approaches to profit scoring

In the next section, we discuss the risk/reward matrix which is being used currently by some lenders as a first approach to optimal profit maximization policies. Here the decisions are made subjectively but one could also use the approach to underpin some models. The assumption is that the state of the borrower does not change over time, nor is it affected by the decision made or any future decision to be made. Thus it is a static approach to profit scoring and the rest of this chapter will then concentrate on two approaches to building dynamic models of profit scoring–Markov chains and survival analysis.

4.2   Profit scoring, risk/reward matrices to customer behaviour dynamics

The profitability of the borrowers to a bank depend on both their risk and reward. The question is how to measure and combine these two aspects of the borrower. The risk measurement is straightforward – the default risk score of the previous chapters is a good measure of risk. The reward part is less clear. We have taken expected profit as the objective in the initial offer/not offer and pricing decisions, and that might be an appropriate measure of reward. In fact, we also looked at the rate of return on capital, which is the expected profit, modified to allow for the amount of capital tied up in the loan and the length of time for which it is tied up. For fixed term loans where the only income stream is the interest paid on the loan the translation from overall expected profit to return on capital and vice versa is easy to do. For credit cards it is more difficult because even though there is a stated interest rate charged on the card balances, there are interest-free periods, which means that transactors pay no interest, and there are other income streams like merchant service charges which are linked to usage (for that reason we will concentrate on expected profit rather than on rate of return on capital when building models in this chapter).

In fact banks recognize that they should be interested not just in the expected profit they make from the borrowers on a loan product, but the expected profit they make from the borrowers because they had the product and that could include profits from other products that were sold on the back of the original loan. Before discussing further how banks measure the return from a borrower, it is worth considering this dual evolution from default scoring to profit scoring and at the same time the change from focusing on a borrower's performance on a product to focusing on the customer's overall performance.

Customer and product level scoring

Banks have evolved their assessment of risk and return so that now there are four different levels at which scoring can be used. These are

1. *Product default scoring*: Scoring the risk of the borrower defaulting on a particular product

2. *Customer default scoring*: Score the risk of the borrower defaulting on any product

3. *Product profit scoring*: Measuring the profitability of the borrower over that product

4. *Customer profit scoring*: Measuring the total profitability of the borrower over all products.

Product default scoring was the original application of credit scoring and is what someone naturally thinks of when credit scoring is mentioned. Customer default scoring has evolved over the last 20 years for customers who have several accounts and loans with a bank, particularly if one of them is a main checking or current account. Profit scoring both at account and customer level is still in its infancy.

So far we have not made the distinction in default scoring whether the score is a product default score or a customer default score. If an organization only has one lending product – car loan firms and finance houses for example – there is no point in distinguishing the two. For firms with more than one product two decisions made during the scorecard development process determine which type of default score it is.

First, what is meant by default? If the borrower only has that loan product with the bank, it is clear it means defaulting on the obligations of that loan. If the borrower has more than one product with a lender, say a mortgage and a credit card, does defaulting on the one mean the borrower should be classified as having defaulted on the other product? Technically it is not a default. Morally and in terms of the conservative approach adopted by and required of banks, it is a default. One is then measuring two different definitions of default – default at the product level and at the customer level – and so could produce two different scorecards.

The second decision to be made by the bank in developing default risk assessment systems, particularly for behavioural scoring systems, is what information to include if the borrower has more than one product (not necessarily all lending products) with the bank. If one has information on the performance of the borrower on other products should this be used as characteristics to forecast the default probability on this product? If so, one will have to segment the population and build different scorecards for those who have other products with you, and those who only have the one product. For lenders with many types of products, this could seem to be turning into a nightmare if one has to build a scorecard for each different combination of products that borrowers might take out. The reality is that the important 'other' information is mostly contained in the checking or current account. Checking accounts, especially if they are the main account where salaries appear to being deposited and from which the 'main' bills are being paid, have many characteristics which are powerful indicators of the financial health of the borrower and hence their risk of defaulting. Thus the question is whether to include this information in estimating if the client will default on other products, such as overdrafts, personal loans, credit cards, car loans, and mortgages. The answer for most banks nowadays is yes and so they develop generic customer default scores, which are measures of whether the customer will default on any loan product. In many instances, these scores are then used as one of the characteristics of a scorecard developed for estimating the risk of default on a specific product and it is no surprise to find that it is usually by far and away the most powerful characteristic.

The reason for this discussion is that this dichotomy between product level and customer level measurements is even more important in trying to assess the return from a borrower. Should this be done at the product level? For fixed term products this is equivalent to working out if and when the borrower will default and so seems to overlap the default score. If prepayment is allowed on the product, then some assessment of how likely this will be to occur, and when it will occur, is needed to estimate the profit. This may take the form of an attrition score.

This still misses out the possibility of cross-selling other products or up-selling the current product and the likely profitability of the borrower if they take up these other products. Hence to get a handle on these possibilities the banks often take the average balance in the customer's checking account as a measure of the level of their finances and of the strength of their relationship with the bank. The implication is that those who have lots of money and keep it in their checking account with that bank are better targets for the bank to sell profitable other products. If the checking account balances are low, it suggests either that the customers have little 'free' reserves or that the main share of their wallet is kept with some other financial organization. Thus banks' systems that use information on several accounts of a borrower to assess their overall profitability are clearly customer profit-scoring systems.

Product profit-scoring systems use information only on the performance of the borrower on that product. The information must include the default risk measures as default has a major impact on profitability and also prepayment risk. Later in this chapter we will see how survival analysis ideas give a much better handle on the time dependence of the risk and hence on the profit of a fixed term loan.

For revolving loan products, like credit cards, one would expect measures of usage (since that relates to the income from the retailers), and balance outstanding, since that indicates how much profit may come from the interest on the balances.

For some products it would also include estimates of whether the borrower will take insurance protection or concierge features of the product, which will provide further income streams. Thus if one is really seeking to estimate the profitability of a borrower either at product or customer level, there are a large number of uncertainties to assess, and it is a very difficult problem to determine how to combine them. So one may need to use a more modest profit system but one which is implementable. Banks just want some way of considering both the risk and the reward of the borrower at the same time.

Risk/reward matrix

As was suggested earlier, one can get a feel for the potential returns from the customers by looking at the average balance in their current account. This is one way of introducing return into a customer profit assessment system. For revolving products, the average balance does the same thing at product level in that it gives some indication of usage and the potential interest repayment stream if the borrower is a revolver. So at both customer and product level one might want to concentrate on behavioural score and average balances. This can be shown as a matrix, the risk/reward matrix, the rows of which are bands of the default score and the columns of which are bands of average balance levels. For each cell in this matrix an operating policy is then decided upon. Table 4.2.1 gives an example where the bank is using the system to decide on the overdraft limits that a customer may be offered.

The strategy in the table makes sense in that the higher the behaviour score (and hence the less risk of default) the higher the overdraft that can be offered. Similarly the higher the average balance, and hence the more potential for profit from the customer, the higher should be the overdraft. However, the choice of level is usually a subjective judgement by the bank's managers with little or no analysis of the likely effect of these decisions on the profitability or the default risk of the borrower. The banding of both the risk and the reward level is normally equally subjective. The split points are sometimes chosen arbitrarily and often because they

TABLE 4.2.1. Example of profit strategy given by a risk/reward matrix.

Overdraft limit	Balance < $1000	Balance £1000– $5000	Balance > $5000
Behavioural score >500	$20,000	$25,000	$30,000
Behavioural score 300–500	$4000	$8000	$20,000
Behavioural score < 300	No overdraft	$1000	$2000

are nicely rounded numbers rather than for any reason of homogeneity of the bands thus formed.

Modelling the optimal decision in a risk/reward matrix

One could use a model to determine the actions one should apply at each to the borrower segment in each cell though, while still meeting some overall portfolio requirement.

Consider the situation where there are m behavioural score risk bands $i = 1, 2, \ldots, m$ with the average probability of being a good in band i being p_i. There are n reward bands $j = 1, 2, \ldots, n$ with the average balance in band j being b_j. If there are n_{ij} borrows in cell (i, j) (risk band i and reward band j), one want to find the credit limit L_{ij} to apply to each borrower in cell (i, j) so as to maximize the expected profit for the portfolio, but with some limits on the risk involved. Assume the reward for the borrowers who remain good is a function $g(b, L)$ of the average balance, b, in their cell and the credit limit, L, being applied to them. The loss registered by a borrower who is a bad is also a function $l(b, L)$ of the average balance and the credit limit in the appropriate cell. Two types of risk constraints are applied to the portfolio. Firstly the total credit extended to risk group i cannot exceed A_i $i = 1, 2, \ldots, m$ and secondly the expected losses from the portfolio should not exceed D. The objective is to choose the credit limits L_{ij} so as to maximize the expected profit (returns minus losses) from the portfolio. This can be expressed as the following non-linear optimization problem:

$$\underset{L_{ij}}{\text{Max}} \sum_{i=1}^{m} \sum_{j=1}^{n} n_{ij} \left(p_i g(b_j, L_{ij}) - (1 - p_i) l(b_j, L_{ij}) \right)$$

$$\text{subject to} \sum_{j=1}^{n} n_{ij} L_{ij} \leq A_i \quad \forall i = 1, 2, \ldots, m \tag{4.2.1}$$

$$\sum_{i=1}^{m} \sum_{j=1}^{n} n_{ij} (1 - p_i) l(b_j, L_{ij}) \leq D$$

$$L_{ij} \geq 0 \quad \forall i = 1, 2, \ldots, m, \quad j = 1, 2, \ldots, n.$$

If the reward and loss functions were linear in the balance and the credit limit, this would reduce to a linear programming problem. A reasonable linear loss function for risk band i would be

$$l(b, L) = b + \alpha_i (L - b), \tag{4.2.2}$$

which suggests that the exposure at default is the average balance plus some risk-dependent credit conversion factor α_i times the balance not drawn down by the average borrower. A reasonable linear reward function for risk band i would be

$$g(b, L) = \gamma b + \delta_i(L - b), \tag{4.2.3}$$

which suggests that the reward is partly related to the average balance (possibly through the merchant service charge) and partly to a risk default factor times the remaining balance which reflects those revolvers who build up their balances and hence have high interest payments. Assuming Eqs. (4.2.2) and (4.2.3) are the respective loss and reward functions, Eq. (4.2.1) reduces to the following linear programming problem:

$$\operatorname*{Max}_{L_{ij}} \sum_{i=1}^{m} \sum_{j=1}^{n} n_{ij} \left((p_i \delta_i - \alpha_i(1 - p_i)) L_{ij} + [p_i(\gamma - \delta_i)b_j - (1 - p_i)(1 - \alpha_i)b_j] \right)$$

$$\text{subject to } \sum_{j=1}^{n} n_{ij} L_{ij} \leq A_i \quad \forall i = 1, 2, \ldots, m$$

$$\sum_{i=1}^{m} \sum_{j=1}^{n} n_{ij}(1 - p_i)\alpha_i L_{ij} \leq D - \sum_{i=1}^{m} \sum_{j=1}^{n} n_{ij}(1 - p_i)(1 - \alpha_i)b_j$$

$$L_{ij} \geq 0 \quad \forall i = 1, 2, \ldots, m, \quad j = 1, 2, \ldots, n. \tag{4.2.4}$$

Notice that if the coefficient of L_{ij} in the objective is negative then the profit can only be maximized if the corresponding credit limit is zero. So that cell will not be offered any loans. This corresponds to the condition that

$$\frac{p_i}{1 - p_i} < \frac{\alpha_i}{\delta_i}. \tag{4.2.5}$$

Example 4.2.1 Portfolio level credit limit decisions

Take a simple example of the linear programming problem given by Eq. (4.2.4). Assume there is a portfolio of 1000 accounts split into two risk bands ($p = 0.95$ and $p = 0.9$) and two reward bands ($b = £500$ and $b = £1000$). We take the parameter values:

$$m = 2, n = 2, p_1 = 0.95, p_2 = 0.9, b_1 = 500, b_2 = 1000,$$

$$n_{11} = 200, n_{12} = 600, n_{21} = 80, n_{22} = 120 \tag{4.2.6}$$

$$\alpha_1 = 0.5, \alpha_2 = 0.9, \delta_1 = 0.1, \delta_2 = 0.4, \gamma = 0.5$$

so there are 200 accounts in the top left cell, 600 in the top right cell, and 100 each in the bottom cells as in Table 4.2.2.

If we set the credit limit for each risk level so that $A_2 = £210,000, A_1 = £1,500,000$, this means we do not want more than £210,000 committed to the riskiest group and a total of £1,710,000 committed to the whole portfolio. Assume

TABLE 4.2.2. Parameter values for Example 4.2.1.

	$B_1 = £500$	$b_2 = £1000$	α	δ	γ
$p_1 = 0.95$	$N_{11} = 200$	$n_{12} = 600$	0.5	0.1	0.5
$p_2 = 0.9$	$N_{21} = 80$	$n_{22} = 120$	0.9	0.4	

TABLE 4.2.3. Credit limit solutions to Example 4.2.3.

	$b_1 = £500$	$b_2 = £1000$
$p_1 = 0.95$	$L_{11} = £750$	$L_{12} = £1833$
$p_2 = 0.9$	$L_{21} = £625$	$L_{22} = £1333$

that the expected losses cannot be more than £70,000 (that is $D = 70,000$). We also will assume that as this is an existing portfolio we cannot really decrease the credit limit too much so we will assume that for those in risk band 1, the credit limit must be at least 1.5 times the average balance (that is £750 and £1500, respectively), while for those in the riskier risk band 2 we will assume the credit limit must be at least 1.25 times the average balance (£625 and £ 1250, respectively). This gives the linear programme

$$\text{Max } 14L_{11} + 42L_{12} + 21.6L_{21} + 32.4L_{22} + 261,300$$

$$\text{subject to } 200L_{11} + 600L_{12} \leq 1,500,000$$

$$100L_{21} + 100L_{22} \leq 210,000 \tag{4.2.7}$$

$$5L_{11} + 15L_{12} + 7.2L_{21} + 10.8L_{22} + 19,100 \leq 70,000$$

$$L_{11} \geq 750, \quad L_{12} \geq 1500, \quad L_{21} \geq 625, \quad L_{22} \geq 1250$$

The solution to this linear programme obtained by using Solver in Excel gives the credit limits in Table 4.2.3.

In this case the profit is £407,600, and the expected losses are exactly £70,000, while exactly £210,000 has been committed to credit limits in the riskier group. The total amount committed in credit limits to the less risky group does not reach the £1,500,000 which was the upper limit. Thus one can use optimization to get a feel for what are the best decisions to make in each cell of a risk/reward matrix.

Dynamics of consumer behaviour

One way of extending the risk/reward matrix approach to allow for the extra factors that affect profitability is to increase the complexity of the reward dimension of the matrix. One exploits the fact that many banks already have a series of scorecards which measure other probabilities relating to the borrower's performance. How likely is it that the borrower can be cross-sold another product? In a revolving product like a credit card, how likely are the borrowers to use the card at all? How likely are they to use it as their main card? How likely are the borrowers to pay-off early a fixed term loan like a mortgage or how likely are they to close their credit card account and move to another lender as soon as the initial attractive offer finishes? Instead of just segmenting the borrowers by risk and a surrogate for reward, they are segmented by their score in several of these probability estimators and different policies applied to each segment.

Extending the dimensions of the risk/reward matrix does not deal with the real difficulty in that approach, which is it only segments according to the current behaviour of the borrower. It does not allow for the fact that borrower's behaviour will change with time and so a borrower is likely to move from cell to cell. This means the subsequent decisions by the bank will also change and this needs to be recognized when making the current decision. Example 4.1.3 was a simple example in that the bank should not increase the credit limit of this period even though it was the optimal one period decision because it wanted the ability to use the lower credit limit in the next period.

There are two well-used approaches in other areas that allow for this stochastic dynamic nature of the borrower's performance to be modelled – Markov chain theory and survival analysis. The first lists the different states the borrower can be in and seeks to estimate the chance of moving from one state to another between one time period and the next. The states can be quite complex as they seek to describe all the aspects of the borrower's position – current default risk, recent repayment behaviour, and recent usage of the product. The Markov property means that the state must also contain all the information needed to estimate the probabilities of which state the borrower may move to next. This means that one needs only to know what the current state of the borrowers is to predict their future behaviour. One can also assume that the transition probabilities between the states are time-independent, which makes the model a lot easier to compute with.

Survival analysis concentrates on when certain events occur and is not interested in the state of the borrower between these events. In the consumer credit context clearly these events would be default, early repayment and purchases of items with the borrowing product. Although survival analysis loses out in that it does not estimate what happens between these events, the argument is that nothing very exciting is happening. Its advantage over Markov chains is that it does not need the Markov assumption. Thus it is particularly useful for fixed term loan products where repayments are predetermined unless there is a default or a prepayment. The Markov chain approach can be used for both fixed and revolving loans but comes into its own in the latter case.

The second difficulty with the static risk/reward matrix approach is that it ignores that there will be subsequent decisions made which will affect the overall profitability of the borrower. One can allow for this in the Markov chain approach by extending it to include the decisions so that it becomes what is called a Markov decision process (MDP). In this one allows decisions to be made in each time period and these affect the return from the borrowers and the probabilities of which behavioural state they move to next. This approach is useful for revolving products, where one is always thinking of adjusting credit limits (be it only the 'shadow' ones in the background) or marketing other products to the borrower. Superficially survival analysis does not seem to take the subsequent decisions into account but it does do so since it models the probabilities of the important events like default occurring as functions of time and the history of the borrower–lender relationship up to that point. Moreover, the idea of competing risks in survival analysis says that that all the events are competing against one another to be the first to happen and when the first event happens this may stop other events happening or make other events possible for the first time.

One of the bonuses of these dynamic approaches to profit scoring is that both will allow the variations in the state of the economy to be part of the model if one so wishes. It certainly seems reasonable to assume the profitability of a product does depend on the impact of the economy on consumers. Since the borrowing products in consumer credit can take several years or decades to maturity or in the case of revolving products might last the lifetime of the borrower, it is important to be able to allow the models to input the banks' forecasts of what will happen to the economy over such extended periods.

Anyhow, enough of the adverts; in the rest of this chapter, we will examine how these two approaches can be used to aid banks make profitable account management decisions.

4.3   Markov chain models of account behaviour

The idea of building a dynamic model of the behaviour of an account was first suggested in the early 1960s. However, the success of the static approach of default-based scoring to estimating risk meant that it is only recently with the move towards profitability as a criterion that such an approach has been implemented in practice. In a Markov chain approach, one identifies the different 'states' that the account can be in and estimates the chance of the account moving from one state during a given base time period. Typically the base time period would be the 1-month billing period for credit card accounts but a quarter or even a year may be more appropriate in some other applications. The state of the account should include all the information needed for the classification or the measurement one wants to make on that account. So for example the state might be the behaviour score of the account or for debt forecasting purposes it might just be the number of periods the account is in arrears.

Definition of Markov chain

The Markov assumption is that the process is memoryless. This means that the probability of which state the account moves to next depends only on which state it is in at present and does not depend on the history of which states it was in previously. This puts quite a burden on the state definition but it also leads to a model which allows one to make useful forecasts of what is likely to happen to that account and hence to the portfolio of accounts held by the lender. More formally, one says that the stochastic process X_n, where $n = 0, 1, 2, \ldots$, defining a dynamic model is a Markov chain if it has the following property.

Definition 4.3.1

Let $\{X_0, X_1, X_2, X_3, \ldots\}$ be a collection of random variables which take values in one of the I states. The process is said to be a finite-valued Markov chain if

$$\Pr\{X_{n+1} = j | X_0 = k_0, \quad X_1 = k_1, \ldots, X_{n-1} = k_{n-1}, \quad X_n = i\}$$
$$= \Pr\{X_{n+1} = j | X_n = i\} \quad \text{for } \forall n \text{ and } i, j \text{ where } 1 \leq i, j \leq I. \quad (4.3.1)$$

The conditional probability $\Pr\{X_n = j | X_{n-1} = i\}$ are called transition probabilities and represented $p_n(i, j)$. The probability properties mean that one requires that $p_n(i, j) \geq 0$ and $\sum_j p_n(i, j) = 1$.

The matrix of these probabilities is denoted by P_n so $(P_n)(i, j) = p_n(i, j)$. The Markov property (4.3.1) means that one can obtain the distribution of X_2, the state in period 2, given the process started in period 0 in the initial state i by saying

$$\Pr\{X_2 = j | X_0 = i\} = \sum_k \Pr\{X_2 = j | X_1 = k\} \times \Pr\{X_1 = k | X_0 = i\}$$
$$= \sum_k p_1(i, k) p_2(k, j) = (P_1 * P_2)(i, j). \quad (4.3.2)$$

Here we denote $(P_1 * P_2)$ to represent matrix multiplication where the value in the kth column of the ith row of the first matrix is multiplied by the value in the kth row of the jth column of the second matrix and these products summed (as defined in Eq. (4.3.2)) over all k. This idea extends so it is possible to calculate the distribution of X_n, the probability of which state the system is in after n periods given the value of X_0 by multiplying the matrices $P_1, P_2, \ldots, P_n$ together since

$$P\{X_n = j|X_0 = i\} = \sum_{k(1),\dots,k(n-1)} P\{X_n = j|X_{n-1} = k(n-1)\}P\{X_{n-1}$$

$$= k(n-1)|X_{n-2} = k(n-2\}\dots$$

$$\dots P\{X_2 = k(2)|X_1 = k(1)\}P\{X_1 = k(1)|X_0 = i\}$$

$$= \sum_{k(1),\dots,k(n-1)} p_1(i,k(1))p_2(k(1),k(2))\dots p_n(k(n-1),j)$$

$$= (P_{1*}P_{2*}\dots_*P_n)(i,j). \tag{4.3.3}$$

If $p_n(i,j) = p(i,j)$ for all n, i, and j, the process is said to be a stationary Markov chain.

In that case, the n-stage transition probabilities are obtained by multiplying P by itself n times so

$$P\{X_n = j|X_0 = i\} = \sum_{k(1),\dots,k(n-1)} p(i,k(1))p(k(1),k(2)),\dots,p(k(n-1),j)$$

$$= (P_*P_*\dots_*P)(i,j) = P^n(i,j). \tag{4.3.4}$$

If π_n is the distribution of X_n, so $\pi_n(i) = \Pr(X_n = i)$, then one can relate the distribution at time $(n+1)$ to that at time n by

$$P\{X_{n+1} = j\} = \sum_i P\{X_n = i\}P\{X_{n+1} = j|X_n = i\}. \tag{4.3.5}$$

This, together with (4.3.4), corresponds to

$$\pi_{n+1} = \pi_n P = \pi_0 P^{n+1} \tag{4.3.6}$$

in vector notation. An aperiodic Markov chain is one in which there is no periodicity where periodicity means that one can only get from one particular state to another particular state in a multiple of a certain number of periods. Formally this means there is no $k \geq 2$, so the $p^n(i,j) \neq 0$ for some i, j only if k divides n exactly. Almost all Markov chains are aperiodic and for them in the long-run π_n converges to a long-run distribution π^*. Replacing π_n and π_{n+1} by π^* in Eq. (4.3.6) shows that π^* must satisfy

$$\pi^* = \pi^* P. \tag{4.3.7}$$

The states of the Markov chain divide into persistent and transient ones. Persistent states i are ones which the chain is certain to return to and correspond to states where $\pi_i^* > 0$, that is, there is a positive probability of being in them in the long run. A persistent state which the chain can never subsequently leave is called an absorbing state. Transient states i are ones where the chain has a probability of less than 1 of ever returning to and corresponding to states where $\pi^*_i = 0$.

Examples of consumer credit Markov chain models

Example 4.3.1 Behavioural score bands

Suppose the behavioural score is split into two groups – high (H) and low (L) – which is similar to the behavioural score models in Section 4.1. In each period, 95% of those with high behavioural scores stay high at the next period while 5% drop to low scores. For those with low scores, 90% stay with low scores in the next period but 10% move to the high score band. The states of the Markov chain that describe this dynamic process are high (H) and low (L) and the transition probability matrix between one period and the next is given by

$$P = \begin{array}{c} \\ H \\ L \end{array} \begin{array}{cc} H & L \\ \begin{pmatrix} 0.95 & 0.05 \\ 0.1 & 0.9 \end{pmatrix} \end{array}. \tag{4.3.8}$$

For individuals starting with a high score $\pi_0 = (1, 0)$, then the probability of what score band they will be in after 1, 2, 3, and 4 periods π_1, π_2, π_3, and π_4 are given by

$$\pi_1 = \pi_0 P = \begin{pmatrix} 1 & 0 \end{pmatrix} \begin{pmatrix} 0.95 & 0.05 \\ 0.1 & 0.9 \end{pmatrix} = \begin{pmatrix} 0.95 & 0.05 \end{pmatrix}$$

$$\pi_2 = \pi_0 P^2 = \pi_1 P = \begin{pmatrix} 0.95 & 0.05 \end{pmatrix} \begin{pmatrix} 0.95 & 0.05 \\ 0.1 & 0.9 \end{pmatrix} = \begin{pmatrix} 0.9075 & 0.0925 \end{pmatrix}$$

$$\pi_3 = \pi_0 P^3 = \pi_2 P = \begin{pmatrix} 0.9075 & 0.0925 \end{pmatrix} \begin{pmatrix} 0.95 & 0.05 \\ 0.1 & 0.9 \end{pmatrix} = \begin{pmatrix} 0.8714 & 0.1286 \end{pmatrix}$$

$$\pi_4 = \pi_0 P^4 = \pi_3 P = \begin{pmatrix} 0.8714 & 0.1286 \end{pmatrix} \begin{pmatrix} 0.95 & 0.05 \\ 0.1 & 0.9 \end{pmatrix} = \begin{pmatrix} 0.8407 & 0.1593 \end{pmatrix}.$$

$$\tag{4.3.9}$$

Similarly, for someone starting with a low behavioural score, the initial distribution is $\pi_0 = (0, 1)$ and so at the subsequent periods the probability distribution of the score bands is

$$\pi_1 = \pi_0 P = \begin{pmatrix} 0 & 1 \end{pmatrix} \begin{pmatrix} 0.95 & 0.05 \\ 0.1 & 0.9 \end{pmatrix} = \begin{pmatrix} 0.1 & 0.9 \end{pmatrix}$$

$$\pi_2 = \pi_0 P^2 = \pi_1 P = \begin{pmatrix} 0.1 & 0.9 \end{pmatrix} \begin{pmatrix} 0.95 & 0.05 \\ 0.1 & 0.9 \end{pmatrix} = \begin{pmatrix} 0.185 & 0.815 \end{pmatrix}$$

$$\pi_3 = \pi_0 P^3 = \pi_2 P = \begin{pmatrix} 0.185 & 0.815 \end{pmatrix} \begin{pmatrix} 0.95 & 0.05 \\ 0.1 & 0.9 \end{pmatrix} = \begin{pmatrix} 0.2572 & 0.7428 \end{pmatrix}$$

$$\pi_4 = \pi_0 P^4 = \pi_3 P = \begin{pmatrix} 0.2572 & 0.7428 \end{pmatrix} \begin{pmatrix} 0.95 & 0.05 \\ 0.1 & 0.9 \end{pmatrix} = \begin{pmatrix} 0.3187 & 0.6813 \end{pmatrix}$$

$$(4.3.10)$$

One could also get a feel for the distribution of score bands over the whole population. If initially 60% of the population has high scores and 40% has low scores, one can describe this by saying that the initial distribution is $\pi_0 = (0.6, 0.4)$ Then the distribution of scores in the population after 1, 2, 3, and 4 periods is

$$\pi_1 = \pi_0 P = \begin{pmatrix} 0.6 & 0.4 \end{pmatrix} \begin{pmatrix} 0.95 & 0.05 \\ 0.1 & 0.9 \end{pmatrix} = \begin{pmatrix} 0.61 & 0.39 \end{pmatrix}$$

$$\pi_2 = \pi_0 P^2 = \pi_1 P = \begin{pmatrix} 0.61 & 0.39 \end{pmatrix} \begin{pmatrix} 0.95 & 0.05 \\ 0.1 & 0.9 \end{pmatrix} = \begin{pmatrix} 0.6185 & 0.3815 \end{pmatrix}$$

$$\pi_3 = \pi_0 P^3 = \pi_2 P = \begin{pmatrix} 0.6185 & 0.3815 \end{pmatrix} \begin{pmatrix} 0.95 & 0.05 \\ 0.1 & 0.9 \end{pmatrix} = \begin{pmatrix} 0.6257 & 0.3743 \end{pmatrix}$$

$$\pi_4 = \pi_0 P^4 = \pi_3 P = \begin{pmatrix} 0.6257 & 0.3743 \end{pmatrix} \begin{pmatrix} 0.95 & 0.05 \\ 0.1 & 0.9 \end{pmatrix} = \begin{pmatrix} 0.6319 & 0.3681 \end{pmatrix}$$

$$(4.3.11)$$

The probability distribution can be interpreted in one of two ways. For an individual it is the probability of what their state will be in the future; for a population it is the distribution of the population in future time periods.

Since the transition probability matrix is independent of time in this example, this is a stationary Markov chain and so settles down to the long-run distribution π^* where $\pi^* = \pi^* P$ or

$$\pi^*(H) = 0.95\pi^*(H) + 0.1\pi^*(L)$$
$$\pi^*(L) = 0.05\pi^*(H) + 0.9\pi^*(L)$$
$$\text{with } \pi^*(H) + \pi^*(L) = 1$$
$$\Rightarrow \pi^*(H) = 2/3, \pi^*(L) = 1/3$$

$$(4.3.12)$$

Notice how the distributions π_t approach the 'long-run' distribution and even after four periods the population split in Eq. (4.3.11) is close to (2/3,1/3). All the above calculations can be extended to allow for far more than just two score bands.

Example 4.3.2 Behavioural score bands with profits

One could use the calculations of Example 4.3.1 to estimate the profitability of a borrower or a portfolio of borrowers. In Example 4.1.2 we assumed that the profitability of borrowers, who were good in the next period, depended on their behavioural score and was $r(H)$ and $r(L)$, respectively. Suppose $r(H) = 10$ and $r(L) = 2$, then the expected profit from a borrower in the period n from now is $10\pi_n(H) + 2\pi_n(L)$. For someone starting with a high behavioural score the expected profit over the next few periods would be

$$10\pi_0(H) + 2\pi_0(L) = 10$$
$$10\pi_1(H) + 2\pi_1(L) = 10(0.95) + 2(0.05) = 9.6 \qquad (4.3.13)$$
$$10\pi_2(H) + 2\pi_2(L) = 10(0.9075) + 2(0.0925) = 9.26.$$

Lenders are most interested in the expected cumulative profitability of the borrower. The cumulative profitability over n periods must depend on whether their behavioural score at the start of the n periods was H or L and we denote these respective expected cumulative profitabilities over n periods by $v_n(H)$ and $v_n(L)$. We can split this profit into that generated in the first of the n periods and that generated in the remaining $(n-1)$ periods and this leads to the equations

$$v_n(H) = 10 + 0.95v_{n-1}(H) + 0.05v_{n-1}(L)$$
$$v_n(L) = 2 + 0.1v_{n-1}(H) + 0.9v_{n-1}(L) \qquad (4.3.14)$$

where the v_{n-1} terms reflect which state the borrowers are in at the end of the first period and hence are multiplied by how likely are they to be in that state.

One can solve these equations iteratively starting with v_1 and hence solving v_2 is as follows:

$$v_1(H) = 10; \; v_1(L) = 2$$
$$v_2(H) = 10 + 0.95v_1(H) + 0.05v_1(L) = 19.6$$
$$v_2(L) = 2 + 0.1v_1(H) + 0.9v_1(L) = 4.8 \qquad (4.3.15)$$
$$v_3(H) = 10 + 0.95v_2(H) + 0.05v_2(L) = 28.86$$
$$v_3(L) = 2 + 0.1v_2(H) + 0.9v_2(L) = 8.28.$$

Notice that the increase in the $v_n(H)$ profitability as the time periods increase $19.6 - 10 = 9.6, 28.86 - 19.6 = 9.26$ agrees with the individual period profits calculates above. Since the long-run distribution is $(2/3, 1/3)$, this means that after some time the average profitability per period for borrowers settles down at $2/3(10) + 1/3(2) = 7.33$. This is what happens as we let n go towards infinity in the equations above. Again these results can be interpreted at either individual or at group level.

In the general case one can repeat this idea of conditioning the expected total profit over n periods by which state transitions occur in the first period, recognizing that the remaining profit is that gained over $(n-1)$ periods starting with the result of this transition. Formally that leads to the equation:

$$v_n(i) = r(i) + \sum_j p(i,j)v_{n-1}(j). \tag{4.3.16}$$

The solution process involves solving for v_1 initially and using this to solve for v_2, and so on.

Example 4.3.3 Behavioural score bands with profit and default

One unrealistic feature of the previous examples was that there was no chance of default. One can add an extra default state D to the model and estimate the probability of defaulting from each behavioural score band. This would involve the transformation of score to default probability outlined in Sections 1.5 and 1.6 if the transition periods are the horizon times used in estimating default. If they are smaller than this horizon, the transition probabilities to default have to be derived empirically. Suppose that in Example 4.3.2 there is in fact no chance that a borrower with a high behavioural score can move into default in the next period but there is a 2% chance that a borrower with a low behavioural score will default next period. We keep the chance of a borrower moving from a low behavioural score to a high score next period as 10% so there is a 88% chance a borrower will remain with a low behavioural score from one period to the next. If a borrower moves into default we assume there is a one-off loss of 1000, the average loss given default on an account. Notice this is a one-off cost compared with the recurring rewards of 10 and 2 ($r(H) = 10$, $r(L) = 2$) which occur if the borrowers are still up to date in their payments in the two behavioural score states. So there are three states in the Markov chain now, H, L, and D (for default) and the transition matrix is

$$P = \begin{array}{c} \\ H \\ L \\ D \end{array} \begin{array}{c} \begin{array}{ccc} H & L & D \end{array} \\ \begin{pmatrix} 0.95 & 0.05 & 0 \\ 0.1 & 0.88 & 0.02 \\ 0 & 0 & 1 \end{pmatrix} \end{array}. \tag{4.3.17}$$

If $v_n(H), v_n(L), v_n(D)$ are the expected cumulative profit over n periods starting in states H, L, and D, respectively, then we can again split those into the profit in the first period plus that in the remaining $(n-1)$ periods to get the recursive equations:

$$\begin{aligned} v_n(H) &= 10 + 0.95v_{n-1}(H) + 0.05v_{n-1}(L) \\ v_n(L) &= 2 + 0.1v_{n-1}(H) + 0.88v_{n-1}(L) + 0.02(-1000 + v_{n-1}(D)) \\ v_n(D) &= v_{n-1}(D) \equiv 0. \end{aligned} \tag{4.3.18}$$

TABLE 4.3.1. Results of Example 4.3.3.

Horizon	$v_1(\cdot)$	$v_2(\cdot)$	$v_3(\cdot)$	$v_4(\cdot)$	$v_{10}(\cdot)$	$v_{25}(\cdot)$	$v_{100}(\cdot)$	$v_{200}(\cdot)$	$v_\infty(\cdot)$
State H	10	18.60	26.03	38.09	57.86	86.39	165.40	227.01	300.0
State L	-18	-32.84	-45.04	-55.03	-85.31	-85.68	-18.18	35.92	100.0
State D	0	0	0	0	0	0	0	0	0

Solving these iteratively starting with $v_0(\cdot) \equiv 0$, since there is no reward if there is no time interval, and then solving for $v_1(\cdot), v_2(\cdot), \ldots, v_n(\cdot)$ in turn gives the values in Table 4.3.1.

Note though that the long-run stationary probability of which state the borrower ends up in is $\pi^* = (0, 0, 1)$ since the borrower is bound eventually to default if the loan continues for long enough. D is the only absorbing state in the system. However, the expected profit for the bank can be positive since there is a steady reward from the borrower while there is no default which more than compensates for the loss at default. The expected profit starting in the high behavioural score state increases as the number of periods increases and eventually converges to 300. This is because the total expected profit from a borrower while they are non-defaulters is 1300 which exceeds the 1000 loss that will occur on default. For a borrower starting in the low state, the expected profit when there is a short-time horizon is negative and getting more negative as the number of periods increases because the chance of defaulting in this period increases. At a time horizon of 19, the profit from those who have not defaulted over 19 periods outweighs the increase in losses from the increased chance of defaulting in 19 rather than 18 periods and so the expected profit starts to increase. Eventually it stabilizes at an expected profit of 100.

Example 4.3.4 Account status with default

A common application which includes a default state is to model the dynamics of the account status of the borrower. Suppose the lender classifies a borrower as having defaulted if they are three periods overdue with their repayments, then the state of an account can be up to date (state 0), 1 period overdue (state 1), 2 periods overdue (state 2), or 3 or more months overdue (state 3). Once a borrower reaches state 3 they are deemed to have defaulted, the product is withdrawn and so they cannot leave that state.

Assume that the transition probabilities between the states are given by the following matrix:

$$P = \begin{pmatrix} 0.95 & 0.05 & 0 & 0 \\ 0.75 & 0.05 & 0.2 & 0 \\ 0.2 & 0.1 & 0.1 & 0.6 \\ 0 & 0 & 0 & 1 \end{pmatrix}. \tag{4.3.19}$$

Note that in the first row, corresponding to transitions from the up to date state, the definition of the states implies that there is no chance of moving to the 2 months overdue or 3 months overdue states. These are called structural zeros. Similarly in row 2 when one is 1 month overdue one cannot go immediately to the 3 months overdue state, though by not paying one moves to 2 months overdue, and by paying the full amount owed one can move back to the up to date state. If only 1 month's repayment on the loan is paid, then the borrower is classified as remaining in the '1 month overdue' state. The last row is the result of saying that once borrowers are 3 months overdue they have defaulted and will remain in that state. This is an absorbing (sometimes called a 'coffin') state. Again we can calculate the distribution of the future account status and incidentally the chance of defaulting of the borrowers who are currently up to date in their repayments as follows:

$$\pi_1 = \pi_0 P = \begin{pmatrix} 1 & 0 & 0 & 0 \end{pmatrix} \begin{pmatrix} 0.95 & 0.05 & 0 & 0 \\ 0.75 & 0.05 & 0.2 & 0 \\ 0.2 & 0.1 & 0.1 & 0.6 \\ 0 & 0 & 0 & 1 \end{pmatrix} = \begin{pmatrix} 0.95 & 0.05 & 0 & 0 \end{pmatrix}$$

$$\pi_2 = \pi_0 P^2 = \pi_1 P = \begin{pmatrix} 0.95 & 0.05 & 0 & 0 \end{pmatrix} \begin{pmatrix} 0.95 & 0.05 & 0 & 0 \\ 0.75 & 0.05 & 0.2 & 0 \\ 0.2 & 0.1 & 0.1 & 0.6 \\ 0 & 0 & 0 & 1 \end{pmatrix}$$

$$= \begin{pmatrix} 0.94 & 0.05 & 0.01 & 0 \end{pmatrix}$$

$$\pi_3 = \pi_0 P^3 = \pi_2 P = \begin{pmatrix} 0.932 & 0.051 & 0.011 & 0.006 \end{pmatrix}$$

$$\pi_4 = \pi_0 P^4 = \pi_3 P = \begin{pmatrix} 0.926 & 0.050 & 0.011 & 0.013 \end{pmatrix}.$$

$$(4.3.20)$$

The problem with this model is that the long-run average distribution is $\pi^* = (0, 0, 0, 1)$, that is eventually one is bound to default. This always follows if there are absorbing states in a Markov chain. One always ends up in an absorbing state. It is possible to calculate how long before this happens by thinking of one getting a profit of 1 each period one has not defaulted and 0 once one has defaulted and then to use the profit calculation of Example 4.3.2. The times until default, T, depend on the state one is in, that is, $T(0)$, $T(1)$, and $T(2)$ and these satisfy

$$T(0) = 1 + 0.95T(0) + 0.05T(1)$$
$$T(1) = 1 + 0.75T(0) + 0.05T(1) + 0.2T(2)$$
$$T(2) = 1 + 0.2T(0) + 0.1T(1) + 0.1T(2)$$

$$(4.3.21)$$

$$\Rightarrow T(0) = 146.8; \quad T(1) = 126.8; \quad T(2) = 46.8.$$

This is not a full description of what can happen because the borrowers may complete their repayments (fixed loan) or close their account in good status (revolving loans) and hence we ought to add another absorbing state – close account in good standing.

Suppose that there is a 1% chance of those who are up to date closing their account each period, a 95% chance they stay up to date and a 4% chance they will slip to one period overdue. If the other transition probabilities stay the same as in Eq. (4.3.19), this gives a five-state Markov chain with states $(C,0,1,2,3)$ where C is closed account in good status. The transition matrix will then become:

$$
\begin{array}{ccccc}
0 & 0 & 0 & 0 & 1 \\
0.01 & 0.95 & 0.04 & 0 & 0 \\
0 & 0.75 & 0.05 & 0.2 & 0 \\
0 & 0.2 & 0.1 & 0.1 & 0.6 \\
0 & 0 & 0 & 0 & 1
\end{array}
\qquad (4.3.22)
$$

In this case there are two absorbing states and the important thing is to estimate how likely a borrower is to end up in the defaulting state. This can be calculated by giving a 'profit' of 1 if the borrowers arrive in the defaulting state, 0 if they arrive in the closed account state with no 'profit' also in the intermediate states. Define $d(i)$ to be the probability of defaulting given the borrower is in state i then one can then use conditioning on the first periods transitions to connect these probabilities. This gives the equations

$$
\begin{aligned}
d(C) &= 0 \\
d(3) &= 1 \\
d(0) &= 0.01d(C) + 0.95d(0) + 0.04d(1) \\
d(1) &= 0.75d(0) + 0.05d(1) + 0.2d(2) \\
d(2) &= 0.2d(0) + 0.1d(1) + 0.1d(2) + 0.6d(3) \\
\Rightarrow d(0) &= 0.3649; \quad d(1) = 0.4562; \quad d(2) = 0.7985.
\end{aligned}
\qquad (4.3.23)
$$

This probability of default is the chance that the borrowers will default at all (that is before they close their account). To calculate the probability of defaulting in the next n periods which is the definition used in default-based scoring, one has to allow the default probabilities to depend both on the current state and the length of time to go until the end of the n periods. Define $d_n(i)$ as the probability of the borrowers defaulting in the next n periods given they are currently in state i, then conditioning yet again on what happens in this period leads to the equations

$$
d_n(C) = 0 \quad \text{and} \quad d_n(3) = 1 \; \forall n
$$
$$
d_0(i) = 0 \quad \text{for } i = C, 0, 1, \text{ and } 2
$$

$$d_n(0) = 0.01d_{n-1}(C) + 0.95d_{n-1}(0) + 0.04d_{n-1}(1)$$
$$d_n(1) = 0.75d_{n-1}(0) + 0.05d_{n-1}(1) + 0.2d_{n-1}(2)$$
$$d_n(2) = 0.2d_{n-1}(0) + 0.1d_{n-1}(1) + 0.1d_{n-1}(2) + 0.6d_{n-1}(3)$$
$$\Rightarrow d_{12}(0) = 0.0508; \quad d_{12}(1) = 0.1824; \quad d_{12}(2) = 0.6965. \tag{4.3.24}$$

Example 4.3.5 Multi-dimensional state spaces

The states describing a borrower on a fixed loan should include the time since the last payment, the current balance of the loan, and indications of the probability of the borrower defaulting, like a behavioural score. In such a case the state space of the borrower would have three dimensions, namely $i = (b, n, s)$ where b is the balance outstanding, n is the number of successive periods of non-payment, and s describes other characteristics or the behavioural score. Using a sample of histories of previous borrowers allows one to estimate

$t(i, a)$ – the probability an account in state i makes a repayment of a next period

$w(i, s')$ – the probability an account in state i changes its other characteristics to s' next period

Assume that default corresponds to N successive periods of non-payment, and that r is the interest per period charged on the loan. Let $d(b, n, s)$ be the probability that a borrower currently in state (b, n, s) will eventually default. Then by definition,

$$d(b, N, s) = 1 \quad \text{for all } b, s \text{ and } d(0, n, s) = 0 \quad \text{for all } s, n < N \tag{4.3.25}$$

One can connect the default probabilities in the other states by conditioning on what happens at the next period to get:

$$d(b, n, s) = \sum_{s', a \neq 0} t(i, a)w(i, s')d(b(1 + r) - a, 0, s')$$
$$+ \sum_{s'} t(i, 0)w(i, s')d(b(1 + r), n + 1, s') \tag{4.3.26}$$

One can use Eqs. (4.3.25) and (4.3.26) to calculate $d(b, n, s)$ for each state. Figure 4.3.1 shows the jumps as the borrower's state moves either closer to the bottom of the grid (if there is a payment and so the borrower becomes more likely to pay-off in good status) or closer to the right-hand side (RHS; if there was no payment and so the borrower becomes more likely to default). Since the value of $d(b, n, s)$ is known at these boundaries one can solve first for those states where the balance is one more repayment and then for the states where it is two repayments, and so on.

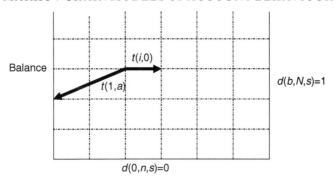

FIG. 4.3.1. Calculation of default probabilities.

It is obvious that the chance of default $d(b, n, s)$ increases as the balance b increases, if n and s are kept fixed, since there has to be more repayments before the balance is paid off. If the bank's policy is to offer loans provided the default rate is below d^*, then one could give a rule for the amount one could loan to those with a score of s, namely,

Loan up to $b^*(s)$ where $b^*(s) = \max\{b | d(b, 0, s) \leq d^*\}$.

So this gives a way of banks determining the maximum amount they are willing to loan to a borrower as a function of the credit score of the borrower.

Example 4.3.6 Numerical example based on multi-dimensional state space

Consider a very simple example of this fixed loan repayment where the loan is repaid in b repayment of 1 unit each and the time between repayments is so small that one can ignore the interest charged on the loan $(r = 0)$. Assume the other characteristics of the borrower do not affect the repayment behaviour, so the state space of a borrower is simply (b, n)– the number of repayments still to be made and the number of successive periods of non-payment. If the probability of repayment is 80% no matter what the state of the borrower, we get $t(i, 1) = 0.8; t(i, 0) = 0.2$. If we assume that default occurs when there are two successive periods of missed payments $(N = 2)$, Eq. (4.3.26) which is satisfied by the default probabilities $d(b, n)$ reduces to

$$d(b, n) = 0.8d(b - 1, 0) + 0.2d(b, n + 1)$$
$$\text{with } d(0, n) = 0 \ d(b, 2) = 1. \tag{4.3.27}$$

So to calculate the default probability if a borrower is just about to start paying off a loan of three repayment, $d(3, 0)$ we undertake the following calculation in sequence:

$$d(1,1) = 0.2$$
$$d(1,0) = 0.2d(1,1) = 0.04$$
$$d(2,1) = 0.2 + 0.8d(1,0) = 0.232$$
$$d(2,0) = 0.8d(1,0) + 0.2d(2,1) = 0.0784$$
$$d(3,1) = 0.2 + 0.8d(2,0) = 0.26272$$
$$d(3,0) = 0.8d(2,0) + 0.2d(3,1) = 0.11616$$

(4.3.28)

Thus, the probability of the borrower defaulting on the loan is 11.6%.

Example 4.3.7 Profitability of a portfolio of consumer loans

In the previous examples, we concentrated on the probability of default of one individual. If one wanted to use this Markov chain model for the whole population there is an obvious difficulty because of the absorbing states, which imply that eventually everyone leaves the lender. The Markov chain is modelling the cohort of the population who were borrowing at the start of the period being considered. It is not considering the borrowers whose loans begin after this time and now are part of the current population. If one wants to get a handle on this population, there is a trick to change the Markov chain with absorbing states into one without.

Suppose the borrowing population is essentially constant in size and that all new borrowers by definition must be up to date when they join. This is equivalent to assuming that everyone who leaves the population either in good standing or because they have defaulted changes into a new borrower who is in the 'up to date' state. This means one can transform the transition probabilities of the five-state Markov chain given by Eq. (4.3.22) into

$$P = \begin{matrix} 1 & 0 & 0 & 0 & 0 \\ 0.01 & 0.95 & 0.04 & 0 & 0 \\ 0 & 0.75 & 0.05 & 0.2 & 0 \\ 0 & 0.2 & 0.1 & 0.1 & 0.6 \\ 0 & 0 & 0 & 0 & 1 \end{matrix} \Rightarrow \tilde{P} = \begin{matrix} 0 & 1 & 0 & 0 & 0 \\ 0.01 & 0.95 & 0.04 & 0 & 0 \\ 0 & 0.75 & 0.05 & 0.2 & 0 \\ 0 & 0.2 & 0.1 & 0.1 & 0.6 \\ 0 & 1 & 0 & 0 & 0 \end{matrix} \quad (4.3.29)$$

In this new model the states 3 and C correspond to borrowers in the current population who have just defaulted or left in that current period not the cumulative percentage of a cohort who have already defaulted or left.

Suppose that in the current population, 2% of the population left last month in good standing, 3% defaulted last month, 80% are up to date, 10% are 1 month overdue, and 5% are 2 months overdue. This corresponds to the probability distribution $\pi_0 = (0.02, 0.8, 0.1, 0.05, 0.03)$ in the Markov chain with transition matrix $\tilde{P}$. The subsequent changes to the population can be calculated using the standard Markov chain updating equations:

$$\pi_1 = \pi_0 \tilde{P} = (0.02, 0.8, 0.1, 0.05, 0.03.)\tilde{P} = (0.008, 0.895, 0.042, 0.025, 0.03)$$

$$\pi_2 = \pi_0 \tilde{P}^2 = \pi_1 \tilde{P} = (0.008, 0.895, 0.042, 0.025, 0.03)\tilde{P}$$
$$= (0.009, 0.925, 0.040, 0.011, 0.015)$$

$$\pi_3 = \pi_0 \tilde{P}^3 = \pi_2 \tilde{P} = (0.009, 0.925, 0.040, 0.011, 0.015)\tilde{P}$$
$$= (0.009, 0.935, 0.040, 0.009, 0.007)$$

In the limit we get $\pi^* = \pi^* \tilde{P} \Rightarrow \pi^* = (0.009, 0.936, 0.040, 0.009, 0.005)$.

$$(4.3.30)$$

Thus, in the long run the population will have about 0.9% of the borrowers leaving each period in good standing and another 0.5% defaulting each period. Of the population, 93.6% will be up to date in their repayments, 4% will be one period overdue, and 0.9% will be 2 months overdue.

This model could also be used to find the expected profitability of the loan portfolio over some future time horizon allowing for the changes in the portfolio described in this example. Suppose the profit per period $r(i)$ depends on the state, i, of the borrower. If we define the average profit per borrower over the next n periods starting with a distribution π in the population as $v_n(\pi)$ then because the population distribution dynamics is given by $\tilde{P}$ we get

$$v_n(\pi) = \sum_{t=1}^{n} \sum_i r(i)(\pi(\tilde{P})^t)(i) \text{ so if we start with } \pi_0 \text{ and } \pi_t = \pi_0(\tilde{P})^t$$

then $v_n(\pi_0) = \sum_{t=1}^{n} \sum_i r(i)((\pi_t)(i))$.

$$(4.3.31)$$

If we wanted to allow for the time value of money as we did in Example 4.1.2, then we can introduce a discount factor β so that the value of a unit reward next period is only equivalent of getting β in this period. In that case, $v_n^{\beta}(\pi)$ the total discounted reward over n periods for a population whose initial state distribution is π is obtained by modifying Eq. (4.3.31) to

$$v_n^{\beta}(\pi) = \sum_{t=1}^{n} \sum_i \beta^t r(i)(\pi(\tilde{P})^t)(i) \text{ so if we start with } \pi_0 \text{ and } \pi_t = \pi_0(\tilde{P})^t$$

then $v_n^{\beta}(\pi_0) = \sum_{t=1}^{n} \sum_i \beta^t r(i)((\pi_t)(i))$.

$$(4.3.32)$$

Estimating parameters and testing hypotheses for a Markov chain

Given a set of data describing the states (behavioural score, account status) of a sample of borrowers over time, how does one calculate the Markov chain that best fits the data and how does one measure how good a fit it is? Suppose one has the data for T time periods $t = 1, 2, \ldots, T$, then let $n_t(i)$ be the number of cases where the borrower is in state i at time t (we swap our time index from n to t in this section to avoid notational confusion). Similarly define $n_t(i,j)$ be the number of cases where a borrower is in state i at time t and in state j at time $t + 1$. Define

$$n(i) = \sum_{t=1}^{T-1} n_t(i) \text{ and } n(i,j) = \sum_{t=1}^{T-1} n_t(i,j). \qquad (4.3.33)$$

Then the maximum likelihood estimators (Anderson and Goodman 1957) of $p(i,j)$ if the dynamics is given by a stationary Markov chain are

$$\hat{p}(i,j) = \frac{n(i,j)}{n(i)}. \qquad (4.3.34)$$

If the assumption was that the dynamics followed a non-stationary Markov chain, then the maximum likelihood estimators of the transition probabilities $p_t(i,j)$ are given by

$$\hat{p}_t(i,j) = \frac{n_t(i,j)}{n_t(i)}. \qquad (4.3.35)$$

The first question one might want to check on is whether the transitions between the states are Markov. To do this one has to generalize our first-order Markov chains to higher order Markov chains. A second-order Markov chain is one in which the probability of a transition depends not just on the state the process is in but also the one it was in at the previous period. This means the condition (4.3.1) in the definition of Markov chain is relaxed to

$$\Pr\{X_{t+1} = j | X_0 = k_0, X_1 = k_1, \ldots, X_{t-1} = k, X_t = i\}$$
$$= P\{X_{t+1} = j | X_t = i, X_{t-1} = k\}$$
$$= p_t(k,i,j,) \quad \text{for } \forall t \text{ and } k, i, j \quad \text{where } 1 \le k, i, j \le I. \qquad (4.3.36)$$

Notice that this can be considered to be a Markov chain Y_t on $I \times I$ by defining $Y_t = (X_t, X_{t-1})$ and the transition probabilities are $\breve{p}_t(.,.)$ where

$$\breve{p}_t((k,i),(i,j)) = p_t(k,i,j); \quad \breve{p}_t((k,i),(i',j)) = 0 \quad \text{if } i \ne i'. \qquad (4.3.37)$$

If $p_t(k,i,j) = p(k,i,j)$ for all periods t, the process is called a stationary second-order Markov chain. The maximum likelihood estimates for a stationary second-order chain are obtained in the same way as the first order. Define $n_t(k,i,j)$ to the number of cases where a borrower is in state k at time t, i at time $t + 1$, and j at time $t + 2$. Let $n(k, i, j) = \sum_{t=1}^{T-2} n_t(k, i, j)$ be the number of times borrowers have gone from state k to state i and then to state j and let $m(k, i) = \sum_{t=1}^{T-2} n_t(k, i)$ be the number of times borrowers have gone from state k to state i in the first $T-2$ periods (hence different from $n(i, j)$ as defined in Eq. (4.3.31)). The maximum likelihood estimator for $p(k, i, j)$ is then

$$\hat{p}(k, i, j) = \frac{n(k, i, j)}{m(k, i)}. \tag{4.3.38}$$

So now the question about the process being a stationary first-order Markov chain can be translated into the hypothesis that it is first order and not second order, at least for state i, namely,

$$H_0^M(i) : p(1, i, j) = p(2, 1, j) = \cdots = p(I, i, j) \, j = 1, 2, \ldots, I. \tag{4.3.39}$$

The likelihood ratio criterion and the Pearson goodness-of-fit χ^2 statistic can be used to test this hypothesis. Under the former the log likelihood ratio:

$$Y^2 = 2\log \left(\prod_{j=1}^{I} \prod_{k=1}^{I} \left(\frac{\hat{p}(k, i, j)}{\hat{p}(i, j)} \right)^{n(k,i,j)} \right) = 2 \sum_{j=1}^{I} \sum_{k=1}^{I} n(k, i, j) \log \left(\frac{\hat{p}(k, i, j)}{\hat{p}(i, j)} \right)$$

$$= 2 \sum_{j=1}^{I} \sum_{k=1}^{I} n(k, i, j) \log \left(\frac{n(k, i, j) n(i)}{m(k, i) n(i, j)} \right). \tag{4.3.40}$$

has a χ^2 distribution with apparently $(I - 1)^2$ degrees of freedom. However, there may be structural zeros in the transitions – state movements which are not possible or not allowed and each of these removes a degree of freedom.

For the Pearson goodness-of-fit test one defines $e(k, i, j)$ the expected number of transition sequences k, i, j if the hypothesis $H_0(i)$ holds and then calculates the usual chi-squared statistic $\text{CHI}^2(i)$ by

$$e(k, i, j) = m(k, i)\hat{p}(i, j) = \frac{m(k, i) n(i, j)}{n(i)}$$

$$\text{CHI}^2(i) = \sum_{k=1}^{I} \sum_{j=1}^{I} \frac{(n(k, i, j) - e(k, i, j))^2}{e(k, i, j)}. \tag{4.3.41}$$

This again appears to have $(I - 1)^2$ degrees of freedom but we need also to subtract the number of structural zeros.

The hypothesis that the system is a first-order Markov chain can then be thought of as requiring $H_0^M(i)$ hold for all $i = 1, 2, \ldots, I$.

One reason that the hypothesis may not be true is that the Markov chain though first order is non-stationary. This can be checked by considering the hypothesis that the transition probabilities at time t are the same as if the process was stationary.

This corresponds to the following $H^T(i,t)$ with corresponding chi-square statistic $\text{CHI}^2(i,t)$:

$$H^T(i,t): p_t(i,j) = p(i,j) \; \forall j \tag{4.3.42}$$

$$e_{t-1}(k,i,j) = n_{t-1}(k,i)\hat{p}(i,j) = \frac{n_{t-1}(k,i)n(i,j)}{n(i)}$$

$$\text{CHI}^2(i,t) = \sum_{k=1}^{I}\sum_{j=1}^{I} \frac{(n_{t-1}(k,i,j) - e_{t-1}(k,i,j))^2}{e_{t-1}(k,i,j)} \tag{4.3.43}$$

Again one has to be careful with the degrees of freedom if there are structural zeros. The assumption that the Markov chain is really stationary is that the hypotheses $H^T(i, t)$ hold for all i and for all t.

Extensions of the Markov chain models

When Markov chain models are built on real consumer credit data, it is rare that one finds the resulting model satisfies the stationary Markov hypotheses described earlier (see Ho et al. 2004 and references therein). One obvious extension is to allow the model to be second- or third-order Markov. The hypothesis H^M is essentially a test of first order against second order. One way of testing whether a second-order model is more appropriate than a third-order model is to recall that a second-order Markov chain is essentially a first order on a state space $I \times I$. Similarly to check if a rth order chain is suitable, we can check if it is first order on the r-fold product space $I \times I \times \ldots \times I$. Often the second-order chain is a much better fit than the first-order one but the third order is only marginally better than the second-order one. One pays a lot for this better fit. If the first-order chain has 10 states, then there are 100 probabilities one needs to estimate and even if half of the entries in each row are structural zeros that leaves 50 probabilities to estimate. The corresponding second-order chain's transition matrix looks as if it has 100 rows and 100 columns but in each row there are again only five non-zero probabilities. Still that adds up to 500 probabilities to estimate while each higher order adds another factor of 10 to the number of probabilities to be estimated. Thus even with the amount of data available in consumer credit one would find it difficult to build robust models above the second order. There is often more benefit in increasing the size of the original state space by adding an extra dimension of information than in increasing the order of the Markov chain.

A second way of extending the stationary first-order Markov model is to drop the stationarity requirement. One could allow the chain to be seasonal, in that the time periods are representing different times of the year, and the transition matrices in a given season may be assumed to be all the same, but different to the transition matrices in other seasons. The most general form of non-stationarity would occur if the transition matrix is assumed to be different in each time period. Although this model gives maximum flexibility, it is not very useful as a forecasting tool unless we can relate the differences to other variables for which one has forecasts. One way of overcoming this is to then make the transitions probabilities functions of the economic variables describing the underlying economic condition that borrowers are facing. One approach to this, applied in a related problem in the insurance sector, is given in Bozzetto et al. (2005).

One final extension of the standard Markov chain model which has been suggested for consumer credit is to recognize that the dynamics of the borrowing population is not homogenous and in fact some groups in the population do not move at all. Frydman et al. (1985) were the first to suggest that it might be worth segmenting the population not just to improve the classification accuracy of the scorecards but also to improve the goodness-of-fit of the dynamic model of the movements in these scores or account status. They suggested there were segments of the population who 'stay' in the same state all the time – usually a 'good' state like account status up to date or a high behavioural score band. There are other segments who move much more between the different behavioural states.

A simple mover–stayer model would have two segments. Segment one which is s of the population stay in state 1 (the least risky state) all the time. So a fraction $(1 - s)$ of the population is in the mover segment and its dynamics is estimated by the transition probabilities $p(i,j)$ of a Markov chain. Frydman (1984) gives the maximum likelihood estimators for these parameters. Ho et al. (2004) generalize this simple model by allowing there to be several segments of movers depending on how much their states jumped around and they called the ones with only small movements 'twitchers' and 'shakers'.

4.4   Markov decision models of profitability

In the previous section, we saw how Markov chain models can deal with one of the difficulties identified in creating profit scoring systems, namely that the state of the borrower is dynamic and can change over time. We also indicated how it might be possible to introduce the profitability of the borrower to the lender by estimating the profit in each time period as a function of the state of the borrower. However, there remains the challenge that the profitability of a borrower depends on a series of decisions by the bank. One cannot look at one decision without thinking of what the subsequent decisions might be. So as well as the states, describing the repayment performance of the consumers, a probability transition matrix describing the dynamics of the repayment behaviour and a reward function describing the value to the organization of the consumer being in that state, one needs to add another element, the decisions that the lender can make. These decisions will impact both on the immediate reward from the borrower and on the borrower's transitions between the states. Such a model involving a Markov chain describing the dynamics between states, an immediate reward function, and decisions which impact on both these is called an MDP, which is a type of stochastic dynamic programming.

Formally an MDP is a stochastic process X_n, $n = 1, 2, \ldots$ taking values in a state space I. For each state $i \in I$, there is a set of actions, $k \in K_i$, and one of these has to be chosen each time the process enters that state. The result of choosing action k in state i is that there is an immediate reward $r^k(i)$, and with probability $p^k(i,j)$ the system moves into state j at the next period. The objective is to choose the actions $k \in K_i$ so as to maximize some function of the rewards. One criterion is the total reward over a finite number of periods (a finite time horizon). In that case, the optimal value and the optimal actions satisfy what is known as the Bellman optimality equation (see Puterman 1994 for details). For example, if $v_n(i)$ is the optimal total reward over n periods with the system starting in state i, then

$$v_n(i) = \max_{k \in K_i} \left\{ r^k(i) + \sum_j p^k(i,j) v_{n-1}(j) \right\} \qquad \text{for all } i \in I \text{ and all } n = 1, 2 \ldots, T.$$

(4.4.1)

where we assume $v_0(i) = 0$ for all states i. The Bellman optimality principal which underlies this equation is so simple that it is difficult to understand its power. What it says is that if one is interested in the best decision strategy over n time periods then whatever the decision at the first time period thereafter one must have the best decision strategy over the remaining $(n-1)$ periods. Hence in the RHS of the equation if one chooses action k initially one has the reward $r^k(i)$ from the first period and then the best reward over the remaining $(n-1)$ periods given one moves to state j, $v_{n-1}(j)$ weighted by $p^k(i,j)$ which is how likely the system is to move to state j. One then chooses the action k that maximizes this sum of the first period reward and the remaining $(n-1)$ period rewards. Given $v_0(i) = 0$, one can substitute this into the RHS of the equation to get $v_1(\cdot)$ and then repeat this process until one gets to the time horizon T one is interested in. Thus the original problem which involved a sequence of T decisions has been simplified to T problems each involving only one decision. Equation (4.4.1) is called the optimality equation since it shows the way the optimality principal separates out the decisions in the problem and gives an equation which the optimal value function will satisfy.

If one wants to consider the lifetime profitability of a borrower, it would seem one has to look at what happens as T goes to infinity. One has to be slightly subtle about this because as T goes to infinity the total reward under every strategy will be infinite so it is hard to distinguish between them. One possibility is to calculate instead the expected average reward, which is the limit as n goes to infinity of $v_n(i)/n$. Under most realistic conditions (see Puterman 1994 for details), this limit has the form

$$\lim_{n \to \infty} v_n(i) = \bar{r}n + w(i) \tag{4.4.2}$$

where $\bar{r}$ is the optimal average reward per period and $w(i)$ is the bias term. $w(i) - w(j)$ corresponds to the total advantage of starting in state i rather than state j. If one takes the limit of $v_n(\cdot)$ at n goes to infinity and substitutes the expression in Eq. (4.4.2) into Eq. (4.4.1) one would expect that $\bar{r}$ and $w(i)$ would satisfy the optimality equation:

$$\bar{r} + w(i) = \max_{k \in K_i} \left\{ r^k(i) + \sum_j p^k(i,j)w(j) \right\} \quad \text{for all } i \in I. \tag{4.4.3}$$

This is indeed the case under very mild conditions.

The second criterion to use in the infinite horizon case is to discount the future rewards as was discussed in Section 4.1. If the risk-free interest rate is r_F then a profit of 1 unit next period only has a net present value (NPV) of $\beta = 1/(1 + r_F)$ since one could put an amount β into a risk-free investment this period and it would be worth 1 next period. Hence one can measure the expected total discounted reward when a discount factor of β is being used. Let $v(i)$ be the optimal expected total discounted reward given that the borrower starts in state i, then the equivalent optimality equation to (4.4.1) that $v(i)$ must satisfy is

$$v(i) = \max_{k \in K_i} \left\{ r^k(i) + \beta \sum_j p^k(i,j)v(j) \right\} \quad \text{for all } i \in I. \tag{4.4.4}$$

Notice that in this case the optimality function does not depend on the time until the end of the time horizon (it is always infinity) and so the optimal strategy is to perform the same action in a particular state no matter what the time period. Thus the optimal policy is stationary unlike the finite horizon case where the decision of what to do can depend on both the state of the borrower and the time until the end of the horizon. One can solve Eq. (4.4.4) by value iteration which means calculating iterates $v_n^\beta(i)$ which satisfy

$$v_n^\beta(i) = \max_{k \in K_i} \left\{ r^k(i) + \beta \sum_j p^k(i,j)v_{n-1}^\beta(j) \right\} \quad \text{for all } i \in I. \tag{4.4.5}$$

$$v_0^\beta(i) = 0 \quad \text{for all } i \in I.$$

and which converge to the optimal value $v(i)$. In the limit, the optimal actions in Eq. (4.4.5) are also the optimal actions in (4.4.4). One reason this criterion is appropriate for the consumer credit case is that one could reinterpret $(1 - \beta)$ as the chance that the borrower will churn and leave the bank in that period and hence the profitability will stop at that point. In this case $v(i)$ can be thought of as the expected total lifetime profit from the borrower. The discount factor β can be thought of as $\beta = 1 - \alpha/1 + r_F$, where $1/(1 + r_F)$ is the discount factor because the risk-free rate is r_F and α is the attrition rate of borrowers as was argued in Eq. (4.1.2).

So far this has all been theory but let us now consider four examples of profitability models based on the MDP approach.

Example 4.4.1 (Extension of Example 4.3.3) Profitability of model with behavioural score and defaults

Example 4.3.3 considered the situation where a borrower's behaviour was in one of the three states – high behavioural score H, low behavioural score L, and default D. Assume that the rewards and the transition probabilities given there corresponded to when the credit limit was set as level 1 (£1000), but there was an alternative credit limit of level 2 (say £2000). So in terms of the parameters of a MDP we would have

$$r^1(H) = 10, r^1(L) = 2, r^1(D) = 0 \text{ and } r^1(L, D) = -1000$$

and

$$p^1(.,.) = \begin{array}{c} \\ H \\ L \\ D \end{array} \begin{array}{ccc} H & L & D \\ \begin{pmatrix} 0.95 & 0.05 & 0 \\ 0.1 & 0.88 & 0.02 \\ 0 & 0 & 1 \end{pmatrix} \end{array} . \tag{4.4.6}$$

Note that rewards can be defined either in terms of the state the Markov chain or in terms of the transitions between states (the £1000 when the borrower moves from state L to the default state). This is because one could modify the reward in state L to include the expected cost of this transition, namely,

$$\tilde{r}^1(L) = r^1(L) + p^1(L, D)r^1(L, D) = 2 + 0.02(-1000) = -18. \tag{4.4.7}$$

For credit limit 2 (£2000) we will assume the following rewards and transition probabilities:

$$r^2(H) = 15; \quad r^2(L) = 8; \quad r^2(L, D) = -1500$$

and

$$p^2(.,.) = \begin{array}{c} \\ H \\ L \\ D \end{array} \begin{array}{ccc} H & L & D \\ \begin{pmatrix} 0.94 & 0.06 & 0 \\ 0.075 & 0.90 & 0.025 \\ 0 & 0 & 1 \end{pmatrix} \end{array} . \tag{4.4.8}$$

TABLE 4.4.1. Results for Example 4.4.1.

Horizon	$v_1(\cdot)$	$v_2(\cdot)$	$v_3(\cdot)$	$v_4(\cdot)$	$v_{10}(\cdot)$	$v_{25}(\cdot)$	$v_{100}(\cdot)$	$v_{200}(\cdot)$	$v_\infty(\cdot)$
State H	15.00	28.02	39.40	49.42	91.43	150.06	333.33	467.02	600.0
State L	−18	−32.24	−43.66	−52.48	−72.78	−46.38	114.15	232.38	350.00
State D	0	0	0	0	0	0	0	0	0
Credit limit H	2	2	2	2	2	2	2	2	2
Credit limit L	1	1	1	1	1	1	1	1	1

So with this credit limit the rewards in each state are higher than under the lower credit limit but the probabilities of moving to worse states (from H to L and from L to D) are also higher than under the lower credit limit as is the loss if the borrower defaults. Applying the iterative scheme from Eq. (4.4.1) we get the results in Table 4.4.1, which describe both the finite horizon values and the optimal action to take in each state in a period with n more periods until the end of the time horizon.

Notice in this case no matter what the time horizon it is best to set the limit of £2000 for those with the higher behavioural score and a limit of £1000 for those with the lower behavioural score.

In this example, we would drop the credit limit of a borrower if they moved from the higher to the lower behavioural score state. Many banks would not wish to do this as they feel the borrower would move to another lender if this occurred. If one keeps either to the £1000 credit limit in both states or to the £2000 limit in both states, the problem reduces to the calculations in Example 4.3.3 for the £1000 limit with a similar set of calculations for the £2000 credit limits. Undertaking these calculations it is easy to show that the £1000 limit always gives a higher profit than the £2000 limit. If one calculates the profit over an infinite horizon then as Table 4.3.1 showed the expected profits under the £1000 limit are $v_\infty(H) = 300$ and $v_\infty(L) = 100$ while under the £2000 limit the expected profits would be $v_\infty(H) = -190$ and $v_\infty(L) = -440$.

Example 4.4.2 Extension of Example 4.3.5

Consider a revolving credit account where the states of the borrowers' repayment behaviour are $i = (b, n, s)$ where b is the balance outstanding, n is the number of periods since the last payment, and s is any other information which could be the behavioural score. The actions are the credit limit, L, to set in each state. The MDP behavioural scoring system is well determined once we have defined $p^L(i,i')$ and $r^L(i)$. Define $p^L(i,')$ by estimating from past data the following:

> $t^L(i, a)$ – probability account in state i with credit limit L repays a next period
>
> $u^L(i, e)$ – probability account in state i with credit limit L purchases e next period

$w^L(i, s')$ – probability account in state i with credit limit L changes its other information such as behavioural score to s'

Notice that we are assuming independence of these three actions which the borrower can perform. If the interest rate charged on outstanding balances is r, then the transition probabilities can be defined by

$$p^L(b, n, s; (b - a)(1 + r) + e, 0, s') = t^L(i, a)u^L(i, e)w^L(i, s') \quad a > 0,$$
$$(b - a)(1 + r) + e \leq L,$$

(so there are both repayment and new purchase in the period)

$$p^L(b, n, s; (b - a)(1 + r), 0, s') = t^L(i, a)$$

$$\times \left(u^L(i, 0) + \sum_{e \geq L - (b-a)(1+r)} u^L(i, e) \right) w^L(i, s') \quad a > 0$$

(payment but no purchase either because there was no purchase or because it took balance over credit limit L)

$$p^L(b, n, s; (b)(1 + r) + e, n + 1, s') = t^L(i, 0)u^L(i, e)w^L(i, s') \quad b(1 + r) + e \leq L$$

(no repayment but a purchase)

$$p^L(b, n, s; b(1 + r) + e, n + 1, s') = t^L(i, 0)^L(i, e)w^L(s, s') \quad b + e \leq L$$

(no repayment but a purchase)

$$p^L(b, n, s; b(1 + r) + e, n + 1, s') = t^L(i, 0)$$

$$\times \left(u^L(i, 0) + \sum_{e > L - b(1+r)} u^L(i, e) \right) w^L(i, s') \qquad (4.4.9)$$

(no repayment and no purchase either because no purchase or because it went above the credit limit

The reward to the firm in any period is a fraction f of the purchase amount which is like a merchant service charge together with the net (repayment – new borrowing) return from the customer which is $a - e$. If we assume than N consecutive periods of non-payments is what the company considers as default, then,

$$r^L(b, n, s) = \sum_a \sum_e (a - e + fe)t^L(i, a)u^L(i, e) - bt^L(i, 0)\delta(n - (N - 1))$$

$$(4.4.10)$$

where the second term corresponds to a loss of the whole balance if this is the Nth consecutive period of non-payment.

was some part of the previous state that was in the description of the current state of the borrower.

Initially the size of the problem looks impossible $-28,800$ states and 50 actions but the first thing to realize is that there are not $50 \times 28,800 \times 28,800$ transitions to calculate since if one is in state (i, k) and undertakes action k (example moving the credit limit) the probability of moving from (i,k) to (j,k) is $p^k(i,j)$ since part of the new state is an action by the lender and so has no uncertainty in it. However, even with 51,000,000 data points one still cannot hope to get estimates for the $576 \times 576 \times 50 = 16,588,800$ transition probabilities needed for such a MDP. The size of the problem was cut down in two ways. Firstly, closely related states that were seldom reached and had very few transitions out of them were amalgamated into one state. This is not as easy as it sounds when the states have six dimensions and one has to look at 50 different probability transition matrices (one for each action) for each of them. A greedy heuristic was used which cut the number of states from 576 to around 200. Secondly, it was assumed that the action k occurs at the start of the period so that if one is in state (i, k') and undertakes action k it is equivalent to starting the period in state (i, k) and hence all that is needed to calculate is $p((i, k), j) = p^k(i, j)$. This amounts to roughly $50 \times 200 \times 200 = 2,000,000$ transition probabilities. This is still a lot of effort but is now possible to do in practice. Similarly the immediate rewards are $r(i, k) = r^k(i)$. These are the functions of the current behavioural state and the new action and so there are 10,000 of these to estimate.

These rewards and transition probabilities were used in the discounted infinite horizon optimality Eq. (4.4.3) and solved using the value iteration scheme of (4.4.5).

Notice that this calculation only gives the expected profitability of an account under the optimal account strategy. One would also like to get a feel for the possible variation around this mean value. A simulation model was then built using the optimal actions given by (4.4.3) and in each run used the transition probabilities to derive a possible set of movements in the behavioural states. This allowed one to get a feel for the distribution of the profitability of a borrower as well as the optimal mean profitability.

The previous two examples used data on a large number of previous borrowers to estimate the transition probabilities in the MDP. It is possible to take a more 'Bayesian' approach and starting with a certain belief about the repayment behaviour of the borrowers use the information on their own repayment history to update this belief every period. This will make the state space even larger as one has to add the parameters describing the belief about the repayment behaviour to the state space but it does mean one is less open to criticism from the borrower that 'they should be judged on their own merits'. Having said that, the complexity means that there are few such systems that have been implemented.

In the simplest Bayesian models, the uncertain parameter is p the probability of repaying. This is the probability relating to the Bernoulli random variable, $X = 1$ if there is payment and $X = 0$ if there is not. The conjugate family of prior belief

For the optimal profitability strategy over T periods, let $v_n(i)$ be the op expected profit over a n period horizon starting in state i. The optimality equ that $v_n(i)$ must satisfy is

$$v_n(i) = \max_L \left\{ r^L(i) + \sum_j p^L(i,j) v_{n-1}(j) \right\} \quad \text{for all } i \in I \text{ and all } n = 1, 2 \ldots$$

(4

To calculate the lifetime profitability of the customer assuming that the discount factor (churn probability plus discount by interest-free rate) is β, the is after the expected total discounted total profit $v^\beta(i)$ starting in state i whic satisfy the optimality equation Eq. (4.4.5).

Example 4.4.3 Bank one credit cards

The U.S. Operations Research Society gives a prize each year for the exce in operations research in decision analysis and in 2002 this was won by a p using MDP models to build profit scoring systems for the U.S. Bank One (Tre al. 2003) to be applied to its credit card portfolio. The data consisted of 18 r of transactions on 3,000,000 accounts, amounting to 51,000,000 account/r in total. This was used to decide what actions were needed in terms of cl in interest rate charged and credit limit given so as to maximize the ex NPV of the profitability to the bank from each class of borrower. The sta borrower was described in six dimensions, which were not identified speci for proprietary reasons but which covered risk, card usage, revolving a purchase, and payment behaviour. Each variable was split into a small r of bands using classification trees together with the frequency distribution variable. Two of the variables were split into four bands; two more int bands each; and two just into two bands. This meant that the underlying N chain had $4 \times 4 \times 3 \times 3 \times 2 \times 2 = 576$ behavioural states, i. The actions, the level of interest charged together with the credit limit set. The first w into five levels and the latter into 10 levels so that there were 50 different combinations that could be undertaken. However, the state space (i, k) de the current action k–current interest rate and credit limit in use – as well behavioural aspect of the states, i, and so there were $576 \times 50 = 28,80($ in total. To try and ensure the Markovity of the process, some of the va that made up the state had a historical component to them. For example, v the borrowers keep having outstanding balances on their credit card whic interest rate charges (revolvers), whether the borrowers pay off all the l each month (transactors), or whether the borrowers do not use the card (ir involves looking at the history of the account. This division is used as on dimensions on the state space. Other variables involved 3-month averages :

distributions for the Bernoulli random variable is the Beta distributions. Conjugate prior distributions have the nice property that no matter the outcome of the random variable the updated (posterior) distribution of ones belief after the random event has occurred is still in the family. Beta distributions are defined by two parameters (w,m) and the density function of $B(w,m)$ is

$$f_{w \cdot m}(p) = \frac{(m-1)!}{(w-1)!(m-w-1)!} p^{w-1}(1-p)^{m-w-1} \quad 0 \le p \le 1; \ 0 \text{ otherwise.}$$

$$(4.4.12)$$

This is a slightly different parameterization from that normally given but one can show that if a repayment is made when the density function of the prior belief $f_0(p)$ is $B(w,m)$ then the density function of the posterior belief $f_1(p)$ after the outcome X_1 is known to be

$$f_1(p) = \frac{P(X_1 = 1|p)f_0(p)}{P(X_1 = 1)} = \frac{m!}{w!(m-w-1)!} p^w(1-p)^{m-w-1}$$

This follows because $P(X_1 = 1) = \dfrac{(m-1)!}{(w-1)!(m-w-1)!}$

$$\int_0^1 p \, p^{w-1}(1-p)^{m-w-1} dp = w/m$$

and so $f_1(p) = \dfrac{P(X_1 = 1|p)f_0(p)}{P(X_1 = 1)}$

$$= \frac{p((m-1)!/(w-1)!(m-w-1)!)p^{w-1}(1-p)^{m-w-1})}{w/m}$$

$$= \frac{m!}{w!(m-w-1)!} p^w(1-p)^{m-w-1} \qquad (4.4.13)$$

that is, the posterior distribution is $B(w+1, m+1)$.
Similarly if there is no payment,

So $P(X_1 = 0) = \dfrac{(m-1)!}{(w-1)!(m-w-1)!}$

$$\int_0^1 (1-p) p^{w-1}(1-p)^{m-w-1} dp = (m-w)/m$$

and $f_1(p) = \dfrac{P(X_1 = 0|p)f_0(p)}{P(X_1 = 0)}$

$\qquad = \dfrac{(1-p)((m-1)!/(w-1)!(m-w-1)!)p^{w-1}(1-p)^{m-w-1})}{(m-w)/m}$

$\qquad = \dfrac{m!}{w-1!(m-w)!}p^{w-1}(1-p)^{m-w}. \hspace{2cm} (4.4.14)$

This is the density function of $B(w,m+1)$. Thus one can interpret these parameters as m representing the number of periods 'history' one has about this borrower and w the number of payments the borrower has made in that time. Some of this 'history' though will be given by the prior distribution one gives to the borrower.

Before looking at MDP examples of this Bayesian approach, it is useful to look at situation where there is no decision being made to see where using this Bayesian approach makes a difference compared with the situation where the probabilities are fixed since they are estimated from previous data.

Example 4.4.4 Bayesian version of multi-dimensional state space models in Examples 4.3.5 and 4.3.6

In Example 4.3.5, a borrower took out a fixed repayment loan and default was defined as N consecutive periods of non-payments. The states describing the borrower's repayment history were $i = (b, n, s)$ where b is the balance outstanding, n is the number of periods of non-payment, and s is the other characteristics including possibly the behavioural score. The probability of a payment of an amount a was assumed to be $t(i, a)$ which was estimated from historic data. In the numerical Example 4.3.6, the only possible payments were those of one unit and so $t(i, 1) = 0.8, t(i, 0) = 0.2$ and the problem was further simplified by assuming the interest rate $r = 0$. In the Bayesian version of this problem, let $s = (w, m)$ describe the parameters of the Beta distribution $B(w,m)$ which is the belief of the repayment probability. Now the probability of repayment will change as it will depend on the payment history of that particular borrower. The full state for a borrower is then (b,n,w,m) and the probability of defaulting is $d(b,n,r,m)$ if missing N consecutive periods constitutes default. Using Eqs. (4.4.13) and (4.4.14), the default probability will satisfy

$$d(b, n, w, m) = \frac{w}{m}d(b - a, 0, w + 1, m + 1) + \left(1 - \frac{w}{m}\right)d(b, n + 1, w, m + 1)$$

with $d(0, n, w, m) = 0;\ d(b, N, w, m) = 1. \hspace{2cm} (4.4.15)$

Figure 4.4.1 shows how these probabilities of payment and non-payment are updated by the Bayesian formulation.

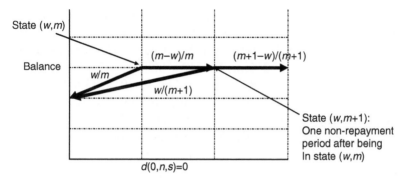

FIG. 4.4.1. Calculation of default probabilities with Bayesian updating.

Example 4.3.6 looked at the case where the borrower had to make three repayments of 1 unit each, and default is defined as two consecutive missed payments. The probability of payment each period for such a borrower was taken to be 80%, and in that case the default probability turned out to be 11.6% from Eq. (4.3.28). Now solve the equivalent Bayesian model which was given above. Assume one starts with a belief $B(4,5)$ about the probability of repayment, which incidentally also has a mean of 0.8. Then the calculations to find the equivalent default probability we are interested in $d(3,0,4,5)$ involves two passes: firstly, a forward pass to identify the states one needs to consider and secondly, a backward pass to solve for these states. These are detailed in Eq. (4.4.16):

$$d(3,0,4,5) = (4/5)d(2,0,5,6) + (1/5)d(3,1,4,6)$$
$$d(3,1,4,6) = (2/6) + (4/6)d(2,0,5,7)$$
$$d(2,0,5,6) = (5/6)d(1,0,6,7) + (1/6)d(2,1,5,7)$$
$$d(2,1,5,7) = (2/7) + (5/7)d(1,0,6,8)$$
$$d(2,0,5,7) = (5/7)d(1,0,6,8) + (2/7)d(2,1,5,8)$$
$$d(2,1,5,8) = (3/8) + (5/8)d(1,0,6,9)$$
$$d(1,0,6,7) = (1/7)d(1,1,6,8)$$
$$d(1,1,6,8) = 2/8$$
$$d(1,0,6,8) = (2/8)d(1,1,6,9)$$
$$d(1,1,6,9) = 3/9$$
$$d(1,0,6,9) = (3/9)d(1,1,6,10)$$
$$d(1,1,6,10) = 4/10$$

(4.4.16)

Forward substitution shows that we need to solve for $d(2,0,5,6)$, $d(3,1,4,6)$, $d(2,0,5,7)$, $d(1,0,6,7)$, $d(2,1,5,7)$, $d(1,0,6,8)$, $d(2,1,5,8)$, $d(1,0,6,9)$, $d(1,1,6,9)$, and $d(1,1,6,10)$. Backward substitution then leads to $d(1,0,6,9)=0.133$, $d(1,0,6,8)=0.083$, $d(1,0,6,7)=0.036$, $d(2,1,5,8)=0.4581$, $d(2,1,5,7)=0.345$, $d(2,0,5,7)=0.1902$, $d(2,0,5,6)=0.0875$, $d(3,1,4,6)=0.4601$, $d(3,0,4,5)=0.1620$. So the chance of defaulting has increased from 11.6% to 16%. If one calculated the expected probability of payment in each period in the Bayes' model, it would still be 0.8; so why has this happened? The reason is that one only gets to the fourth, fifth, and sixth period in the time horizon if there have been some non-repayments which means the subsequent beliefs about the repayment probabilities expect them to be low. Hence only the low repayment probabilities corresponding to these 'bad' paths will occur in these distant periods because path corresponding to borrowers with good repayment histories will have completed all the payments by that time.

Example 4.4.5 Bierman–Hausman charge card model

The first Bayesian model of repayment behaviour was suggested by Bierman and Hausman (1970) in the context of a charge card, where the amount borrowed has to be completely repaid each period, before more can be borrowed the next month. They modelled this as a MDP, where the state space is (w,m), the parameter of the Beta distribution describing the belief of the repayment probability. Let r be the profit in a period on the lending when the correct repayment is made and let l be the loss if there is no repayment.

The assumption made was that one does not add this loss to the balance if no repayment is made. The decision was whether to allow the card to continue for another period or whether to withdraw the borrower's lending facility. Losses and profits were discounted by β each period. Then $v(w, m)$ the maximum expected total profit that can be obtained from a customer in state (w,m) satisfies the equation:

$$v(w, m) = \max\left\{\frac{w}{m}(r + \beta v(w + 1, m + 1)) + \left(\frac{m - w}{m}\right)(-l + \beta v(w, m + 1)); 0\right\}$$

$$(4.4.17)$$

while if one deals with total expected profitability over the next n periods the total profit $v_n(w, m)$ satisfies

$$v_n(w, m) = \max\left\{\frac{w}{m}(r + \beta v_{n-1}(w + 1, m + 1)) \right.$$

$$\left. + \left(\frac{m - w}{m}\right)(-l + \beta v_{n-1}(w, m + 1)); 0\right\}. \qquad (4.4.18)$$

In the case when $n = 2, r = 1, l = 4$ and the initial belief is $B(4,5)$ then these optimality Eqs. (4.4.17) and (4.4.18) become

$$v_3(4, 5) = \max\{(4/5)(1 + v_2(5, 6)) + (1/5)(-4 + v_2(4, 6); 0\}$$

$$v_2(5, 6) = \max\{(5/6)(1 + v_1(6, 7)) + (1/6)(-4 + v_1(5, 7); 0\}$$

$$v_2(4, 6) = \max\{(4/6)(1 + v_1(5, 7)) + (2/6)(-4 + v_1(4, 7); 0\}$$

$$v_1(6, 7) = \max\{(6/7)(1 + v_0(7, 8)) + (1/7)(-4 + v_1(6, 8); 0\}$$

$$v_1(5, 7) = \max\{(5/7)(1 + v_0(6, 8)) + (2/7)(-4 + v_1(5, 8); 0\}$$

$$v_1(4, 7) = \max\{(4/7)(1 + v_0(5, 8)) + (3/7)(-4 + v_1(4, 8); 0\}$$

Since $v_0(.,.) = 0$ then $v_1(4, 7) = v_1(5, 7) = 0; v_1(6, 7) = 0.285.$

Hence $v_2(4, 6) = 0; \quad v_2(5, 6) = 0.214; \quad v_3(4, 5) = 0.171.$ \hfill (4.4.19)

where the non-zero entries correspond to allowing the borrower to continue. Since $v_3(4, 5) = 0.171$, it is worth allowing the borrowers to keep the card if there are three periods to go and the belief about their repayment probability is $B(4,5)$. Note that if there were no updating and the repayment probability were the mean value of 0.8, then expected profit from the borrower each period would be $\max\{1(0.8) + (0.2)(-4); 0\} = 0$ and the bank would always be indifferent between stopping the card or allowing the borrower to use it for another period, since the expected profit under both actions is zero.

Example 4.4.6 Charge card with outstanding balances carried over

The assumption in Example 4.4.5 that the lender keeps wiping off any debt incurred is unrealistic so what happens if this debt is then carried over in the balance outstanding. The difficulty now is that the amount to be repaid each period may be different (as is the case with most revolving credit instruments) and so it seems unrealistic to have just one probability of repayment irrespective of what is owed. Two things have to be estimated–whether a repayment is made and if it is made how much is the repayment.

One way of doing this, suggested in Thomas (1992), is to think of the amount, R, of the repayment as being a random variable which can take one of a number of levels $a_0 = 0; a_1, a_2, \ldots, a_K$. One can define the probability distribution of R by defining a number of conditional or marginal distributions as follows. Assume the payment is at least a_i, then define the conditional distributions R_i to be 1 if the repayment R is greater than a_i, given that it is known it is at least a_i with $R_i = 0$ if the repayment is exactly a_i given that it is known to be at least a_i These conditional distributions are asking the question 'given the borrowers can afford to repay a_i, can they afford to pay back at the next higher level a_{i+1}?'. These are Bernoulli random variables and the corresponding probabilities are

$$p_i = \mathrm{P}\{R_i = 1\} = \mathrm{P}\{R > a_i | R \geq a_i\} \quad \text{for } i = 0, 1, 2, \ldots, K - 1$$

with $p_0 = \mathrm{P}\{R > 0\} = \mathrm{P}\{R_0 = 1\}$ being the probability of some repayment.

So $R_0 = 1$, $R_1 = 1$, and $R_2 = 0$ means that a_2 was the amount repaid. Since the R_i are all Bernoulli random variables and independent of each other, one can describe the belief about each probability p_i by a Beta distribution with parameters (w_i, m_i).

Consider a credit card product where the average spend each period is e units and the fraction of the spend that is a profit to the credit card through merchant service charges is f. Repayments each period can be 0, 1, 2, up to K units and the probability distribution of the repayments is given in terms of the conditional marginal random variables R_i $i = 0, 1, \ldots, K$ described earlier. The interest rate on the credit card is r_L and the bank can borrow the money it lends out at a rate of r_B. So if there is a balance of b left outstanding on the card at the end of the month, it increases to $b(1 + r_L)$ and the profit to the bank because of this interest charged is $(r_L - r_B)b$. Default is defined as N successive periods of non-payments and in that case the bank losses a proportion l_D of the outstanding balance.

Thus the state of a borrower is given by $(b, n, w_0, m_0, w_1, m_1, w_2, m_2, \ldots, w_{K-1}, m_{K-1})$, where b is the current balance, n the number of successive periods of non-payment until the present, and $(w_i, m_i), i = 0, 1, 2, \ldots, K - 1$ are the parameters of the Beta distribution describing the belief about the probabilities p_i of the random variables R_i described earlier. The decision each period is again whether to stop the borrowers using the credit card or let them continue using it. It is assumed that if the card is stopped, the borrower will immediately pay-off the balance and so the bank will not incur any further profit or loss from that borrower. Other conditions of what happens if the credit card is withdrawn can also be considered. The optimal expected profitability over t periods given the borrower starts in $(b, n, w_0, m_0, \ldots, w_{K-1}, m_{K-1})$ is $v_t(b, n, w_0, m_0, \ldots, w_{K-1}, m_{K-1})$ and this satisfies the following optimality equation:

$$v_t(b, n, w_0, m_0, w_1, m_1, \ldots, w_{K-1}, m_{K-1}) = \max \left\{ \left(\frac{m_0 - w_0}{m_0} \right) \right.$$

$$(fe + (r_L - r_B)b + v_{t-1}((1 + r_L)b + e, n + 1, w_0, m_0 + 1, w_1, m_1, \ldots, w_K, m_K))$$

$$+ \sum_{j=0}^{K-1} \prod_{i=0}^{j} \left(\frac{w_i}{m_i} \right) \left(\frac{m_{j+1} - w_{j+1}}{m_{j+1}} \right) \left(fe + ((r_L - r_B)(b - j) + v_{t-1}((1 + r_L)(b - j) \right.$$

$$+ e, 0, w_0 + 1, m_0 + 1, \ldots, w_{j-1} + 1, m_{j-1} + 1, w_j, m_j + 1, w_{j+1}, m_{j+1} \ldots, w_K, m_K))$$

$$+ \prod_{i=0}^{K} \left(\frac{w_i}{m_i} \right) \left(fe + ((r_L - r_B)(b - K) + v_{t-1}((1 + r_L)(b - K) + e, 0, w_0 \right.$$

$$+1, m_0 + 1, \ldots, w_{d+1} + 1, m_{d+1} + 1, \ldots, w_K + 1, m_K + 1)); 0\}$$
$$v_t(b, N, w_0, m_0, w_1, m_1, \ldots, w_{K-1}, m_{K-1}) = -l_D \, b. \qquad (4.4.20)$$

In this optimality equation, there is a choice between extending the credit for another period (the first expression) or stopping it now (0). The first term in the expression corresponds to there being no repayment, the second term corresponds to partial repayments of $l, 2, 3, \ldots, K - 1$, and the final term is the maximum possible repayment of a_K. The final equation describes what is lost when the borrower defaults after N missed payments.

The changes in the Beta distribution parameters correspond to three types of cases:

1. where one does not get to a repayment level because the borrower fails to repay at a lower level, and so there are no changes in either parameter

2. where one gets to a repayment level but the borrower fails to repay more than that amount. This corresponds to there being no increase in the w parameter but the m parameter increases by 1

3. where one gets to a repayment level and repays at that level and in fact repays at a higher level. In that case both the w and the m parameters are updated by 1.

Clearly there are a large number of dimensions to the state space in this type of problem and so running them in practice might be difficult. However, there is no estimation involved (one of the strengths of the Bayesian approach) and so the only problem is whether one can solve the MDP with such a large state space. Since one is able to solve such problems with more than 1,000,000 states, this suggests that one could use such models with three or four dimensions at least.

4.5   Survival analysis-based scoring systems and default estimation

When not if

Once one accepts that borrower's behaviour is dynamic, then one starts considering the time element of their credit status. Instead of asking the question that underlies default-based scoring, 'what is the probability that an applicant will default within a fixed time period in the future?', one could ask 'when will they default?' This is a more difficult question to address because one is trying to estimate a complex probability distribution over time rather than the one fixed time default probability. Also for all the customers, except those who have defaulted, the data in any sample is censored in that the default event did not occur. So for some borrowers, one only knows that they were still good customers at the end date of the sample; for others one knows when they ceased to be borrowers, either because they paid back the loan when it was due, or because they paid it back early perhaps by moving the balance of the loan to another lender. In each of these cases they were not in default when they ceased to repay.

However, there are several substantial advantages in trying to answer this harder question. The foremost advantage is that if we are serious about building a model of the profitability of the customer, then we do need to get estimates of when certain actions which affect the profit will occur, not just if they might occur. It is also the case that estimating the time when defaults occur will give a forecast of the default levels as a function of time. We introduced this idea in Section 1.6 where we introduced a probability survival function and a default hazard rate. These estimates of when defaults will occur are useful for firms' debt provisioning. Such estimates may also guide the decision by the bank on the length of time over which the loan should be required to be repaid. It is also a way of incorporating the future changes in the economic climate into estimates of the default probability and the profitability of the loans as will be discussed in the next section.

This approach to credit scoring, where one tries to estimate how long until default occurs even though in many cases it will not occur, is exactly what the models of survival analysis were designed for, as was recognized in Section 1.6.

Survival analysis

Survival analysis (Kalbfleisch and Prentice 1980; Hosmer and Lemeshow 1998) is concerned with the time until an event occurs. Initially it began as a way of dealing with mortality data, and then became used in industry for estimating the lifetime of equipment. Its usefulness was transformed by two results. Firstly, Kaplan and Meier (1958) developed the product limit estimator which allowed one to estimate the survival function given censored and uncensored data. Then Cox (1972) introduced the idea of the proportional hazard functions which allowed one to easily connect the characteristics of the individual to the time until the event of interest occurred. Immediately its use was taken up in medicine to estimate onset of disease and effects of treatments, in marketing to estimate the times between purchases, and more recently in both corporate and consumer lending to estimate the time until a default occurs. Hereafter, we will discuss survival analysis in this consumer lending context and so keep referring to T as the time until the consumer defaults on a loan.

Let T be the length of time until a borrower defaults on a loan and as in Section 1.6 we will initially think of T as a continuous variable before specializing to the case where it is discrete. In consumer credit, data is usually summarized on a monthly basis and so what is recorded is the month in which a borrower defaulted rather than when in that month the borrower reached the 90-day overdue mark or whatever other criteria the lender uses to define default. So one can consider T to be a discrete time variable or a continuous variable where the data is interval censored, that is, the status of the borrower is only checked at certain time intervals.

This allows us to think of the discrete time survival analysis as a special type of censored continuous time model and move between the two with relative freedom.

Recall that in Section 1.6 we defined the following functions and the relationships between them. Here we extend the definition by assuming the borrower has characteristics $\mathbf{x}$ and including that in all the definitions. Then the probability of a borrower defaulting before time t is

$$P_B(t, \mathbf{x}) = \Pr\{T < t\} \tag{4.5.1}$$

and so the probability of default in $(t, t+\delta t]$ is

$$\Pr\{t < T \le t + \delta t, \mathbf{x}\} = P_B'(t, \mathbf{x})\delta t.$$

The probability survival function that default will occur after t is

$$P_G(t, \mathbf{x}) = 1 - P_B(t, \mathbf{x}) = \Pr\{T \ge t\}$$

$$= \Pr\{\text{default occurs at or after } t\} = \int_t^\infty P_B'(u, \mathbf{x})du. \tag{4.5.2}$$

The default hazard rate, $h(t,\mathbf{x})$, is a rate where $h(t,\mathbf{x})\delta t$ is the conditional probability of default in $(t, t + \delta t]$ given there has been no default in $(0,t]$:

$$h(t, \mathbf{x}) = \Pr\{t \le T < t + \delta t | T \ge t\} \triangleq \frac{P_B'(t, \mathbf{x})}{1 - P_B(t, \mathbf{x})}$$

$$= -\frac{d}{dt} \ln(1 - P_B(t,)) = -\frac{d}{dt} \ln(P_G(t, \mathbf{x})). \tag{4.5.3}$$

Defining the cumulative hazard function by $H(t, \mathbf{x}) \triangleq \int_0^t h(u, \mathbf{x})du$ means one can write the probability survival function as

$$P_G(t, \mathbf{x}) = 1 - P_B(t, \mathbf{x}) = e^{-H(t,\mathbf{x})} \text{ and } P_B'(t, \mathbf{x}) = h(t, \mathbf{x})e^{-H(t,\mathbf{x})}. \tag{4.5.4}$$

Finally, the definition of a log odds score was extended to this context by defining $s(0,\tau|\mathbf{x})$ to be the log of the odds of the chance of being good (that is not defaulting) during the period $[0,\tau)$ divided by the chance of becoming bad (that is defaulting) during that period, and hence having

$$s(0, \tau|\mathbf{x}) = \ln\left(\frac{P_G(\tau, \mathbf{x})}{P_B(\tau, \mathbf{x})}\right) = -\ln\left(e^{H(\tau,\mathbf{x})} - 1\right). \tag{4.5.5}$$

For human mortality and industrial equipment applications, the typical hazard rate has a bath tub shape which consists of three parts. First, a steep drop from a high value at the beginning, since there is a high chance of failure while the item is first used which drops as it is run in. Then, there is a constant low value which is called the steady state before 'ageing' set in and there is a gradual rise in the hazard function. This is shown in the left-hand side figure of Fig. 4.5.1. There is no need

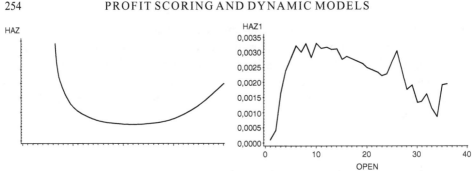

FIG. 4.5.1. Example of hazard functions.

for it to follow such a shape and the RHS figure shows the hazard rate obtained from some consumer default data.

The important point to recognize when using survival data is that for many cases the event of interest will not yet have occurred, that is, they are right censored. So in the consumer credit case many consumers will not have yet defaulted. One does not want to lose the power of such data and this is where the product limit estimator of Kaplan–Meier estimator comes in. It is able to estimate the survival function for any set of data using information from the censored and the uncensored observations. If we consider a sample of n customers payment history each of which consists of one time measured from the start of the loan (t_i), at which either customer i defaulted ($D_i = 1$) or no more payment information was available on customer i ($D_i = 0$). Here we define D_i to be the censoring variable which is 1 if there was full information – that is, the time of the default of the customer is known and 0 if the information was censored – so no default had yet occurred. For each customer, we have values t_i and D_i. Order the n times in increasing order $t_1 \leq t_2 \leq \ldots \leq t_m$ where $m \leq n$ since there may be ties. Assume that at time t_j there were d_j defaults (that is with $D_i = 1$) and c_j borrowers who were censored at that point ($D_i = 0$). At any time t we define the probability survival function in terms of the $k(t)$ entries $t_1 \leq t_2 \leq \ldots \leq t_{k(t)} < t$ by

$$\hat{P}_G(t) = \prod_{j=1}^{j=k(t)} [(n_j - d_j)/(n_j)]$$

where

$$n_j = n - \sum_{k=0}^{j-1} (d_j + c_j). \qquad (4.5.6)$$

This gives a non-parametric maximum likelihood estimator of the survival function from any set of survival data be it continuous or discrete time, though the estimator itself is always a step function.

TABLE 4.5.1. Data for example 4.5.1.

i	1	2	3	4	5	6	7	8	9	10	11	12	13	14	15	16	17	18	19	20
t_i	2	3	3	4	4	4	6	7	9	9	9	10	10	12	12	12	14	15	15	15
d_i	0	1	0	1	1	0	0	1	1	0	0	1	1	1	1	0	1	0	0	0

Example 4.5.1 Probability survival function using Kaplan–Meier estimator

Suppose the data on when they defaulted or were censored from a sample of 20 borrowers over a 15-month period was as given in Table 4.5.1.

Since the lowest t_i value is 2, for both $\hat{P}_G(1) = \hat{P}_G(2) = 1$, since there are no values $t_i < t$ for those two terms. For the rest we recognize that we can rewrite Eq. (4.5.6) as

$$\hat{P}_G(j+1) = \hat{P}_G(j) \left(\frac{n_j - d_j}{n_j} \right)$$

and so

$$n_2 = 20, d_2 = 0, c_2 = 1 \Rightarrow \hat{P}_G(3) = \hat{P}_G(2) \left(\frac{20 - 0}{20} \right) = 1$$

$$n_3 = 19, d_3 = 1, c_3 = 1 \Rightarrow \hat{P}_G(4) = \hat{P}_G(3) \left(\frac{19 - 1}{19} \right) = 18/19 = 0.947$$

$$n_4 = 17, d_4 = 2, c_4 = 1 \Rightarrow \hat{P}_G(5) = \hat{P}_G(4) \left(\frac{17 - 2}{17} \right)$$

$$= 0.947 \times (15/17) = 0.836$$

$$n_5 = n_6 = 14, d_6 = 0, c_6 = 1 \Rightarrow \hat{P}_G(7) = \hat{P}_G(6) \left(\frac{14 - 0}{14} \right)$$

$$= \hat{P}_G(5) \left(\frac{14 - 0}{14} \right) = 0.836$$

$$n_7 = 13, d_7 = 1, c_7 = 1 \Rightarrow \hat{P}_G(8) = \hat{P}_G(7) \left(\frac{13 - 1}{13} \right)$$

$$= 0.836 \times (12/13) = 0.772$$

$$n_9 = n_8 = 12, d_9 = 1, c_9 = 2 \Rightarrow \hat{P}_G(10) = \hat{P}_G(9) \left(\frac{12 - 1}{12} \right)$$

$$= \hat{P}_G(8) \left(\frac{12 - 1}{12} \right) = 0.707$$

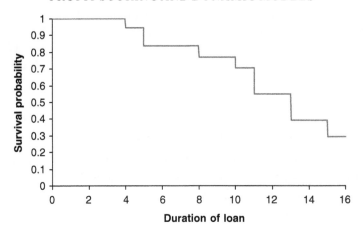

FIG. 4.5.2. Probability survival function of Example 4.5.1.

$$n_{10} = 9, d_{10} = 2, c_{10} = 0 \Rightarrow \hat{P}_G(11) = \hat{P}_G(10) \left(\frac{9-2}{9} \right)$$

$$= 0.707 \times (7/9) = 0.550$$

$$n_{12} = n_{11} = 7, d_{12} = 2, c_{12} = 1 \Rightarrow \hat{P}_G(13) = \hat{P}_G(12) \left(\frac{7-2}{7} \right)$$

$$= \hat{P}_G(11) \left(\frac{7-2}{7} \right) = 0.550 \times (5/7) = 0.393$$

$$n_{14} = n_{13} = 4, d_{14} = 1, c_{14} = 0 \Rightarrow \hat{P}_G(15) = \hat{P}_G(14) \left(\frac{4-1}{4} \right)$$

$$= \hat{P}_G(13) \left(\frac{4-1}{4} \right) = 0.393 \times (3/4) = 0.295.$$

Plotting these estimates of the probability survival function gives the step function in Fig. 4.5.2.

Proportional hazard models

In standard application scoring one assumes the application characteristics affect the probability of default. Similarly in this survival analysis approach, we want models which allow these characteristics to affect the probability of when a customer defaults. The breakthrough in survival analysis in general came when one was able to build survival models where this time until the critical event depended on the characteristics of the individual involved. There are two models which have become the established ways of doing this – proportional hazard models and accelerated life models. By far the more common model is the proportional hazard models introduced by Cox (1972) in the work alluded to above.

The idea behind proportional hazard models is if $\mathbf{x} = (x_1, \ldots, x_p)$ are the application (explanatory) characteristics, then one assumes the hazard rate

$$h(t, \mathbf{x}) = g(\mathbf{x})h_0(t) \qquad (4.5.7)$$

so the characteristics $\mathbf{x}$ have a multiplier effect on some baseline hazard $h_0(t)$ (think of $h_0(t)$ as the hazard for someone with no interesting, if not redeeming, features). Since $h(t, \mathbf{x})$ is a rate, it has to be non-negative as does $h_0(t)$ and so $g(\mathbf{x})$ must be positive. One way of ensuring this is to make $g(\mathbf{x})$ an exponential of a function of $\mathbf{x}$ since exponentials are always positive. The simplest of such a model is to make it the exponential of a linear function of $\mathbf{x}$ and this leads to the formal definition of a proportional hazards model as

$$h(t, \mathbf{x}) = e^{\mathbf{w} \cdot \mathbf{x}} h_0(t). \qquad (4.5.8)$$

The other model used in survival analysis to make the survival functions heterogeneous in the applicants' characteristics is the accelerated life model where one assumes

$$S(t, \mathbf{x}) = S_0(e^{\mathbf{w} \cdot \mathbf{x}} t) \text{ or } h(t) = e^{\mathbf{w} \cdot \mathbf{x}} h_0(e^{\mathbf{w} \cdot \mathbf{x}} t) \qquad (4.5.9)$$

where h_0 and S_0 are again baseline functions so the $\mathbf{x}$ can speed up or slow down the 'ageing' of the account. This model was discussed in the different context of building an acceptance probability function in Section 3.5. The difference between the models is that in proportional hazards the applicants most at risk of defaulting at any one time remain the ones most at risk of defaulting at any other time, whereas in accelerated life models the relative risks change over time. Someone who is slower at ageing could be going through a particularly hazardous part of the lifecycle distribution, while another individual with a higher ageing factor is in a less hazardous part of the distribution, but later on this may be reversed.

One can use a parametric approach to both the proportional hazards and accelerated life models by assuming $h_0(\cdot)$ belongs to a particular family of distributions. It turns out that the negative exponential and the Weibull distributions are the only main distributions that lead to models that are both accelerated life and proportional hazard models – the negative exponential distribution is a special case of the Weibull distribution. From Eqs. (4.5.8) and (4.5.9), a proportional hazards model must satisfy $h(t) = e^{\mathbf{w} \cdot \mathbf{x}} h_0(t)$ and an accelerated life model must satisfy $h(t) = e^{\mathbf{w} \cdot \mathbf{x}} h_0(e^{\mathbf{w} \cdot \mathbf{x}} t)$. Example 1.6.3 showed that the hazard rate for a Weibull distribution was $h_{\lambda, \alpha}(t) = \lambda \alpha^{-\lambda} t^{\lambda - 1}$ and so if $h_0(t) = h_{\lambda, \alpha}(t)$ then

$$e^{\mathbf{w} \cdot \mathbf{x}} h_0(e^{\mathbf{w} \cdot \mathbf{x}} t) = e^{\mathbf{w} \cdot \mathbf{x}} \lambda \alpha^{-\lambda} (e^{\mathbf{w} \cdot \mathbf{x}} t)^{\lambda - 1} = \lambda (\alpha e^{-\mathbf{w} \cdot \mathbf{x}})^{-\lambda} t^{\lambda - 1} = h_{\lambda, \alpha e^{-\mathbf{w} \cdot \mathbf{x}}}(t) \equiv h(t),$$
$$(4.5.10)$$

which satisfies the requirement in Eq. (4.5.9) for an accelerated life model where $h(t, \mathbf{x}) = h_{\lambda, \alpha e^{-\mathbf{w} \cdot \mathbf{x}}}(t)$. Similarly:

$$e^{\mathbf{w} \cdot \mathbf{x}} h_0(t) = e^{\mathbf{w} \cdot \mathbf{x}} \lambda \alpha^{-\lambda}(t)^{\lambda - 1} = \lambda(\alpha e^{-(\mathbf{w}/\lambda) \cdot \mathbf{x}})^{-\lambda} t^{\lambda - 1} = h_{\lambda, \alpha e^{-(\mathbf{w}/\lambda) \cdot \mathbf{x}}}(t) \equiv h(t)$$

$$(4.5.11)$$

shows that a Weibull hazard distribution satisfies the proportional hazards requirements provided we define $h(t, \mathbf{x}) = h_{\lambda, \alpha e^{-\mathbf{w} \cdot \mathbf{x}/\lambda}}(t)$. Note this connection only holds if the characteristics $\mathbf{x}$ are fixed. If we allow them to be time dependent, that is, $\mathbf{x}(t)$, the Weibull distribution is no longer an accelerated life model. Also the Weibull distribution is of less use on consumer credit modelling than in the equipment failure cases. In consumer credit, the typical hazard function is of the form shown in Fig. 4.5.1 and this is impossible to fit using a Weibull distribution because whatever the choice of the parameters of the Weibull distribution the resultant hazard function will be monotone increasing or monotone decreasing.

The proportional hazard approach of estimating the times to default can also give rise to the notion of a score and so is much closer to the idea of a log odds default score which one gets when estimating the chance of default in a given time period than might be first thought. It is the linear risk factor $\mathbf{w} \cdot \mathbf{x}$ of individual borrowers that relates their characteristics to when they are likely to default. So in the proportional hazards approach we define the hazard score s_h for an individual with characteristics $\mathbf{x}$ to be

$$s_h = -\mathbf{w} \cdot \mathbf{x} = -(w_1 x_1 + w_2 x_2 + \cdots + w_m x_m). \qquad (4.5.12)$$

The negative sign is inserted to ensure that those with higher scores are the least likely to default, that is, the lowest risk factor. Then if the definition of 'good' was the standard one of not having defaulted within a time t^*, the probability, p, that an applicant will be good satisfies

$$p = P_G(t^*, \mathbf{x}) = e^{-\int_0^{t^*} h(u, \mathbf{x}) du} = e^{-\int_0^{t^*} e^{\mathbf{w} \cdot \mathbf{x}} h_0(u) du} = \left(e^{-\int_0^{t^*} h_0(u) du} \right)^{e^{\mathbf{w} \cdot \mathbf{x}}}$$

$$(4.5.13)$$

$$= (S_0(t^*))^{e^{\mathbf{w} \cdot \mathbf{x}}} = (S_0(t^*))^{e^{-s_h}}$$

where $S_0(t)$ is the survival function corresponding to the baseline hazard function.
Hence

$$p = c^{e^{-s_h}} \Rightarrow \log p = e^{-s_h} \log c \text{ and we can choose the baseline so:}$$

$$c = S_0(t^*) = e^{-k}$$

Hence $e^{-s_h} = (-\log p)/k \Rightarrow s_h = -\log(-\log(p)/k)$

$$= -\log(-\log(p)) + \log(k) \qquad (4.5.14)$$

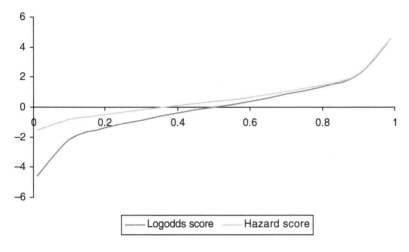

FIG. 4.5.3. Comparison of log odds score and hazard score.

This idea of the hazard score being minus the log of minus the log of the probability of being good can be compared with the standard definition of the log odds score given in Section 1.5 as the log of the odds of being good to being bad. Both transform a probability which takes values between 0 and 1 to a score which can take values from $-\infty$ to ∞. The differences in the transformations is shown in Fig. 4.5.3, where the hazard score is taken with $k = 1$. Whereas in the logodds score, changes in the riskiness of the population mean changes in popodds and adds a constant to the score, in the hazard score, changes in the riskiness of the population affect the value of k but that also results in a constant being added to the score.

So a hazard score is a log–log transform of the probability of default while the log odds default score is a logit transformation of the default probability. Both of these transform the probability region [0,1] into $(-\infty, +\infty)$. The proportional hazard models though have much more information in them because of the $h_0(t)$ part of the expressions.

Cox's proportional hazard models

Cox (1972) pointed out that in proportional hazards one can estimate the weights **w** without any information about the distribution of $h_0(t)$ just by using the ordering of the failure times and the censored times. One only needs to know the order in which customers either defaulted or left the sample. This is called the non-parametric (or correctly the semi-parametric) version of the proportional hazards model because one does not have to define the form of the baseline distribution. This non-parametric approach is useful in the consumer credit context because it means one does not have to assume the baseline hazard function is of a particular family, since in this context it is rarely of a standard form.

If t_j, D_j, x_j are the failure (or censored) times, the binary censoring variable (1 if default, 0 if censored), and the characteristics of borrower j in the sample, order the sample so $t_1 \leq t_2 \leq \ldots \leq t_n$. Let $R(i) = (i, i + 1, i + 2, \ldots, n)$ be the set of customers still in the sample just before time t_i which is a time at which there is a default ($D_i = 1$) then the conditional probability that given a customer will default at time t_i it is customer i is given by

$$\exp\{\mathbf{w} \cdot \mathbf{x}_i\}h_0(t_i) \Big/ \sum_{k \in R(i)} \exp\{\mathbf{w} \cdot \mathbf{x}_k\}h_0(t_i) = \exp\{\mathbf{w} \cdot \mathbf{x}_i\} \Big/ \sum_{k \in R(i)} \exp\{\mathbf{w} \cdot \mathbf{x}_k\},$$

$$(4.5.15)$$

which is independent of h_0. Hence the partial likelihood (joint probability over all the default events) which one has to maximize by a choice of $\mathbf{w}$ is

$$L(\mathbf{w}) = \prod_{i:D_i=1} \frac{\exp\{\mathbf{w} \cdot \mathbf{x}_i\}}{\sum_{j \in R\{i\}} \exp\{\mathbf{w} \cdot \mathbf{x}_j\}}. \qquad (4.5.16)$$

There are two complications when applying this model to consumer credit. As mentioned previously data on who has defaulted tends to be recorded only once a month and so the default time is really discrete not continuous, or at least interval censored if one wants to consider it as continuous. Also because of this monthly recording and the large size of the data sets, there are lots of ties with a large number of customers whose data is censored or they have defaulted in the same month.

Cox (1972) suggested one way of extending proportional hazard models to discrete times by working with the odds of $h(n, \mathbf{x})$, the conditional probability of default in period n given the borrower with characteristics $\mathbf{x}$ has not defaulted before then. If $h_0(n)$ is the equivalent baseline conditional probability, then the assumption is that

$$\frac{h(n, \mathbf{x})}{1 - h(n, \mathbf{x})} = \frac{h_0(n)}{1 - h_0(n)}e^{\mathbf{w} \cdot \mathbf{x}}. \qquad (4.5.17)$$

By taking logs this becomes

$$\ln\left(\frac{h(n, \mathbf{x})}{1 - h(n, \mathbf{x})}\right) = \ln\left(\frac{h_0(n)}{1 - h_0(n)}\right) + \mathbf{w} \cdot \mathbf{x} = \alpha_n + \mathbf{w} \cdot \mathbf{x}. \qquad (4.5.18)$$

This has parallels with the log odds score defined in Section 1.5 except that one is taking the chance of default just over the next period. One could use a logistic regression approach to solve the equation. Transform the data set so that a borrower who has been repaying for k months is considered as k separate data points, one for each month with the target variable being whether or not they defaulted in that month. Note that there is a different constant α_n of the log odds of the baseline conditional default probability for each month.

The alternative way of extending proportional hazard models to discrete time was suggested by Kalbfleisch and Prentice (1980) and uses the form of the probability survival function of proportional hazards namely if

$$h(t, \mathbf{x}) = e^{\mathbf{w}\cdot\mathbf{x}}h_0(t) \Rightarrow P_G(t, \mathbf{x}) = e^{-\int_0^t h(u,\mathbf{x})du} = e^{-e^{\mathbf{w}\cdot\mathbf{x}}\int_0^t h_0(u)du}$$

$$= \left(e^{-\int_0^t h_0(u)du}\right)^{e^{\mathbf{w}\cdot\mathbf{x}}} = S_0(t)^{e^{\mathbf{w}\cdot\mathbf{x}}}.$$

Since for discrete time $P_G(n, \mathbf{x}) = \prod_{i=1}^{n-1}(1 - h(i, \mathbf{x}))$ and $S_0(n) = \prod_{i=1}^{n-1}(1 - h_0(i))$

this implies $(1 - h(i, \mathbf{x})) = (1 - h_0(i))^{e^{\mathbf{w}\cdot\mathbf{x}}}$.   (4.5.19)

Taking logs in this case gives

$$-\log(1 - h(n, \mathbf{x})) = -e^{\mathbf{w}\cdot\mathbf{x}}\log(1 - h_0(n))$$

$$\Rightarrow \log(-\log(1 - h(n, \mathbf{x}))) = \mathbf{w}\cdot\mathbf{x} + \alpha_n \text{ where } \alpha_n = \log(-\log(1 - h_0(n))).$$
                (4.5.20)

This second approach is the same model that is obtained by grouping the continuous time proportional hazard models into time intervals $0 = \tau_0 < \tau_1 < \cdots < \tau_K$. Let $h(n, \mathbf{x})$ be the conditional probability that a borrower with characteristics $\mathbf{x}$ will default between τ_{n-1} and τ_n. Let $h_0(n)$ be the similar definition for the 'baseline' borrower, then

$$h(n, \mathbf{x}) = 1 - \Pr\{T > \tau_n | T > \tau_{n-1}\} = 1 - e^{-\int_{\tau_{n-1}}^{\tau_n} h(u,\mathbf{x})du}$$

$$= 1 - e^{-\int_{\tau_{n-1}}^{\tau_n} e^{\mathbf{w}\cdot\mathbf{x}}h_0(u)du} = 1 - \left(e^{-\int_{\tau_{n-1}}^{\tau_n} h_0(u)du}\right)^{e^{\mathbf{w}\cdot\mathbf{x}}} = 1 - (1 - h_0(n))^{e^{\mathbf{w}\cdot\mathbf{x}}}.$$
                (4.5.21)

So it has become standard to use this second extension to discrete time proportional hazard models since it means one can use the standard proportional hazard models in most software packages.

The second difficulty that a discrete time model brings is that it means there will be lots of ties when several consumers default or are censored at the same time. This causes the following computational problem when calculating the $\mathbf{w}$ by maximizing the likelihood function. If d_i are the number of defaults ('failures') at time t_i, let $R(t_i, d_i)$ be the set of all subsets of d_i borrowers taken from the risk set

$R(i)$ – the borrowers who could default at time t_i. Let R be any such subset of d_i borrowers in $R(t_i,d_i)$ and let A be the set of the d_i borrowers who actually defaulted at t_i. The likelihood function Eq. (4.5.15) arising from this model is then

$$\prod_{i=1}^{K} \left(\sum_{r \in A} \exp(\mathbf{w} \cdot \mathbf{s}_r) \middle/ \sum_{R \in R(t_i,d_i)} \sum_{r \in R} \exp(\mathbf{w} \cdot \mathbf{s}_r) \right). \qquad (4.5.22)$$

Maximizing this is difficult because of the large number of sets that have to be summed over in the denominator. Breslow (1974) and Efron (1977) have suggested simplifying approximations, the former involving less calculation but the latter is more accurate.

Once one has calculated the weights $\mathbf{w}$ of the hazard score function one can use the Kaplan–Meier product limit estimation procedure, suitably modified to allow for the different risk factors that each individual has to get an estimate for the baseline survival function. Let $(t_i, D_i, \mathbf{x}_i)$ be the failure/censor times, the censor variable, and the individual characteristics of a sample of previous borrowers ordered so that t_i is increasing in i. In the standard Kaplan–Meier estimator the critical point is that $S(t_i)/S(t_{i-1}) = 1 - h_i$ where h_i is the conditional probability of defaulting at t_i given the borrower has not defaulted before. Similarly in proportional hazards the critical point is that $S_0(t_i)/S_0(t_{i-1}) = 1 - h_0(t_i)$. Since from Eq. (4.5.19) $(1 - h(t_i, \mathbf{x})) = (1 - h_0(t_i))^{e^{\mathbf{w} \cdot \mathbf{x}}}$ then if $R(i)$ is the set of borrowers at risk just before time t_i of which $A(i)$ are the set who defaulted at that time, then the likelihood of getting this group to default at this time is

$$\prod_{j \in R(i)-A(i)} (1 - h_0(t_i))^{e^{\mathbf{w} \cdot \mathbf{x}_j}} \prod_{k \in A(i)} \left(1 - (1 - h_0(t_i))^{e^{\mathbf{w} \cdot \mathbf{x}_j}}\right). \qquad (4.5.23)$$

Taking logs and differentiating with respect to $h_0(t_i)$ to find the maximum likelihood estimator gives

$$\sum_{j \in R(i)-A(i)} \frac{e^{\mathbf{w} \cdot \mathbf{x}_j}}{1 - h_0(t_i)} - \sum_{j \in A(i)} \frac{e^{\mathbf{w} \cdot \mathbf{x}_j}(1 - h_0(t_i))^{e^{\mathbf{w} \cdot \mathbf{x}_j}-1}}{1 - (1 - h_0(t_i))^{e^{\mathbf{w} \cdot \mathbf{x}_j}}} = 0$$

$$\Rightarrow \sum_{j \in R(i)-A(i)} e^{\mathbf{w} \cdot \mathbf{x}_j} = \sum_{j \in A(i)} \frac{e^{\mathbf{w} \cdot \mathbf{x}_j}(1 - h_0(t_i))^{e^{\mathbf{w} \cdot \mathbf{x}_j}}}{1 - (1 - h_0(t_i))^{e^{\mathbf{w} \cdot \mathbf{x}_j}}}$$

$$\Rightarrow \sum_{j \in R(i)} e^{\mathbf{w} \cdot \mathbf{x}_j} = \sum_{j \in A(i)} \frac{\left(e^{\mathbf{w} \cdot \mathbf{x}_j}(1 - h_o(t_i))^{e^{\mathbf{w} \cdot \mathbf{x}_j}} \right) + e^{\mathbf{w} \cdot \mathbf{x}_j} \left(1 - (1 - h_o(t_i))^{e^{\mathbf{w} \cdot \mathbf{x}_j}} \right)}{1 - (1 - h_o(t_i))^{e^{\mathbf{w} \cdot \mathbf{x}_j}}}$$

$$= \sum_{j \in A(i)} \frac{e^{\mathbf{w} \cdot \mathbf{x}_j}}{1 - (1 - h_o(t_i))^{e^{\mathbf{w} \cdot \mathbf{x}_j}}}. \tag{4.5.24}$$

Equation (4.5.24) can be used to estimate $h_0(t_i)$
In the case when there is only one entry in $A(i)$, this reduces to

$$1 - h_0(t_i) = \left(1 - \frac{e^{\mathbf{w} \cdot \mathbf{x}_i}}{\sum_{r \in R(i)} e^{\mathbf{w} \cdot \mathbf{x}_r}} \right)^{e^{-\mathbf{w} \cdot \mathbf{x}_i}}. \tag{4.5.25}$$

Having estimated $h_0(t_i)$ by $\hat{h}_0(t_i)$, one can estimate the baseline survival function by

$$\hat{S}_0(t) = \prod_{t_i \le t} \left(1 - \hat{h}_0(t_i) \right) \tag{4.5.26}$$

The Breslow approximation to the partial likelihood function if there are ties mentioned above is equivalent to assuming that $(1 - h_0(t_i))^{e^{\mathbf{w} \cdot \mathbf{x}}} = 1 + e^{\mathbf{w} \cdot \mathbf{x}}$ $\ln(1 - h_0(t_i))$ and substituting that into Eq. (4.5.26) gives the estimator

$$\left(1 - \hat{h}_0(t_i) \right) = \exp \left(\frac{-d_i}{\sum_{r \in R(i)} e^{\mathbf{w} \cdot \mathbf{x}_r}} \right) \tag{4.5.27}$$

where d_i is the number of defaulters at time t_i.

Building proportional hazard models

In using the proportional hazards models with its advantage of an arbitrary time horizon over which default is measured, it is important to ensure that this time horizon does not creep in elsewhere into the calculations. As was discussed in Section 1.8, coarse classification is used in building default scores to deal with non-monotonicity of risk in continuous characteristics and to avoid having too many attributes for categorical characteristics. In coarse classification, each characteristic is split into bins which are either intervals for continuous characteristics or groups of attributes for categorical characteristics. Each bin is then replaced with a binary dummy variable.

The usual way of finding these bins is to look at the good:bad ratios or related measures, like weights of evidence for each of a fine (many groups) division of the attributes that the characteristic takes and then grouping together attributes with similar good:bad ratios. Inherent in this approach is the choice of a time horizon so that defaults before that time horizon are 'bad' while ones that default after it or do not default at all are 'good'. To avoid the horizon creeping back in this way when building survival analysis type scorecards, one can use the proportional hazards models to coarse classify the characteristics as well as to build the final model so there is no need for a preferred time horizon. One way of doing this was the following:

1. Split the characteristic into a fine classification (maybe 10–20 equal percentile groups for a continuous characteristic and all the categories, unless they are a minute proportion of the sample, for a categorical characteristic)

2. Create a binary variable for each group

3. Fit the proportional hazard model using only the binary variables from that characteristic

4. Choose the coarse classification by grouping together the fine bands whose coefficients in three are similar.

Using this approach one has a way of modelling the default distribution of a consumer over all time periods without putting emphasis on any particular time horizon.

Having coarse classified the characteristics, one can then use Cox's proportional hazard approach to obtain the coefficients **w** in the hazard score or risk function by maximizing the partial likelihood estimator given by Eq. (4.5.16). This gives the discrimination between the different borrowers but to get a prediction of the probability of their default in any given time interval one would need to use the Kaplan–Meier estimators suggested by Eqs. (4.5.24) to (4.5.27). We undertake these calculations for a very simple case in the next example.

Example 4.5.2 Construction of a proportional hazards model

Suppose one has a data set consisting of six borrowers where the only characteristic for each borrower is whether they are an owner ($x = 1$) or not an owner ($x = 0$). Table 4.5.2 gives the data on the six borrowers, three of whom have defaulted, one paid off completely after 6 months, and the other two were still repaying at the end of the data set month 12 and month 14, respectively. Let the coefficient of being an owner be w, then the only defaults occur at times 4, 8, and 10 and the risk

TABLE 4.5.2. Data for example 4.5.2.

t_i	4	6	8	10	12	14
D_i	1	0	1	1	0	0
x_i	0	1	0	1	1	0

sets, respectively, are $R(4) = \{3$ owners and 3 non-owners$]$, $R(8) = \{2$ owners and 2 non-owners$]$, and $R(10) = \{2$ owners and 1 non-owner$]$. So the partial likelihood from Eq. (4.5.16) is

$$\frac{1}{3 + 3e^w} \times \frac{1}{2 + 2e^w} \times \frac{e^w}{1 + 2e^w} \qquad (4.5.28)$$

This is maximized at $w = -0.941$ so the hazard score is 0.941 for owners and 0 for non-owners.

To calculate the baseline survival function, we use Eq. (4.5.25) since there are no ties. The only time the survival function $P_G(t)$ changes and so one has hazard rates less than 1 is at the default times $t = 4, 8$, and 10. Applying Eq. (4.5.25) gives

$$1 - \left(1 - \hat{h}_4\right) = \hat{h}_4 = \frac{1}{3 + 3e^w} = \frac{1}{3 + 3e^{-0.941}} = 0.240$$

$$1 - \left(1 - \hat{h}_8\right) = \hat{h}_8 = \frac{1}{2 + 2e^w} = \frac{1}{2 + 2e^{-0.941}} = 0.360$$

$$1 - \left(1 - \hat{h}_{10}\right)^{e^{-0.941}} = \frac{e^w}{1 + 2e^w} = \frac{e^{-0.941}}{1 + 2e^{-0.941}} = 0.219 \Rightarrow 1 - \hat{h}_{10} = 0.5305$$

$$(4.5.29)$$

Hence the baseline survival function is

$$S_0(t) = \begin{cases} 1 & t < 4 \\ 0.760 & 4 \le t < 8 \\ 0.487 = (0.760 \times 0.640) & 8 \le t < 10 \\ 0.258 = (0.487 \times 0.258) & 10 \le t \end{cases} \qquad (4.5.30)$$

To compare proportional hazard-based discrimination with standard default-based scorecards, one has to revert to a fixed time horizon so that the latter can be constructed. Figure 4.5.4 shows the results (Stepanova and Thomas 2002) of comparing a proportional hazard model based on personal loan data with two separate logistic regression models. The first model takes the whole population of borrowers and defines 'bad' to be defaulted in the first 12 months of the loan while the second takes the population as those who had not defaulted in the first 12 months and defines 'bad' to be a default in the second 12 months. One has to build two completely separate logistic regression scorecards for these but one can get the two calculations from the same proportional hazards models since the probability of being good in the former case is $S(12)$ and in the latter case it is

$$\Pr(T > 24|T > 12) = \Pr(T > 24)/\Pr(T > 12) = S(24)/S(12)$$

The resulting receiver operating characteristic (ROC) curves s are shown in Fig. 4.5.4 and suggest that the proportional hazards model seems to be almost as good a discriminator as the two logistic regression models.

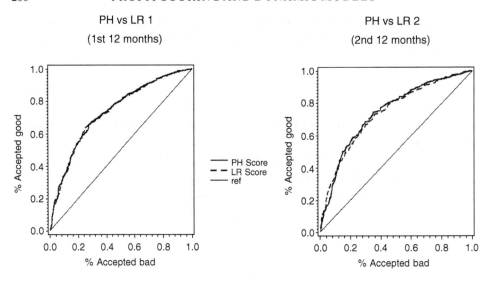

FIG. 4.5.4. ROC curves for proportional hazards and logistic regression models predicting default.

The proportional hazards assumption, that a particular characteristic has the same effect on the hazard rate at all times of the loan, is a very strong one and may not always be appropriate for consumer lending. One can use the plots of residuals, like the Schoenfeld residual, to test either by eye or using statistical tests whether the assumption is true. If it is not, then all is not lost. Instead one can introduce time varying coefficients as follows. For each characteristic x_1 that one believes the proportionality may not be time dependent, introduce a second variable x_{1t} which at time t of the loan has value $x_1 \times t$. If w_1 and w_2 are the respective coefficients, then their impact on the score is

$$s = -(w_1 x_1 + w_2 x_{1t} + \cdots) = -((w_1 + w_2 t)x_1 + \cdots), \qquad (4.5.31)$$

which allows the impact of x_1 to change over time. This is very useful for variables like purpose of loan where refinancing is a very negative characteristic early on but its effect diminishes the longer the loan is being repaid. This is also a good way of checking if the proportional hazard assumption is holding because if the coefficients of the variables which are products of time and original characteristics are insignificant then the assumption is valid.

So far we have concentrated on Cox's semi-parametric approach to apply survival analysis to consumer default data, but as mentioned earlier one could also use the fully parametric approach by assuming the baseline hazard function is of a particular type. The parametric models tend to give more robustness in their estimates but lose the flexibility of the non-parametric approach in allowing any form of the baseline hazard function. Usually this extra flexibility means the Cox's approach gives better fits to the data but there is one area where the parametric approach is advantageous (Banasik et al. 1999). If one is building a scorecard for a new product with little or no previous data, then can one use the default information in the very early months to build a scorecard? The standard default approaches will not work because there is not enough history available and the Cox approach also has insufficient information to model sensibly into the future. Using the parametric approach though one can use the form of the parametric distribution to connect early estimates of the weights w and the parameters of the baseline distribution to forecasts of default probabilities at later periods. Hand and Kelly (2001) give an example of this approach in action.

PHaB (Proportional HAzard Behavioural) Scores

So far we have concentrated on how survival analysis can be used as a way of extending application scorecards, but the approach can also be used with some modifications for behavioural scorecards. If the lending arrangement has been running for a time a already, that is, the loan is of age a, then one wants to estimate how much longer before it will default. Figure 4.5.5 shows the situation and in behavioural scores one uses the information in the payment period, the current credit bureau information, and the application information to estimate such a default. The standard approach is again to ask what is the chance that the loan will default within a fixed time, usually 12 months, from the present. Notice in this formulation, lending arrangements that have been running for 3 months, 3 years, and 30 years are all considered at the same time and the only way they are separated is that there may be a variable indicating if it is a fairly recent loan or not. To apply the proportional hazards approach to behavioural scoring, one separates out these loans and defines a hazard function $h^a(t)$ – which depends on the age, a, of the loan.

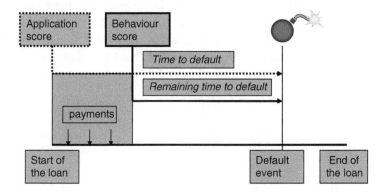

FIG. 4.5.5. Time line for PHaB scores.

Thus for a PHaB score – a proportional hazards behavioural score–one defines the hazard function as follows. Suppose it is a periods since the start of the loan and $\mathbf{y}(\mathbf{a})$ are the behavioural characteristics in period a and the application characteristics are $\mathbf{x}$, then the hazard rate for defaulting in another t periods time, that is $t + a$ since the start of the loan, is given by

$$h^a(t) = e^{\mathbf{w_y}(\mathbf{a})\cdot\mathbf{y}(\mathbf{a})+\mathbf{w_x}(a)\mathbf{x}}h_0^a(t). \qquad (4.5.32)$$

Thus the baseline hazard function will change depending on the age of the loan, and the coefficients of the behavioural and application characteristics can also change with the age of the loan. So, at the next period when the loan is of age $a + 1$, the comparable hazard rate would be that for $t - 1$ more periods to go, that is,

$$h^{a+1}(t - 1) = e^{\mathbf{w_y}(a+1)\cdot\mathbf{Y}(a+1)+\mathbf{w_x}(a+1)\mathbf{x}}h_0^{a+1}(t - 1). \qquad (4.5.33)$$

Thus the coefficients $w(a)$ have to be estimated separately for each period a, using only the data in the data set that has survived up to period a. As it stands these coefficients could change significantly from one period to the next. One way of smoothing out these changes would be to make the behavioural score at the last period, one of the characteristics for the current period. So suppose $\mathbf{x} = (x_1, \ldots, x_p)$ were the application characteristics and $\mathbf{y}(\mathbf{a}) = (y(a)_1, \ldots, y(a)_q)$ were the behavioural characteristics at period a, one defines a series of behavioural scores by $s(0) = -\mathbf{w} \cdot \mathbf{x}$ where $e^{\mathbf{w}\cdot\mathbf{x}}h_0^0(t)$ is the default rate hazard function at time 0. At time 1, the hazard function for the time from now until default is $e^{-(\mathbf{w}_0^1 s(0)+\mathbf{w}(1)\cdot\mathbf{y}(1))}h_0^1(t)$ and define $s(1) = w_0(1)s(0) + \mathbf{w}(1)\mathbf{y}(1)$. Repeating this procedure leads to behaviour scores at age a satisfying $s(a) = w_0(a)s(a - 1) + \mathbf{w}(a) \cdot \mathbf{y}(a)$. Details of this analysis can be found in Stepanova and Thomas (2001).

There are other ways of defining the time dependency in proportional hazards versions of behavioural scores. Thus t might be defined also from the start of the loan and so one can only define hazard functions $h^a(t)$ for $t \geq a$ and Eq. (4.5.32) would describe the form of the proportional hazard model at age a. However, if the loan ages one more month the comparable hazard function for that particular month into the loan would not then be Eq. (4.5.33) but instead would be

$$h^{a+1}(t) = e^{\mathbf{w_y}(a+1)\cdot\mathbf{y}(a+1)+\mathbf{w_x}(a+1)\cdot\mathbf{x}}h_0^{a+1}(t). \qquad (4.5.34)$$

Up to now we have considered the hazard score to be a function of the characteristics of the individual and the loan. However, there is no reason not to include economic variables into this hazard score. This will lead to proportional hazard models where the characteristics are time-dependent, which means one needs to deal with the economic variables in the same way as one deals with behavioural characteristics in the above models.

4.6 Survival analysis-based profit models, including attrition and prepayment

Using survival analysis models for profitability calculations

One of the real advantages of having estimates of when a borrower will default is that one can now get more accurate estimates of the profitability of a loan or a credit card than those obtained in Section 1.7 where one ignored the probability of default.

Consider a fixed repayment loan of L_0 over n time periods where the lending rate charged is r_L and the risk-free rate is r_F. If one ignores defaulting then as in Eq. (1.7.16) the amount a to be repaid each period can be calculated. In the usual case, the interest is charged on the outstanding balance of the loan at each period. The relationship between a and L_0 can be obtained by discounting the value of all repayments back to the start of the loan. Thus for such decreasing loan cases:

$$L_0 - \sum_{i=1}^{N} (1+r_L)^{-i} a = 0 \Rightarrow a = L_0 \frac{r_L}{1 - (1+r_L)^{-N}}. \tag{4.6.1}$$

The NPV, V, and the present discounted worth of the loan, W_P are given, respectively, by the calculation leading to Eq. (1.7.18), namely

$$W_P(N, r_L, r_F) = a \sum_{n=1}^{N} \frac{1}{(1+r_F)^n} = a \left(\frac{1 - (1+r_F)^{-N}}{r_F} \right)$$

$$= L_0 \left(\frac{r_L}{r_F} \frac{1 - (1+r_F)^{-N}}{1 - (1+r_L)^{-N}} \right) > L_0 \qquad r_L > r_F$$

$$NPV = V_P(N, r_L, r_F) = W_P(N, r_L, r_F) - L_0 = L_0 \left(\frac{r_L}{r_F} \frac{1 - (1+r_F)^{-N}}{1 - (1+r_L)^{-N}} - 1 \right). \tag{4.6.2}$$

However, this does not allow for the possibility of the borrower defaulting. One can allow for the impact of possible defaulting by using the estimates of the survival function probability $P_G(k)$ that a default has not occurred by period k.

We need to be slightly careful in that in Section 4.5 we were using $P_G(t)$ to define the distribution of T the time when default occurred. Normally in consumer credit, default is defined as 90 days or 3 months overdue which if one assumes normal repayment followed by no repayment, the last payment occurred at month $T - 3$. The profitability of the loan depends on the time of the last payment and so we need to be able to express the distribution of the time of the last payment in terms of the distribution of when default occurred. One can move from one distribution to the other by defining the survival function for last payment by

$$S_{\text{last payment}}(t) = S_{\text{default}}(t + N_{\text{D}}) = P_{\text{G}}(t + N_{\text{D}}) \tag{4.6.3}$$

if default is defined to be N_{D} periods of non-payment. We will assume that the default time distribution has been obtained using a proportional hazards model so that a borrower with characteristics $\mathbf{x}$ will have a probability of survival function $P_{\text{G}}(t, \mathbf{x})$ and a hazard rate function $h(t, \mathbf{x})$ related to the baseline survival function $S_0(t)$ and baseline hazard rate $h_0(t)$ by

$$P_{\text{G}}(t, \mathbf{x}) = S(t, \mathbf{x}) = S_0(t)^{\mathrm{e}^{-s_{\text{h}}(\mathbf{x})}}$$
$$h(t, \mathbf{x}) = \mathrm{e}^{-s_{\text{h}}(\mathbf{x})} h_0(t) \tag{4.6.4}$$

where $s_{\text{h}}(\mathbf{x})$ is the hazard score for a borrower with characteristics $\mathbf{x}$.

The profitability of the loan depends on the probability distribution of the default times, the balance of the loan outstanding at default (or at last payment), and the loss given default l_{D} which is the fraction of the loan outstanding at default that is not recovered during the subsequent collections process. For ease of notation we will in fact take l_{D} to be the fraction of the loan outstanding at the time of the last payment that is not recovered. If we assume full repayments are made for k time periods and then no subsequent payments are made the balance of the loan after the last payment is given by Eq. (1.7.17) namely

$$L_k = L_0 \frac{1 - (1 + r_{\text{L}})^{-(N-k)}}{1 - (1 + r_{\text{L}})^{-N}} \qquad 1 \le k \le N. \tag{4.6.5}$$

Putting these calculations together gives the NPV allowing for defaulting for the loan to a borrower with hazard score of s_{h} of

$$V_{\text{P}}(s_h(\mathbf{x})) = \sum_{k=1}^{n} \left(\frac{\begin{array}{c} P_{\text{G}}(k + N_{\text{D}}, \mathbf{x})a + P_{\text{G}}(k + N_{\text{D}} - 1, \mathbf{x}) \\ \times h(k + N_{\text{D}}, \mathbf{x})(1 - l_{\text{D}})L_{k-1} \end{array}}{(1 + r_{\text{F}})^k} \right) - L_0$$

$$= \sum_{k=1}^{n} \left(\frac{\begin{array}{c} (S_0(k + N_{\text{D}}))^{\mathrm{e}^{-s_{\text{h}}(\mathbf{x})}} a + (S_0(k + N_{\text{D}} - 1))^{\mathrm{e}^{-s_{\text{h}}(\mathbf{x})}} \\ \times \mathrm{e}^{-s_{\text{h}}(\mathbf{x})} h_0(k + N_{\text{D}})(1 - l_{\text{D}})L_{k-1} \end{array}}{(1 + r_{\text{F}})^k} \right) - L_0$$

$$= \frac{L_0}{(1 - (1 + r_L)^{-N})}$$

$$\sum_{k=1}^{n} \left(\frac{(S_0(k + N_D))e^{-s_h(x)} r_L + (S_0(k + N_D - 1))e^{-s_h(x)}}{\times e^{-s_h(x)} h_0(k + N_D)(1 - l_D)(1 - (1 + r_L)^{-(N-k+1)})}{(1 + r_F)^k} \right) - L_0.$$

$$(4.6.6)$$

Example 4.6.1 Impact of default on NPV of loan

To understand the impact of allowing default estimation to be part of the profitability calculation, take a very simple example to see the difference between the NPV value in Eq. (4.6.2) and Eq. (4.6.6). Assume the bank gives a loan of £100 to be repaid over three time periods where the lending rate is taken as $r_L = 0.10$ while the risk-free interest rate is $r_F = 0.05$. If there is no default considered, then from Eq. (4.6.1) there should be three repayments of

$$a = L_0 \frac{r_L}{1 - (1 + r_L)^{-N}} = 100 \frac{0.1}{1 - (1 + 0.1)^{-3}} = £40.21 \qquad (4.6.7)$$

and the profitability of the loan leads to a NPV of

$$NPV = V_P(3, 0.1, 0.05) = L_0 \left(\frac{r_L}{r_F} \frac{1 - (1 + r_F)^{-N}}{1 - (1 + r_L)^{-N}} - 1 \right)$$

$$= 100 \left(\frac{0.1}{0.05} \frac{1 - (1 + 0.05)^{-3}}{1 - (1 + 0.1)^{-3}} - 1 \right) = £9.51. \qquad (4.6.8)$$

Assume that default corresponds to three periods of non-payment and the baseline default hazard rate is constant of value 0.1, for all $h_0(t), t > 3$. Thus once the first three periods have occurred the baseline default function is the equivalent of an exponential lifetime distribution with mean of 10 periods and a baseline survival function $S_0(1) = S_0(2) = S_0(3) = 1, S_0(4) = 0.9, S_0(5) = 0.81, S_0(6) = 0.729$. For a borrower who has hazard score of $s_h = 0$, the actual probability survival function and the actual default rate coincide with the baseline expression. Assuming that $l_D = 1$, (the worst possible loss), then the profitability of the loan is given by Eq. (4.6.6):

$$
V_P(s_h(\mathbf{x}) = 0)
$$

$$
= \sum_{k=1}^{3} \left(\frac{(S_0(k + N_D))e^{-s_h(\mathbf{x})}a + (S_0(k + N_D - 1))e^{-s_h(\mathbf{x})} \times e^{-s_h(\mathbf{x})}h_0(k + N_D)(1 - l_D)L_{k-1}}{(1 + r_F)^k} \right) - L
$$

$$
= \sum_{k=1}^{3} \left(\frac{(S_0(k + 3))e^0(40.21)}{(1 + 0.05)^k} \right) - 100 = \frac{(0.9)^0}{1.05} 40.21
$$

$$
+ \frac{(0.81)^0}{(1.05)^2} 40.21 + \frac{(0.729)^0}{(1.05)^3} 40.21 - 100 = £10.67. \tag{4.6.9}
$$

So in this case the loan is not expected to be profitable to the lender.

If the loan is given to a borrower with hazard score of $s_h(\mathbf{x}) = 1$, then the expected profitability would be

$$
V_P(s_h(\mathbf{x}) = 1)
$$

$$
= \sum_{k=1}^{3} \left(\frac{(S_0(k + N_D))e^{-s_h(\mathbf{x})}a + (S_0(k + N_D - 1))e^{-s_h(\mathbf{x})} \times e^{-s_h(\mathbf{x})}h_0(k + N_D)(1 - l_D)L_{k-1}}{(1 + r_F)^k} \right) - L_0
$$

$$
= \sum_{k=1}^{3} \left(\frac{(S_0(k + 3))e^{-1}(40.21)}{(1 + 0.05)^k} \right) - 100 = \frac{(0.9)^{e^{-1}}}{1.05} 40.21
$$

$$
+ \frac{(0.81)^{e^{-1}}}{(1.05)^2} 40.21 + \frac{(0.729)^{e^{-1}}}{(1.05)^3} 40.21 - 100 = £1.51. \tag{4.6.10}
$$

So for these less risky borrowers the loan is just profitable to the lender.

One use of these calculations is to determine the most profitable term of a loan to offer a borrower. Now that one has included the possibility of default then the profitability of a loan of a given term will vary according to the hazard score of the customer and this variation will differ from term to term. One could envisage that for riskier borrowers, giving them loans with shorter terms will mean they have less time in which to default. Figure 4.6.1 is the profit functions obtained from personal

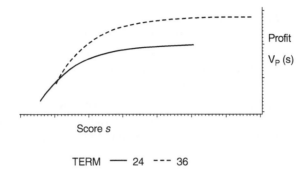

FIG. 4.6.1. Profitability of loans of different duration as hazard score varies.

loan data when applied to loans of 24- and 36-month terms. It shows that as one would expect most of the time the loan with a repayment period of 36 months is more profitable than the 24-month term loan but for those with low scores (the most likely to default) the profits are reversed. Thus the lender may wish to give shorter loans to those with lower hazard scores. This analysis does not consider any affordability issues though.

With revolving credit products, like credit cards, consider the situation where the average profit per period, g, and the likely exposure at default, l, of a customer stays constant over time. In that case if again one has a non-default survival probability distribution $P_G(k)$ with hazard function $h(k)$ given by a proportional hazards model, the expected future profitability $V_P(k, s_h)$ of the customer if their hazard score is s_h and they have had the product for k periods already is given by

$$
\begin{aligned}
V_P(k, s_h) &= \frac{S(k+1)}{S(k)}\left(g + \frac{V_P(k+1, s_h)}{1+r_F}\right) + \left(1 - \frac{S(k+1)}{S(k)}\right)(1 - l_D)l \\
&= \left(\frac{S_0(k+1)}{S_0(k)}\right)^{e^{s_h}}\left(g + \frac{V_P(k+1, s_h)}{1+r_F}\right) \\
&\quad + \left(1 - \left(\frac{S_0(k+1)}{S_0(k)}\right)^{e^s}\right)(1 - l_D)l.
\end{aligned}
\tag{4.6.11}
$$

From this recursion one can calculate the total future discounted profitability of the customer. Note that has a strong connection with the MDP models looked at earlier.

Competing risks

So far we have assumed that the only thing that can go wrong with the loan is that the borrower will default. However, the profit can be affected if the borrower pays the loan off early (prepayment) or moves to another lender (attrition). The former is more usual in mortgages and auto finance where traditionally it came about because the borrower moved house or purchased another car. In the early 2000s, competition in the mortgage market has meant borrowers move to another lender who has a more attractive offer when the initial discounts on their present mortgage finish. How mortgage lenders have managed to promote a situation where there are penalties rather than discounts for loyalty defies rational explanation but they have in the UK at least. In the US borrowers tend to switch to a new fixed interest rate mortgage, when the interest rates are particularly attractive. The plethora of competing attractive alternatives until the credit crunch of 2008 is also the reason for attrition in the credit card market and there are some borrowers, known colloquially as 'rate tarts' who will change credit cards every 6 months so as to keep the interest they pay as low as possible.

Survival analysis has been used to dealing with this idea of there being several types of events that can occur but one will only see the first that happens. In the medical area it corresponds to there being several different ailments that can cause death in an individual and one is trying to estimate the time to occurrence for each one separately even though only one with ever actually occur. This problem goes under the name of competing risks. The assumption is that the person or item can fail and there are K different causes of failure labelled $i = 1, 2, \ldots, K$. T_i is the net lifetime of the unit due to cause i. The net lifetime of the unit due to cause i is the lifetime of the unit if only that cause of failure is possible. The actual lifetime of the unit is then T where

$$T = \min\{T_1, T_2, \ldots, T_K\}.$$

However, what one can measure is the crude lifetimes, Y_i, that is, that there is a failure at time t due to risk i. One can connect the two sets of variables by the equation:

$$\Pr\{Y_j \geq t\} = \Pr\{T_j \geq t, T_j < T_i \text{ for all } i \neq j\}. \qquad (4.6.12)$$

As it stands one cannot estimate the T_i from the Y_i. However if one assumes the risks are independent, then one can rewrite this connection as

$$\Pr\{Y_j \geq t\} = \Pr\{T_j \geq t, T_j < T_i \text{ for all } i \neq j\} = \Pr\{T_j \geq t\} \prod_{i:i \neq j} \Pr\{t < T_i\}$$

$$(4.6.13)$$

and hence get the distribution of risk j by assuming that if the unit fails for some other reason it is just censored as far as risk j is concerned. One can never disprove this independent risk assumption no matter what data one is given, and so there is no loss of mathematical generality in assuming it is true. One can then derive proportional hazard models for each of the risks separately and use Kaplan–Meier estimates to get the survival function and hazard rate for each risk.

One might want to use competing risks in the credit scoring context if one is trying to identify why someone defaults on a loan as well as when is the default. Is default due to fraud, financial naivety, breakdown of family relationships, or loss of employment? The time to default under the different causes is likely to have quite different lifetime distributions. However, a much more relevant application is to estimate prepayment (fixed term loans) and attrition (revolving credit) as a competing risk to default. In that case one takes as the event to measure the early repayment of the loan or the credit card customer moving to another lender. One can construct proportional hazard models and accelerated life models of when these events occur in exactly the same way as for the defaulting events. This means one must start the coarse classifying exercise again and it is very common for the optimal splits for the early repayment to be quite different to those for default. We will define the survival function for the early repayment event as $P_e(k)$, the hazard rate to be $h_e(k)$ and the score if we use a proportional hazard model for early repayment to be s_e. The corresponding values for the baseline hazards of the early repayments are $S_{e,0}(k), h_{e,0}(k)$.

The expected profitability of the loans under default and possible early repayment follows from Eq. (4.6.6) by recognizing that the existing pay-off at period k will only occur if there has been no early repayment at the end of period k, that is with probability $S_{e,0}(k)$. If there is early repayment in period k, which will happen with probability $S_{e,0}(k-1)h_{e,0}(k)$, this payment will consist of the normal payment plus the balance of the loan remaining at the end of period k, that is $a+L_k$. Thus the expected profitability of the loan is given by Eq. (4.6.14),

$$V_P(s_h(\mathbf{x}), s_e(\mathbf{x}))$$

$$= \sum_{k=1}^{n} \left(\frac{\begin{array}{c} S_e(k, \mathbf{x})\,(P_G(k+N_D, \mathbf{x})a + P_G(k+N_D - 1, \mathbf{x}) \\ \times h(k+N_D, \mathbf{x})(1 - l_D)L_{k-1}) + S_e(k-1, \mathbf{x})h_e(k, \mathbf{x})(L_k + a) \end{array}}{(1 + r_F)^k} \right) - L_0$$

$$= \sum_{k=1}^{n} \left(\frac{\begin{array}{c} S_{e,0}(k)^{e^{-s_e(\mathbf{x})}} \left((S_0(k+N_D))^{e^{-s_h(\mathbf{x})}} a + (S_0(k+N_D - 1))^{e^{-s_h(\mathbf{x})}} \right. \\ \left. \times e^{-s_h(\mathbf{x})} h_0(k+N_D)(1 - l_D)L_{k-1} \right) \\ + S_{e,0}(k-1)^{e^{-s_e(\mathbf{x})}} e^{-s_e(\mathbf{x})} h_{e,0}(k)(L_k + a) \end{array}}{(1 + r_F)^k} \right) - L_0$$

$$= -L_0 + \frac{L_0}{\left(1 - (1 + r_L)^{-N}\right)}$$

$$\times \sum_{k=1}^{n} \left(\frac{\begin{array}{l} S_{e,0}(k)e^{-s_e(x)}\left((S_0(k + N_D))e^{-s_h(x)}r_L + (S_0(k + N_D - 1))e^{-s_h(x)}\right. \\ \times e^{-s_h(x)}h_0(k + N_D)(1 - l_D)\left(1 - (1 + r_L)^{-(N-k+1)}\right)\big) \\ + S_{e,0}(k - 1)e^{-s_e(x)}e^{-s_e(x)}h_{e,0}(k)(r_L + \left(1 - (1 + r_L)^{-(N-k)}\right)) \end{array}}{(1 + r_F)^k} \right)$$

(4.6.14)

When building models of early repayment, it is not obvious that the important time is how long the loan has been in place. Stepanova and Thomas (2001) for example found that when they built a model for early repayment using loans of different term the results were disappointing.

As Fig. 4.6.2 shows, the hazard rates for early repayment using the length of time the loan had been running was quite different for loans of different terms, and the resulting proportional hazards model gave poor discrimination. However, when the survival function was built using time until the loan was to have terminated (that is with time running backwards), the results were much more encouraging as the plots of the hazard rates for the loans of different terms in Fig. 4.6.3 show. Not surprisingly the corresponding proportional hazards model proved to be much more discriminating.

In the case of revolving credit, which involves credit and store cards, there is no such thing as early repayment, but there is still the chance of attrition where the

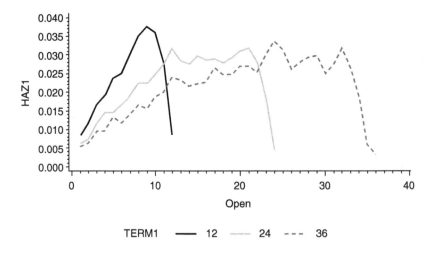

FIG. 4.6.2. Early repayment hazard rate for loans of different length.

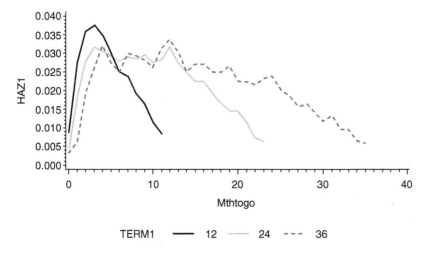

FIG. 4.6.3. Early repayment hazard rate versus time to loan maturity.

customer moves to another lender with a corresponding loss in profit. Using the same notation – survival function $P_e(k)$, the hazard rate $h_e(k)$, and score s_e – as for the early repayment case, the future profitability of a customer who has had the revolving product for k periods and whose hazard default score is s_h and hazard attrition score is s_e can be obtained by modifying the recursion in (4.6.11). Thus the expected future profit of such a customer is $V_P(k, s_h, s_e)$ where

$$
V_P(k, s_h(\mathbf{x}), s_e(\mathbf{x})) = \left(\frac{P_e(k+1, \mathbf{x})}{P_e(k, \mathbf{x})} \right) \left(\frac{P_G(k+1, \mathbf{x})}{P_G(k, \mathbf{x})} \right) \left(g_k + \frac{V_P(k+1, s_h(\mathbf{x}), s_e(\mathbf{x}))}{1 + r_F} \right)
$$
$$
+ \left(1 - \frac{P_G(k+1)}{P_G(k)} \right) (1 - l_D) l_k \Big)
$$
$$
= \left(\frac{S_{e,0}(k+1)}{S_{e,0}(k)} \right)^{e^{-s_e(\mathbf{x})}} \left(\left(\frac{S_0(k+1)}{S_0(k)} \right)^{e^{-s_h(\mathbf{x})}} \left(g_k + \frac{V_P(k+1, s_h(\mathbf{x}), s_e(\mathbf{x}))}{1 + r_F} \right) \right.
$$
$$
+ \left(1 - \left(\frac{S_0(k+1)}{S_0(k)} \right)^{e^{-s_h(\mathbf{x})}} \right) (1 - l_D) l_k \Big) . \tag{4.6.15}
$$

The probability of no attrition in a period can be thought of as a discount factor applied to the future rewards. An obvious extension to the model is to let the profits each period, g_k, and the balance if a default occurs, l_k, depend on the age k of the account. In an era with offers which are very attractive to the borrower in the initial period and so $g_k < 0$ for $k = 1, 2, \ldots, 6$, say, this is certainly the case as far as the profits are concerned and it is in these cases that the attrition score becomes so important.

5

Portfolio credit risk and the Basel Accord

5.1   Portfolio credit risk

Portfolio level measures

The previous chapters of this book have concentrated on the profitability and default risk of individual accounts. This is because the decisions a lender makes on accepting or rejecting an applicant, or adjusting the credit limit or interest rate of a current borrower, are made at the account level. However, the business measures that lenders use to assess their success look at the impact at the portfolio level of these decisions. Banks are interested in what is the total profitability of their portfolio and what is the credit risk of their portfolio. The question is how these are related to the profitability and credit risk of each account separately. For example, if one lends £1000 to accounts whose default probability is 5%, the expected loss will be £50. If one has lent £1 to 1000 separate accounts, it is likely by the central limit theorem that the actual loss will not be that different from £50. However if one lends all £1000 to the same account, then the losses will either be £0 or close to £1000. Thus the distribution of the losses is quite different in the two cases even though both have the same mean. Thus, it is necessary to consider how models developed at account level can deal with the portfolio level questions.

There are two current pressures that are forcing this requirement for portfolio level modelling – the growth in securitization of retail loan portfolios and the new rules, based on internal rating models, governing the regulatory capital that banks will need to keep to cover their lending risks. These rules are in the new Basel Capital Accord, which was introduced in 2007 to regulate banks' lending. The internal-rating based (IRB) models allowed in these regulations let the banks develop their own models of the probability of default (PD) and the loss given default (LGD) of lending to consumers. Regulators then use the resulting estimates in a corporate credit risk-type model to assign how much regulatory capital a bank must hold to cover unexpected credit losses in the bank's loan portfolio, in its corporate, sovereign, and consumer lending. As mentioned in Chapter 2, the Basel Accord has highlighted the need to develop accurate estimates of default probabilities of individual accounts. It also means lenders need to be able to segment their loan portfolio in such a way that the estimates of the default rates for each segment can be validated. The Basel Accord has also pointed out that analysts and researchers had not developed adequate models of the credit risk of portfolios of consumer loans and so the regulators have had to impose a corporate credit risk model with arbitrarily chosen correlation parameters. Consumer credit modellers need to decide whether such models are appropriate for portfolios of consumer loans and, if not, will need to develop appropriate models over time.

The other pressure to improve the models for understanding credit risk of portfolios of consumer loans comes from the increase in volume of securitization of such loans. In securitization, the loans outstanding at a given date are bundled together by the lender and sold to a third party often called a special purpose vehicle (SPV). The SPV then issues tranched bonds in the public marketplace, where the repayment of the coupons and the principal of these bonds are covered by the cash flow from the repayments of the loans. The bonds are sold in tranches with the highest priority tranche having first call on being repaid, while those in the lowest tranche are most at risk of not being able to be repaid. The bond holders then 'own' the debt outstanding and the interest stream on it but also the risk of default (or early repayment) from this portfolio of borrowings. The price that one should pay for a bundled portfolio and hence the charge for the tranched bonds issued depends on the credit risk involved. So there are two decisions to make in this process. Firstly, which borrowings to bundle together in the portfolio for securitization, and secondly, how to decide on the tranches and the price of each tranche. The first is a decision by the lender but the second involves the credit rating agencies since their rating of the credit risk of each tranche is the main indicator of the price to be charged. Although the credit score distribution of the loans is considered when the securitized portfolio is constructed and when the tranches are chosen there does not seem to be any agreed models of how to make either decision. Currently both decisions tend to be made by subjective judgement using historical precedence and current market conditions. The way the US sub-prime mortgage crisis of 2007 developed into a 'credit crunch' is partly due to there not be accurate modelling of what were the credit risks and hence the price for the sub-prime mortgage backed securities that had been sold into the market. Models that link account level credit risk with portfolio level credit risks would clearly be of use in supporting these pricing decisions.

Probability of default at portfolio level

Suppose there are N borrower accounts in the bank's loan portfolio or portfolio segment. Let D_i be the indicator variable of default for account i so $D_i = 1$ if that account defaults and $D_i = 0$ if there is no default, with $\Pr\{D_i = 0\} = p_i$ is the probability the borrower is good.

Each D_i is a Bernoulli random variable with parameter $1 - p_i$. Let D_{port} be the random variable describing the PD in the portfolio, which is the proportion of the account population in the portfolio who will default. Then,

$$D_{\text{port}} = \frac{D_1 + D_2 + \cdots + D_N}{N}$$

and so

$$E[D_{\text{port}}] = \left(\sum_{i=1}^{N} E(D_i)\right) \bigg/ N = \sum_{i=1}^{N} (1 - p_i)/N = 1 - \sum_{i=1}^{N} p_i/N ; \quad (5.1.1)$$

that is, the mean of the portfolio default probability is the average of the individual default probabilities.

If there is a log odds score, s, defined on the portfolio, so account i has score s_i, then from Section 1.5 we have

$$p_i = \frac{1}{1 + e^{-s_i}}; \quad 1 - p_i = \frac{1}{1 + e^{s_i}}. \quad (5.1.2)$$

If the distribution of scores in the portfolio is given by a density function $f(s)$, then the expected portfolio default rate would be

$$E\{D_{\text{port}}\} = \int \frac{f(s)}{1 + e^s} ds \quad (5.1.3)$$

or its discrete equivalent.

All these results hold irrespective of what is the dependence or the correlations between the defaults of the different borrows in the portfolio, but in order to describe the distribution D_{port} further, one has to make some assumptions about this dependence.

The simplest assumption is that the defaults of the different borrowers, D_i, are independent of one another. In that case for a reasonably sized portfolio, D_{port} is the sum of a large number of independent variables and so the central limit theorem would imply the distribution is close to being normal, though of course D_{port} can only take values between 0 and 1. In this case,

$$\text{Var}[D_{\text{port}}] = \text{Var}\left(\sum_{i=1}^{N} D_i/N\right) = \sum_{i=1}^{N} \text{Var}(D_i/N) = \sum_{i=1}^{N} \text{Var}(D_i)/N^2$$

$$= \left(\sum_{i=1}^{N} p_i(1 - p_i)\right) \bigg/ N^2 \quad (5.1.4)$$

where the second equality depends on the independence of the D_i.

This result only holds because of the independent assumptions. If that does not hold, then one needs lots more information to connect account and portfolio level default estimates. For example, assume the PD of account i and j are not independent and their covariance is $\text{Cov}(D_i, D_j) = \sigma_{ij}$, then the mean and variance of the portfolio default probability which were given in (5.1.1) and (5.1.4) become:

$$E[D_{\text{port}}] = \left(\sum_{i=1}^{N} E(D_i) \right) \bigg/ N = \sum_{i=1}^{N} (1 - p_i)/N = 1 - \sum_{i=1}^{N} p_i/N \text{ but}$$

$$\text{Var}[D_{\text{port}}] = \text{Var}\left(\sum_{i=1}^{N} D_i/N \right) = \frac{\sum_{i=1}^{N} (\text{Var}(D_i)) + 2 \sum_{i,j:i>j} \text{Cov}(D_i, D_j)^2}{N^2}$$

$$= \frac{1}{N^2} \left(\sum_{i=1}^{N} p_i(1 - p_i) \right) + 2 \sum_{i,j:i>j} \sigma_{ij}^2. \qquad (5.1.5)$$

If log odds scores are used as forecasts of the PD of individual borrowers, there is an inherent correlation assumed in the corresponding default variables. Recall from Section 1.5 that the log odds score for a borrower with characteristics $\mathbf{x}$ can be written as

$$s(\mathbf{x}) = \ln o(G|\mathbf{x}) = \ln \left(\frac{p_G f(\mathbf{x}|G)}{p_B f(\mathbf{x}|B)} \right) = \ln \left(\frac{p_G}{p_B} \right) + \ln \left(\frac{f(\mathbf{x}|G)}{f(\mathbf{x}|B)} \right)$$

$$= \ln o_{\text{Pop}} + \ln I(\mathbf{x}) = s_{\text{Pop}} + s_{\text{Inf}}(\mathbf{x}). \qquad (5.1.6)$$

The $s_{\text{Inf}}(\mathbf{x})$ part of the score depends only on the information about that individual borrower, but the s_{Pop} part is common to all the individuals. If over time the population odds change, then theoretically this should be reflected by a change from s_{Pop} to s'_{Pop} (that is adding a constant to every borrower's score). The assumption is that this change should not affect the $s_{\text{Inf}}(\mathbf{x})$ part of the score. So using a score implies that default for individual borrowers is considered to be a one factor model and conditional on the value of this factor – the current population odds – borrowers' default probabilities should be independent of one another.

Example 5.1.1 Calculation of correlations implicit in population odds

Take a very simple example where there are two borrowers in the portfolio and we are unsure about what the population odds next year might be. So assume that

$$s_{\text{Inf}}(\mathbf{x}_1) = 1, s_{\text{Inf}}(\mathbf{x}_2) = 2; \quad s_{\text{Pop}} = 0 \text{ or } 5, \text{ each with probability } 0.5.$$

Then using the relationship between probability of defaulting and score given in Eq. (5.1.2), we get

$$E[D_1] = 0.5 \left(\frac{1}{1 + e^{0+1}} \right) + 0.5 \left(\frac{1}{1 + e^{5+1}} \right) = 0.136$$

$$E[D_2] = 0.5 \left(\frac{1}{1 + e^{0+2}} \right) + 0.5 \left(\frac{1}{1 + e^{5+2}} \right) = 0.060$$

$$E[D_1 D_2] = 0.5 \left(\frac{1}{1 + e^{0+1}} \right) \left(\frac{1}{1 + e^{0+2}} \right)$$

$$+ 0.5 \left(\frac{1}{1 + e^{5+1}} \right) \left(\frac{1}{1 + e^{5+2}} \right) = 0.016$$

$$E[D_1 D_2] = 0.016 \neq E[D_1]E[D_2] = 0.008.$$

(5.1.7)

So there is a positive correlation between the individual default variables D_1, D_2.

The population odds can depend on economic factors such as unemployment, interest rates, consumer confidence, and gross domestic production (GDP), and so this is one way of introducing economic variables into the credit risk of a portfolio of consumer loans.

Thus the main problem in going from account level models which are so useful in aiding the day to day decision making in consumer credit to portfolio level models which are useful at the strategic level for assessing and understanding the overall risks that the lender faces is to understand what is the dependence between the credit risks of different accounts. When are these dependencies important, when can they be ignored, and what is the underlying cause of the dependences between the default risks of different accounts?

Considering the last of these issues – what connects the defaulting of different accounts – one needs to consider why accounts default. Each account default has its own special circumstances but one could crudely classify them into four reasons:

1. Fraud, where the intention of the borrower is to default on the loan

2. Financial naivety, where the borrower does not understand the actual or potential financial implications of the repayment regime required to service the loan or revolving account

3. Loss of job, where the loss of part or all of the expected income stream means the loan repayments cannot be serviced

4. Marital breakdown (or the 'modern day' equivalent), where the loss of a second income stream and the extra costs involved in running two households mean the ability to repay the loan is squeezed.

If fraud or financial naivety are the causes of correlations in default probability, then this suggests that either the marketing of the product or the initial fraud checks with credit bureaus and the like are deficient. So in some senses these could be considered operational risks rather than credit risks. Financial naivety is often caused by a coalition of optimism between the borrower and the lender. For example, the sub-prime mortgage crisis in 2007 was partially caused because both lenders and borrowers believed that house prices would keep increasing and thus borrowers could keep remortgaging to translate this extra equity into cash with which to fund the mortgages repayments. The drop in house prices exposed this naïve financial thinking.

It is clear why loss of job might be the cause of correlations in default risk. Employment rates are very dependent on the state of the economy and hence a downturn in the economy can lead to an increase in unemployment and hence to increases in the default rates on consumer credit products. The connections could be more sophisticated than just through the national unemployment rate. It might involve rises in unemployment in certain geographical regions or in certain types of occupations. On the surface, marital breakdown seems not to be something that could underpin dependencies between the defaulting of different accounts. However, it is true that economic stress does impact on marriage break-up and so again could give rise to default dependencies for this reason.

The reasons for an account defaulting are rarely recorded and so it is difficult to substantiate these suggestions. However, it is likely that defaulting because of fraud happens very early in the loan period. How long financial naivety will take to impact on the default status of a loan can depend on the type of borrowing involve. With unemployment and marital breakdown as the cause of defaulting, there seems little reason for the time of default to have much bearing on the time since the loan began. One might therefore be able to use the competing risks approach of survival analysis to identify the reasons for default by modelling when into the loan such defaults occurred.

Loss given default and portfolio level losses

If we look at the losses from the portfolio, one has further added uncertainties. Assume that each account borrows one unit and if the borrower defaults, the default would be for that amount. To calculate the losses, consider the fraction of the amount lost if there is a default. This is needed because some of the defaulted amount may be recovered subsequently. We define $l_{D,i}$ to be the fraction of the amount lost if borrower i defaults. This is called the loss given default (LGD) for account i. This LGD for borrower i is not known until several years after default has occurred when the collection process is completed. Before then we assume it is given by a random variable L_i. The total loss on the portfolio L_{port} is given by

$$L_{port} = \sum_{i=1}^{N} L_i D_i. \tag{5.1.8}$$

The distribution function of L_i, LGD, has not been studied much up to now. Even in the corporate credit risk case which has been more widely researched than in the consumer case, it is only in the last decade that one has some empirical evidence on the mean of the variable (Altman et al. 2005a). In consumer credit it is accepted that different credit products have different LGD means with residential mortgages having a distribution highly skewed towards zero and with a high probability mass value at 0. This is because if borrowers default on a mortgage, the property is repossessed and can usually be sold for a price that covers the cost of the original loan. Likewise secured loans like auto finance are likely to have lower LGD values than unsecured lending like personal loans and credit cards because if one can repossess the car this will aid recovery of part of the loan. Overdrafts tend to have the lowest recovery fraction.

If one can assume independence not just between the different L_i variables but also between the LGD and the PD for the same individual (L_i and D_i), then one can get an expression for the expected loss of the portfolio in terms of the account level variables. Suppose in fact the LGD distribution is the same for all borrowers $L_i = L$, then

$$E[L_{port}] = E\left(\sum_{i=1}^{N} L_i D_i\right) = \sum_{i=1}^{N} E(L_i D_i) = \sum_{i=1}^{N} E(L_i)E(D_i)$$

$$= E(L)\sum_{i=1}^{N} E(D_i) = NE(L)E(D_{port}) = E(L)\left(\sum_{i=1}^{N}(1 - p_i)\right) \quad (5.1.9)$$

where the third equality follows from the independence of L_i and D_i.

However, this assumption about independence between L_i and D_i is again something that is not borne out when looking at historical data. As was mentioned earlier little work has been done on modelling LGD for consumer lending, but it is clear from UK mortgage data that in the last major recession around 1990, both default rates and LGD increased substantially. In corporate lending there is much more evidence. Figure 5.1.1 shows how the recovery rate $(1-LGD)$ varies over time for the United States corporate loans during the period 1982 to 2003. In the recession periods around 1990 and 2000, the recovery rate dropped substantially and so the LGD must have increased commensurately. At the same time, the default rates increased substantially so there is no doubt of the dependence between L_i and D_i. It is changes in the economy that caused this correlation between PD and LGD both in the corporate but also in consumer lending portfolios.

One can relax the assumption that all the loans in the portfolio are of the same amount. For portfolio losses, what is important is how much is still owed at default, which is called the exposure at default (EAD). For loan i denote this amount by the variable E_i. With this addition the total loss in the portfolio changes from Eq. (5.1.8) to

$$L_{port} = \sum_{i=1}^{N} E_i L_i D_i \quad (5.1.10)$$

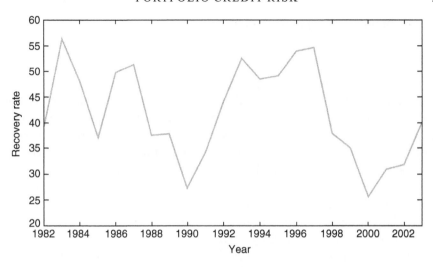

FIG. 5.1.1. Impact of economy on recovery rates (1−LGD): Moody's KMV
1982–2003 data set.

and hence if there is independence between E_i, L_j, D_k for any i, j, k. Equation (5.1.9)
becomes:

$$E[L_{\text{port}}] = E\left(\sum_{i=1}^{N} E_i L_i D_i\right) = \sum_{i=1}^{N} E(E_i L_i D_i)$$

$$= \sum_{i=1}^{N} E(E_i)(E(L_i)E(D_i)) = E(L)\sum_{i=1}^{N} E(E_i)E(D_i)) \qquad (5.1.11)$$

$$= E(L)\left(\sum_{i=1}^{N} E(E)_i\right)(1 - p_i)$$

In the rest of this chapter we concentrate on why credit scoring was essential
for the introduction of the Basel regulations but also how the introduction of these
regulations has required both modelling and technical developments in credit scoring. The Basel Accord has forced the development of modelling risk for consumer
lending at the portfolio level since the regulatory capital required by the regulations depends on such models. However, it also highlighted the need to develop
more appropriate models for the credit risk of portfolios of consumer loans than the
corporate-based models which underpin the Basel Accord. Before concentrating
on the Basel Accord, it is worth differentiating between regulatory and economic
capital since these terms are sometimes used interchangeably by banks.

5.2   Economic and regulatory capital

Assets and liabilities

Part of a bank's business is repackaging loans. A bank receives money from its customers through their savings and their current accounts and from money markets by issuing financial instruments like bonds, which allow it to borrow from other lenders. It then repackages this money and lends it to its borrowers. If they are consumers they may require mortgages or credit card loans; if they are companies they may require bank loans and overdrafts. Of course not all the bank's money has been 'borrowed', since some comes from retained earnings and some from equity which the bank's shareholders have provided by buying its shares. Equity is essentially a long-term loan in that the bank has to produce dividends for the shareholders, which is like paying interest on a loan.

Thus a bank like any other business has to balance its assets – the cash it has on hand and the lending it has made at both low and high risk – against its liabilities – the money it has borrowed both short and long term and the equity in the firm. As Fig. 5.2.1 suggests these should balance out.

In order for this to happen then the lending by the bank needs to be at a higher rate than the borrowing so that the lending is profitable. To ensure higher rates though the banks need to decide what loan portfolios to create. It also needs to worry about the term of the lending and the borrowing. Ideally it would like to borrow money over a long term and lend it on short-term loans – the 'borrow long, lend short' dictum – so there is no problem about having to refinance the lending it has made while the loans are still active. Unfortunately it is very hard to do this as depositors with a bank can take back their money on very short notice usually. Thus the bank should be concerned with the liquidity of its assets. Could these be realized quickly enough to pay back its liabilities if it had to do so. This was the

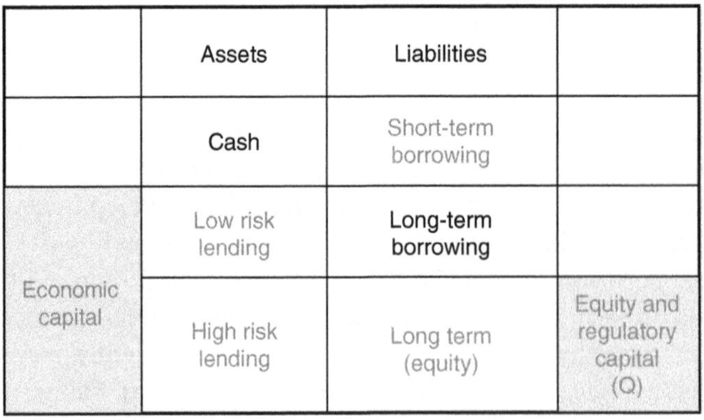

	Assets	Liabilities	
	Cash	Short-term borrowing	
Economic capital	Low risk lending	Long-term borrowing	
	High risk lending	Long term (equity)	Equity and regulatory capital (Q)

FIG. 5.2.1. Assets versus liabilities in a bank.

problem that occurred with Northern Rock, a major mortgage lender in the UK in 2007. It borrowed so much of its money by short-term securitization of its assets that when the 'credit crunch' meant other banks were not interested in repurchasing these short-term securities, the depositors also took out their money from the bank and the UK government had to step in. However, the real problem is to ensure the risk and return of the lending made by the banks means it is profitable.

Risk in lending

So far in this book, the decision criteria has always been expected profit or expected return. It was only in the last section when we started to discuss portfolio level business measures that we recognized that the profit or return is not deterministic but can vary and so looked at both the mean and the variance of the portfolio losses. The point is that even if the expected return from a loan portfolio is highly positive, it could turn out that the actual return in the next few years is so negative that the bank does not have enough capital to cover the losses and so collapses. Thus banks need to find a way of including the riskiness of the loans they are making into both their decision making and their contingency planning.

One approach used by banks to include risk and return in determining what portfolio of assets to construct is the mean–variance approach suggested by Markowitz (1952) as the foundation of modern portfolio theory. For each portfolio, if X is the random return on a portfolio, then one looks at $(E[X], -\text{Var}[X])$ and seeks to find the portfolios that are Pareto optimal. These are the ones where there is no other portfolio that is greater than this one in both dimensions or greater than it in one dimension and the same in the other. Variance though is a measure of the spread of the returns which is not quite the same as the riskiness of the returns. For example, returns much higher than the mean value would be welcomed by the bank but would increase the variance. Other measures like semi-variance have been considered and finding a suitable way of determining risk in this context remains an active research area.

A second popular way of addressing risk, when building decision models in finance is to add a risk premium to the normal risk-free rate when considering the net worth or net present value of an investment. Suppose the cash flow from an investment is expected to be $(c_1, c_2, \ldots, c_n)$ over the n periods of the investment. If the risk-free interest rate is r_F per period, then the decision maker will instead discount the cash by a rate $r = r_F + r_P > r_F$. This means the net worth of the investment is

$$\sum_{i=1}^{n} \frac{c_i}{(1+r)^i} = \sum_{i=1}^{n} \left(\frac{1+r_F}{1+r}\right)^i \frac{c_i}{(1+r_F)^i} = \sum_{i=1}^{n} (1-h)^i \frac{c_i}{(1+r_F)^i} \qquad (5.2.1)$$

where $h = (r - r_F)/(1 + r)$. This has similarities to Eq. (4.6.6) which looked at the net present value if there were defaults given by a hazard function. So one can reinterpret Eq. (5.2.1) by saying it is as if there is a constant default hazard rate of $h = (r - r_F)/(1 + r)$.

However, these approaches only help in the initial decision making. Once the portfolio exists how does the bank protect against the risk that the losses on the portfolio of assets are so catastrophic that the bank will become insolvent. This is where economic and regulatory capital enter.

Regulatory and economic capital

Regulatory capital is the minimum amount of capital that the bank regulator of a country (the Federal Reserve in the United States, the Financial Services Authority in the United Kingdom, and the Bundesbank in Germany) says is required to cover the possible losses on loans so that the depositors in the bank can get their deposits back. The capital to be set aside can consist of the bank's equity (Tier 1) and some types of very long-term borrowing (Tier 2) since in the case of a crisis the equity holders should be the last people paid off. So in Fig. 5.2.1, we show the regulatory capital alongside the equity of the firm as that is what that equity needs to be used for. The way of determining the appropriate amount of regulatory capital has since 1988 been agreed internationally by a committee of the Bank of International Settlement under two Basel Accords. The rest of this chapter will go into much more details about these Accords.

Economic capital on the other hand is determined by the firm itself. It is the capital which the firm thinks it needs to cover the risks it is running and still keep on as a going concern. Thus, in Fig. 5.2.1, we set it against the risky lending of the bank because it has to cover the problems that arise there. For a given portfolio this has come to mean how much capital is needed to cover the possible losses from that portfolio in a given future time period with a pre-specified probability. This is often called the value at risk (VaR), a concept which has come across from market risk where the concerns are that changes in the share prices of an equity portfolio may lead to substantial losses. Typically the probabilities considered are 99%, 95%, or sometime 99.9%. Note that there is no requirement on the bank to actually set this capital aside, but most prudent banks do use these calculations to determine how much risk capital to set aside. In fact one of the problems when the new regulatory capital rules were introduced in 2007 was that many banks felt they had more sophisticated models for determining the risk capital they actually set aside than those that underpinned the regulatory capital.

Economic capital can also be used when comparing loan portfolios as a way of measuring the risk of the portfolio, just as variance was used initially in modern portfolio theory. This is also a continuing area of research especially because it has been recognized that VaR is not coherent. This means one can combine two portfolios and the resultant VaR is greater than the sum of the VaRs in the two original portfolios, whereas one would expect diversification to reduce risk. Thus other concepts such as conditional VaR (CVaR), where one is concerned with the expected value of the losses in the worst $p\%$ of the future scenarios are considered as ways of assessing the risk involved.

5.3   Summary of Basel Capital Accords

History

The Bank of International Settlements was established in 1930 in Basel to oversee war reparation payments but quickly became the forum for cooperation between the Central Banks on monetary and financial stability. In 1974 after the failure of several large international banking organizations, it set up the Basel Committee on Banking Supervision to formulate supervisory standards and guidelines. The committee cannot enforce these but expects its members (the central banks of Belgium, France, Germany, Netherlands, United States, United Kingdom, Canada, Italy, Spain, Sweden, and Japan, plus Luxembourg and Switzerland) to implement the principles in whichever way is most appropriate for them. So successful has this approach been that when the Committee published a set of Minimum Standards for supervision in 1992, the central banks of almost all the countries in the world endorsed the guidelines suggested by the Committee.

Basel 1

The topic which has been highest on the Committee's agenda in the last three decades has been the capital adequacy of banks. In the early 1980s it was recognized that the capital ratios of the main international banks were deteriorating just at the time that the risks of lending, particularly to heavily indebted countries, were rising. The first formal attempt at dealing with this problem was the 1988 Basel Accord (henceforth Basel 1), which set out a regulatory framework for the required or regulatory capital needed on commercial bank lending. With hindsight this a very broad brush approach in that the regulatory capital that banks had to set aside to cover all the risks in their lending was a uniform 8% of the loan face value. There were one or two exceptions; the largest in the consumer lending area was that for residential mortgages only 4% had to be set aside. The money set aside had to be at least 50% of core (Tier 1) capital, which is essentially equity shares and retained earnings, while the rest had to be Tier 2 supplementary capital which included perpetual preferred stock, undisclosed reserves, and subordinate debt. One should not underestimate the importance of Basel 1 in that it was the first time regulators had required banks to set aside capital to deal with unexpected risks. When the Accord was introduced the 8% charge was thought to be 'about right on average' for a typical bank portfolio. However, the failure to distinguish among commercial loans of different degrees of risk created the incentive to move the less risky loans off the balance sheet and retain only the riskier lending. This 'regulatory arbitrage' undermined the effectiveness of the Capital Accord and so a new Basel Accord was developed during the first 5 years of this millennium through a series of consultative papers and surveys, with implementation beginning in 2007.

Basel 2

This second Accord (BCBS 2005, 2006) separates the risks involved in lending into market risk (which had been separated out in a supplement to Basel 1 in the mid-1990s), credit risk, and operational risk. In the case of credit risk, banks can either elect to stay with a slight modification of the existing 8% of value of the loan rule – the standardized approach – or move to an Internal Ratings Based (IRB) approach. In this approach the loans are grouped into segments and the bank has to produce models that give estimates of the default parameters for each segment which meet the approval of the regulators. These parameters are then used in a formula developed by the Basel committee to identify the regulatory capital required for that segment of the lending. The regulatory capital that the banks need to set aside is then the sum of the regulatory capital for each segment. As well as this minimum capital requirement (MCR), which is called Pillar 1 in the Accord, the Basel 2 Accord details what a country's banking supervisory body must examine in its annual supervisory review of the models. It has to check that banks have a process for assessing their capital adequacy and the credit risks they are taking; that they have strategies for setting and attaining the appropriate levels of capital adequacy; and the supervisors have the right where appropriate to require banks to hold more capital than the MCR. This supervisory review is called Pillar 2 in the Accord. Finally the Accord also has rules about market discipline, which is called Pillar 3, and which involve the levels of disclosure that banks must make public about both their levels of regulatory capital and the process they use to calculate these.

The major segmentation required in the IRB approach is between five sectors of lending – sovereign, corporate, retail, bank, and equity – and all consumer lending falls into the retail sector. So we will concentrate on this. The model used in the Accord to assess the regulatory capital needed holds for all the five sectors; so we will review that first.

Expected losses, unexpected losses, regulatory capital, and value at risk

In Section 5.1, we pointed out that L_{port} the loss on a portfolio over a fixed time horizon (hereafter considered to be 1 year) is a random variable. Lenders see this

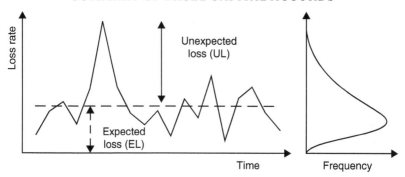

FIG. 5.3.1. Historical losses for a loan portfolio.

randomness in the variation in the actual amount lost in a year as displayed in Fig. 5.3.1.

From this historical data one can derive a distribution of the amount of the annual losses and hence find the expected loss which is the mean of that distribution. Alternatively one can build up this annual loss distribution from the information on the individual accounts, maybe with suitable independence assumptions, as was done in Section 5.1.

A lender is concerned when the actual loss in a year is higher than the mean values and these are referred to as unexpected losses (note that if the loss is lower than the mean that is not an unexpected loss). The lender is most concerned when there is an extremely high unexpected loss – a peak in Fig. 5.3.1. As was shown in Chapter 3 on risk-based pricing, lenders price their product to ensure that the returns cover the expected losses and produce a real profit. In these peak loss years, the returns will not cover the losses and so one has to have capital available to do so. Recall from the previous section that when this is imposed on the lender from a governing body it is referred to as regulatory capital and when it is calculated by the lender for internal decision-making purposes it is called economic capital. In the Basel context we will refer to it as regulatory capital.

It is conceivable, though highly improbable, that a lender could lose the whole amount lent in the portfolio. Holding enough capital to cover such an event would be economically inefficient and yet the less capital the lending organization holds the more likely for it to become insolvent, in that its profit plus the capital held would not cover the losses incurred.

The Basel 1 rule, where the regulatory capital is a fixed percentage of the loan, is rather a crude instrument for dealing with this. Figure 5.3.2a shows an example where the variations in losses are so small that the 8% of the loan value set aside is always too much, while in Fig. 5.3.2b the loss distribution has a higher variance, and in many years the losses exceed the capital set aside and insolvency is likely.

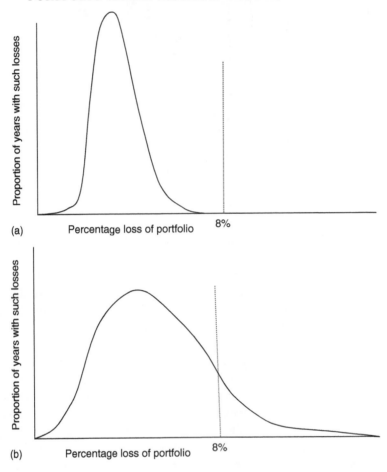

FIG. 5.3.2. (a) Loss distribution with low variance. (b) Loss distribution with high variance.

In the Basel 2 Accord, the formulae to determine the regulatory capital are based on estimating the distribution of the losses and then setting the regulatory capital so that the chances of losses being greater than it are some fixed predefined probability (this could be reinterpreted as the proportion of insolvency the regulators are prepared to accept). Figure 5.3.3 shows this, where the shaded area is the probability that the losses will exceed the given regulatory capital, and the latter has been chosen so that this probability is at the pre-defined level. This is the same approach as is used in VaR calculations to set economic capital in corporate lending. In that case, the probability of the losses not exceeding the capital threshold is called the confidence level and the threshold is called the VaR at that confidence level. Thus if supervisors decide that they will accept that losses exceed regulatory capital

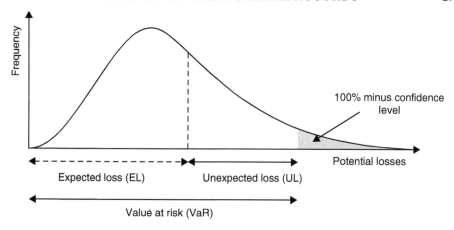

FIG. 5.3.3. Expected loss (EL), unexpected loss (UL), and value at risk (VaR).

with probability p, they will set the regulatory capital RC_p equal to the difference between the VaR at a confidence level $1-p$ and the expected losses, $E[L_{\text{port}}]$.

$$RC_p = (\text{VaR})_{1-p} - E[L_{\text{port}}]. \qquad (5.3.1)$$

Portfolio invariance

It is clear from the analysis of Section 5.1 that the loss distribution of a portfolio depends on the dependencies between the default probabilities of the different loans that make it up. To model this accurately would be extremely difficult and for a regulator to validate such a model even more so. Moreover, if such a model with direct dependencies between the characteristics of the individual loans is used in deciding whether to make a particular loan it would have the unfortunate property that the decision would depend on the other loans in the portfolio, and so one day it would be sensible to make the loan, but the next day it would not be sensible. The Basel committee therefore decided that any model they used for setting RC_p had to be portfolio invariant. This means that the capital required for any loan should depend only on the risks involved in that loan and must not depend on the portfolio it is added to.

Portfolio invariance is therefore a very necessary requirement to provide a workable regulatory model but it is a restrictive condition on the models that can be used. Gordy (2003) showed that one had to make two strong assumptions if one wanted a portfolio invariant rule for calculating the regulatory capital of confidence level p. The first was that the portfolio should consist of an infinite number of loans each of infinitely small amounts. This was to ensure that one could get exactly the confidence level p. If one is willing to accept that one has a confidence level of almost p (between $p - \varepsilon$ and $p + \varepsilon$ for small ε), one can relax this to only requiring that the portfolio has a large number of loans none of which is too large a fraction of the portfolio. Portfolios of consumer loans all tend to have this property.

The second assumption is that there can only be one risk factor which affects all the loans. Portfolio invariance implies that one cannot model all the interactions between the different loans in the portfolio but this condition says that any interaction between the default probabilities of loans has to be through this one factor, which we can think of as the state of the 'global economy'. For consumer credit portfolios consisting of the same type of loan instrument to consumers in the same country this may be acceptable but for corporate loan portfolios where one is lending to companies in different countries and different industries this is less acceptable. In fact international banks have traditionally built multifactor models reflecting the fact that the economies of different countries are growing at different rates and that different industry sectors are affected by changes in the economy in different ways. For these reasons such lenders would diversify these industry and geographic specific risks away by lending to different countries and industries. The one factor model does not recognize the need for such divergence because it says the 'economy' acts on every firm in the same way.

Putting the two assumptions together means that any idiosyncratic risks associated with individual loans tend to cancel each other out because of the large numbers of very small exposures; so it is only the systemic risk caused by the one factor that will really affect the losses in the portfolio. So all the uncertainty is related to this risk factor.

So far we have looked at portfolios in their totality but in the previous section we built models of the losses in a portfolio by starting with the individual loans. In fact we need to connect the two approaches. Portfolio invariance says that the regulatory capital, RC_{port}, for a portfolio is the sum of the regulatory capital $RC(i)$ for each loan i in the portfolio, while in Section 5.1 we identified three factors which make up the risk of loss in a specific loan. These are:

- the PD where $PD_i = 1 - p_i$ if p_i is the probability of being 'good' and not defaulting (we use this odd connection in notation since PD has become the standard nomenclature of Basel 2);

- the LGD, $l_{D,i}$, which gives the fraction (given as a percentage) of the loan that will be lost on default allowing for recovery costs; and

- the EAD which is the estimate of the amount outstanding when a borrower defaults. Although this factor has less uncertainty than the other two, one cannot be sure of its value as it can include future draw downs in the case of credit cards and overdrafts and accumulated interest on missed payments in the case of personal loans and mortgages.

This means that if the portfolio consists of N loans then the regulatory capital RC_{port} is the sum of the regulatory capital $RC(i)$ for each loan where each of them is a function of PD, LGD, and EAD and so the portfolio regulatory capital satisfies

$$RC_{port} = \sum_{i=1}^{N} RC(i) = \sum_{i=1}^{N} RC(PD_i, LGD_i, EAD_i)$$

$$= \sum_{i=1}^{N} RC(1 - p_i, l_{D,i}, EAD_i). \tag{5.3.2}$$

One problem with thinking of each loan completely independently of the others is that it would be hard to verify that the estimates made about that loan were correct. The obvious way to overcome this is to group loans with similar values of the estimators – particularly of PD and LGD. One can then use the default and loss outcomes of a group to validate the parameter estimates of the group. This means one segments the portfolio into groups $s \in S$ with similar values of PD (and possibly LGD) for the loans in each segment and seeks to derive the regulatory capital for each segment. Suppose the portfolio is split into such segments based on PD bands and assume all the loans in segment s have a PD of PD_s then the regulatory capital requirement can be written as

$$RC_{port} = \sum_{i=1}^{N} RC(PD_i, LGD_i, EAD_i) = \sum_{s \in S} \sum_{i:PD_i=PD_s} RC(PD_i, LGD_i, EAD_i)$$

$$= \sum_{s \in S} \sum_{i:PD_i=1-p_s} RC(1 - p_s, l_{D,i}, EAD_i). \tag{5.3.3}$$

One advantage of segmenting in this way is that one can calculate the expected losses for the portfolio by using the same segmentation. It is not unreasonable to assume that in such a segment the LGD L_i for the different loans conditioned on them all having the same PD value are independent of one another. If one also makes the reasonable assumption that the exposures at default on loans are independent of one another and of the LGD assuming the PD is fixed, then the expression for the expected loss in the portfolio simplifies considerably, since

$$E[L_{port}] = E\left(\sum_{i=1}^{N} (EAD)_i L_i D_i\right) = \sum_{s \in S} \sum_{i:PD_i=PD_s=1-p_s} E((EAD)_i L_i D_i)$$

$$= \sum_{s \in S} \sum_{i:PD_i=PD_s=1-p_s} E((EAD)_i)E(L_i)E(D_i)$$

$$= \sum_{s \in S} (1 - p_s) \sum_{i:PD_i=PD_s=1-p_s} E((EAD)_i)E(L_i). \tag{5.3.4}$$

Now though, we need to look at the regulatory capital needed in each segment.

Conditional and unconditional probabilities of default

Portfolio invariance means there is only one factor allowed in the model used to determine regulatory capital. This factor can be used to connect two default probabilities that are important in modelling how much regulatory capital is needed, namely the long-run average PD and the PD occurring in an economic downturn. The average PD is the expected default rate under normal business conditions and is the one that lenders estimate by looking at the historical average default rates of the loans they make. However, regulatory capital is designed to cover the losses that occur when the PD is that conditioned on the one 'economic' factor taking some very conservative (that is poor) value. So what happens is that the Basel formula maps the average PD value onto a conservative PD value K(PD), corresponding to the default probability conditioned on when the economic conditions are in this poor state.

Basel model underlying regulatory capital expression

The model used to derive the regulatory capital expression is based on Merton's (1974) original model of the credit risk of a corporate loan. This was generalized by Vasicek (2002) to a single factor model of the credit risk of a portfolio of such loans. The point is that the model is one for corporate lending which has been widely used in that context, but in the Basel Accord is being used in retail (consumer) lending as well as corporate lending. In subsequent section we will look at whether such a model is appropriate in this context.

Merton's model assumes that a company will default on its loans if its debts exceed its assets. Consider a one period discrete time model with a portfolio (or a segment of a portfolio) of loans lent to $i = 1, 2, \ldots, N$ companies. The debt of company i is d_i and at the start of the period its assets are $a_{i,0}$. These initial assets are not known but can be assumed to be fixed. However, the assets of company i at the end of the period $A_{i,1}$ are stochastic. It is assumed that the assets follow a log normal distribution which means that the asset value change after one time period, R_i is normally distributed ($R_i/a_{i,0}$ can be thought of as the return on the initial assets). So the asset value change satisfies:

$$R_i = A_{i,1} - a_{i,0} \sim N(\mu_i, \sigma_i^2) \quad \text{where } E(R_i|a_{i,0}) = \mu_i; \quad \text{Var}(R_i|a_{i,0}) = \sigma_i^2$$

$$(5.3.5)$$

The one factor assumption means that the return consists of sum of three components – the deterministic part, the factor X, which affects all returns simultaneously, and the idiosyncratic factor U_i so

$$R_i = \mu_i + bX + cU_i$$

where

$$X \sim N(0, 1), \ U_i \sim N(0, 1). \tag{5.3.6}$$

Note that the impact, b, of the common factor is the same for all firms within a segment. Since all the random variables X, U_i are independent with zero mean, the variance, covariance, and correlation coefficient becomes

$$\sigma_i^2 = \text{Var}(R_i) = \text{Var}(\mu_i + bX + cU_i) = \text{Var}(\mu_i) + \text{Var}(bX) + \text{Var}(cU_i)$$

$$= b^2\text{Var}(X) + c^2\text{Var}(U_i) = b^2 + c^2 = \sigma^2$$

$$\sigma_{ij}^2 = \text{Cov}(R_i, R_j) = E((\mu_i + bX + cU_i)(\mu_j + bX + cU_j)) - E(R_i)E(R_j)$$

$$= \mu_i\mu_j + b(\mu_i + \mu_j)E(X) + c(\mu_i E(U_j) + \mu_j E(U_i)) + bc(E(X)(E(U_i)$$

$$+ E(U_j)) + E((bX)^2) + c^2 E(U_i U_j) - \mu_i\mu_j = E((bX)^2) = b^2$$

$$\rho_{ij} = R = \frac{\sigma_{ij}^2}{\sigma_i\sigma_j} = \left(\frac{b}{\sigma}\right)^2. \tag{5.3.7}$$

Let PD_i be the probability that company i will default on its loan in the period under consideration. From Merton's assumption

$$PD_i = P\{A_{i,1} < d_i\} = P\{R_i < d_i - a_0\} = P\left\{\frac{R_i - \mu_i}{\sigma} < \frac{d_i - a_0 - \mu_i}{\sigma}\right\} \tag{5.3.8}$$

and since $\frac{R_i - \mu_i}{\sigma}$ is $N(0, 1)$, that is, standard normal, if we define $N(\cdot)$ to be the cumulative standard normal distribution function then

$$PD_i = N\left(\frac{d_i - a_0 - \mu_i}{\sigma}\right). \tag{5.3.9}$$

This gives us an expression for the unconditional PD. What we want to do is to connect this with the $PD_i(x)$ conditioned on the factor X having an extremely poor outcome x, so that the portfolio or segment losses are likely to be extreme. This can de done by showing

$$PD_i(x) = P\{A_{i,1} < d_i | X = x\} = P\{\mu_i + bx + cU_i + a_{i,0} < d_i\}$$

$$= P\left\{U_i < \frac{d_i - a_{i,0} - \mu_i - bx}{c}\right\} = P\left\{U_i < \frac{\frac{d_i - a_{i,0} - \mu_i}{\sigma} - \frac{bx}{\sigma}}{c/\sigma}\right\}$$

$$= N\left(\frac{\frac{d_i - a_{i,0} - \mu_i}{\sigma} - \frac{bx}{\sigma}}{c/\sigma}\right) = N\left(\frac{N^{-1}(PD_i) - bx/\sigma}{\left(1 - (b/\sigma)^2\right)^{1/2}}\right)$$

$$= N\left(\frac{N^{-1}(PD_i) - R^{1/2}x}{(1 - R)^{1/2}}\right) \tag{5.3.10}$$

where again N is the cumulative standard normal distribution function and N^{-1} is its inverse function. All the regulator needs to do now is to choose what is the extreme value of x that the regulatory capital must cover and then to determine the correlation coefficient R. The Basel regulators have decided that they want regulatory capital to cover all but the worst 0.1% of the economic conditions (that is those that on average happen once every 1000 years). By the symmetry of a standard normal distribution, if $-x$ does this then $+x$ has the property that there is only a 0.1% chance that the standard normal distribution will choose a value greater than it. Thus x is $N^{-1}(0.999)$ and so for any average PD_i the regulatory capital requires that one turns it into the conservative conditional:

$$PD_i(N^{-1}(0.001)) = PD_i(-N^{-1}(0.999))$$

$$\text{where } PD_i\left(N^{-1}(0.001)\right) = N\left(\frac{N^{-1}(PD_i) + R^{1/2}N^{-1}(0.999)}{(1-R)^{1/2}}\right). \qquad (5.3.11)$$

Basel formula for consumer lending

Having calculated the PD under these extreme conditions, it is now straightforward to identify the regulatory capital needed to cover the expected losses on the loans in a segment of the portfolio. One starts with the amount of money at risk, the EAD. This is multiplied by the PD in these extreme conditions, which is equivalent to the proportion of the exposure that will default (recall that because of the infinite number of small loans assumption, the segment can be considered to have EAD loans each of 1 unit lent). This gives the expected amount defaulted upon, but not all of this is lost because the lender can recover much of it – a mortgage company can repossess a house and sell it to recover the money lent. LGD reflects the proportion that is not recoverable. Hence the expected loss conditional on these extreme conditions is K(PD) × LGD × EAD but PD × LGD × EAD of this, the unconditional expected loss should be covered by the lending profits. So for a segment, the regulatory capital set aside should be

$$K(PD) \times LGD \times EAD - PD \times LGD \times EAD. \qquad (5.3.12)$$

Or for each unit of lending exposure, it is

$$K(PD) \times LGD - PD \times LGD. \qquad (5.3.13)$$

Formally, Basel 2 splits consumer loans into three groups – residential (mortgages), revolving (credit cards), and others – and in all three cases the formula for the capital to be set aside as a percentage of the estimated EAD is

Regulatory capital $\tilde{K} = LGD \times K(PD)$

$$= LGD \times N\left(\left(\frac{1}{1-R}\right)^{1/2} N^{-1}(PD) + \left(\frac{R}{1-R}\right)^{1/2} N^{-1}(0.999)\right) - LGD \times PD$$

$$\qquad (5.3.14)$$

where N is the cumulative standard normal distribution function and N^{-1} is its inverse. In our notation this reads as

$$\tilde{K}(p) = l_D \times N\left(\left(\frac{1}{1-R}\right)^{1/2} N^{-1}(1-p) + \left(\frac{R}{1-R}\right)^{1/2} N^{-1}(0.999)\right)$$
$$- l_D(1-p) \tag{5.3.15}$$

where we define the total capital needed to cover the losses (expected and unexpected) to be

$$\mathrm{TC}(p) = \tilde{K}(p) + (1-p)l_D. \tag{5.3.16}$$

For residential loans the correlation is taken to be $R = 0.15$, for revolving credits the correlation is to be $R = 0.04$ while for other retail exposures (like personal loans and overdrafts) the correlation is assumed to vary according to the PD and the corresponding formula is

$$R = 0.03\left(\frac{1-e^{-35PD}}{1-e^{-35}}\right) + 0.16\left(1 - \frac{1-e^{-35PD}}{1-e^{-35}}\right) \tag{5.3.17}$$

Figure 5.3.4 shows the capital K required as a function of the PD in the case when LGD $= 0.5$ for the three groups, together with the capital requirements on the corporate loans as a reference. One will be expecting lenders to operate with segments having PDs less than 0.1 but notice that for very high expected levels

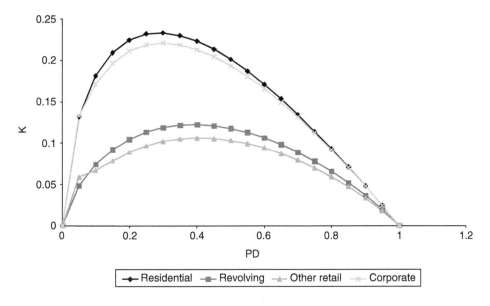

FIG. 5.3.4. Basel capital requirements $K(p)$ when LGD $= 0.5$.

of default the amount of regulatory capital starts to fall. This is because more and more of the losses are expected and so should be covered from the profits, though it does lead to the surprising requirement that for defaulted loans no capital need to be set aside. The effect of this has been modified in the final Accord by recognizing that the LGD on defaulted loans is still uncertain for a considerable time after default. Residential mortgages have the highest R because defaults on mortgages are more highly correlated with each other through the impact of worsening economic conditions and drops in house prices. The figure also seems to imply that one needs to set more capital aside for mortgages than for other forms of consumer loans. This is not the case though because the typical PD for mortgages is much lower than the PD for the other forms of consumer credit.

The choice of the correlations used in the Basel formula (Eq. (5.3.15)) for the consumer lending $-R = 0.15$ for mortgages, $R = 0.04$ for revolving credit, and the expression in (5.3.17) for other retail exposures (like personal loans and overdrafts) – is driven by the need to obtain capital requirements that look right when compared with empirical data. There is no economic rational for the particular values chosen. The reason is that this is a corporate credit risk model applied to a different lending context. So all that can be done is to choose correlations to make the results empirically acceptable. We will investigate some of the difficulties that this leads to in the next section.

Figure 5.3.5 shows the total capital needed to cover both the expected losses ($EL = EAD \times LGD \times PD$) and the unexpected losses ($UL = EAD \times LGD \times K(PD)$) in the case when $EAD = 1$ and $LGD = 1$. This is simply $K(PD) + PD$ and does have the other property that in all cases it is 0 if $PD = 0$.

The 'other retail' loans category includes loans to small businesses up to 1 million Euros. There is a transitional formula for loans to businesses with sales of between 1 and 50 million euros. The corporate model function is used for loans to companies with sales over 50 million euros. This transitional formula has an extra term in it – the maturity M – which is also used in the corporate loan Basel formula and reflects the impact that changes in interest rate have on loans which are repaid over long periods of time. The maturity of a loan is defined so that the impact of a shift in the risk-free interest rate on the net present value of the loan repayments is the same as the impact of the same shift on a loan where the whole amount is repaid at the maturity date. What is surprising in Fig. 5.3.5 is that though for the consumer products the capital set aside is 1 if $PD = 1$, for small corporate loans, which come under the retail sector formula, the capital set aside is actually slightly greater than 1 because of this maturity term.

Summary

So to summarize, the New Accord has three pillars to it – a MCR, which is what we have concentrated on, a supervisory review, and a role for market discipline.

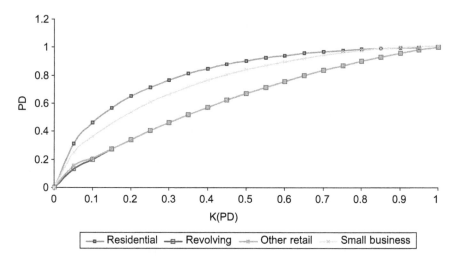

FIG. 5.3.5. Expected loss + regulatory capital, EL + UL, as function of p when LGD $= 1$.

The supervisory review requires that the banking regulators review each bank's risk management models and systems. In the light of such a review, a regulator could require the bank increase its regulatory capital above the minimum or decrease its lending portfolio. The review must cover several areas including a usage test to ensure that the bank is using its models in its operating decisions; analysis of the bank's stress tests to see what impact adverse operating conditions would have on a bank's requirement for capital; ensuring the model estimates are built on suffi- ciently long data sets (5 to 7 years of history depending on what is being estimated) and that the bank has experience in operating the models and systems; and ensur- ing that senior management are responsible for and aware of the results of the modelling. The market discipline pillar outlines what details of the risk manage- ment systems and the outcomes of the models therein have to be reported publicly in order that investors can make informed decisions about the bank's attitude to risk.

The regulations covering the assessment of market risk remain essentially as they are under the current regulations while those covering operational risk require either that the capital to be set aside is some proportion of the average annual income or, if the bank has sophisticated operational risk models, the capital suggested by these may be allowed. Modelling operational risk in financial institutions is in its infancy and so there is incentive for considerable research in this topic which is outside the scope of this book.

For credit risk, the regulations split the lending portfolio into five sectors – corporate, retail, sovereign, bank, and equity. A bank can choose to use the standard regulations (essentially the existing situation that regulatory capital is 8% of loan value) or two variants of IRB regulations – one where a bank provides only an estimate of the PD, and another where it provides both PD and LGD estimates. For retail lending, which includes all consumer lending, only this second advanced version of the IRB regulations is allowed and if a bank uses the IRB approach for one form of lending it has to provide a timetable on when it will use the IRB approach for all other forms of lending.

When using the IRB regulations for retail lending, a bank has to split its retail loan portfolio into a number of segments and provide PD, LGD, and EAD estimates for each segment. There is a fundamental difference in how PD and LGD are measured. PD is the long-run probability of a loan defaulting in the next 12 months. As was shown earlier there is no need to worry about what happens to PD in recessions because $K(PD)$ gives the equivalent downturn probability. The problem though is that a credit scoring system estimates the point in time (PIT) PD, which is the chance of default in the next 12 months. The Basel Accord regulations require the PD estimate to be the average long-run PD, which is the average of PIT PDs over an economic cycle. This can be difficult to do in practice because the credit scorecard may be recalibrated or even rebuilt several times in an economic cycle. How one can transform PIT PDs to long-run PDs continues to be an area of debate for regulators and lenders. We will return to this issue in the next section.

LGD on the other hand appears in the regulations formula as is, and so the LGD estimate should reflect the LGD in an economic downturn. There is no comparable transformation of average LGD to downturn LGD as there is for PD. The expected loss in a segment is taken to be EL = PD × LGD × EAD and this predictable loss is expected to be covered by the profits of the lending and so no extra capital needs to be set aside (note though that this predictable loss includes the downturn LGD). The unexpected loss is $(K(PD) - PD) \times LGD \times EAD$ and this is the minimum amount of capital the IRB regulations require to be set aside.

The choice of which and how many segments is clearly very important. Basel 2 requires that such lending be first split into three classes – residential mortgages, revolving credit, and other retail lending (personal loans, overdrafts) because different correlations are applied in the $K(PD)$ formula. Within each of these classes, the regulation suggests that different types of lending be separated out and also that defaulted loans have to be a separate segment. Lenders tend to segment further by PD bands and some occasionally by LGD bands as well, though the regulations mean that there is a floor of 0.03% allowed on any PD band in any type of consumer loan and of 10% on any LGD value used in residential mortgages. In the next two sections, we look at some of the implications of the new Basel Accord on credit scoring systems and their operation.

5.4   Basel II regulations and their impact on credit scoring

Three-way relationship

There is a three-way relationship between the new Basel capital adequacy regulation, the use of credit scoring in consumer lending, and the operational decision in these retail credit portfolios as shown in Fig. 5.4.1. It has long been recognized that credit scoring with its default risk score is an excellent tool for measuring and hence controlling credit risk (risk of consumers defaulting) through the operating decisions in retail portfolios. It is only now being recognized that operating decisions will have an effect on the way one builds credit scorecards in the future. Up to now since most lenders have had the same product and the same operating regime the operating decisions have had little impact on their default scores, but as lending becomes more customized this will change. The resulting problem of policy inference – what would have happened under a 'vanilla' operating policy – will make reject inference look like a minor difficulty.

In the next two sections we look at how the Basel regulations will impact firstly on credit scoring itself and then on the operating decisions it supports. Without credit scoring one could not use the IRB approach of the Basel regulations to portfolios of consumer loans and as Table 5.4.1, from the fifth quantitative impact study commissioned by the Basel Committee, shows this is the area where one can make the most savings under IRB for major international banks. As it stands there is a saving of 10.6% in the regulatory capital required for international banks and 21% for national banks under the then current Basel 2 proposals compared with the

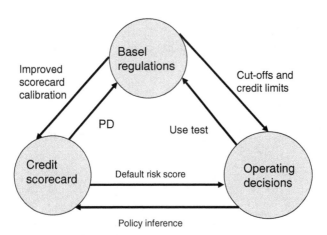

FIG. 5.4.1. Relationship between Basel regulations, credit scorecards, and operating decisions.

TABLE 5.4.1. Results from QIS5 of impact of Basel 2 on capital requirements.

Portfolio	International banks			National banks		
	% of capital requirement (1988)	% increase caused by advanced IRB	% increase in total capital requirement	% of capital requirement (1988)	% increase caused by advanced IRB	% increase in total capital requirement
Corporate	28	−18	−5	21	−18	−4
Sovereign	0.5	240	1	0.4	140	0.6
Bank	4	10	0.4	4	2.4	0.1
Retail (total)	18	−46	−8	34	−51	−17
Mortgage part of retail	12	−64	−7.6	22	−58	−12
Non-mortgage part of retail	9	−22	−2	12	−42	−4
SME (corporate)	7	−19	−1.3	15	−15	2.2
Equity	3	85	2	3	130	3.6
Market risk	3	−7	−0.2	2	0.4	0
Operational risk			6			7.5
Overall change			−4.6			−14

existing rules. This exceeds the extra 6% (7%, respectively) increase in regulatory capital needed to cover operational risk that was not covered before. Thus there is an advantage in banks moving to the IRB approach. However, closer examination shows that the vast majority of this saving (8% of the 10% and 17% of the 21% depending on the type of bank) comes from using IRB in the retail area and without that economic carrot less lenders might move to the new system. It is the use of IRB in consumer lending based on credit scoring systems that makes Basel 2 attractive to lenders.

Default definition

Much of standard credit scoring approaches immediately satisfy the Basel IRB requirements. Default is taken to be that the borrower is 90 days overdue or unlikely to repay in full. This 90-day definition is what is traditionally used in credit scoring and so the scores seem to measure what the Basel Accord wants to estimate. Some regulators (the United Kingdom for example) have changed the definition of default though to being 180 days in arrears. This causes some difficulties because directly building a scoring system to identify who will be 180 days overdue is hard because far fewer borrowers reach this level compared with the 90-day overdue level. Also lenders have usually intervened long before this level is reached. So one often estimates the effectiveness of the lender's collection process as well as the riskiness of the borrower. Most lenders deal with this extended definition by building a scorecard on the 90-day overdue definition of bad and then checking whether the scorecard still discriminates well on the 180-day overdue definition. If it does, it is only a matter of recalibrating the score to log odds relationship for this new definition of bad.

Point in time and through the cycle probabilities of default

The standard for consumer credit default scores is to measure the probability of a loan defaulting over a fixed future time horizon, which is almost always the next 12 months. Again this is the time horizon suggested in the Basel definition of PD, pace the question of whether one is measuring through the cycle (TTC) PD or a PIT PD. (Heitfeld 2005). Consumer credit scores are traditionally PIT measures in that one is interested in the chance of default in the next 12 months, but the external ratings agencies such as Moodys and Standard and Poor rate corporate lending such as bonds on a TTC approach. In this, one tries to estimate the chance of default in the next 12 months on average through an economic cycle. So such ratings should not change because of economic conditions but only because of the idiosyncratic factors affecting the individual company. Since risk management in most international banks has been led from the corporate lending side, this has been traditionally the most common philosophy considered. It is not surprising therefore that this is the philosophy proposed in the Basel Accord, where the PD is taken as the long-run average of the probability of the borrower defaulting in the next 12 months.

Thus to use consumer credit scorecards for Basel purposes, the bank needs to translate a PIT PD into a TTC PD estimate. As alluded to earlier, how to do this satisfactorily is a matter of debate between regulators and lenders, especially if the lenders have insufficient historical data to plot the PD of their borrower populations through an economic cycle. Even if such data were available, it is questionable whether it would be of much use for consumer lending since it is highly unlikely that the features and price of the loan, the application channels used, and the lenders' marketing and operating policies would stay constant over such a time period. Hence the type of borrowers applying for a particular loan product and the way they perform with it are likely to change considerably and trying to separate out this from changes due to the economic cycle is difficult. Despite these caveats, lenders have to determine what is an appropriate PIT PD to TTC PD transformation if they want to use credit scores for regulatory capital purposes. Let $PD_t(s, t_0)$ be the PIT PD at time t for the segment of the consumer loan portfolio who had a default score of s at time t_0, where the score is a log odds score. The lender is required to calculate $\overline{PD}(s, t_0)$, which is the long-run average TTC PD for the same segment of loans. If we assume the length of a cycle is T then

$$\overline{PD}(s, t_0) = \frac{1}{T} \int_0^T PD_t(s, t_0) dt. \qquad (5.4.1)$$

One possible approach is to exploit the decomposition of score into log of population odds and log of information odds described in Eq. (1.5.17). Let the proportion of defaults (bads) and non-defaults (goods) in the population at time t be $p_B(t)$ and $p_G(t) = 1 - p_B(t)$, respectively. If the log odds score s is built on a set of characteristics $\mathbf{x}$ and we define $P_t(B|\mathbf{x})$ and $P_t(G|\mathbf{x})$ to be the proportions of those with characteristics $\mathbf{x}$ who are bad (defaulters) or good (non defaulters) at time t, then Bayes' theorem and the definition of a log odds score would give that the score $s_t(\mathbf{x})$ at time t satisfies

$$s_t(\mathbf{x}) = \ln\left(\frac{P_t(G|\mathbf{x})}{P_t(B|\mathbf{x})}\right) = \ln\left(\frac{p_G(t)}{p_B(t)}\right) + \ln\left(\frac{f_t(\mathbf{x}|G)}{f_t(\mathbf{x}|B)}\right) = s_t^{Pop} + s_t^{Inf}(\mathbf{x})$$

where

$$s_t^{Pop} = \ln\left(\frac{p_G(t)}{p_B(t)}\right); \quad s_t^{Inf}(\mathbf{x}) = \ln\left(\frac{f_t(\mathbf{x}|G)}{f_t(\mathbf{x}|B)}\right) \qquad (5.4.2)$$

and $f_t(\mathbf{x}|G)$ is the likelihood in the population at time t of having characteristics $\mathbf{x}$.

One simple but intuitively reasonable assumption to make is that the information part of the score that depends on the individuals' characteristics does not change over time so that

$$s_t^{\text{Inf}}(\mathbf{x}) = \ln\left(\frac{f_t(\mathbf{x}|G)}{f_t(\mathbf{x}|B)}\right) = \ln\left(\frac{f(\mathbf{x}|G)}{f(\mathbf{x}|B)}\right) = s^{\text{Inf}}(\mathbf{x})$$

$$\text{so } s_t(\mathbf{x}) = s_t^{\text{Pop}} + s^{\text{Inf}}(\mathbf{x}). \tag{5.4.3}$$

If we define $X(s, t_0) = \{\mathbf{x} : s_{t_0}(\mathbf{x}) = s\} = \{\mathbf{x} : s_{t_0}^{\text{Inf}}(\mathbf{x}) = s - s_{t_0}^{\text{Pop}} = \tilde{s}\}$ this is the segment of the population we are interested at time t and we can define

$$P_t(B|X_{t_0}(s)) \equiv P_t(B|s, t_0) \equiv \text{PD}_t(s, t_0); P_t(G|X_{t_0}(s)) \equiv P_t(G|s, t_0)$$
$$= 1 - \text{PD}_t(s, t_0).$$

With abuse of notation we will write (s, t_0) instead of $X(s, t_0)$ hereafter. Applying Eq. (5.4.2) with the assumption in (5.4.3) to the whole set $X(s, t_0)$ gives the equation

$$s_t(s, t_0) = \ln\left(\frac{P_t(G|s, t_0)}{P_t(B|s, t_0)}\right) = \ln\left(\frac{p_G(t)}{p_B(t)}\right) + \ln\left(\frac{f(s, t_0|G)}{f(s, t_0|B)}\right) = s_t^{\text{Pop}} + s^{\text{Inf}}(\tilde{s})$$

$$= \ln\left(\frac{1 - \text{PD}_t(s, t_0)}{\text{PD}_t(s, t_0)}\right) = \ln\left(\frac{p_G(t)}{p_B(t)}\right) + s^{\text{Inf}}(\tilde{s})$$

$$\Rightarrow \text{PD}_t(s, t_0) = \frac{1}{1 + e^{s_t(s, t_0)}} = \frac{1}{1 + \frac{p_G(t)}{p_B(t)} e^{s_{\text{Inf}}(\tilde{s})}}. \tag{5.4.4}$$

Since at time t_0, the score s for the segment under consideration satisfies

$$s = s_{t_0}^{\text{Pop}} + s_{\text{Inf}}(\tilde{s}) = \ln\left(\frac{p_G(t_0)}{p_B(t_0)}\right) + s_{\text{Inf}}(\tilde{s}),$$

then

$$\text{PD}_t(s, t_0) = \frac{1}{1 + \frac{p_G(t)p_B(t_0)}{p_B(t)p_G(t_0)} e^s} \Rightarrow \overline{\text{PD}}(s, t_0) = \frac{1}{T}\int_0^T \text{PD}_t(s, t_0)dt$$

$$= \frac{1}{T}\int_0^T \frac{1}{1 + \frac{p_G(t)p_B(t_0)}{p_B(t)p_G(t_0)} e^s} dt. \tag{5.4.5}$$

Thus to perform this transformation one needs the population odds of goods and bads over the whole cycle. The transformation depends on the assumption that the information odds do not change over time and in reality this does not often occur. In particular for behavioural scores one often finds that the dominant characteristics are a bureau generic score and whether the loan is arrears. The bureau score has the population odds implicit in it and so is likely to change over time. Still this is a useful first approximation to considering how to translate PIT PDs to long-run average PDs and shows how the transformation even in this simple case does not involve multiplying the current PDs by a common conversion factor. A specific example follows.

Example 5.4.1 Score decomposition transformation of PIT PD to TTC PD

Suppose the economic cycle consists of four periods – a good time when the population odds of non-defaulters to defaulters is 1000:1, two average periods when the population odds of defaulters to non-defaulters is 50:1, and one recession period where the non-default:default odds in the population is 10:1.

Consider three different segments in the good period. Segment 1 corresponds to PD = 0.001 or a score of $s = \ln(0.999/0.001) = 6.906$. As there are only four periods the integral in Eq. (5.4.5) becomes a sum and so

$$\overline{\text{PD}}(\text{Score} = 6.906, \text{Good}) = \frac{1}{4}\left(\frac{1}{1 + \frac{100}{1} \times \frac{1}{100} \times 999} + \frac{2}{1 + \frac{50}{1} \times \frac{1}{100} \times 999}\right.$$

$$\left. + \frac{1}{1 + \frac{10}{1} \times \frac{1}{100} \times 999}\right) = 0.0037.$$

Segment 2 corresponds to PD = 0.01 or a score of $s = \ln(0.99/0.01) = 4.595$. Then the long-run average becomes

$$\overline{\text{PD}}(\text{Score} = 4.595, \text{Good}) = \frac{1}{4}\left(\frac{1}{1 + \frac{100}{1} \times \frac{1}{100} \times 99} + \frac{2}{1 + \frac{50}{1} \times \frac{1}{100} \times 99}\right.$$

$$\left. + \frac{1}{1 + \frac{10}{1} \times \frac{1}{100} \times 99}\right) = 0.0353.$$

The final segment corresponds to loans where PD = 0.1 in the good period, that is the score then is $s = \ln(0.9/0.1) = 2.197$. The long-run average for this group becomes

$$\overline{\text{PD}}(\text{Score} = 2.197, \text{Good}) = \frac{1}{4}\left(\frac{1}{1 + \frac{100}{1} \times \frac{1}{100} \times 9} + \frac{2}{1 + \frac{50}{1} \times \frac{1}{100} \times 9}\right.$$

$$\left. + \frac{1}{1 + \frac{10}{1} \times \frac{1}{100} \times 9}\right) = 0.247.$$

It is clear that the transformation is not equivalent to multiplying each PIT PD by an identical constant.

A second approach has been developed if all that is available is the average default rate of the whole portfolio over the economic cycle. In particular this can be used if industry wide default rates are available through a whole cycle but the bank may only have the default rate for its portfolio through part of the cycle. It benchmarks its default rate against the industry level on the period it has information for and uses this benchmark to project back an estimated default rate for its portfolio for the whole of the cycle. The assumption is that during the cycle the loans will migrate through different behavioural score bands and also that the score to PD transformation will also change.

Assume that one has the long-run average portfolio level default rate $\overline{PD}_{port}$ for a whole economic cycle. Assume also that the portfolio has been split into score bands s and $\pi_t(s)$ is the proportion of the portfolio in scoreband s at time t. As in Section 4.3 one can describe the dynamics of the behavioural scores by a Markov chain with transition matrix $P(s, s')$. In particular one can use the approach in Example 4.3.7 where one only looked at the active states of the borrower, and excluded the states where the borrower closed the account or defaulted. This was done by assuming that for each such account that was closed or defaulted another one opened. If one knows the score band probability distribution of new accounts, then one can think of each closed account moving with this probability to the appropriate band. With this adjustment the state space describes the movement of the borrowers in the portfolio between the different behavioural score bands. This means that the proportions of the portfolio in each band satisfy

$$\pi_{t+1}(s') = \sum_s \pi_t(s)P(s, s') \tag{5.4.6}$$

while in the long-run (stationary) distribution the proportions of the population in each band $\pi^*(s)$ satisfy

$$\pi^*(s') = \sum_s \pi^*(s)P(s, s'). \tag{5.4.7}$$

If as before we define $\overline{PD}(s)$ as the long-run average TTC PD for a segment of loans which are in scoreband s, then one would expect given the definition of $\pi^*(s)$ that

$$\overline{PD}_{port} = \sum_s \pi^*(s)\overline{PD}(s). \tag{5.4.8}$$

In order to make this work one assume that the long-run average PD in score band s is some factor of the current PD (time t_0) of that score band, $PD_{t_0}(s, t_0)$. So one chooses α so that if $\overline{PD}(s) = \alpha PD_{t_0}(s, t_0)$ then

$$\overline{PD}_{port} = \sum_s \pi^*(s)\overline{PD}(s) = \sum_s \pi^*(s)\alpha PD_{t_0}(s, t_0). \tag{5.4.9}$$

Calibration

The Basel regulations have pointed out several deficiencies in credit scoring and the first is in the calibration of the scores. In Chapter 2 we looked at the ways that one could measure scoring systems and recognized there are three different aspects of the systems that are important – prediction, discrimination, and calibration. In prediction, one looks at the decisions that one makes using a scoring system including the cut-off score and measures how many of these are the correct decisions to have made. One is comparing the actual good/bad status of a consumer in the sample with the predicted status and measuring the difference using percentage correctly classified (PCC) or divergence (2×2) tables. In discrimination, it is the ranking given by the scores which is important and a cut-off or the final decision does not appear. Measures like receiver operating characteristic (ROC) curves and Gini coefficient reflect how well the score separates the two groups when one ranks the borrowers by their score. These are the two aspects that have been traditionally assessed in credit scoring – discrimination to measure the power of a scorecard and prediction to compare cut-offs and scoring systems. Whether the score accurately reflects the PD is less important than the ranking accuracy of the scores since one wants to accept the 'best' customers. Even the cut-off score is often chosen subjectively by managers using other issues than just the PD of those marginal customers.

In the Basel regulations though, it is the value of the PD that is used in the regulatory capital equations. So for Basel, it is calibration – whether the estimated default probabilities accurately reflect the actual default probabilities – that is critical. One needs a group of similar loans to obtain actual default probabilities and so one checks calibration by taking a segment of loans with similar estimated PDs and comparing this with the default rate subsequently observed in the segment. As Tasche (2005) points out this is not easy to do because one is never sure if any variation is due to systematic errors in the scoring system or purely random fluctuations and there are only a few tests that one can use. The comparison of score against actual good:bad log odds is regularly used in credit scoring to ensure the scorecard is 'well calibrated' but in this case it involves comparing the score with the good:bad odds of the sample of borrowers on which it was built. Basel calibration requires one to compare the score with the future default odds of the borrower segment all of whom have estimated default values in a given PD band. There is a need for credit scorers to learn from forecasting theory the techniques and measures which enable this to be done accurately.

The Basel regulations insist that the lender have enough historic data (at least 5 years) to be able to make such calibration estimates. Lenders have not traditionally held data for such long time periods and so one might ask how can this increase in information be used to improve the way scorecards are built as well as being used to calibrate them more accurately. One possibility is to introduce economic variables into the scorecards where previously it was assumed that the observation and performance periods were too short for there to be major changes in the economy.

Using a corporate model in a consumer context

However, there are also problems because the Basel 2 formula is essentially a corporate credit risk model forced into the consumer lending context with its parameters calibrated empirically. There are a number of properties that one would expect of the regulatory capital set aside to cover the credit risk of a loan, namely:

- the capital set aside for unexpected loss plus the expected loss should not exceed the value of the loan or the estimated EAD for revolving loans; and

- if one is able to segment the portfolio into a larger and more precise set of segments according to PD then this extra information should mean the capital set aside to cover unexpected losses would decrease, and this capital plus the expected loss should decrease.

Neither of these properties is always true. Figure 5.3.5 (and a magnifying glass) shows that in the case of the small business loans where the formulae is used to make a transition between the consumer and corporate formulae, one can have $EL + UL$ being more than 100% if $LGD = 1$. The problem is the maturity term which does not come into consumer loans but is part of the corporate loan formula.

If we enlarge Fig. 5.3.4, the graph of the Basel capital required as a function of PD in the region where the PD is small, we get Fig. 5.4.2. Here it is clear that the capital required in the 'other retail' categories is not concave around the 0.05 PD region (it is still not concave if one adds in the expected loss).

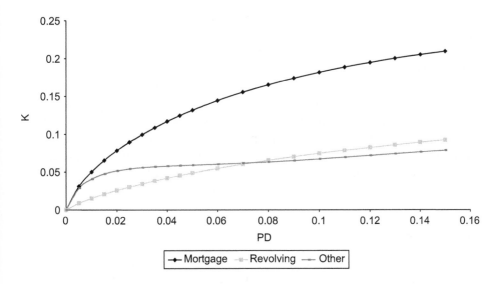

FIG. 5.4.2. Capital required to cover unexpected losses for low values of PD.

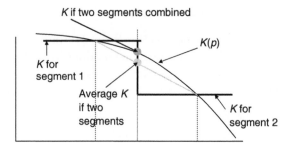

FIG. 5.4.3. Capital required if segments combined using concave $K(p)$.

TABLE 5.4.2. Example of capital needed in non-concave region

PD value	Loan amount	$\tilde{K}(PD)$	Capital needed if LGD $= 1$
0.06	1,000,000	0.060205	60,205
0.08	1,000,000	0.063182	63,182
Total	2,000,000		123,387
0.07	2,000,000	0.061561	123,122

If the capital function $\tilde{K}(PD)$ is concave, then Fig. 5.4.3 shows that keeping segments separated always results in lower regulatory capital. However, since there is a region where $\tilde{K}(PD))$ is not concave then in this region finding more precise risk categories does not cut down the capital needed. This is really the case as Table 5.4.2 shows. If one compares having one segment of PD $= 6\%$ with loans of 1,000,000 units and one segment of loans with PD $= 8\%$ also with loans worth 1,000,000 with combining the two segments into one large segment containing 2,000,000 loans where the average PD is 7%, then one gets the results in that table. So by having more precise risk categories – two instead of one – one actually has to set aside £265 more capital. This is not what one would normally expect.

These difficulties arise because one is using a corporate credit risk model in a consumer credit situation where the parameters have been chosen empirically. However, these problems with the Basel model highlight another failure in consumer credit modelling – the lack of models of the credit risk of portfolios of consumer loans. We return to this issue in Section 5.6.

Exposure at default

So far we have concentrated on the impact that the Basel regulation have had on the PD estimation implicit in credit scoring but there are two other estimates needed to implement IRB systems – EAD and LGD. In most cases EAD estimates look to be fairly straightforward and possibly deterministic. One knows the current balance outstanding and can calculate the number of missed payments and the interest on these payments that are needed to trigger default. The sum of these is likely to be a good estimate of EAD though one needs to make some assumptions about whether any payment made before default actually cut the balance outstanding or just cover the interest generated. The exception is for revolving credit – credit cards and overdrafts – where one has both the current balance outstanding and the current credit limit. How much of the extra credit available – the difference between the credit limit and the actual balance – is likely to be drawn down before default? How is this percentage draw down affected by economic conditions or the type of loan product? One could model this using regression, probit or hazard approaches, or seek to build Markov chain models of the situation. Whichever models prove most effective, it is another area of credit scoring that will be receiving more attention because of the Basel regulations.

Loss given default

Estimating LGD has received far less attention than PD estimating even though in some ways it has a larger impact on the regulatory capital formula. It is only since 2000 that researchers in corporate credit risk have started to model LGD as anything than a fixed value obtained from historical averages and invariant to economic conditions, and type and seniority of debt. The research into the comparable measure in the consumer case has been almost zero except for mortgage repossessions, mainly because recovery data has not been combined with application and transactional data available before default. Now it is being recognized that LGD and PD are correlated (Altman et al. 2005b) and that one needs to modify existing models to deal with these facts (Bennett et al. 2005). The difficulty with modelling LGD is data or rather the lack of it, especially with loan products where the default rates are historically low. The problem of dealing with low default portfolios (LDP) has been recognized by the setting up of working parties by several regulators. For PD estimates in such portfolios, one can do something by taking every possible default no matter how long ago or how far into the loan duration and using survival analysis ideas to recalibrate the results to the standard 12-month PD. For LGD estimates though one has no way out if there is no information which allows one to construct the true losses on the few default there have been. The one exception to this dearth of data is usually the mortgage portfolio where default usually results in repossession and subsequent resale and one can hope to build some realistic models by estimating what are the factors that affect that resale value. In unsecured consumer credit there is an impetus to model the collection processes more closely as a way of getting to grips with LGD estimation (Matuszyk et al. 2007).

Thus although the current scoring systems are essential for lenders to be able to use the Basel IRB approach on their consumer loan portfolio, the same Basel calculations have identified a number of different areas of consumer credit risk modelling which require further research.

5.5　Regulatory capital and optimal cut-off policies

Deciding which applicants to accept for a loan is one of the most important operating decisions a bank has to make. This was the problem first modelled in Section 1.4 using a decision tree and then looked at again in Section 1.7 in terms of the rates of return on the loan, and the loss if the loan defaults. In this section, we return to this problem and examine what impact the Basel Accord requirements for regulatory capital have on the decision.

Modelling the acceptance decision on an individual loan

Consider a loan of one unit (dollar, pound, or euro) by a bank to a borrower with credit score s, which translates into a probability of being a good of $p(s)$ (and so probability of defaulting PD of $1 - p(s)$). If the score is a log odds score, then as in Eq. (1.5.16) $p(s) = 1/1 + e^{-s}$. The rate charged by the bank on the loan is r_L and if the loan defaults, the LGD will be l_D. Initially, we assume that the funds loaned by the bank are in fact borrowed from the money markets and depositors at a rate $r_B, r_B < r_L$. In that case, the expected profit $E[P_A | p(s)]$ to the bank on this account loaned to a borrower with probability $p(s)$ of being good is

$$E[P_A | p(s)] = (1 + r_L)p(s) + (1 - l_D)(1 - p(s)) - (1 + r_B)$$
$$= r_L p(s) - l_D(1 - p(s)) - r_B. \tag{5.5.1}$$

The Basel Accord requires the bank to set aside regulatory capital to cover unexpected losses on this loan. The MCR per unit of loan with a default risk of $1 - p(s)$ is defined as $l_D K(p(s))$. We consider three different MCRs in this section:

- Basel 0: Describes the situation pre-1998 when there were no requirements so

$$K(p) = K_0 = 0. \tag{5.5.2}$$

- Basel 1: Describes the MCR between 1988 and 2007 under the first Basel Accord where

$$K(p) = \begin{cases} K_1 = 0.08/l_D \text{ (for most consumer loans)} \\ K_1^{mort} = 0.04/l_D \text{ (for residential mortgages).} \end{cases} \tag{5.5.3}$$

- Basel 2: Describes the MCR under the IRB approach of the second Basel Accord. As was defined in Eq. (5.3.15) this means that if the LGD is l_D, then the amount set aside is

$$l_D K_2(p) = l_D N \left(\left(\frac{1}{1-R} \right)^{1/2} N^{-1}(1-p) + \left(\frac{R}{1-R} \right)^{1/2} N^{-1}(0.999) \right)$$
$$- l_D(1-p)$$

where $R = 0.15$ (mortgages); $= 0.04$ (credit cards);

$$= 0.03 \left(\frac{1 - e^{-35(1-p)}}{1 - e^{-35}} \right) + 0.16 \left(1 - \frac{1 - e^{-35(1-p)}}{1 - e^{-35}} \right) \text{ (other retail)}$$

$$(5.5.4)$$

$N(\cdot)$ is the cumulative normal distribution and $N^{-1}(\cdot)$ is the inverse cumulative normal distribution.

We will assume that this regulatory capital has to be provided by equity capital. Note this is the only capital the equity holders have to provide to support this lending operation but we will also allow the possibility that some of the equity capital can be used to fund the lending. Assume that a percentage b of the loan is funded by borrowing and a percentage $1-b$ is funded by equity capital. Let r_Q be the required return on equity (ROE) capital. This means that the dividends to shareholders plus the increase in the bank's share price should be at least at this level. If it falls below such a level, equity holders will want to sell their shares and the bank will be unable to obtain further capital (or even maintain this capital) on the equity market. This means there is an extra cost to be added to Eq. (5.5.1), namely, the cost of regulatory capital $r_Q l_D K(p(s))$ while the borrowing cost now becomes $b r_B + (1-b)r_Q$. Hence the expected profit from a unit loan to a borrower whose probability of being good is $p(s)$ becomes

$$E[P_A | p(s)] = r_L p(s) - l_D(1 - p(s)) - r_Q l_D K(p(s)) - b r_B - (1-b)r_Q. \quad (5.5.5)$$

The decision of how much of the lending to finance by borrowing and how much by equity is clear from Eq. (5.5.5). If $r_B > r_Q$ fund it all by equity and so $b = 0$; if $r_B \le r_Q$ then fund it all by borrowing so $b = 1$. As $p(s)$ increases $K(p(s))$ decreases or is constant provided $p(s)$ is greater than 0.7 (see Fig. 5.3.4), and so under the three regimes considered (Basel 0, 1, and 2) $E[P_A | p(s)]$ increases as $p(s)$ increases. This leads to the definition of a cut-off probability $p(s_c)$ and cut-off score s_c, which is the score at which the expected profit in Eq. (5.5.5) is zero. The bank should accept all the loans with scores above s_c because they all have positive expected profit; the bank should reject all the loans with scores s_c or lower because these will all be unprofitable or have zero profit. The cut-off score s_c satisfies

$$r_L p(s_c) - l_D(1 - p(s_c)) - r_Q l_D K(p(s_c)) - b r_B - (1-b)r_Q = 0$$
$$\Rightarrow p(s_c) = \frac{b r_B + (1-b)r_Q + l_D + r_Q l_D K(p(s_c))}{r_L + l_D}$$

$$\Rightarrow o(s_c) = \frac{p(s_c)}{1 - p(s_c)} = \frac{(br_B + (1-b)r_Q) + l_D + r_Q l_D K(p(s_c))}{r_L - (br_B + (1-b)r_Q) - r_Q l_D K(p(s_c))}$$

$$> \frac{(br_B + (1-b)r_Q) + l_D}{r_L - (br_B + (1-b)r_Q)} > \frac{l_D}{r_L}.$$

(5.5.6)

The second line of Eq. (5.5.6) has $p(s_c)$ on both sides of the equation. As s increases, $K(p(s))$ decreases or is constant, which means the left-hand side (LHS) of the equation increases but the right-hand side (RHS) decreases. So there can only be one cut-off point s_c which satisfies this equation. Moreover since $K(p(s))$ is positive under the regulatory capital regimes, Basel 1 and Basel 2, one gets the first inequality in the last line of Eq. (5.5.6). This shows that under these regimes the cut-off odds and hence the cut-off score are higher than when the regime was not in operation. Moreover whichever way the banks funds the lending – through borrowing or through equity capital – the final inequality shows that accounting for the cost of funding the loans increases the cut-off score compared with ignoring the funding.

Example 5.5.1 Borrowing rate above equity rate

Consider an example where $r_L = 0.1, r_B = 0.05, l_D = 0.5$ so the bank lends at 10%, borrows at 5%, and for those who default 50% of the balance outstanding will eventually be lost. Initially we assume $r_Q = 0.04$ so the return required on equity has to be 4%. In that case it is clear the bank will use equity capital to fund the borrowing as well as covering the regulatory capital since it is a lower rate and so $b = 0$. We will assume the loan portfolio is of credit cards and so under the Basel 1 requirements the regulatory capital is $K(p) = K_1 = 0.08/l_D$ while the correlation in the Basel 2 requirement in Eq. (5.5.4) is $R = 0.04$. We can now apply the results in Eq. (5.5.6) under the three regulatory regimes.

Under Basel 0, Eq. (5.5.6) gives

$$p(s_c) = \frac{0.04 + 0.5}{0.1 + 0.5} = 0.9$$

$$\Rightarrow o(s_c) = \frac{0.9}{1 - 0.9} = 9 \Rightarrow s_c = \ln(o(s_c)) = 2.197.$$

(5.5.7)

Under Basel 1, we get from Eq. (5.5.6)

$$p(s_c) = \frac{0.04 + 0.5 + 0.04 \times 0.08}{0.1 + 0.5} = 0.9053$$

$$\Rightarrow o(s_c) = \frac{0.9053}{1 - 0.9053} = 9.56 \Rightarrow s_c = \ln(o(s_c)) = 2.258.$$

(5.5.8)

Under Basel 2, one has to solve the equation

$$p(s_c) = \frac{0.04 + 0.5 + 0.04 \times 0.5 \times K(p(s_c))}{0.1 + 0.5} = 0.904$$

$$\Rightarrow o(s_c) = \frac{0.904}{1 - 0.904} = 9.508 \Rightarrow s_c = \ln(o(s_c)) = 2.252.$$

(5.5.9)

The solution of Eq. (5.5.9) can be obtained using the Solver function in Excel. So in this situation the cut-off score for Basel 2 is between than for Basel 0 and Basel 1. It is the Basel 1 regulations that restrict the size of the portfolio most.

Example 5.5.2 Equity rate above borrowing rate

One can repeat these calculations with the same lending and borrowing rates and LGD values in the case when the equity rate is $r_Q = 0.075$, that is, investors expect their ROE to be 7.5%. As the borrowing rate is now below the equity rate, the funding for the lending should come from borrowing, $b = 1$, and the equity is only used to cover the regulatory requirements. In this case, the calculations in Eq. (5.5.6) give under the different regulatory regimes

For Basel 0,

$$p(s_c) = \frac{0.05 + 0.5}{0.1 + 0.5} = 0.9167$$

$$\Rightarrow o(s_c) = \frac{0.9167}{1 - 0.9167} = 11 \Rightarrow s_c = \ln(o(s_c)) = 2.398.$$

(5.5.10)

For Basel 1,

$$p(s_c) = \frac{0.05 + 0.5 + 0.075 \times 0.08}{0.1 + 0.5} = 0.9267$$

$$\Rightarrow o(s_c) = \frac{0.9267}{1 - 0.9267} = 12.63 \Rightarrow s_c = \ln(o(s_c)) = 2.537.$$

(5.5.11)

While for Basel 2,

$$p(s_c) = \frac{0.05 + 0.5 + 0.075 \times 0.5 \times K(p(s_c))}{0.1 + 0.5} = 0.925$$

$$\Rightarrow o(s_c) = \frac{0.925}{1 - 0.925} = 12.256 \Rightarrow s_c = \ln(o(s_c)) = 2.506.$$

(5.5.12)

As is expected in all three cases the extra cost of equity means that the cut-off scores are higher and less borrowers are accepted for credit cards. Again in this case the Basel 2 cut-off score is higher than the Basel 0 cut-off score but below the Basel 1 cut-off score.

Optimal cut-offs in portfolio level model with predetermined equity capital

The previous model looked at what cut-off rule to apply to the application score for an individual loan assuming a known required rate of ROE. A more realistic model of how lenders make these cut-off decisions is to consider the problem at the portfolio level not at the individual loan level and to recognize there is no known acceptable ROE. Instead assume that the bank decides in advance how much of its equity capital can be used to cover the requirements of a particular loan portfolio – say its residential mortgage portfolio. Initially we also assume that b the fraction of funds for the portfolio that is raised by borrowing from the market (at a rate of r_B) is fixed. This reduces the three decisions involved in setting up the lending portfolio – the amount of equity capital set aside, Q, the split b between the borrowed and equity funds used for lending, and the cut-off score s_c for the accept/reject decision – to just the last of these decisions.

The unconditional expected profit derived from a portfolio of loan assets is obtained from the conditional account profit by integrating over the risk profile of booked accounts, that is, those above the cut-off score, s_c. Let p_G, (p_B), $p_G + p_B = 1$ be the proportional of goods and bads (defaulters) in the application population. We define $F(s|G)$ ($F(s|B)$) to be the conditional probability of a good (bad) having a score of s or lower while $F(s) = F(s|G)p_G + F(s|B)p_B$ is the proportion of the whole applicant population who have score of s or lower. $dF(s)(= f(s)ds$ as we assume $F(s)$ is differentiable) denotes the fraction of accounts with risk score in the interval $(s, s+ ds]$ and the tail or complementary score distribution is denoted by $F^{(c)}(\cdot)$. Similarly one defines $f(s|G)$ and $f(s|B)$ to be the density functions of the score distributions of the goods and bads, respectively. The size of all the loans is the same and we define the monetary units so that 1 unit is the total amount lent if the bank accepted everyone who applied. Thus the total value of the loans in the actual portfolio lent is a fraction $F^c(s_c)$ between 0 and 1 if the cut-off score is s_c.

With these adjustments and ignoring the regulatory capital and the cost of funding some of the borrowing from equity, the profit from a loan with score s is modified from Eq. (5.5.5) to

$$E[\tilde{P}_A | p(s)] = r_L P(G|s) - l_D(P(B|s)) - br_B$$
$$= (r_L - br_B)P(G|s) - (l_D + r_B)(P(B|s)). \qquad (5.5.13)$$

The other extra cost at the portfolio level not considered at the individual level is that there is a fixed operating cost, C_F involved in running the lending operation (one might also think that part of the operating cost is proportional to the number of accounts in the portfolio but this can be subtracted from the lending rate r_L).

Thus, if we define $E[P_{\text{port}}(s)]$ to be the expected profit (revenue minus fixed and borrowing costs) from a portfolio with cut-off score s, we find

$$E[P_{\text{port}}(s)] \triangleq \int_{s}^{\infty} E[\tilde{P}_A | p(u)] dF(u) - C_F$$

$$= \int_{s}^{\infty} ((r_L - br_B)P(G|u) - (l_D + br_B)P(B|u)) \, f(u) du - C_F$$

$$= \int_{s}^{\infty} ((r_L - br_B)p_G f(u|G) - (l_D + br_B)p_B f(u|B)) \, du - C_F$$

$$= (r_L - br_B)p_G F^{(c)}(s|G) - (l_D + br_B)p_B F^{(c)}(s|B) - C_F \quad (5.5.14)$$

where from Bayes's theorem

$$P(G|u)f(u) = p_G f(u|G) = \Pr\{\text{borrower is good and score "is" } u\}$$

The regulatory capital set aside to cover such a portfolio where all loans of score at least s are accepted is $\Re(s)$ where

$$\Re(s) \triangleq l_D \int_{s}^{\infty} K(p(u)) dF(u) \quad (5.5.15)$$

The regulatory capital plus the equity capital used to finance the loans $(1 - b)F^c(s)$ cannot exceed the equity capital Q set aside for this portfolio. Thus in order to maximize the expected profit from the portfolio given the limit on the equity capital provided, one needs to solve the following constrained non-linear optimization problem.

$$\underset{s}{\text{Max}} \, E[P_{\text{port}}(s)] = \underset{s}{\text{Max}}[(r_L - br_B)p_G F^{(c)}(s|G) - (l_D + br_B)p_B F^{(c)}(s|B) - C_F]$$
$$(5.5.16)$$

subject to

$$\lambda \geq 0 : \Re(s) + (1 - b)F^{(c)}(s) \leq Q. \quad (5.5.17)$$

This is equivalent (Anderson et al. 2002) to solving the unconstrained problem in two variables – cut-off score s and 'price' of the constraint λ where the Lagrangian function that must be maximized is

$$L(s, \lambda) = E[P_{\text{port}}(s)] - \lambda(\Re(s) + (1 - b)F^c(s) - Q). \quad (5.5.18)$$

Finding a local maximum of $L(s, \lambda)$ is equivalent to differentiating (5.5.18) with respect to λ and s. Differentiating with respect to λ gives either $\lambda = 0$, which means $L(s, \lambda) = E[P_{\text{port}}(s)]$ and one finds the unconstrained maximum, or that $\Re(s) + (1 - b)F^{(c)}(s) = Q$ and the constraint is tightly satisfied. In that case, differentiating $L(s, \lambda)$ with respect to s will find the maximum of $E[P_{\text{port}}(s)]$ on this tight constraint, while λ gives the increase in the expected portfolio profit if the equity capital is increased by 1. Differentiating Eq. (5.5.18) with respect to s gives a necessary condition for optimality of the maximization in (5.5.17), namely that the optimal cut-off s_c and the optimal shadow price λ^* satisfy

$$\frac{\partial L(s, \lambda)}{\partial s} = -(r_L - br_B)p_G f(s\,|\,G) + (l_D + br_B)p_B f(s\,|\,B)$$

$$+ (1 - b)\lambda^* f(s) + \lambda^* l_D K(p(s))f(s) = 0$$

$$\Rightarrow o(s_c) = \frac{P(G|s_c)}{P(B|s_c)} = \frac{(l_D + br_B + (1 - b)\lambda^*) + \lambda^* l_D K(p(s_c))f(s_c)}{(r_L - br_B - (1 - b)\lambda^*) - \lambda^* l_D K(p(s_c))f(s_c)} \quad (5.5.19)$$

$$\geq \frac{(l_D + br_B + (1 - b)\lambda^*)}{(r_L - br_B - (1 - b)\lambda^*)} \quad \lambda^* \geq 0.$$

Both sides of Eq. (5.5.19) depend on the optimal cut-off score so it is not always possible to obtain a closed form solution. However the solution is always unique since $o(s) = P(G|s)/P(B|s)$ is increasing in s and so the LHS of Eq. (5.5.19) increases in s, while, since $K(p(s))$ is decreasing (or constant) in s, the RHS of Eq. (5.5.19) is decreasing or constant in s. Hence there can only be one value at which the two expressions are equal. Moreover, the cut-off score is always greater or equal to that under the Basel 0 conditions when there is no regulatory capital as the final inequality shows.

There are two different types of situations that arise in the solution of Eq. (5.5.19). In case (i), the equity capital constraint is a strict inequality and so the shadow price λ^* is zero. This is the unconstrained or Basel 0 solution where the cut-off s_c^0 is

$$o^0 = o(s_c^0) = \frac{p_G f(s_c^0|G)}{p_B f(s_c^0|B)} = \frac{l_D + br_B}{r_L - br_B} \Rightarrow s_c^0 = \ln\left(\frac{l_D + br_B}{r_L - br_B}\right). \quad (5.5.20)$$

In that case the expected portfolio profit is

$$E[P_{port}(s_c^0)] = (r_L - br_B)p_G F^{(c)}(s_c^0|G) - (l_D + br_B)p_B F^{(c)}(s_c^0|B) - C_F. \quad (5.5.21)$$

In case (ii) there is insufficient equity capital to meet the regulatory requirements and set aside the required fraction to fund the lending. Thus, there is a value λ^* for each extra unit of equity capital made available for the portfolio, and the equity capital constraint is tight. Thus the optimal cut-off is now given by this tight constraint namely

$$\Re(s_c) + (1 - b)F^{(c)}(s_c) = \int_{s_c}^{\infty} l_D K(p(s))f(s)ds + (1 - b)F^{(c)}(s_c) = Q. \quad (5.5.22)$$

Note that the borrowing and lending rate do not come into calculating the optimal cut-off odds in this case. Moreover the shadow price for one extra unit of equity capital is given by rearranging Eq. (5.5.19) to get

$$\lambda^* \left(1 - b + l_\mathrm{D}K(p(s_\mathrm{c}))\right) f(s_\mathrm{c}) = (r_\mathrm{L} - br_\mathrm{B})p_\mathrm{G}f(s_\mathrm{c}|G) - (l_\mathrm{D} + r_\mathrm{B})p_\mathrm{B}f(s_\mathrm{c}|B)$$

$$\Rightarrow \lambda^* = \frac{(r_\mathrm{L} - br_\mathrm{B})P(G|s_\mathrm{c})f(s_\mathrm{c}) - (l_\mathrm{D} + r_\mathrm{B})P(B|s_\mathrm{c})f(s_\mathrm{c})}{\left(1 - b + l_\mathrm{D}K(p(s_\mathrm{c}))\right) f(s_\mathrm{c})}$$

$$= \frac{E[\tilde{P}_\mathrm{A}|p(s_\mathrm{c})]}{1 - b + l_\mathrm{D}K(p(s_\mathrm{c}))} \geq 0. \tag{5.5.23}$$

where we use the definition of the profit of an account in Eq. (5.5.13). So the numerator is the expected profit of the next acquisition if the cut-off is extended from s_c, while the denominator is the additional equity needed, both in funding and regulatory capital required to acquire that account. So the optimal price of equity is the marginal ROE – the ratio of the marginal expected profit to the marginal increase in equity at the optimal cut-off. Thus unlike the earlier part of this section there is no market price of equity, it comes from the marginal ROE at the optimal cut-off. Putting the two cases together, we can write the optimal solution to this cut-off problem as follows:

$$\lambda^* = \begin{cases} 0 & \text{with } s_\mathrm{c} = \ln \dfrac{l_\mathrm{D} + br_\mathrm{B}}{r_\mathrm{L} - br_\mathrm{B}} : \text{sufficient equity} \\[2em] \dfrac{E[\tilde{P}_\mathrm{A}|p(s_\mathrm{c})]}{1 - b + l_\mathrm{D}K(p(s_\mathrm{c}))} & \text{with } s_\mathrm{c} \text{ solution of } \Re(s_\mathrm{c}) + (1 - b) F^{(\mathrm{c})}(s_\mathrm{c}) \\[1em] & \qquad = Q : \text{insufficient equity}. \end{cases}$$

$$\tag{5.5.24}$$

Since λ^* is the marginal profit increase for an extra unit of equity, it will help the bank decide whether or not to expand the retail credit portfolio in preference to other investments by comparing its value with the market price of equity.

In this model we have assumed the equity available and the fraction of funds borrowed are fixed and from that found the cut-off that gives the optimal expected profit from the portfolio. In fact because the equity is fixed this cut-off also gives the optimal ROE because ROE equals profit divided by a fixed Q.

If we allow the borrowing fraction to vary, it is fairly obvious what is the optimal fraction. It cannot ever be optimal to have unused equity capital; so when the equity available exceeds the required regulatory capital, one can increase the profit and the ROE by decreasing b, the fraction of borrowed funds until all the equity is used up. So the obvious strategy is to start with $b = 1$, all the lending funded by borrowed capital. If in this case the cut-off $s_\mathrm{c}^0 = \ln(l_\mathrm{D} + r_\mathrm{B}/r_\mathrm{L} - r_\mathrm{B})$ is such that there is sufficient equity ($\mathfrak{R}(s_c^0) < Q$), then we can start to decrease b by using some of the equity to fund the lending. From Eq. (5.5.24) this will drop the optimal cut-off score and so require more regulatory capital. Thus the spare equity capital is being used up both to increase the amount of the lending funded by equity and to cover the increase in regulatory requirements. Eventually one will reach a borrowing level b where the equity constraint is tight for that particular b. That is the optimal decision on how much of the lending to cover from the equity. It is possible of course that so much equity is provided that even with all the lending being funded by equity ($b = 0$), there is still spare equity at the optimal cut-off, s_c^0 when $b = 0$. This corresponds to the condition that $\mathfrak{R}(s_c^0) + F^c(s_c^0) < Q$. The third possibility is that even in the case $b = 1$ where all the lending is funded by borrowing there is insufficient equity available with an optimal cut-off $s_c^1 = \ln(l_D/r_L)$ to cover the regulatory capital (that is $\mathfrak{R}(s_c^1) > Q$). Then one has to fund all the lending by borrowing and the optimal cut-off is given by

$$\mathfrak{R}(s_c) = Q$$

Optimal cut-offs in portfolio level model with variable levels of equity capital

So far it has been assumed that the equity ascribed to the loan portfolio has been predetermined. Consider now what happens if one can also change the amount of equity available as well as the cut-off score. To simplify matters a little we start by considering the extreme case when all funds that source loans are borrowed, $b = 1$ but we still assume that the fixed cost C_F is positive. Figure 5.5.1 describes what happens to the expected profit as the equity capital set aside for a portfolio is

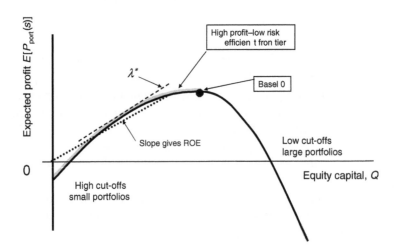

FIG. 5.5.1. Expected portfolio profit versus equity capital.

increased from zero. Using Eqs. (5.5.16) and (5.5.17) this graph plots

$$E[P_{\text{port}}(s_c)] = (r_L - r_B)p_G F^{(c)}(s_c|G) - (l_D + r_B)p_B F^{(c)}(s_c|B) - C_F$$

where $\Re(s_c) = l_D \int_{s_c}^{\infty} K(p(u))dF(u) = Q$

as a function of Q. When equity capital is small the optimal cut-off is high and the portfolio size is so small that its profit does not cover the fixed operating cost, and so the expected profit is negative. As equity capital increases, so does the portfolio size and even though the cut-off score drops with an increase in the number of defaulters this is more than compensated for by the increase in the goods. Hence the expected portfolio profit increases. Eventually though the cut-off score will be so low that the expected losses on the bad borrowers accepted at the cut-off score is greater than the expected profit from the goods accepted at that score. At this point the expected portfolio profit will start to drop. This is the cut-off score under the Basel 0 regulation, namely $s_c^0 = \ln(l_D + r_B/r_L - r_B)$. One should not increase the equity capital beyond this point but if the bank were to do so and continue to drop the cut-off score, the expected profit would eventually become negative.

In Fig. 5.5.1, the tangent to the slope of the curve which is given by a dashed line shows the marginal ROE (which is the value of the shadow price λ given in Eq. (5.5.24)). This keeps decreasing as the amount of equity increases and becomes negative once one reaches the Basel 0 solution.

The actual ROE is the slope of the line joining each point on the line to the origin (since ROE is expected profit divided by equity capital), which is the dotted line in Fig. 5.5.1. In Fig. 5.5.2 we plot what happens to the ROE as equity capital increases. Initially it is negative but rapidly increases and reaches a maximum when the ROE slope line in Fig. 5.5.1 is a tangent to the curve. This will occur before the expected profit is maximized. Thereafter the ROE will gradually drop as equity capital is increased. The dotted line in Fig. 5.5.2 shows the marginal ROE, which is always decreasing as equity increases and equals the ROE when the latter is at its maximum. The marginal ROE remains below ROE and is zero at the Basel solution when the expected portfolio profit is maximized.

In the case when $b \neq 1$ one gets similar results to the case above, except that the axes are stretched in both directions. Thus along the equity capital axes one would be plotting $\Re(s) + (1 - b)F^c(s)$ rather than just $\Re(s)$. Along the expected profit axes, the profit would be increased by an amount $r_B(1 - b)F^c(s)$ since there is saving on the cost of funds. However, this makes very little difference to the shape of the curves and the relationship between them.

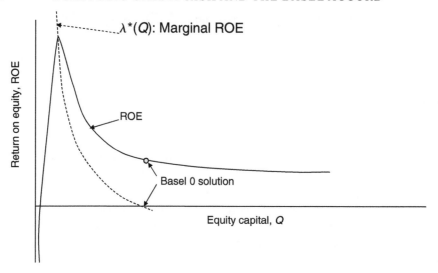

FIG. 5.5.2. Return on equity as a function of equity capital.

Impact of Basel regulations on ROC curve

In Section 2.3 we described how business measures can be identified from the ROC curve – the graph of the cumulative distribution of bads below a given score ($F(s|B)$) against the cumulative distribution of goods below that score ($F(s|G)$). Expected profit is such that the lines of constant profit are straight lines with slope given by

$$\frac{F(s_c|B)}{F(s_c|G)} = \frac{p_G(r_L - br_B)}{p_B(l_D + br_B)} \qquad (5.5.25)$$

This is a modification of the result in Eq. (2.3.14) since now we are including the cost of borrowing. In this unconstrained or Basel 0 situation as far as equity capital is concerned, the optimal cut-off is obtained when a line with this slope is tangent to the ROC curve because that is the furthest to the top left – the direction of maximum profit – that this curve goes. The tangent to the ROC curve at the point with cut-off score s is $f(s|B)/f(s|G)$ and so the maximum profit is the point on the ROC curve where

$$\frac{f(s|B)}{f(s|G)} = \eta_0 = \frac{p_G(r_L - br_B)}{p_B(l_D + br_B)}. \qquad (5.5.26)$$

With the Basel 1 regulations then one can rewrite Eq. (5.5.19) so that the slope of the line of constant profit is

$$
\eta_1 = \frac{F(s|\text{B})}{F(s|\text{G})} = \frac{p_\text{G}P(\text{G}|s)}{p_\text{B}P(\text{B}|s)}
$$
$$
= \frac{p_\text{G}}{p_\text{B}} \frac{(r_\text{L} - br_\text{B} - (1-b)\lambda^*) - 0.08\lambda^*}{(f_\text{D} + br_\text{B} + (1-b)\lambda^*) + 0.08\lambda^*} \le \eta_0 \quad \lambda^* \ge 0. \tag{5.5.27}
$$

In this case, the slope $\eta_1 \le \eta_0$ and since the optimal point under this regulation is when the tangent to the curve $f(s|\text{B})/f(s|\text{G})$ equals η_1 this point will be at the same point as the Basel 0 one if $\lambda^* = 0$ or further to the right if the regulatory capital constraint is tight. This corresponds to a higher cut-off and so a lower size of portfolio. In this case, when the regulatory capital constraint is tight, the optimal cut-off is determined by Eq. (5.5.22), namely,

$$
s_\text{c}^1 = F^{-1}\left(1 - \frac{Q}{1 - b + 0.08}\right). \tag{5.5.28}
$$

This is shown in Fig. 5.5.3 where the Basel 1 cut-off point is further up the ROC curve than the Basel 0 one.

Under the Basel 2 regulations the optimal cut-off s_c^2 is such that the tangent at that point has the same slope as the constant profit line:

$$
\eta_2 = \frac{p_\text{G}}{p_\text{B}} \frac{(r_\text{L} - br_\text{B} - (1-b)\lambda^*) - \lambda^* l_\text{D} K(p(s_\text{c}^2))}{(f_\text{D} + br_\text{B} + (1-b)\lambda^*) + \lambda^* l_\text{D} K(p(s_\text{c}^2))} \le \eta_0 \quad \lambda^* \ge 0. \tag{5.5.29}
$$

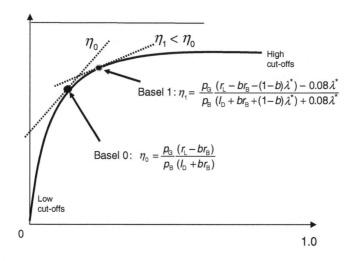

FIG. 5.5.3. The effect of regulatory capital requirements on the ROC operating point.

Since this slope is lower or the same as that under the Basel 0 regulations the corresponding optimal cut-off point will be either the same as the Basel 0 one (if the regulatory conditions are not tight) or further up the ROC curve. Such points correspond to higher cut-offs and lower portfolio sizes. There is though no obvious relationship between the Basel 1 and Basel 2 cut-off points as $\eta_1 < \eta_2$ only if $l_D K(p(s_c^2)) < 0.08$. This may or may not be the case depending a lot on the value of l_D. We illustrate these results by a number of examples.

Comparison of Basel 0, Basel 1, and Basel 2

We conclude the section by calculating the optimal cut-offs in this portfolio level analysis under the different Basel conditions.

Example 5.5.3 Optimal cut-off on portfolio level model with fixed equity capital

In these final examples we take the same lending and borrowing rates and the LGD as in Example 5.5.1, namely, $r_B = 0.05, r_L = 0.1, l_D = 0.5$. However, we assume all the loans are funded through borrowing $b = 1$ and that we have a personal loan portfolio. For such a portfolio, the Basel 1 requirement remains as in Example 5.5.1 at $K(p) = K_1 = 0.08/l_D$ and though the Basel 2 regulatory capital requirement remains as in Eq. (5.5.4), we use the 'other' retail correlation of

$$\rho = 0.03 \left(\frac{1 - e^{-35(1-p)}}{1 - e^{-35}} \right) + 0.16 \left(1 - \frac{1 - e^{-35(1-p)}}{1 - e^{-35}} \right).$$

To undertake the calculations at portfolio level, we have to describe the marginal and full density functions of the score distributions. It is easier to describe the equivalent density functions of the probability of being a good $- f(p|G), f(p|B), f(p) -$ and then use the standard log odds score transformation $s = \ln(p/1 - p)$ to get the equivalent score distributions. One family of distributions that has the appropriate properties is the Beta distributions, which are described by two parameters m and n. Let the density function of the probability of being a good in the whole population be $B(m,n)$ which is denoted by $f_{n,m}(p)$ where

$$f_{n,m}(p) \propto p^{m-1}(1-p)^{n-1} \left[= \frac{(m+n-1)! p^{m-1}(1-p)^{n-1}}{(m-1)!(n-1)!} \right]$$

$$\Rightarrow \tilde{f}_{n,m}(s) \propto ((1+e^{-s})^{-1})^{m-1}(1 - (1+e^{-s})^{-1})^{n-1}. \qquad (5.5.30)$$

It is easy then to show that the density function of the scores among the goods and the bads are equivalent to the density functions over the probabilities of being a good being given by Beta distributions with parameters $(n+1, m)$ and $(n, m+1)$, respectively, since

$$\Pr\{\text{score is "}p\text{"}|G\} \propto p \times f_{n,m}(p) \propto p^m (1-p)^{n-1}$$
$$\Pr\{\text{score is "}p\text{"}|B\} \propto (1-p) \times f_{n,m}(p) \propto p^m (1-p)^n. \tag{5.5.31}$$

Take $m = 17$ and $n = 3$ which gives the expected probability of being good in the full population, $p_G = 0.85$, which would correspond to a default rate of 15% if every applicant was taken.

Assume that the bank sets aside equity of $Q = 0.01$ for this portfolio and that the fixed cost for running the portfolio is $C_F = 0.001$ (recall that the unit of money is the total amount that would be lent if every applicant was accepted).

Basel 0: When there were no regulatory requirements and so $K(p) = K_0 = 0$, one had the situation in Eq. (5.5.20) where

$$o_c^0 = \frac{l_D + r_B}{r_L - r_B} = \frac{0.5 + 0.05}{0.1 - 0.05} = 11 \Rightarrow s_c^0 = \ln o_c^0 = 2.398$$

$$p(G|s_c^0) = p^0 = \frac{o_c^0}{1 + o_c^0} = 0.917; \quad p(B|s_c^0) = 1 - p^0 = 0.083$$

$$E[V(s_c^0)] = F^{(c)}(p(s_c^0)) = 1 - F_{\text{Beta}(17,3)}(0.917) = 0.207$$

$$E[P_{\text{port}}(s_c^0)] = (r_L - r_B)p_G F^{(c)}(s_c^0|G) - (l_D + r_B)p_B F^{(c)}(s_c^0|B) - C_F$$

$$= 0.05 \times 0.85 \times F_{\text{Beta}(18,3)}^c(0.917) - 0.55 \times 0.15 \times F_{\text{Beta}(17,4)}^c$$

$$(0.917) - 0.001 = 0.002203$$

$$\text{ROE} = \frac{0.002203}{0.01} = 0.220. \tag{5.5.32}$$

where $E[V(s_c^0)]$ is the volume of accounts accepted. So approximately 20% of the total original application population were accepted at the optimal cut-off. The expected portfolio profits and the size of the portfolio do not depend on regulatory capital and are independent of Q but ROE decreases inversely with Q.

Basel 1: The regulatory capital for other loans under the Basel 1 regime was a constant $l_D K_1 = 0.08$ independent of the probability of the score of the accounts. It was noted that the optimal cut-off odds are either higher than the Basel 0 case because there is insufficient regulatory capital or is equal to the Basel 0 case when there is ample capital. This latter situation would occur when the capital is at least $Q_1 = 0.08 \times F^c(s_c^0) = 0.08(0.207) = 0.0166$. Substituting the relevant values into Eq. (5.5.24) and the three previous equations gives for any given amount of equity capital Q, the optimal cut-off and the shadow price of equity as follows:

$$s_1^* = \ln o_1^* = \ln \frac{(l_D + r_B) + l_D K_1 \lambda_1^*}{(r_L - r_B) - l_D K_1 \lambda_1^*} = \ln \frac{0.55 + 0.08\lambda^*}{0.05 - 0.08\lambda^*}$$

$$\lambda_1^* = \frac{E[P_E|s_c^1]}{l_D K_1} > 0 \Rightarrow Q = K(s_c^1) = 0.08 F^{(c)}(s_c^1) \text{ or } s_c^1$$

$$= F^{-1}(1 - 12.5Q). \tag{5.5.33}$$

If $Q = 0.01$ there is insufficient equity for the Basel 0 (profit maximizing) solution to hold and so the optimal cut-off is determined by the Basel 1 capital requirements. So the optimal cut-off is larger than that which maximized the expected profit with no regulatory requirement (Basel 0). The solution in this case is given by

$$Q = 0.01 = 0.08 F^{(c)}\left(p\left(s_c^1\right)\right) \Rightarrow F_{\text{Beta}(17,3)}\left(p\left(s_c^1\right)\right) = 1 - \frac{0.01}{0.08}$$

$$\Rightarrow p(s_c^1) = 0.934$$

$$o_c^1 = 0.934/0.056 = 14.23 \Rightarrow s_c^1 = \ln\left(o_c^1\right) = 2.656$$

$$\lambda_1^* = \frac{E\left[\tilde{P}_A|p\left(s_c^1\right)\right]}{l_D K\left(p\left(s_c^1\right)\right)} = \frac{0.05p\left(s_c^1\right) - 0.55\left(1 - p\left(s_c^1\right)\right)}{0.08}$$

$$= \frac{0.01061}{0.08} = 0.1327$$

$$E\left[V\left(s_c^1\right)\right] = F^{(c)}(p(s_c^1)) = \frac{K_1}{Q} = 0.125$$

$$E\left[P_{\text{port}}\left(s_c^1\right)\right] = (r_L - r_B)p_G F^{(c)}\left(s_c^1|G\right) - (l_D + r_B)p_B F^{(c)}\left(s_c^1|B\right) - C_F$$

$$= 0.05 \times 0.85 \times F^c_{\text{Beta}(18,3)}(0.934) - 0.55 \times 0.15$$

$$\times F^c_{\text{Beta}(17,4)}(0.934) - 0.001 = 0.001778$$

$$\text{ROE} = \frac{E\left[P_{\text{port}}\left(s_c^1\right)\right]}{Q} = \frac{0.001778}{0.01} = 0.1778. \tag{5.5.34}$$

So, as one would expect, compared with the Basel 0 situation, the cut-off score is higher, the size of the portfolio is lower, the expected profit and the ROE are lower.

Basel 2: Under the Basel 2 regulations for 'other retail' the regulatory capital is given in Eq. (5.5.4). Applying this in Eqs. (5.5.19) and (5.5.24) gives

$$o_2^* = \frac{(l_D + r_B) + \lambda_2^* l_D K\left(p\left(s_c^2\right)\right)}{(r_L - r_B) - \lambda_2^* l_D K\left(p\left(s_c^2\right)\right)} = \frac{0.55 + \lambda_2^* l_D K\left(p\left(s_c^2\right)\right)}{0.05 - \lambda_2^* l_D K\left(p\left(s_c^2\right)\right)}$$

$$\lambda_2^* = \frac{E\left[\tilde{P}_A|s_c^2\right]}{l_D K\left(p\left(s_c^2\right)\right)} > 0 \Rightarrow Q = \Re\left(p\left(s_c^2\right)\right) = l_D \int_{s_c^2}^{\infty} K(p(s))dF(s).$$

$$\tag{5.5.35}$$

With a capital restriction of $Q = 0.01$, the optimal score cut-off for Basel 2 is lower than that for Basel 1 because the Basel 2 capital requirement is lower than that of Basel 1. In the Basel 2 case the equity level at which we can meet the unconstrained Basel 0 requirements is $Q_2 = \Re(s_c^0) = \Re(2.398) = 0.012$. So if we only have $Q = 0.01$ then we are in constrained situation. The cut-offs, shadow prices, and ROE in this case are given by

$$Q = 0.01 = \Re\left(p\left(s_c^2\right)\right) = \int_{p(s_c^2)}^{1} l_D K(p) f_{\text{Beta}(17,3)}(p) dp; \; p\left(s_c^2\right) = 0.924$$

$$o_c^2 = 0.924/0.924 0.066 0.066 = 12.158 \Rightarrow s_c^2 = \ln\left(o_c^2\right) = 2.498$$

$$\lambda_2^* = \frac{E\left[\tilde{P}_A | p\left(s_c^2\right)\right]}{l_D K\left(p\left(s_c^2\right)\right)} = \frac{0.05 p\left(s_c^2\right) - 0.55\left(1 - p\left(s_c^2\right)\right)}{0.5 \times (0.128)}$$

$$= \frac{0.0044}{0.064} = 0.0687$$

$$E\left[V\left(s_c^2\right)\right] = F^{(c)}\left(p\left(s_c^2\right)\right) = 1 - F_{\text{Beta}(17,3)}(0.924) = 0.172$$

$$E\left[P_{\text{port}}\left(s_c^2\right)\right] = (r_L - r_B) p_G F^{(c)}\left(s_c^2 | G\right) - (l_D + r_B) p_B F^{(c)}\left(s_c^2 | B\right) - C_F$$

$$= 0.05 \times 0.85 \times F_{\text{Beta}(18,3)}^c(0.924) - 0.55$$

$$\times 0.15 \times F_{\text{Beta}(17,4)}^c(0.924) - 0.001 = 0.002125$$

$$\text{ROE} = \frac{E\left[P_{\text{port}}(s_c^2)\right]}{Q} = \frac{0.002125}{0.01} = 0.2125 \tag{5.5.36}$$

The hardest part of this calculation is estimating $p(s_c^2)$ since this involves finding the lower value of an integral of the product of the Basel regulatory function and the density function of the Beta distribution. This was done by numerical approximation. The rest of the calculations then follow as in the Basel 0 and Basel 1 calculations. Because the cut-off lies between the Basel 0 and Basel 1 solutions, the ROE, expected portfolio size, and shadow price for new equity capital also lie between their respective Basel 0 and Basel 1 values.

Example 5.5.4 In which Basel 2 leads to more restrictive conditions than Basel 1

Since the Basel 2 regulatory capital requirements depend on the LGD whereas the Basel 1 requirements did not, it is not surprising that they will lead to a more conservative portfolio than Basel 1 when the LGD is large. To illustrate such a case we examine the solutions when $r_L = 0.15, l_D = 0.75, Q = 0.02$. Much of the

TABLE 5.5.1. Optimal solutions with $r_L = 0.15$, $l_D = 0.75$, $Q = 0.02$.

$r_L = 0.15$, $r_B = 0.15$, $l_D = 0.75$, $Q = 0.02$	Basel 0	Basel 1	Basel 2
Score cut-off, s^*	2.079	2.290	2.364
Probability of good $p(s^*)$	0.889	0.908	0.914
Shadow price, λ^*	N/A	0.170	0.235
$E[V(s^*)]$	0.375	0.252	0.220
ROE	0.585	0.545	0.515

analysis of this section follows the paper by Oliver and Thomas (2005) and this example is given in that paper. The results are summarized in Table 5.5.1. In this and the other examples it is assumed that equity is only used to cover the regulatory capital. In reality, banks often have equity capital which exceeds that needed to cover the Basel 2 regulatory requirements and so the returns on equity given in these examples may appear to be unrealistically large.

These models show that the introduction of regulatory capital both in Basel 1 and Basel 2 means that the cut-off scores which maximize the expected profit over the portfolio of loans accepted need to increase with a consequent drop in the expected profits, portfolio size, and ROE. The expected profit on a portfolio is maximized at the 'Basel 0' cut-off score. Depending on the parameters, particularly the LGD in the portfolio, the Basel 2 cut-off which maximizes expected profit can be higher or lower than the Basel 1 maximal profit cut-off. If there is not enough equity available to provide regulatory capital to cover the 'Basel 0' profit maximizing portfolio, there is a shadow price one is willing to pay for extra equity. This price is derived from the needs of the portfolio itself and can be different from the market price, which the market is willing to pay for taking on such risks. With sufficient regulatory capital the expected profits and ROE will yield the Basel 0 case. If extra equity is available this can be used to start funding part of the capital that is being lent out.

Assuming there are fixed costs in running a loan portfolio, at low levels of equity capital, ROE will be smaller than the high shadow price of new equity and the two objectives of increasing ROE and portfolio size are aligned. It is sensible to acquire extra equity capital to meet the regulatory requirements of the consumer credit portfolio. Eventually the level of equity capital is such that the shadow price of additional equity equals the current ROE. Adding further equity to the portfolio means both the optimal shadow price and ROE decrease. So at this point increasing the portfolio size will decrease ROE even though it continues to increase expected profits until the unconstrained optimal Basel 0 portfolio is reached.

5.6   Modelling credit risk for portfolios of consumer and corporate loans

The formulae used to determine the minimum regulatory capital requirement in the Basel Accord are derived from a structural model of the credit risk of portfolios of corporate loans, first formulated by Merton (1974). As this formula is then used in the case of consumer loans, one needs to confirm the appropriateness of these corporate models in consumer lending.

There are a number of differences between consumer and corporate lending. The market in corporate bonds is well established with the bonds in a company often being bought and sold many times during their duration. In the bond market the originating firm has little control over changes in the repayment structure initially agreed upon apart from occasional well-defined dates on which some bonds can be bought back or converted into stock shares.

With consumer loans, on the other hand, there is no market mechanism for continuously trading in such loans and hence no continuously available market price to value the return on an individual loan. There has been considerable growth though in the securitization of consumer loan portfolios, which converts them into tradable assets. Tranches of this securitized portfolio are then sold in the market. What tends to happen though is that the company initiating the securitization adds risk protection mechanisms to the loans so that the rating agencies will ascribe a particular rating grade to that tranche. The subsequent price of the tranche of loans in the market is then driven by the market price of equivalently rated bonds in the bond market. Thus the ratings agencies have tended to take a top down approach by subjectively identifying the properties of the portfolio when setting the price. In doing this, one loses the bottom-up information of the credit risk attrition risk and repayment rules of the various loans. As the credit crunch of 2008 has shown, this top-down approach has led to considerable mis-pricing of the risks involved, leading to a freezing of the whole credit market – not just in asset-backed securities but also in other loan products. Those buying the securitized product did not know or did not recognize that in some case there would be a fourfold increase in the interest rate charged 1 year into the loan and that this might affect the credit risk (see the models developed in Section 3.3). This is one of the fundamental errors caused by top down pricing. The important point for us though is that the price charged in such securitization did not feedback in any meaningful way to give a price for the individual loans which make up the portfolio and so there was no mechanism of continuously pricing the underlying consumer loans.

Consumer and corporate lending and the way they are modelled differ in two other aspects as well. Firstly in the consumer market the individual consumers who make up the portfolio can decide at any time to cease using that lending product with consequent changes to the value and composition of the portfolio. For mortgages, there is prepayment where consumers pay-off the mortgages and move to another lender; for credit cards consumers can just stop using their card for purchases, as well as attrition where they cancel the card and move to another lender. Secondly, the structural models of corporate credit risk, developed from Merton's model, assume that a firm will default when its debts exceed some proportion of its assets. For consumers on the other hand, default on a loan is much more related to cash flow and income being insufficient to service the loan since few consumers can calculate, let alone realize, their assets. The correlations between defaults of bonds of different companies are assumed to be related to the correlations in their asset movements and it is assumed that the correlations in the share prices of the companies reflect the correlations in the asset movements. There is however no consumer equivalent of a share price measuring a consumer's assets. So are these corporate models appropriate for the credit risk of consumer loans and if not what models would be?

Variants of corporate credit risk models

There are a number of well-established corporate credit risk models widely used by financial organizations, but no such established consumer credit risk models for consumer loans. Hence it may be easier to get a modified or reinterpreted corporate credit risk model accepted by the industry than to develop completely new consumer loan credit models. If it is necessary, it needs to be done in time for Basel 3. We first review the approaches to credit risk modelling for corporate loan portfolios before examining whether any of these can be used in the consumer loan case.

Corporate bonds are the way lending to large companies is structured and losses occur with these (a) because the company defaults; (b) because the rating of the loan is lowered by rating agencies, like Standard and Power or Moodys, and hence the loan is worth less in the market because of the increased risk of default; (c) the difference between the value of bonds of a given rating and the value of the highest rated bond – the credit spread – increases. This last problem affects the whole bond market and so is considered to be a market risk rather than a credit risk. The first split in models is between those which only try to estimate the chance of default, called default mode (DM) models, and those which try to estimate both the chance of default and of ratings changed, called mark-to-market (MTM) models. The second split is between structural models which relate the value of a bond and its default probability to the capital and debt structure of the firm, and the reduced form models, which model the default process and/or the rating change process directly using historical estimates. Lastly there is split between static models which can only model the credit over a fixed time interval and dynamic models which allow one to model over any time interval.

The Merton (1974) model provides the foundation for structural models with its assumption that a firm defaults when at the maturity of the loan to the firm, the debts of the firm exceed its assets. Thus when a bank lends to a firm it is equivalent to writing a put option on the assets of the firm. A put option is when one buys the right to sell an item, usually a share, at some fixed price in the future. The writer of a put option sells the buyer of the option that right (that is guarantees to buy the item at the agreed price if the other party wants to sell). In this case it is as if the bank sets a price on the firm by the amount of money it lends it and at the maturity of the loan, the firm's shareholders and management have to decide whether to 'sell' the firm to the bank by defaulting on the loan, or not to sell the firm by paying back the loan. Thus the Merton model used the Black–Scholes approach to pricing the value of options to price the value of such loans or bonds. In it the value of the firm's assets were assumed to follow a random process, often a geometric Brownian random walk with a drift. In continuous time, this would mean the assets A_t and returns R_t satisfy the equation

$$R_t = d \log(A_t) = \frac{dA_t}{A_t} = \mu_t + cdw_t \qquad (5.6.1)$$

where w_t is a Brownian random walk. Later models allowed variations of the original model the most important being the first passage model (Black and Cox 1976) where the first crossing of the debt threshold signifies default even if the bond has not yet matured. Other extensions sought to allow jumps in the movements of the asset values, or to assume the asset value of the firm or the debt threshold are unknown variables until default. The Longstaff–Schwartz model (Longstaff and Schwartz 1995) includes interest rate risk as well as default risk into the pricing of the loans or bonds. Vasicek (1987) extended Merton's model to allow for a common risk factor, X_t, as in Eq. (5.6.2) which can be thought of as the state of the economy. This became the basis of the Basel formula and reduced in the discrete time one period case to the model in Eq. (5.3.5):

$$R_t = d \log(A_t) = \frac{dA_t}{A_t} = \mu_t + bX_t + cdw_t. \qquad (5.6.2)$$

The reduced form approach developed from the idea of Pye (1974) that one could use an actuarial approach and model the default rate of a group of bonds over time in a similar way to mortality tables for humans' lifetime. There are obvious connections between mortality models and the survival analysis approach to credit scoring discussed in Section 4.5, but Pye's approach also has strong similarities with the basic consumer credit models of Chapter 1.

Example 5.6.1 Simplified version of Pye approach

Suppose one has a group of bonds with a constant PD of $1 - p$ each year, and l_D is the LGD on the face value of the bond. If there is no default the bond holders receive in dividends and increase in bond value a return r_L, which is the risk-free borrowing rate r_F plus a default premium of r_P. If one were indifferent between lending 1 unit in this way or putting it into a risk-free investment and get $1 + r_F$ at the end of the period, this gives a way of calculating what the risk premium should be by saying there is no arbitrage opportunity in the market. If there was no default then the return is $1 + r_L$ and if there is default one gets $1 - l_D$. Hence for a risk-neutral lender indifference occurs when

$$1 + r_F = (1 + r_L)p + (1 - l_D)(1 - p) = (1 + r_F + r_P)p + (1 - l_D(1 - p))$$

So $r_P = \dfrac{(r_F + l_D)(1 - p)}{p}$ \hfill (5.6.3)

which has considerable similarities with the decision tree calculations in Eq. (1.7.6).

This is a static, one period or infinite period model (if one thinks of the one period being infinitely repeated). Jarrow and Turnbull (1997) were able to extend the idea to a dynamic model by replacing the fixed PD by a hazard rate (or intensity rate as it is called in this literature) which we have already discussed in the consumer profit scoring context in Section 4.5. This is a DM model. By modelling the dynamics of the process in terms of a Markov chain model on the rating grades including a defaulted ratings grade, Jarrow et al. (1997) were able to develop a MTM version of this approach.

There is now a realization that the difference in these models is more in the information available. Guo et al. (2005) pointed out that structural models are based on the information on asset values and liabilities available only to the firm's management while reduced form models are based on information available in the market, where there is only indirect information on a firm's assets and liabilities. Reconciliation models have been developed (see the survey by Elizalde 2005) which do not have complete information on the dynamics of the process that triggers default in the structural models and hence leads to cumulative rates of default as in reduced form models.

This reduced form approach like the structural approaches is a 'bottom-up' approach in that one seeks to estimate the credit risk for each firm separately or within small groups and then puts them together to estimate the credit risk in a portfolio. Putting them together means dealing with the correlation between the default probabilities of different loans. This is done in one of two ways. In one, the Brownian random walk processes in the different loans are assumed to be from a multi-dimensional normal distribution with suitable correlations. The second way is to use economic variables or other common factors which appear in the models of all the loans to give the correlation between defaults for the different loans. This is the same approach as the Vasicek extension takes in the structural models (which gives the Basel formula) where the common factor – 'the overall economic condition' – drives the correlations between the defaults probabilities of the different loans.

There is an alternative development of the actuarial approach which concentrated on 'top-down' models which model at portfolio or segment of portfolio level directly and make no assumptions concerning correlations between individual firms default risk. This meant that the models were much closer to those from the original actuarial applications with much more emphasis on historical data and far less assumptions made about the details of the model.

Finally, there are static scorecard models which seek to estimate the PD in a fixed period of time as a function of accounting ratios of firms, and now also include other market information. These are DM models and are essentially credit scoring applied to firms rather than consumers. It was pioneered by Altman (1968) who has continued to be one of the leading developers of the approach. More recent models (Chava and Jarrow 2004) seek to connect the results of this approach with the hazard rate estimates necessary for the reduced form models.

A number of well-established commercial products have been developed to implement these ideas. These products have developed to incorporate aspects of more than one type of approach, but a rough matching of product to approach would suggest the following classification.

Credit Metrics, introduced in 1997 by J. P. Morgan, is a MTM version of the structural approach, which uses information on the loan's rating, the probability of change in rating, the LGD estimates, and credit spreads to calculate the mean and variance of the asset process. This gives a distribution of the value of the portfolio (the equivalent of a VaR curve) which is the output of a Merton model. One then fits the rating grades of the loan to intervals in this VaR curve to obtain a MTM model. This is extended to a portfolio level model by using a multi-normal distribution for the assets of a portfolio of loans where the default correlations between the loans are obtained by using a multifactor model of the equity returns of the individual firms.

Moody's KMV Portfolio Manager is a structural model which can be used for MTM outcomes or just in DM. For each individual loan, the KMV model uses data on assets and loans to measure the distance to default (DD) $(DD = $ value of assets $-$ value of debt/standard deviation of assets$)$. This translates into an expected default frequency (EDF) in the DM case and to changes in credit rating, including moving to default, in the MTM version. The credit risk of loans at the portfolio level is obtained by estimating the individual asset returns using the Basic KMV model and then uses a multifactor model with global, regional, and industrial sector factors to obtain the correlations. One of the strengths of this approach is the proprietary database which gives the default frequencies for a large number of unrated firms, since some of the other approaches require the firm to have a rating for the model to be applied.

CreditPortfolio View, originally developed by McKinsey but now independent, is a MTM reduced form model which concentrates on modelling the transition probability matrix of the Markov chain which describes the dynamics of the rating movements of a loan. It recognizes that these probabilities depend on the state of the economy and has two different approaches of dealing with this. Firstly the past sample is split into normal and stressed years and different transition matrices are built on each. A more sophisticated version is to fit a model of the transition probabilities to economic factor and to shocks in the economy – the latter being random events. This is done by transforming the historic transition matrices by shift factors into probabilities conditioned on the economic variable values. Monte Carlo simulation then allows one to simulate the dynamics of the Markov chain transition probabilities and hence of the chain itself. The correlation between different loans is given by putting each loan into appropriate industry–country segments and for each such segment building regression models of default rates on the important economic variables. Then the correlations in default and rating migration are given by them depending on common economic factors. Thus this approach involves building a large number of industry/country/risk grade-specific regression models with a consequent need for large amounts of economic data.

Credit Risk Plus developed by Credit Suisse is an example of a DM top-down actuarial approach. It models at the portfolio segment level and uses historical information to estimate the continuous variable of default rate in a segment as opposed to the probability of the binary events of an individual loan defaulting or changing grade. It is also one of the first approaches to model the equivalent of LGD × EAD – the severity of the losses. It has much simpler assumptions than the other models and the results can be obtained analytically rather than by using simulation.

The scoring approaches such as Altman's z-scores are static DM approaches as opposed to all the other above models which are dynamic. They measure the PD over a given future time horizon – usually 1 year. The approach is almost identical to consumer credit scoring, which preceded it by a dozen years, but in the subsequent 40 years it has proved less successful and less widely used. This is for two reasons. It is hard to get the large populations of homogeneous firms one needs to segment by industry, size, and country. Also, the scorecards depend on accounting information, which, no disrespect to the auditors, is less accurate especially just before a firm defaults than the transactional information used in behavioural scorecards. Moreover the scorecards ignore any correlation in the default rate of different firms, which is exactly the problem that has been ignored in consumer credit scoring until now.

So can these credit risk approaches be used in the context of consumer lending portfolios? If not can they be reinterpreted or modified to make sense in this context or can the different information available in the consumer case – more detailed individual characteristics, very detailed transactional data, but no market pricing data – allow new approaches to be used. These are the issues we will concentrate on in the rest of this section.

Consumer structural model based on reputation

Andrade and Thomas (2007) suggested that whereas the corporate structural models assumed that the shareholders have a put option on the assets of the firms one could construct a consumer structural model by assuming that the borrowers have a call option on their reputation; that is, the borrowers have the opportunity to keep or lose their reputation for credit worthiness. One can construct a model using this approach where one uses the behavioural score as a surrogate for the reputation for credit worthiness of the borrower.

Assume that for borrower i, there is an unobservable quantity Q_i, the borrower's credit worthiness. This includes all the information about the borrowers that is needed to assess their credit risk. Lenders have information from both internal and external sources, such as credit bureaus, about the financial condition and the repayment performance of the borrower. This information is usually translated into behavioural scores and it seems reasonable to take these as a proxy for the creditworthiness Q_i.

It seems reasonable to assume that the probability of consumer i being accepted as a client by a lending institution, q_i^a, is a strictly increasing function of Q_i, $q_i^a = f(Q_i)$. Moreover if the borrower defaults on the loan, the information is quickly passed to the credit bureaus and hence to all other lenders. Thus the consumers will lose their 'reputation' for credit worthiness and will have no access to credit in the immediate future. This access to credit is clearly of value to a borrower and this value is related to the amount of credit to which the borrower has access. Define this value as R_i the value of the borrower's reputation. It is a reasonable assumption that this value is a strictly increasing function of q_i^a, $R_i = h(q_i^a)$.

With these assumptions one can construct an option-based model for the credit risk of an individual borrower. If the value of borrowers i's reputation R_i is higher than their debt D_i, then the borrowers will seek to repay the debt. If $R_i < D_i$ then the borrower will default. The lending institution will report this to the market via the credit reference bureaus and the borrower's reputation will be lost along with access to credit. Thus we can think of the borrowers as having a put option on their reputation with the strike price being the amount of debt owed.

Since it is reasonable to assume $f(\cdot)$ and $h(\cdot)$ are strictly increasing functions of Q_i and q_i^a, R_i is a strictly increasing function of Q_i:

$$R_i = h(f(Q_i)) = g(Q_i). \tag{5.6.4}$$

Thus, there is a unique one-to-one correspondence between the values of R_i and the values of Q_i, and vice versa. In particular let $K_{Q,i}$ be the credit worthiness which corresponds to having a reputational value of D_i. Thus, the option analogy can be applied also in the creditworthiness dimension. The borrowers will default if their creditworthiness is below $K_{Q,i}$ and continue to repay if their creditworthiness is above $K_{Q,i}$.

Credit worthiness is unobservable but lenders do use behavioural scores as a surrogate for it. If that is the case, default will correspond to the behavioural score $S_i(t)$ for borrower i at time t, dropping below a threshold value $K_{S,i}$. To complete the model we need to derive the dynamics of the behavioural score $S_i(t)$.

In Section 4.3, we developed Markov chain model of such dynamics, but in keeping with the Merton style corporate credit risk Andrade and Thomas (2007) considered credit worthiness to be the discrete time equivalent a continuous time diffusion process with jumps. Thus $S(t)$ satisfies

$$dS_i(t) = \mu_i + \sigma_i dW + a_t dY_t \qquad (5.6.5)$$

where μ_i is the drift of the process, $\sigma_i dW$ is a Brownian motion, and dY_t is a Poisson jump process. Although the process is written in continuous time, when it comes to estimating the parameters, one should use a discrete time equivalent with time intervals of 1 month. The idea is that μ_i corresponds to a natural drift in credit worthiness caused in part by the account ageing. This is related to the change in the hazard rates as functions of months on books that was discussed in Section 4.5. The Brownian motion described the natural variation in behavioural score while the Poisson jump term is included to model jumps in behavioural scores due to major events like loss of job.

Given a time series of behavioural scores for a sample of borrowers, one can then estimate the parameters $\mu_i \sigma_i$ for each consumer and a_t for the whole population either using Bayesian Markov Chain Monte Carlo (MCMC) techniques or by maximum likelihood estimates. All that is left is to estimate $K_{S,i}$ the behavioural score level at which default is triggered. This can be done by Monte Carlo simulations of the behavioural score paths. For borrowers we have their historical scores and can apply simulation to obtain score paths for the next few periods. This is done a number of times for each individual and if we consider a possible default value $K_{S,1}$, then we can calculate the number of paths that go below that value (see Fig. 5.6.1). This gives the estimated default probability for that borrower. To make the model tractable the same value K_S is used for all borrowers, and so we have a default probability for each individual for each value of K considered. One can then choose the value of K_S to ensure good calibration or good discrimination. In the former case, one sets K_S so that the simulated default rate in the portfolio is equal to the actual default rate. In the latter case, K_S is chosen to maximize a measure of discrimination such as Kolmogorov–Smirnov statistic or the Gini coefficient. Note that the estimation of K_S and the estimation of the process parameters are tackled separately. The later estimates the dynamics of credit worthiness and the former estimates what default threshold gives the appropriate default behaviour.

Andrade and Thomas (2007) built such a model using Brazilian data on behavioural scores over a 3-year period and chose the K_S value that maximized the Kolmogorov–Smirnov distance. They did this for five different models; the most recent behavioural score which essentially ignores the dynamics and the four models given by including or dropping the drift term and the jump process. Table 5.6.1 shows the results. As one would expect, and hope, all the dynamic models gave superior discrimination to the static model with the KS statistic increasing

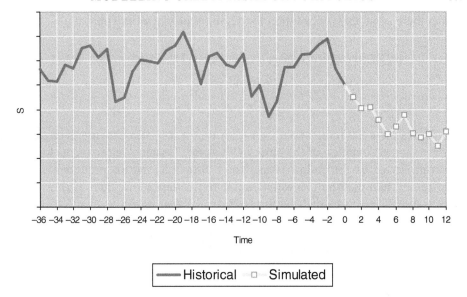

FIG. 5.6.1. Default prediction in a simulation score path.

TABLE 5.6.1. KS results for alternative models.

Model	KS	Increase in KS
Behavioural Score (at last observation time)	0.410	0.000
Diffusion with drift and jump process	0.444	0.034
Diffusion with drift but no jump process	0.459	0.049
Diffusion with no drift but jump process	0.448	0.038
Diffusion without drift and no jump process	0.466	0.056

by between 0.001 and 0.044. The surprise was that the best discrimination was in the model with no drift and no jump process, and so the dynamics was purely a random walk:

$$dS_i(t) = \sigma_i dW. \qquad (5.6.6)$$

The results do not prove that this basic model is always better than the other models, but do suggest that it is competitive. Using the principle of Occam's razor – that one should choose the simplest explanation – this would be the model to use. If one built models on other data, particularly from countries with lower average default rates, the result could be different.

The advantage of using (5.6.6) (rather than its discrete equivalent (5.6.7))

$$P\{S_i(t+1) - S_i(t) = \sigma\} = p; \quad P\{S_i(t+1) - S_i(t) = -\sigma\} = 1 - p \qquad (5.6.7)$$

is that there is an analytic solution for default within the time horizon t.

$$P(\text{default occurred by } t | S(0) = S_0) = \Pr\{S(s) \le K \text{ for some } s$$

$$\le t\} = P(t) = 2N\left(\frac{K - S_0}{\sigma\sqrt{t}}\right) \quad S_0 > K \tag{5.6.8}$$

where K is the default threshold. S_0 is the current ($t = 0$) behavioural score and σ is the standard deviation of the borrower's score. This can be proved as follows.

From Eq. (5.6.6), it follows that since a Brownian motion process has, after a time t, a normal distribution with mean 0 and variance $\sigma^2 t$, then $S_i(t) - S_i(0) = S_i(t) - S_0 = Z_i(t)$ has a distribution $N(0, \sigma_i^2 t)$ and so $Z_i(t) / \sigma_i\sqrt{t}$ is $N(0,1)$. So

$$\Pr\{S_i(t) \le K\} = \Pr\{Z_i(t) - S_0 \le K\} = \Pr\left\{\frac{Z_i(t)}{\sigma_i\sqrt{t}} \le \frac{K - S_0}{\sigma_i\sqrt{t}}\right\} = N\left(\frac{K - S_0}{\sigma_i\sqrt{t}}\right).$$
$$\tag{5.6.9}$$

Here though comes the lovely trick. What we want to know is not whether $S_i(t)$ is below K at time t but was it ever below K at any time before t. The trick is to recognize that Brownian motion has the property that at every time t it is equally likely to move up and down by the same amount. Suppose that one path of $S_i(.)$ hits K at time s, then from that instant onwards for every move up or down it makes there is an equally likely path making the opposite move. So if its subsequent path was $K - f(s + u)$, there is an equally likely path of the form $K + f(s + u)$ (see Fig. 5.6.2a).

In that case, if at time t the path was below K there is a partner path which hit the barrier at k at the same time and is not above K. This partner path has the same probability as the original one. Moreover if, as in Fig. 5.6.2b, the path hit K, went below it but at time t is now above K, there is a partner path which is below K at time t. Thus for every path below K at time t (which must therefore have hit the barrier at K before time t), there is a partner path with an equal probability of occurring which is above K at time t. Hence,

$$\Pr\{S_i(s) \le K \text{ for some } s \le t\} = 2\Pr\{S_i(t) \le K\} = 2N\left(\frac{K - S_0}{\sigma\sqrt{t}}\right). \tag{5.6.10}$$

Note that $(S_0 - K)/\sigma$ gives the same ranking of customers as that given by the probability of defaulting within time t, and so is akin to the DD used in the Portfolio Manager approach to corporate credit risk modelling.

This approach is not yet a portfolio credit risk model as we need to combine the credit risks of the individual loans. The standard way of doing this is to take a multivariable version of the basic structural Eq. (5.6.6) where each variable

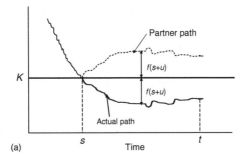

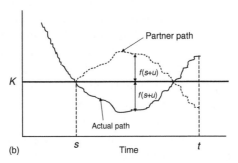

FIG. 5.6.2. (a) Example of partner path. (b) Example of double crossing partner path.

corresponds to one loan or one class of loan. The simplest such model is to use a multivariate normal distribution with a correlation matrix Σ describing the joint movement of the credit worthiness proxies. There are standard ways of simulating such distributions (for example Cholesk transformations) and for each simulation run one can estimate the PD of the portfolio by counting the number of loans that default during that run (hit the default barrier K). Repeating the simulation many times gives a distribution for the default probability PD. Since the calibration is most important in this context, one should choose K so as the empirical and simulated probabilities of default match.

Surprisingly when this was done using the Brazilian data described above the pairwise correlation of behavioural scores (the creditworthiness proxies) was 0.00095 – very close to 0. This poses a dilemma because it is clear the defaults of individual loans in any given time period are correlated. One way to model this is to assume the credit worthiness of the individual loan consists of an idiosyncratic part which is the behavioural score and a systemic part which is due to economic conditions and is not captured by the behavioural scores as they do not contain economic factors. This suggests that the generic scorecard being used in this case did not have the population odds component in it. Thus, if we define $Q_i(t, e_t)$ as the creditworthiness of consumer i at time t if the economic state is e_t by

$$Q_i(t, e_t) = \tilde{Q}_i(t) + f(e_t) = S_i(t) + f(e_t) \tag{5.6.11}$$

where $S_i(t)$ is the behavioural score of borrower i at time t and $f(e)$ is the impact of the economic state on the credit worthiness of i. Default occurs if

$$Q_i(t, e_t) < K_Q \Leftrightarrow \tilde{S}_i(t) + f(e_t) < K_S \Leftrightarrow \tilde{S}_i(t) < K_S - f(e_t). \tag{5.6.12}$$

The factor $f(\cdot)$ could be reinterpreted as the way the changes in the economic conditions affect the default thresholds. An analogy would be that the behavioural score of a consumer (their idiosyncratic creditworthiness) is moving up and down according to a random walk, but if it falls below the water level K_S the borrowers drown in their debt. The water level itself moves up and down according to the economic conditions. When it is high, a lot of borrowers will drown at the same time; when it is low very few will drown. Hence the correlations between defaulters are given by these changes in the economic conditions.

The economic states e_i and the related factors $f(e_i)$ are used to model the dynamics of the economy and its connection with default rates. Central banks (and some credit bureaus) keep data on default rates DR (t) usually as a quarterly series and these could be connected to macroeconomic variables to identify which combinations of the latter affect default rates. One can partition the economic situations into a number of states each having sets of economic conditions with similar default rates and use historic data to build a Markov chain describing the transitions between these different economic states. Thus one can complete the dynamics of the model by defining these transition probabilities:

$$P(e_{t+1} = i | e_t = j) = p_{ij}. \tag{5.6.13}$$

Since as outlined in Section 1.5, the normal relationship between the behavioural score s and the probability of being 'good', p, is given by $s = \log(p/1 - p)$, we could use this relationship to define the factors $f(e_i)$ which is added to the behaviour score. Suppose we have information on DR(t) for $t = 1, \ldots, T$, then an empirical estimate for the log odds of good when the economy is in state e_i which occurs n_i times in that period is

$$\log \left(\frac{1 - \left(\sum_{t \in e_i} DR(t) \bigg/ n_i \right)}{\sum_{t \in e_i} DR(t) \bigg/ n_i} \right). \tag{5.6.14}$$

Then defining $f(e_i)$ to be the weights of evidence when the state of the economy is in state e_i gives

$$
f(e_i) = \log\left(\frac{1 - \left(\sum_{t\in e_i} DR(t) \Big/ n_i\right)}{\sum_{t\in e_i} DR(t) \Big/ n_i}\right) - \log\left(\frac{1 - \left(\sum_{t\in e_i}^{T} DR(t) \Big/ T\right)}{\sum_{t\in e_i}^{T} DR(t) \Big/ T}\right)
$$

(5.6.15)

where the second term is the long-run average default rate. With $f(e_i)$ describing the state of the economy, one can simulate the distribution of defaults in a portfolio over a given time period in the future. First one simulates the path of the Markov chain which describes the economy and then one can simulate the dynamics of each individual's behaviour score and hence the number of defaults in the portfolio.

Consumer structural models based on affordability

It has been argued that consumers default more because of cash flow problems than because their debts exceed their assets as a consumer's assets are not easily realizable. Thus one could build a structural model on whether the consumer can afford to service the loan. In some countries there is a requirement on lenders to build such models. A simple version of the model relates the variables at time $t+1$ to those at time t by

$$
(\text{Realizable assets})_{t+1} = (\text{Realizable asset})_t + (\text{Income})_t - (\text{Expenditure})_t
$$
$$
- (\text{Loan Repayment})_t \qquad\qquad (5.6.16)
$$

where default occurs if realizable asset becomes negative. One approach to estimate income and expenditure is to use a survey of borrowers' expenditure and income and then to use this data to build regression models of expenditure and income against consumer characteristics and where necessary behaviour scores. If the lender is a bank which has access to the details of the borrower's current account, then it could use the total value of credits in month t as an estimate of income and total value of debits as an estimate of expenditure.

This model can then follow the Merton idea of default occurring when debts exceed realizable assets. It may be necessary to estimate the total debt of a borrower since one lender may only see a fraction of the total actual debts. Default can be defined to occur if assets drop below some level related to the total debts, though it will be necessary to estimate what this level should be. Next the dynamics of the realizable assets process would need to be modelled. Both these last two steps – estimating the relationship between assets, debts and the trigger level for default, and the dynamics of the asset process – are difficult to do and so it is not surprising that this approach is currently rarely implemented. One way of building the correlation between the defaults of different borrowers is to make the dynamics of the asset process, including the income and expenditure to be functions of economic conditions or other common factors.

Consumer reduced form models based on hazard functions

One can develop the equivalent of reduced form credit risk models for portfolios of consumer loans by developing the survival-based scoring models of Sections 4.5 and 4.6. The hazard models of Section 4.5 have strong parallels with the DM intensity-based corporate credit risk models. Recall that in the hazard-based application scoring models of that section, using the discrete time notation, then at the nth period since the start of the loan, the probability a borrower defaults is given by a hazard function $h(n) = e^{\mathbf{w}' \cdot \mathbf{x}} h_0(n) = e^{-s_h(\mathbf{x})} h_0(n)$ where $\mathbf{x} = (x_1, x_2, \ldots, x_m)$ is a vector of the borrower's social-demographic characteristics at application which can be combined in the score s.

The correlation between the default distributions of different borrowers can be introduced by adding common factors to the score function. The most obvious common factors are the variables that describe the external economic conditions. Thus one can extend the basic hazard-based default model by allowing two types of characteristics $x_1, x_2, \ldots, x_r$ and $y_1(s), y_2(s), \ldots, y_m(s)$ where $\mathbf{x} = (x_1, x_2, \ldots, x_r)$ is the vector of social-demographic characteristics describing the static characteristics (which will mainly be the socio-demographic information of the borrowers) and $\mathbf{y}(s) = (y_1(s), y_2(s), \ldots, y_m(s))$ is the vector of external economic condition variables at time s.

The proportional hazards assumption is that if the borrower's lending facility was opened at time t_0 then the chance the loan will default after a further n periods given it has not defaulted earlier is given by the hazard rate $h_{t_0}(n)$ if the individual and environment characteristics are given by $\mathbf{x}, \mathbf{y}(\cdot)$, is

$$h^{t_0}(n) = h_0(n) \exp\left(\mathbf{w}' \cdot \mathbf{x} + \mathbf{v}' \cdot \mathbf{y}(t_0 + n)\right) \tag{5.6.17}$$

where $h_0(n)$ terms represents the baseline hazard, that is, the propensity of a default occurring when all the independent variables $\mathbf{x}, \mathbf{y}(\cdot)$ are equal to zero. Recall there are two approaches in defining $h_0(\cdot)$, $\mathbf{w}$, and $\mathbf{v}$ – the parametric approach and the non-parametric (or at least the semi-parametric) approach. In the parametric approach the lifetime distribution and hence the hazard rate is chosen to be of a certain form; for example, if exponential then $h_0(t) = \lambda$; if Weibull with shape parameter k and scale parameter λ, then $h_0(t) = k(\lambda t)^{k-1}$. The parameters of the distribution as well as $\mathbf{w}$ and $\mathbf{v}$ coefficients are then estimated from the data. The more commonly used approach is the semi-parametric one of Cox's proportional hazard function (Cox 1972; Kalbfleisch and Prentice 1980) where the coefficients $\mathbf{w}$ and $\mathbf{v}$ can be estimated without having to assume a specific distributional form for $h_0(t)$, and the latter can be backed out of the data using the Kaplan–Meier estimation procedure. The fact the same economic conditions affect all the consumers allows correlations between the default probabilities. Of course the common variables in the risk scores of the different borrowers do not have to be the economic conditions. One could use other factors such as geographical area or type of employment category to introduce the correlation.

In the simplest model, borrowers i's relative hazard rate (their hazard 'score') at time t, $(s_h(i, t))$, is a linear combination of the two types of factors so that $s_h(i, t) = -\mathbf{w}'\mathbf{x}^i - \mathbf{v}'\mathbf{y}(t)$ where the personal characteristics of consumer i are $\mathbf{x}^i$. Notice that this means $s_h(i, t_1) - s_h(j, t_1) = s_h(i, t_2) - s_h(j, t_2)$ so that the ranking of the individual scores stays the same in all time periods. Thus it is only the personal characteristics that affect the ordering of how likely a borrower is to default and this ordering is the same for all time periods. A more powerful model would use both sets of variables to affect this relative ranking of the borrowers. There are two ways of doing this in this context. The first is to make the coefficients of the variables (or at least the borrower characteristics) time dependent. Thus borrower i's 'hazard' score at time t on a loan begun at time t_0 would be

$$s_h(i, t) = -(\mathbf{w}_0 + t\,\mathbf{w}_1)'\mathbf{x}^i - \mathbf{v}'\mathbf{y}(t_0 + t). \qquad (5.6.18)$$

This can be calculated by introducing variable $t \times x_i$ as well as x_i into the hazard function and their coefficients are the $\mathbf{w}_1$. The second approach is to introduce borrower–economy interaction variables. Assuming that the borrower characteristics are binary, then one can define an interaction variable $x_i^* y_j(t)$ to be the variable that takes the values $y_j(t)$ for the borrowers who have $x_i = 1$ and takes the value 0 for the borrowers with $x_i = 0$.

So far we have assumed the borrower's characteristics are constant as occurs in application scorecards. In the survival analysis equivalent of the behavioural score, then the behavioural characteristics will also change over time. The hazard probability $h^{t_0}(n)$ for a loan beginning at time t_0 is the PD during period n given that there has been no default before then. If we define for periods $m, m \le n$, the behavioural characteristics to be $\mathbf{b}(\mathbf{m})$, the economic variable values to be $\mathbf{y}(t_0 + m)$, and the fixed borrower characteristics to be $\mathbf{x}$, then the proportional hazard probability would satisfy

$$h^{t_0}(n) = e^{\mathbf{w}.\mathbf{x} + \mathbf{v}\mathbf{y}(t_0 + n) + \mathbf{u}\mathbf{b}(\mathbf{n})} h_0(n) = e^{-s_h(\mathbf{x},\, n)} h_0(n). \qquad (5.6.19)$$

So if we know the current characteristics $\mathbf{b}(\mathbf{n})$, and the current economic conditions $\mathbf{y}(t_0 + n)$, one has an estimate of the default probability $h^{t_0}(n)$ in the next period. One can also use such a model to forecast more than one period ahead in two ways. The first way is to build a model to forecast the future values of the economic variables, which is a standard econometric problem, and also one to forecast the dynamics of the behavioural variables, which is not something commonly done at present. The second way is to take lagged economic variables and behavioural characteristics in the hazard function, so that to estimate $h^{t_0}(n)$ one might need $\mathbf{b(n-k)}$, and $\mathbf{y(t_0+n-\ k)}$. This will give a model where one can always forecast up to k period ahead.

In these variants of the hazard function models, one can model the correlations between the different borrowers by the fact they have common economic variables (or possibly other common factors) affecting their hazard rates. So one can then use Monte Carlo simulation to obtain estimates of the credit risk for a portfolio of such consumer loans (see Malik and Thomas 2007). An extension of this approach is the frailty models, first introduced but not named by Clayton (1978), which assume that there is also an unknown factor that is connecting the default probabilities of the different borrowers. One adds this to the model by multiplying the hazard function by this frailty term and the most common models are when this frailty term is assumed to have the Gamma distribution.

We have concentrated in this section on how one can extend the application scoring hazard-based models of Section 4.5 to consumer credit risk portfolio models. One can do exactly the same for the behavioural scoring hazard-based models outlined in that section.

Consumer reduced form models based on Markov chains

MTM reduced form models in corporate credit risk use the information available in the marketplace about the current rating of the corporate loans to price the credit losses which occur because of the drop in a loans rating as well as when the loan defaults. Thus they allow one to use the most recent estimate of the PD of the loan which is exactly what behavioural scoring does in the consumer context. Thus one can seek to develop consumer loan equivalents of those models.

The Markov chain models described in Section 4.3 describe the current state of the borrowers account. The states can be the current default status – up to date, 30 days overdue, 60 days overdue, and so on – bands of behavioural scores or more complex situations involving frequency and recency of payment and usage and current balances. The ones most directly related to credit risk would be the Markov chains based on default status or behavioural score bands. In both cases one needs to identify states which correspond to default. In the default status models, default is already defined as one of the states but in the behavioural score band models one needs to add a default state. Section 4.3 developed a series of Markov chain models based on the transition probabilities $p_t(i, j)$ of moving from state i to state j during period t. These allow one to estimate the probability of an individual borrower defaulting in any time interval. In fact they give the probability distribution π_t of which state the borrower will be in at time t. This distribution function π_t can also be reinterpreted via the ergodic theorem as the proportion of the loans in any portfolio which are in the different states at that time. This appears to give the estimates of the credit risks for a portfolio of such loans.

The one difficulty in this is that there is an implicit assumption that the default status of different borrowers are independent of one another. There is no correlation between the defaults of different loans. How can one introduce correlations into such a model? The answer again is to make the transitions probabilities depend on other parameters which hold for all or at least some segment of the borrowers at the same time. If these parameters are not known but themselves satisfy a Markov chain, this is a hidden Markov chain process of which there is a large literature (Cappe et al. 2005). A simpler model would be to make the Markov chains transitions $p_t(i,j)$ depend on the economic parameters $\mathbf{y}(t)$ which hold at that period. The most common approach to doing this is to assume the transition probabilities form a cumulative logistic transformation of the underlying economic variables. First, define the cumulative transition distribution by

$$P_t(i,k) = \sum_{j=1}^{k} p_t(i,j). \tag{5.6.20}$$

The cumulative logistic transition models then connects these cumulative probability distribution to the economic variables by

$$\log\left(\frac{P_t(i,k)}{1 - P_t(i,k)}\right) = \alpha_{i,k} + \sum_{m} \beta_{i,m} y_m(t) \tag{5.6.21}$$

where the constants α are chosen to ensure the transition probabilities are all positive. For more details of this approach in a different context, see Allison's (1999) book.

5.7   Basel stress testing of consumer portfolios: static and dynamic approaches

In the last section, ways of modelling the credit risk of portfolios of consumer loans were discussed. There are several reasons for developing such models. One is to assist lenders make comparisons of the risks of lending to different portfolios of borrowers by developing economic capital models for all types of lending including retail lending. A second reason, which has come to the fore since the 'credit crunch' of 2008, is to develop pricing models for securitized products based on consumer loans. The third reason for developing such models though is the requirement in the Basel Accord to be able to stress test both the models that lenders are building to estimate PD, LGD, and EAD, and the levels of regulatory capital that these models suggest are needed. Models built for stress testing will describe how default rates vary as economic conditions vary and so could also be useful in calculating the relationship between current PIT estimate of PD and the estimates of long-run average PD, which was described briefly in Section 5.4. In this final section of the chapter, we concentrate on what is meant by stress testing in the Basel Accord, how lenders can undertake such stress tests, and where the portfolio level credit risk models might be appropriate.

Stress testing in the Basel Accord

Stress testing is a risk management tool used to evaluate the potential impact on a firm of specific event and/or movement in a set of financial variables.

BIS Working Group Report 2005

This book has concentrated on the use of models to assess and manage risk in the financial sector and in this chapter it has looked at how models can be used under the regulations in the Basel Capital Accord. An advantage of modelling is that one can ask 'what if questions', that is investigate the outcome of situations which have not yet arisen. Stress testing is exactly this. It asks what does a model suggest occurs in particularly difficult lending conditions.

Stress testing is an adjunct to statistical models such as VaR, the major tool used in risk assessment, particularly of market risk. In VaR one estimates the distribution of the probability of the losses (or gains) of a portfolio of loans and then identifies for what value there is a 5% (or a 1%) chance that losses will be worse than that value. Figure 5.7.1 represents such a probability distribution of profits (losses) and the VaR value is such that the probability the loss is worse than this value exceeds some pre-assigned level. The distribution of the losses in VaR

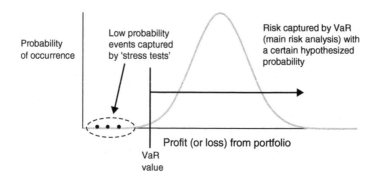

FIG. 5.7.1. Stress tests capture exceptional but plausible events.

is obtained from a model which assumes a specific form of the loss distribution – log normal, for example, and so it is not clear that the very extreme events are accurately represented. Stress testing looks at the extreme tail of the losses and asks what could cause such an outcome and how would the lending be affected in such circumstances. The difference in the two approaches is that VaR is a statistical description of the returns on a portfolio based on historical data and so there is no connection between the actual events and the unexpected losses. Looking at potential situations in more detail, by considering the impact of certain events or changes in the values of financial and economic variables, allows more realism. One can then investigate if there are correlations between the losses in different parts of the overall loan portfolio, and what a lender could do to mitigate the worst effects of these stressed situations.

Stress testing is emphasized by regulators as an essential component of risk management and is also an integral part of the Basel Accord regulations. One can identify four interrelated objectives in risk regulation where stress testing should be used:

- To prepare bank management to respond to future events that could put the organization under pressure (non-Basel).
- General stress testing of MCRs (as part of the Basel Pillar 1, IRB).
- Specific credit risk/economic cycle stress tests for those requirements (Basel Pillar 1 IRB).
- Scenario analysis as part of the supervisory review process (Basel Pillar 2, Supervisory Review).

The first of these is not in the Basel Accord but bank regulators are keen to ensure that senior managers in banks do consider the possible events which could impact negatively on their business and how they might cope with them. This applies both to on-going business and when determining whether to undertake new lending opportunities. Senior managers should be able to articulate their firm's appetite for risk and understand the implication of stressed events that may occur because of this level of risk in their business strategy. They should be involved in identifying the scenarios which could lead to these stressed events and there should be good reporting procedures so they are aware of the results of any stress testing undertaken on such scenarios.

In the Basel context, specific stress testing is needed to be undertaken by those lenders who are using the IRB approach, because the MCR adds together the capital needed to cover market risk, credit risk, and operational risk, which implies they are independent of one another. In extreme situations, it is clear these risks are not independent as problems with credit risk can induce major market fluctuations and problems of liquidity. There are correlations between the risks but these need not be all positive correlations and stress testing is needed to ensure that in realistic extreme scenarios the total MCR covers all the losses whatever their causes.

Even with credit risk the Basel regulations add together the capital needed in the different risk segments. This would be the situation if the default risk in the different segments is independent but of course there will be correlations between the segments. These are assumed to be dealt with by all segments having a given correlation, R^2 with the one factor which is assumed to affect all segments of all types of loans. But does this work? The stress tests examine how well the capital requirement can cope with these inter-segment correlations in extreme conditions.

Stress testing is also used to ensure that the models which generate PD, LGD, and EAD estimates for the IRB formula are sound in that the results they give in mildly stressed economic conditions are reasonable – two periods of zero growth is the condition suggested by the Basel regulations but this is being modified some what by several regulators. These stress tests are part of the validation of these PD models since there is subjective judgement involved in building these models. Similar tests are advocated for other risks, for example illiquidity, concentration, and collateral risks when they occur.

Some regulators require these credit risk stress tests focus also on the impact of changes during the economic cycle. So they want to check what happens to the MCR at all stages of an economic cycle, particularly during the equivalent of an economic recession which is as bad as a one in 25-year event. This means looking at the way the forecasts of score and PD ratings of the borrowers obtained from the models the banks have developed migrate as economic conditions change. These migrations should be independent of changes in the size and composition of the overall portfolio. It is as if there was a one-off shock of this proportion to the economy.

The final objective of stress testing reinforces the first objective of ensuring good risk management procedures by senior managers in the bank. The supervisory review regulations in the Basel Accord require the regulators to assess whether a bank's decision makers have processes which help them understand the risks they are taking, and that the capital set aside by the MCR covers the potential losses if the extreme risks identified did occur. Thus it is as much a matter of process and risk identification as of analysis. Is the information on the impacts of the extreme risks being considered by the decision makers, and are appropriate precautionary actions in place to deal with them? If not, the regulators have the right to impose capital requirements above those of the MCR formula.

The objective is not to demand that lenders have enough regulatory capital to cope with such an event today, but rather that if it occurred 2 or 3 years in the future, with indications beforehand that the economy was worsening, then lenders could manage their way through the difficult period. This managing could involve retaining more profits beforehand, scaling back the size of the portfolio, or using hedging mechanisms to alleviate the potential losses.

Types of stress testing in general: sensitivity analysis and scenario analysis

Stress testing has been widely used in the market risk area for more than 20 years and there are two main approaches. Sensitivity type tests are where a single factor like the exchange rate or the yield curve is changed and the implications for the portfolio examined. This allows one to validate the model describing the performance of the portfolio. This validation works in two ways. Firstly it is clear from experience and logic in which direction the change in a parameter value should move the final result even if the magnitude of the change is not obvious. Secondly extreme parameter values often lead to simplified situations where the outcome is obvious even if not realistic. These sensitivity tests are an integral part of model building but they are useful outputs when the model is applied in real situations. They identify how much the outcome changes when there are changes in the parameter values. For example, a mortgage lender certainly would be interested in what the impact of a 10% drop in house prices on the profitability of its loan portfolio is.

Sensitivity tests have the advantage that it is easy to understand the results as there is only change in one parameter and so all the impact on the portfolio must come from this adjustment. The problem is that it rarely occurs that just one economic or financial factor will change in isolation to the others. In multifactor sensitivity analysis, one examines what happens if several of the economic parameters change at the same time. The problem then is to recognize which of these changes is having the major effect. However, the main difficulty with multifactor stress tests is that in reality there are relationships between the movement in one factor and another. To avoid the multifactor stress testing being an irrelevant exercise, one really needs to identify these connections when building scenarios of the situations.

The second approach to stress testing is to build scenarios. These can be historical ones of actual events and hence involve few judgements on what happens to the various economic factors, but may be inappropriate for the current portfolio. Alternatively hypothetical scenarios can be constructed, which are probably more relevant but are very labour intensive and involve a lot of expert judgement.

Historical scenarios have the advantage that one knows what exactly happened and how the different risks interacted. Thus they require few subjective judgements by the scenario builders. The disadvantage is that financial organizations do not usually obey Santayana's quotation that 'those who cannot remember the past are condemned to repeat it'. Thus it is likely that the current lending portfolio is quite different from the positions being held during that historical scenario, and also the financial markets will react in a different way now because they have learnt from those events.

Hypothetical scenarios are more relevant to the current situation but there is considerable time and expertise needed in deciding what sequence of events will occur in a scenario and how the different risks will interact. Ensuring that no important risk factor is omitted and combining the changes in each risk factor in a way that makes economic sense is a difficult task. One can start with the actual portfolio and construct these hypothetical scenarios for that specific portfolios or one can start with current risks and then build scenarios of how these risks would impact on lending portfolios. Whichever approach is taken there is always a difficult trade-off between realism and comprehensibility.

Note that in the Basel Accord the first two areas where stress testing is suggested – part of the supervisory review process and general stress testing of the MCRs – are ones where it would seem scenario analysis is more appropriate, while the third area –stressing the specific credit risks – is closer to the sensitivity analysis approach. For the scenario analysis approach, one wants to connect the economic scenario to the resultant change in the PD.

Approaches to stress testing probability of default in the Basel Accord

There are three approaches to stress testing the models which give PD estimates required for the IRB approach to credit risk in the Basel New Accord. These are the static approach which is essentially sensitivity analysis, a dynamic approach based on the correlation between PD and economic factors, and one that uses a dynamic model of the credit risk of portfolios of consumer loans. The last one is essentially scenario based. Using correlations between PD and economic factors is the most common approach of stress testing for corporate portfolios.

Static approach

This is essentially the sensitivity type tests where some parameters are flexed and the resultant impact identified. In the case of stress testing, the PD one could make the following changes:

- Change the PD value for a given segment by adding a fixed amount to the original PD or multiplying that value by a given factor.
- Use the parameters in the transformation of the behavioural scores to the PD values to increase the PDs for a given score.
- Drop all loans by one score band or apply some other form of loan migration.

The advantage of these static approaches is that they are very easy to implement and understand. The difficulty is that it is hard to defend why specific changes in the PD value should correspond to specific scenarios on economic conditions unless one uses the historic-based migration matrices. Also these approaches do not allow for the migration of the loans between the score bands. Recall that in a PIT PD model, there will be lots of migration of loans while in a TTC PD model there should be very little change in the rating of a loan. Since most retail Basel systems for estimating PD are more PIT than TTC, one should expect such migration. These limitations can be overcome if one has dynamic models where all the historic data available can be used in building a model.

Dynamic correlation approach

Dynamic correlation-based approaches use historical data to build regression models to identify the impact of changes in economic variables on default rates. It is important to recognize that this impact varies considerably between different types of lending and also between different degrees of risk within the same type of lending. Although Fig. 5.7.2 shows this difference in terms of corporate bonds, because the data on them is publicly available, the same changes in that high default groups are more affected by recessions than low risk groups also holds on the consumer side.

It is clear that the US recessions around 1990 and 2002 increased the default rates for all types of bonds but whereas the change for investment grade bonds is minimal there were major changes in the rate for speculative grade bonds. The fact that economic changes affect default rates is evident whatever data is examined. Figure 5.7.3 for example show the changes in UK interest rates and UK mortgage default rates (the latter multiplied 10-fold to show on a comparable scale to interest rates), using the Council of Mortgage Lenders figures of loans 6+ months in arrears as a proxy for default. Thus one can build single factor or multivariate models which connect the default rate for risk segment A, B, C, and so on to economic variables

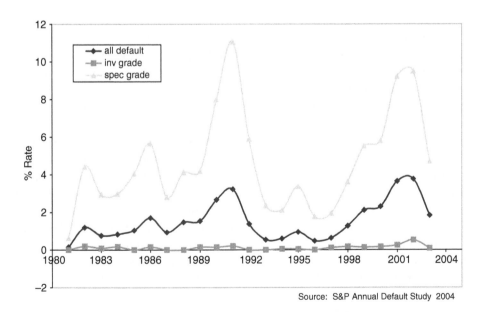

Source: S&P Annual Default Study 2004

FIG. 5.7.2. Effect of economy on bond default rates 1980-2003.

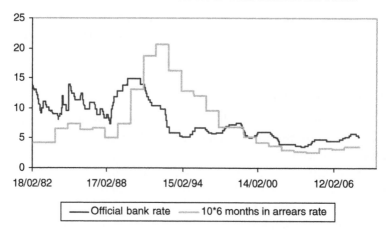

Fig. 5.7.3. Relationship between UK bank rate and 6 months in arrears mortgage rate.

as in (5.7.1):

$$PD_A = \beta_0 + \beta_1 GDP \text{ (single factor model)}$$

$$PD_A = \beta_0 + \beta_1 GDP + \beta_2 \text{ inflation } \beta_3 \text{ (house price index)} \qquad (5.7.1)$$

$$\text{(multivariate model)}$$

This is harder than it looks because the calculation of PD_i is not straightforward as the loans that are in that segment keep changing from period to period. Another issue is which economic variables to use and which version of them is appropriate. One can get help in this quest by looking at the variables that econometricians and financial forecasters have found most useful when they make their economic forecasts.

There are still two issues that are of concern with using this approach for stress testing. The first is whether the correlations that are found in normal times break down when the economy is stressed. Earlier we thought of this when considering multifactor sensitivity tests and realizing one needs to consider what the correlations between the factors might be. In building hypothetical scenarios, the concern is that the relationship between the default rate and the economic variables found when there are minor changes in the economy may not hold when the changes are more severe. There is also the perennial question 'Is the next recession going to be like the last ones?' Obviously it will not be, so is it sensible to use the relationships found in these previous recessions? So for example the relationship between default rate and interest rate found in Fig. 5.7.3 may not hold in the next recession.

Dynamic model-based approach

The third approach to stress testing is to use the models of credit for portfolios of consumer loans as outlined in the previous section. These models relate portfolio default rates to the parameters of economic variables. This is exactly what is required in stress testing and unlike the static models relates the economic conditions directly to the impact on default. Their advantage over the correlation approaches is that the models are built to reflect the fact that the impact of the economy on default rates is not linear in the economic variable variants that is being used. Although they have a unified model for the impact of the economy on the portfolio within that they ensure that the different risk segments are treated in different ways.

In a structural reputation based model (Eqs. (5.6.4) to (5.6.14)), the economy comes into the default levels since these depend on economic factors. Recall that $S_i(t)$ is the behavioural score of borrower i and satisfied a simple random walk:

$$dS_i(t) = \sigma dW(t). \tag{5.7.2}$$

Define

$$D_i(t) = \begin{cases} 1 & \text{if borrower } i \text{ defaults at time } t \\ 0 & \text{if no default by borrower } i \text{ at time } t. \end{cases}$$

If the economic factors which impinge on default levels are $F_1(t), F_2(t), \ldots, F_r(t)$ then defaults occurs when

$$D_i(t) = \Pr\{S_i(t) < K_t\}$$

$$\text{where } \Pr\{K_t = k | K_{t-1} = j\} = p_{jk}(f_1(t), f_2(t), \ldots, f_r(t)) \tag{5.7.3}$$

where the random default level K_t is a Markov chain whose transition probabilities depend on the economic factors, whose specific values at time t were $f_1(t), f_2(t), \ldots, f_r(t)$.

To estimate PD one can build a time series model of the dynamics of the factors $F_i(t)$. For stress testing one can choose a particular set of downturn scenarios by choosing a sequence of values for $f_1(t), f_2(t), \ldots, f_r(t), t \in [t_s, t_e]$ which are compatible with the dynamics of the factor models and spread over the downturn period which starts at t_s and ends at t_e.

In the hazard rate-reduced form models, one can introduce the economic variables into the hazard score as was suggested in Eq. (5.6.19). Using coarse classification of the economic variables and introducing interaction terms between these variables and the applicant characteristics would allow the economic impact to have different effects in expansionary and recessionary times. Thus one can use this type of model to develop stress tests as follows. Define $D_i(t), \mathbf{F(t)} = (F_1(t), F_2(t), \ldots, F_r(t))$ as before then the hazard function for borrower i, $h(t, i)$ is defined by

$$h(t, i) = \Pr\{D_i(t) = 1 | D_i(s) = 0, \forall s < t\} \tag{5.7.4}$$

where t is the maturity of the loan – the time since the loan started. If we assume the loan started at calendar time t_0, then the proportional hazards model outlines in Eq. (5.6.19) becomes

$$h^{t_0}(t, i) = e^{\mathbf{a} \cdot \mathbf{X^i}(t) + \mathbf{b} \cdot \mathbf{F}(t+t_0) + \mathbf{c} \cdot (\mathbf{X^i}(t) * \mathbf{F}(t+t_0))} h_0(t) \tag{5.7.5}$$

where $\mathbf{X^i}(t)$ can be the both the fixed characteristics of borrower i which can be part of the application score and the dynamic characteristics of the borrower which are used in the behavioural scores. $\mathbf{X^i}(t) * \mathbf{F}(t + t_0)$ describes the interaction terms between the individual borrower's characteristics and the economic factors.

To use this model for stress testing, one should choose a series of scenarios describing the movement of the economic factors $\mathbf{F}(t)$ over a number of periods which represent the economic downturn situation. Then use these to estimate the hazard functions for a portfolio of borrowers, which gives the probability of each borrower defaulting in each period of the scenario. One can then use Monte Carlo simulation to obtain the distribution of the default levels in the scenario either with one particular scenario repeated many times or allowing for a number of different scenarios each with a certain probability. Again this allows the lender to understand what is likely to happen if there is an economic downturn.

In the Markov chain-based reduced form models, the economic factors can affect the transition probabilities of movement from different risk grades in different ways. There are several advantages to these Markov chain models defined in Section 4.3 and then in the Basel context in Eqs. (5.6.20) and (5.6.21). Firstly because they model the whole portfolio and allow for the dynamical changes in the portfolio they use all the data, including the movement between non-defaulting states, on all the loans in the portfolio to build the model. The disadvantage is the Markov property which says that all that is important about a borrower is their current state and not how they got there. Suppose the state of borrower i a time t, which may be just the behavioural score is given by $X^i(t)$ and the dynamics of $X^i(t)$ is given by a Markov chain with states $j = 1, 2, \ldots, D$ where D is the state that implies the borrower has defaulted. Assuming the economic factors are again given by $\mathbf{F}(t) = (F_1(t), F_2(t), \ldots, F_r(t))$ with specific values at any time being $f_1(t), f_2(t), \ldots, f_r(t)$ these impact on the model by assuming the transition probabilities are function of them, so

$$\Pr\{X^i(t) = k | X^i(t-1) = j\} = p_t(j, k | f_1(t), f_2(t), \ldots, f_r(t)) \tag{5.7.6}$$

One usually uses logistic regression to estimate these probabilities. This can be done by estimating each transition separately, so

$$\ln\left(\frac{p^t(j,k|F_1(t),F_2(t),\ldots,F_r(t))}{1-p^t(j,k|\,F_1(t),F_2(t),\ldots,F_r(t))}\right) = w_0^{j,k,t} + \sum_l w_l^{j,k,t} F_l(t) \quad (5.7.7)$$

though the probabilities will then need to be normalized so that the row sums in the transition matrix add up to one. An alternative which smoothes the data somewhat is to use cumulative logistic regression as follows:

$$P^t(j,k|\mathbf{F}(t)) = \sum_{l=1}^{k} p^t(j,l|\mathbf{F}(t))$$

$$\ln\left(\frac{P^t(j,k|\mathbf{F}(t))}{1-P^t(j,k|\mathbf{F}(t))}\right) = w_0^{j,t}(k) + \sum_l w_l^{j,t} F_l(t)$$

$$(5.7.8)$$

The scorecard-based approach can also be used to stress test model but only for a fixed period ahead. Suppose a risk scorecard is built using a time horizon of t periods, then at time t_0 defining the default probability for borrower i by $\Pr\{D_i(t+t_0) = 1\} = p_i(t+t_0)$, the scorecard satisfies

$$\ln\left(\frac{1-p_i(t+t_0)}{p_i(t+t_0)}\right) = s_{\text{Pop}}(t+t_0) + s_{\text{Inf}} \quad (5.7.9)$$

which is the form of the score described in Section 1.5. In this simple model, one can define the population odds part of the score as a sum of economic factors, namely:

$$s_{\text{Pop}}(t+t_0) = w_1 F_1(t+t_0) + w_2 F_2(t+t_0) + \cdots + w_r F_r(t+t_0) \quad (5.7.10)$$

Thus one can estimate the default rate t periods into the future if one assume what economic scenario will be occurring then. Note though that this form of stress testing is only like making a constant adjustment to the credit score for that time period. Thus using the basic scorecard approach to stress testing really reduces to a sensitivity analysis approach rather than a scenario analysis approach.

There are several advantages to using models for stress testing. Firstly models cover the whole portfolio of loans and use all the data on all the loans in building the model, rather than directly estimating the impact of a set of economic conditions on the default rate of one risk group. In the latter case there is only one pillar of data that one is basing one's conclusion on and hence that pillar had better be very wide to bear the weight of the conclusions. If one has a model then it has many pillars of data and provided the model which one can think of as the beams that connect the pillars together is valid then one does not have to have each of the pillars so wide since the weight of the conclusions is distributed over them. Granted one has the extra task of validating the model assumptions but this is usually worth it for the fact one can end up with much stronger conclusions.

Stress testing LGD and EAD

The Basel Accord requires stress testing not just of the PD estimate, but also of the LGD, and EAD estimates. The three approaches suggested for PD – static sensitivity tests, correlations with economic variables, and economy dependent dynamic models could also be used for these contexts. The correlation approach makes a lot of sense in the LGD and EAD cases as one can apply the regression at the individual loan level if one wanted to do so. The main modelling approach though is to separate the collections and recovery process into a sequence of events and estimate the likelihood of each event and the likely recoveries for each of these events. For example in the mortgage recovery process after default, first there is the uncertainty about whether the property will need to be repossessed or not, and if so when and for how much will it be resold. If these probabilities and monetary values are functions of economic conditions, like house prices, then one can use these models for stress analysis.

One obvious question is if LGD is supposed to be the value that one gets in a downturn, why bother to stress test it? The regulators do acknowledge this by accepting 'there is an overlap between down turn conditions assumed for estimating LGD and those adopted in some forms of stress tests. Where a firm assumes the stress and down turn conditions are similar, then the LGD estimates used in both context might also be similar' (FSA 2006).

The Basel regulations require that as part of the 'downturn' LGD estimation one compares the result with that of the long-run average LGD estimation. So one needs a model of LGD so that one can estimate both the downturn and the long-run average LGD.

EAD is normally estimated by some deterministic process for fixed term loans where there is little chance of further exposure and the repayment levels are known. So it is only in the case of revolving loans, like credit cards and overdrafts that a model is required. Even in that case there are no established ways of incorporating economic factors into the model and so the correlation approach seems the most appropriate.

This section has concentrated on stress testing credit risk but the Basel Accord requires stress testing for all the risks that impact on the banks' ability to survive. Thus in the market risk section of the Accord, it is expected that stress testing will be used with VaR models to assess that there is enough capital to cope with extreme market conditions. Other risks which affect the lender's capital requirements and so require stress testing are illiquidity risk, counterparty credit risk, and concentration risk. In this last risk, there are a group of exposures that would all be affected by the same geographic or industry sector downturn, or the same individual borrower defaulting and which could produce large enough losses to affect the core operations of the lender. Arguably illiquidity and counterparty credit risk have been the major causes of bank failures.

In this book we have tried to show how models based on credit scoring can be used for three of the most important areas of consumer lending – pricing, profit, and portfolio risk. There can be no doubt that such credit scoring-based models will continue to be refined and developed for as the English satirist Samuel Butler said 'All progress is based upon a universal innate desire on the part of every organism to live beyond its income'.

Appendices

A Scores and runbook example

Score	Number of Goods	Number of Bads	Marginal Odds	Number Cumul-ative Goods	Number Cumul-ative Bads	% Cumul-ative Goods	% Cumul-ative Bads	Cumul-ative odds
143	0	4	0.00	0	4	0.0%	0.5%	0.0
146	0	3	0.00	0	7	0.0%	0.8%	0.0
147–168	0	10	0.00	0	17	0.0%	1.9%	0.0
169	4	10	0.40	4	27	0.0%	3.1%	0.1
172	2	6	0.33	6	33	0.0%	3.7%	0.2
178	2	3	0.67	8	36	0.0%	4.1%	0.2
179–180	8	32	0.25	16	68	0.1%	7.7%	0.2
190–199	28	32	0.88	44	100	0.2%	11.3%	0.4
200–202	16	11	1.45	60	111	0.3%	12.6%	0.5
203–205	10	14	0.71	70	125	0.4%	14.2%	0.6
206–208	14	8	1.75	84	133	0.5%	15.1%	0.6
209–211	16	21	0.76	100	154	0.5%	17.4%	0.6
212–214	6	11	0.55	106	165	0.6%	18.7%	0.6
215–217	52	24	2.17	158	189	0.9%	21.4%	0.8
218–220	52	37	1.41	210	226	1.2%	25.6%	0.9
221–223	30	21	1.43	240	247	1.3%	28.0%	1.0
224–226	34	20	1.70	274	267	1.5%	30.2%	1.0
227–229	94	38	2.47	368	305	2.0%	34.5%	1.2
230–232	68	26	2.62	436	331	2.4%	37.5%	1.3
233–235	84	35	2.40	520	366	2.9%	41.4%	1.4
236–238	90	28	3.21	610	394	3.3%	44.6%	1.5
239–241	70	15	4.67	680	409	3.7%	46.3%	1.7
242–244	82	16	5.13	762	425	4.2%	48.1%	1.8
245–247	98	19	5.16	860	444	4.7%	50.3%	1.9
248–250	92	15	6.13	952	459	5.2%	52.0%	2.1
251–253	74	22	3.36	1026	481	5.6%	54.5%	2.1
254–256	158	32	4.94	1184	513	6.5%	58.1%	2.3
257–259	118	13	9.08	1302	526	7.1%	59.6%	2.5
260–262	210	40	5.25	1512	566	8.3%	64.1%	2.7
263–265	146	19	7.68	1658	585	9.1%	66.3%	2.8
266–268	156	17	9.18	1814	602	9.9%	68.2%	3.0
269–271	172	21	8.19	1986	623	10.9%	70.6%	3.2
272–274	306	18	17.00	2292	641	12.6%	72.6%	3.6
275–277	322	26	12.38	2614	667	14.3%	75.5%	3.9
278–280	166	11	15.09	2780	678	15.2%	76.8%	4.1
281–283	194	15	12.93	2974	693	16.3%	78.5%	4.3
284–286	172	19	9.05	3146	712	17.3%	80.6%	4.4
287–289	210	14	15.00	3356	726	18.4%	82.2%	4.6

(*continued*)

Table (*continued*)

Score	Number of Goods	Number of Bads	Marginal Odds	Number Cumulative Goods	Number Cumulative Bads	% Cumulative Goods	% Cumulative Bads	Cumulative odds
290–292	238	10	23.80	3594	736	19.7%	83.4%	4.9
293–295	380	18	21.11	3974	754	21.8%	85.4%	5.3
296–298	462	11	42.00	4436	765	24.3%	86.6%	5.8
299–301	194	7	27.71	4630	772	25.4%	87.4%	6.0
302–304	318	10	31.80	4948	782	27.1%	88.6%	6.3
305–307	340	8	42.50	5288	790	29.0%	89.5%	6.7
308–310	306	7	43.71	5594	797	30.7%	90.3%	7.0
311–313	270	7	38.57	5864	804	32.2%	91.1%	7.3
314–316	310	7	44.29	6174	811	33.9%	91.8%	7.6
317–319	200	6	33.33	6374	817	35.0%	92.5%	7.8
320–322	508	7	72.57	6882	824	37.7%	93.3%	8.4
323–325	364	2	182.00	7246	826	39.7%	93.5%	8.8
326–328	362	6	60.33	7608	832	41.7%	94.2%	9.1
329–331	312	6	52.00	7920	838	43.4%	94.9%	9.5
332–334	390	6	65.00	8310	844	45.6%	95.6%	9.8
335–337	490	7	70.00	8800	851	48.3%	96.4%	10.3
338–340	376	3	125.33	9176	854	50.3%	96.7%	10.7
341–343	214	4	53.50	9390	858	51.5%	97.2%	10.9
344–346	386	2	193.00	9776	860	53.6%	97.4%	11.4
347–349	536	2	268.00	10312	862	56.6%	97.6%	12.0
350–352	360	2	180.00	10672	864	58.5%	97.8%	12.4
353–355	440	2	220.00	11112	866	60.9%	98.1%	12.8
356–358	370	3	123.33	11482	869	63.0%	98.4%	13.2
359–361	358	1	358.00	11840	870	64.9%	98.5%	13.6
362–364	414	1	414.00	12254	871	67.2%	98.6%	14.1
365–367	346	0		12600	871	69.1%	98.6%	14.5
368–370	264	2	132.00	12864	873	70.5%	98.9%	14.7
371–373	382	2	191.00	13246	875	72.6%	99.1%	15.1
374–376	274	1	274.00	13520	876	74.1%	99.2%	15.4
377–379	434	1	434.00	13954	877	76.5%	99.3%	15.9
380–382	310	0		14264	877	78.2%	99.3%	16.3
383–385	300	1	300.00	14564	878	79.9%	99.4%	16.6
386–388	224	0		14788	878	81.1%	99.4%	16.8
389–391	272	1	272.00	15060	879	82.6%	99.5%	17.1
392–394	222	0		15282	879	83.8%	99.5%	17.4
395–297	236	2	118.00	15518	881	85.1%	99.8%	17.6
398–400	208	0		15726	881	86.2%	99.8%	17.9
401–403	128	0		15854	881	86.9%	99.8%	18.0
404–406	356	1	356.00	16210	882	88.9%	99.9%	18.4
407–409	184	0		16394	882	89.9%	99.9%	18.6
410–412	140	0		16534	882	90.7%	99.9%	18.7
413–415	164	1	164.00	16698	883	91.6%	100.0%	18.9
416–418	210	0		16908	883	92.7%	100.0%	19.1
419–448	1074	0		17982	883	98.6%	100.0%	20.4
449–	252	0		18234	883	100.0%	100.0%	20.7

B Southampton bank application data

yes (cc)

	Under 30 g	Under 30 b	30–39 g	30–39 b	40–49 g	40–49 b	Over 50 g	Over 50 b	Numbers	Two-dimensional marginal odds	Total numbers	One-dimensional marginal odds
Owner g	50		110		110		200		470	23.5	570	19
Owner b		3		5		5		7	20		30	
Renter g	40		10		15		55		120	4	150	3
Renter b		9		4		3		14	30		50	
Other g	50		15		10		75		150	15	180	9
Other b		4		1		2		3	10		20	
Numbers	140	16	135	10	135	10	330	24	800		1000	
Two-dimensional marginal odds	8.75		13.5		13.5		13.75					

no (cc)

	Under 30 g	Under 30 b	30–39 g	30–39 b	40–49 g	40–49 b	Over 50 g	Over 50 b	Numbers	Two-dimensional marginal odds
Owner g	15		15		35		35		100	10
Owner b		2		3		3		2	10	
Renter g	13		10		2		5		30	1.5
Renter b		7		10		1		2	20	
Other g	7		15		3		5		30	3
Other b		1		7		1		1	10	
Numbers	35	10	40	20	40	15	45	5	200	
Two-dimensional marginal odds	3.5		2		8		9			
Total numbers	175	26	175	30	175	15	375	29	1000	
One-dimensional marginal odds	6.730769		5.833333		11.66667		12.93103			

	cc				
		yes		no		popodds
		g	b	g	b	
Total numbers		740	60	160	40	9
One-dimensional marginal odds	12.33333			4		

Three-dimensional marginal odds

cc yes	Under 30	30–39	40–49	Over 50
Owner	16.66667	22	22	28.57143
Renter	4.444444	2.5	5	3.928571
Other	12.5	15	5	25

cc no	Under 30	30–39	40–49	Over 50
Owner	7.5	5	11.66667	17.5
Renter	1.857143	1	2	2.5
Other	7	2.142857	3	5

References

Allison P.D. (1999), *Logistic Regression using the SAS system: Theory and Applications*, SAS Publications.

Altman E.I. (1968), Financial ratios, discriminant analysis and the prediction of corporate bankruptcy, *The Journal of Finance* 23, 589–609.

Altman E., Resti A., Sironi A. (2005a), *Recovery Risk*, Risk Books, London.

Altman E.I., Brady B., Resti A., Sironi A. (2005b), The link between default and recovery rates; theory, empirical evidence and implications, *Journal of Business* 78, 2203–2222.

Anderson D.R., Sweeney D.J., Williams T.A. (2002), *Introduction to Management Science: A Quantitative Approach to Decision Making*, Thomson South Western, Mason, Ohio.

Anderson R. (2007), *The Credit Scoring Toolkit Theory and Practice for Retail Credit Risk Management and Decision Automation*, Oxford University Press, Oxford.

Anderson T.W., Goodman L.A. (1957), Statistical inference about Markov chains, *Annals of Mathematical Statistics* 28, 89–109.

Andrade F.W.M., Thomas L.C. (2007), Structural models in consumer credit, *European Journal of Operational Research* 183, 1569–1581.

Bamber D. (1975), The area above the ordinal dominance graph and the area below the receiver operating characteristic graph, *Journal of Mathematical Psychology* 12, 387–415.

Banasik J., Crook J.N., Thomas L.C. (1999) Not if but when borrowers default, *Journal of Operational Research Society* 50, 1185–1190.

Basel Committee on Banking Supervision (BCBS) (2005, comprehensive version 2006), *International Convergence of Capital Measurement and Capital Standards—A Revised Framework*, Bank for International Settlements, Basel.

Bennett R.L., Catarineu E., Moral G. (2005), *Loss Given Default Validation, Studies on the Validation of Internal Rating Systems*, Working Paper 14, Basel Committee on Banking Supervision, Basel, pp. 60–76.

Bierman H., Hausman W.H. (1970) The credit granting decision, *Management Science* 16, 519–532.

Black F., Cox J.C. (1976), Valuing corporate securities. Some effects of bond indenture provisions, *Journal of Finance* 31, 351–368.

Bozzetto J.-F., Tang L., Thomas S., Thomas L.C. (2005), *Modelling the Purchase Dynamics of Insurance Customers using Markov Chains*, Discussion Paper CORMSIS-05-02, School of Management, University of Southampton, Southampton.

Breiman L. (2001), Random forests, *Machine Learning* 45, 5–32.

Breiman L., Friedman J.H., Olshen R.A., Stone C.J. (1984), *Classification and Regression Trees*, Wadsworth, Belmont, California.

Breslow N. (1974), Covariance analysis of censored survival data, *Biometrics* 30, 89–99.

Cappe O., Moulines E., Ryden T. (2005), *Inference in Hidden Markov Models*, Springer, Heidelberg.

Chava S., Jarrow R. A. (2004), Bankruptcy failure with industry effects, *Review of Finance* **8**, 532–569.

Clayton D. (1978), A model for association in bivariate life tables and its application in epidemiological studies of familial tendency in chronic disease incidence, *Biometrika* 65, 141–151.

Cox D.R. (1972), Regression models and life tables (with discussion), *Journal of Royal Statistical Society* Series B, 187–220.

Crook J.N., Banasik J. (2004), Does reject inference really improve the performance of application scoring models? *Journal of Banking and Finance* 28, 857–874.

Durand D. (1941), *Risk Elements in Consumer Installment Financing*, National Bureau of Economic Research, New York.

Edgeworth F.Y. (1881), *Mathematical Psychics: An Essay on the Application of Mathematics to the Moral Sciences*, Kegan Paul & Co., pp. viii, 150.

Efron B. (1977), The efficiency of Cox's likelihood function for censored data, *Journal of American Statistical Association* 72, 557–565.

Elizalde A. (2005), *Credit Risk Models III; Reconciliation Structural-Reduced Models*, www.abelelizalde.com

Feelders A.J. (2000), Credit scoring and reject inference with mixture models, *International Journal of Intelligent Systems in Accounting, Finance and Management* 9, 1–8.

Fisher R.A. (1936), The use of multiple measurements in taxonomic problems, *Annals of Eugenics* 7, 179–188.

Freed N., Glover F. (1981a) A linear programming approach to the discriminant problem, *Decision Sciences* 12, 68–74.

Freed N., Glover F. (1981b) Simple but powerful goal programming formulations for the discriminant problem, *European Journal of Operational Research* 7, 44–60.

Freed N., Glover F. (1986a), Evaluating alternative linear programming models to solve the two-group discriminant problem, *Decision Sciences* 17, 151–162.

Freed N., Glover F. (1986b), Resolving certain difficulties and improving classification power of LP discriminant analysis formulations, *Decision Sciences* 17, 589–595.

Frydman H. (1984), Maximum likelihood estimation in the Mover–Stayer model, *Journal of American Statistical Association* 79, 632–638.

Frydman H., Kallberg J.G., Kao D.-L. (1985), Testing the adequacy of Markov chains and Mover–Stayer models as representations of credit behaviour, *Operations Research* 33, 1203–1214.

Gelfand I.M., Fomin, S.V. (2000), *Calculus of Variations*, Dover, Mineola, New York.

Gordy M.B. (2003), A risk factor model foundation for ratings-based bank capital rules, *Journal of Financial Intermediation* 3, 199–232.

Guo X., Jarrow R.A., Zeng Y. (2005), *Information Reduction in Credit Risk Models*, Working Paper, School of Operations Research and Industrial Engineering, Cornell University, Ithaca.

Hand D.J., Henley W.E. (1993), Can reject inference ever work? *IMA Journal of Mathematics Applied in Business and Industry* 5, 45–55.

Hand D.J., Kelly M.G. (2001), Look ahead scorecards for new fixed term credit products, *Journal of the Operational Research Society* 52, 989–996.

Heitfeld E.A. (2005), *Dynamics of Rating Systems, Studies on the Validation of Internal Rating Systems*, Working Paper 14, Basel Committee on Banking Supervision, Basel, pp. 10–20.

Ho J., Pomrey T.A., Scherer W.T., Thomas L.C. (2004), Segmenting in Markov chain consumer behaviour models, in *Readings in Credit Scoring*, Eds. L.C. Thomas, D.B. Edelman, J.N. Crook, Oxford University Press, Oxford, pp. 295–307.

Hosmer D.W., Lemeshow S. (1980), A goodness of fit test for the multiple logistic regression model, *Communications in Statistics* A10, 1043–1069.

Hosmer D.W., Lemeshow S. (1989, 2000 2nd edition), *Applied Logistic Regression*, Wiley, New York.

Hosmer D.W., Lemeshow S. (1998), *Applied Survival Analysis*, Wiley, New York.

Jarrow R.A., Lando D., Turnbul S. (1997), A Markov model for the term structure of credit risk spreads, *Review of Financial Studies* 10, 481–523.

Jarrow R.A., Turnbull S. (1995), Pricing derivatives on financial securities subject to credit risk, *Journal of Finance* 50, 53–86.

Jung K.M., Thomas L.C. (2008), A note on coarse classifying in acceptance scoring, *Journal of Operational Research Society* 59, 714–718.

Kalbfleisch J.D., Prentice R.L. (1980), *The Statistical Analysis of Failure Time Data*, Wiley, New York.

Kaplan E.L., Meier P. (1958), Nonparametric estimation from incomplete observations, *Journal of American Statistical Association* 53, 457–481.

Keeney R.L., Oliver R.M. (2005), Designing win–win financial loan products for consumers and businesses, improving lender offers using consumer preferences, *Journal of Operational Research Society* 56, 1030–1040.

Kullback S., Leibler R.A. (1951), On information and sufficiency, *Annals of Mathematical Statistics* 22, 79–86.

Lewis E. M. (1992), *An Introduction to Credit Scoring*, Athena Press, San Rafael, California.

Longstaff F.A., Schwartz E.S. (1995), A simple approach to valuing risky fixed and floating rate debt, *Journal of Finance* 50, 789–819.

Malik M., Thomas L.C. (2007), *Modelling Credit Risk of Portfolio of Consumer Loans*, Working Papers CORMSIS 07–07, Centre for Operational Research, Management Science, and Information Systems, School of Management, University of Southampton, Southampton.

Markowitz H.M. (1952), Portfolio selection, *Journal of Finance* 7, 77–91.

Matuszyk A., Mues C., Thomas L.C. (2007), *Modelling LGD for Unsecured Personal Loans; Decision Tree Approach*, Working Paper CORMSIS 07-07, School of Management, University of Southampton, Southampton.

Mays E. (1998), *Credit Risk Modeling, Design and Application*, Fitzroy Dearborn publishers, Chicago.

Mays E. (2004), *Credit Scoring for Risk Managers, The Handbook for Lenders*, Thomson South Western, Mason, Ohio.

McNab H., Wynn A. (2000), *Principles and Practice of Consumer Credit Risk Management*, CIB Publishing, Canterbury.

Merton R.C. (1974), On the pricing of corporate debt: the risk structure of interest rates, *Journal of Finance* 29, 449–470.

Mizen P. (2002), *Consumer Credit and Outstanding Debt in Europe*, Opening Address, Joint Workshop between Chair in Finance and Consumption (EVI) and ET CEM Centre, Nottingham, and EVI, Florence.

Oliver R.M., Thomas L.C. (2005), *Optimal Score Cut-offs and Regulatory Capital in Retail Credit Portfolios*, Working Paper, School of Management, University of Southampton, Southampton.

Phillips R.L. (2005), *Pricing and Revenue Optimization*, Stanford Business Books, Stanford, California.

Puterman M.L. (1994), *Markov Decision Processes*, Wiley, New York.

Pye G. (1974), Gauging the default process, *Financial Analysts Journal* January–March, 49–52.

Quinlan J.R. (1993), *C4.5: Programs for Machine Learning*, Morgan Kaufman, San Mateo, California.

Safavian R., Landgrebe D. (1991), A survey of decision tree classifier methodology, *IEEE Transactions on Systems, Man, and Cybernetics* 21, 660–674.

Siddiqi N. (2005), *Credit Risk Scorecards, Developing and Implementing Intelligent Credit Scoring*, Wiley, New York.

Stepanova M., Thomas L.C. (2002), Survival analysis methods for personal loan data, *Operations Research* 50, 277–289.

Stepanova M., Thomas L.C. (2001), PHAB scores: proportional hazards analysis behavioural scores, *Journal of Operational Research Society* 52, 1007–1016.

Tasche D. (2005), *Rating and Probability of Default Validation, Studies on the Validation of Internal Rating Systems*, Working Paper 14, Basel Committee on Banking Supervision, Basel, pp. 25–59.

Thomas L.C. (1992), Financial risk management models, in *Risk Analysis, Assessment and Management*, Eds. J. Ansell, F. Wharton, Wiley, Chichester.

Thomas L.C., Crook J.N., Edelman D.B. (1992), *Credit Scoring and Credit Control*, Oxford University Press, Oxford.

Thomas L.C., Edelman D.B., Crook J.N. (2002), *Credit Scoring and its Applications*, SIAM, Philadelphia.

Thomas L.C., Edelman D.B., Crook, J.N. (2004), *Readings in Credit Scoring*, Oxford University Press, Oxford.

Thomas L.C., Jung K.M., Thomas, S.D.A., Wu Y. (2006), Modelling consumer acceptance probabilities, *Expert Systems and their Applications* 30, 507–518.

Trench M.S., Pederson S.P., Lau E.T., Ma L., Wang H., Nair S.K. (2003), Managing credit lines and prices for Bank One credit cards, *Interfaces*, 33, 4–21.

Vasicek O.A. (1987), *Probability of Loss on Loan Portfolio*, KMV Corporation. San Francisco.

Vasicek O.A. (2002), Loan portfolio value, *Risk* December, 160–162.

Von Neumann J., Morgernstern O. (1944), *Theory of Games and Economic Behaviour*, Princeton University Press, Princeton.

Index